DAILY GUIDEPOSTS

2009

Guideposts®

New York, New York

Daily Guideposts 2009
ISBN-13: 978-0-8249-4738-5
Published by Guideposts
16 East 34th Street
New York, New York 10016
www.guideposts.com

ACKNOWLEDGMENTS

Every attempt has been made to credit the sources of copyrighted material used in this book. If any such acknowledgment has been inadvertently omitted or miscredited, receipt of such information would be appreciated.

All Scripture quotations, unless otherwise noted, are taken from *The King James Version of the Bible*.

Scripture quotations marked (AMP) are taken from *The Amplified Bible*, © 1965 by Zondervan Publishing House. All rights reserved.

Scripture quotations marked (CEV) are taken from *The Holy Bible, Contemporary English Version*. Copyright © 1995 American Bible Society. All rights reserved.

Scripture quotations marked (EB) are taken from *The Holy Bible, New Century Version* [*The Everyday Bible*], copyright © 1987, 1988, 1991 by Word Publishing, Nashville, TN. Used by permission.

Scripture quotations marked (GNB) are taken from *Good News Bible: Today's English Version*. Copyright © 1966, 1971, 1976 American Bible Society. All rights reserved.

Scripture quotations marked (JB) are taken from *The Jerusalem Bible*, © 1966, 1967 and 1968 by Darton, Longman & Todd Ltd. and Doubleday, a division of Random House, Inc. All rights reserved.

Scripture quotations marked (MSG) are taken from *The Message*. Copyright © 1993, 1994, 1995, 1996, 2000, 2001, 2002 by Eugene H. Peterson.

Scripture quotations marked (NAS) are taken from the *New American Standard Bible*, © The Lockman Foundation, 1960, 1962, 1963, 1968, 1971, 1972, 1973, 1975, 1977. Used by permission.

Scripture quotations marked (NEB) are taken from *The New English Bible*. Copyright © The Delegates of the Oxford University Press and the Syndics of the Cambridge University Press 1961, 1970.

Scripture quotations marked (NIV) are taken from *The Holy Bible, New International Version*. Copyright © 1973, 1978, 1984 International Bible Society. Used by permission of Zondervan Bible Publishers.

Scripture quotations marked (NKJV) are taken from *The Holy Bible, New King James Version*. Copyright © 1997, 1990, 1985, 1983 by Thomas Nelson, Inc.

Scripture quotations marked (NLT) are taken from the *Holy Bible*, New Living Translation. Copyright © 1996. Used by permission of Tyndale House Publishers, Inc., Wheaton, Illinois 60189. All rights reserved.

Scripture quotations marked (NRSV) are taken from the *New Revised Standard Version Bible*. Copyright © 1989 by the Division of Christian Education of the National Council of the Churches of Christ in the U.S.A. Used by permission. All rights reserved.

Scripture quotations marked (RSV) are taken from the *Revised Standard Version of the Bible*. Copyright © 1946, 1952, 1971 by Division of Christian Education of the National Council of Churches of Christ in the U.S.A. Used by permission.

Scripture quotations marked (TLB) are taken from *The Living Bible*. Copyright © 1971 by Tyndale House Publishers, Wheaton, IL 60187. All rights reserved.

"Reader's Room" by Jack Brewer, Betty Crow, Ruth Dabney, Suzanne DeBoer, Diane Francis, Linda Grazulis, Carolyn Malion, Janet Markoff, Vicky Orlowski, Carlisle Parsons, Kurt Sampson and Carolyn Schemahorn are reprinted with permission from the authors.

Brian Doyle's photo by Jerry Hart. Oscar Greene's photo copyright © 2001 by Olan Mills, Inc. Rick Hamlin's photo by Lilly Dong. Roberta Messner's photo by Jan D. Witter/Camelot Photography. Elizabeth Sherrill's and John Sherrill's photos by Gerardo Somoza.

Design by The DesignWorks Group, David Uttley, www.thedesignworksgroup.com
Indexed by Patricia Woodruff
Typeset by Planet Patti Inc.

Printed and bound in the United States of America

"The word is nigh thee," says the apostle Paul, quoting Deuteronomy 30:14, "even in thy mouth, and in thy heart" (Romans 10:8). For us as believers, in the twenty-first century as in the first, the Word of God is a constant presence in our lives. We encounter the Word in the person of Jesus, in the words of Scripture, in the prayers the Spirit prays in and through us, in the words God sends us through loved ones, friends, colleagues, pastors and even strangers, and in the "still, small voice" that speaks to us in the silence of our hearts. So our theme for Daily Guideposts 2009, our thirty-third annual edition, is "Living the Word."

Our encounter with the Living Word gives us life, and our lives find their shape and their beauty as we let the Word transform us in God's likeness. So we've asked our fifty-eight writers—old friends like Fred Bauer, Elizabeth Sherrill, Daniel Schantz, Marion Bond West, Oscar Greene, Carol Kuykendall and Scott Walker, and some newer members of the family like Joshua Sundquist, Patricia Pusey and Pablo Diaz—to explore the many ways they live their faith in the encounters and events, large and small, that God brings all of us every day. They'll help you live the Word more deeply in your daily walk, whether it's by hearing an unexpected word of wisdom from the lips of a child, putting a Scripture verse to work to make a difficult situation better, finding consolation in a Psalm or receiving a word of encouragement from a coworker.

Living the Word means being alive to new opportunities and new challenges, so we've redesigned *Daily Guideposts* this year to make it simpler to use and, we hope, even easier to read. But you'll still find everything you've come to expect: a verse of Scripture; a true, first-person story of the ways God speaks to us in the events of our daily lives; a brief prayer to help you put the day's message to work in your life. And you'll find special series throughout the year, including reflections for Holy Week and Easter and Advent devotionals to help you get the most out of your Christmas celebration.

One of the hardest things to do is to say farewell to those who have walked ahead of us to our journey's end. On July 2, 2007, we lost Phyllis Hobe, who had been a part of our family since 1983. On January 31, 2008, Roberta Rogers, who joined us in 1997, died after a brief but intense battle with cancer. One week earlier, on January 24, Van Varner, former editor-in-chief of *Guideposts* magazine, died in California, where he was to have boarded a ship bound for the South Pacific. It would be hard to overstate the impact Van had on everyone here at Guideposts by his kindness, his courtesy, his skill as a writer and editor, and his concern for everyone who was privileged to know him.

Finally, on February 6, 2008, we said good-bye to our cofounder Ruth Stafford Peale. Guideposts began more than sixty years ago at Dr. and Mrs. Peale's kitchen table, and over the years Mrs. Peale's dedication to Guideposts' mission, her deep faith in the providence of God and the power of prayer, and her positive approach to whatever challenges came her way in a life that spanned 101 years have inspired all of us and left a legacy that will be with us always. To the memory of Mrs. Peale, Van, Roberta, Phyllis, and with our prayers for their families and friends, we dedicate *Daily Guideposts 2009*.

Whether you've just discovered *Daily Guideposts* or joined us many times before, our prayer is that sharing this year with us will help renew your faith in the Word that is near us and in us and with us, and will put new strength in your stride as the whole *Daily Guideposts* family—almost a million strong—walks the days from January to December together.

—ANDREW ATTAWAY
Editor, *Daily Guideposts*

DAILY GUIDEPOSTS DEVOTIONALS IN YOUR IN-BOX

Receive each day's devotional in your in-box or read it online!

Visit OurPrayer.org/DGP2009 and enter this code:

DGP2009

JANUARY

In the beginning was the Word,
and the Word was with God,
and the Word was God.

—JOHN 1:1

Editor's Note: Have you ever tried making a list of all the ways that God speaks to you in your life? Scripture and prayer would rightly head most of our lists, but are there some other ways? We invite you to join Daniel Schantz at the beginning of each month this year as he shares some of the many ways God has spoken to him.

THU
1

"This Book of the Law shall not depart from your mouth. . . . For then you will make your way prosperous, and then you will have good success."

—Joshua 1:8 (NKJV)

The new year is a good time to learn a new skill. I learned to fly an airplane in the month of January. The air was brittle-cold, and the airport was blanketed with three inches of snow.

God Speaks
through His Law

Flying a plane is not like driving a car. Up in the atmosphere there are no traffic lights, no road signs and no patrolmen. And yet there are laws, even in the atmosphere: speed limits, load limits, prohibited air space and more.

Flying is about learning to obey the laws of flight, such as lift and gravity, thrust and drag. Often my instructor had to yell at me, "Watch your heading!" "Get that nose down!" "Watch out for that commercial jet!" "No, no, no, no!"

At times I wanted to cry and at other times I wanted to bark back at him, but I was paying him good money to yell at me. I knew it wasn't personal; he was just trying to save my life—and his.

I find the Bible to be a bit like my flight instructor. It's filled with blunt warnings and commands: "Do not steal!" "Do not lie!" "Do not kill!"

Obedience comes hard for me some days, but learning to listen and obey is the key to learning any new skill, whether it's driving a car, playing a musical instrument or learning to live with a new bride.

When I respect God's Word and the moral laws that He's built into the universe, I can soar into the future.

Father, in this new year, help me to see Your love, crafted in the form of law.
—Daniel Schantz

Editor's Note: Please let us know some of the ways God speaks to you. You can write them down in "My Living Words," the journal pages at the end of every month.

"But in their time of trouble they cried to you and you heard them. . . ."
—Nehemiah 9:27 (TLB)

The ice storm hit Kansas on December 29 while my husband Don and I were visiting family in Texas. When we arrived home, the temperature was twelve degrees. The power lines were sagging or snapped, coated in ice and laden with icicles. We had no heat, no lights and because our well has an electric pump, no water.

Don started a fire while I gathered up flashlights, candles and blankets. We could heat food on our gas burner, and the fireplace would supply enough heat to keep the upstairs temperature tolerable. Power outages are common in our rural area, but they're always short.

This one was different. And it seemed worse because of another storm: Don's health. He was having heart problems and was scheduled to see a cardiologist on January 2. On New Year's Day we drove four hours to Wichita. Don went from the doctor's office to the hospital for an angioplasty and stent to open an artery that was ninety-eight percent blocked. The procedure was frightening but successful. Twenty-four hours later he was discharged and, exhausted, we returned to our still-powerless house. I was so grateful that Don was going to be okay that it seemed petty to complain. But I longed for a hot shower!

About 7:00 PM, after several flickers, the power came on to stay. "How many hours until we have hot water?" I asked.

"Just turn on the tap!" Don replied. "The water was always hot. It just took that electric spark to pump it out."

Just like God, I thought, as steaming shower water cascaded over me. His power, care and love are always available. And the spark that lets them flow out is simple: a prayer.

Gracious God, thank You for the blessing of Your presence in the storms of life.
—Penney Schwab

"Ask and it will be given to you; seek and you will find; knock and the door will be opened to you. For everyone who asks receives; he who seeks finds; and to him who knocks, the door will be opened."

—MATTHEW 7:7–8 (NIV)

For as long as I can remember, I've made lists. There's a list for what I need to pick up at the grocery store, a daily appointment schedule; I've even taken time to think well into the future with five- and ten-year goals.

When our children lived at home, I wrote up goal worksheets for them. Every January 1, we sat around the dining room table, filled out the worksheets and read the ones from the previous year. The tradition continues: My husband Wayne and I spend part of the first day of the year talking about the twelve months ahead. We chat about commitments we've already made and set time aside for people we want to see and places we plan to visit. We have financial goals, recreational ones, personal goals and spiritual ones. It's our way of laying out the year before God, telling Him the things we'd like to accomplish and asking for His blessing in order to see it come to pass.

This last time, though, I had trouble focusing on my goals. Naturally, I want everything I do to be wildly successful, but so many factors are in play that the final outcome is completely out of my control. Some of my goals seemed more like wishes.

Then one day, shortly after the first of the year, I drove past a billboard that read, "Some things need to be believed in order to be seen."

I have a new category for my goal worksheets now: "Needs to Be Believed." It's a list that's growing longer every year.

FATHER GOD, THANK YOU FOR THE DREAMS YOU'VE PLANTED IN MY HEART.

—DEBBIE MACOMBER

I am the bread of life.

—JOHN 6:48 (NIV)

Bread was a big thing in my childhood. Not just those balloon-embellished loaves of store-bought white bread, but homemade cornbread and biscuits. Biscuits were mostly for breakfast and special occasions; cornbread was a daily affair. And on really special occasions, my sister would make her cloverleaf yeast rolls. Bread has always been something that does more than fill the belly; it comforts and consoles and assures me that despite whatever particular drama may be consuming me, life is normal after all.

That's why I've always appreciated Jesus' affirmation "I am the bread of life." Not the Oreo of life or the chopped steak of life or even the cream cheese of life, but the *bread* of life—the basic, daily, constant ingredient. The thing we start with, the thing we crave, the thing that satisfies us in a way nothing else can. Always.

That's a comforting and amazing thought. I think I'll ponder it for a while . . . and toast myself a bagel.

You, God, sustain and nourish my soul. Keep me from the "junk food" of foolish philosophies and wandering loyalties.   —Mary Lou Carney

---

MON
5

Follow that which is good, both among yourselves, and to all men.
—I Thessalonians 5:15

When I rediscovered that wonderful childhood poem "The Cupboard" by Walter de la Mare, in an old poetry book, I had no idea what fun it would become for my five-year-old grandson Caleb and me. We were visiting my son in his new home. Phil had, to a child's mind, a "portal to another kingdom" in his kitchen—a tall white cupboard in which he stockpiled just about every kind of candy there is.

Caleb would have cleaned him out if I hadn't declared, "I am in charge of the cupboard."

"I have a small fat grandmama," I quoted,
"With a very slippery knee,
And she's Keeper of the Cupboard,
With the key, key, key.
And when I'm very good, my dear,
As good as good can be,
There's Banbury Cakes, and Lollipops
For me, me, me."

I even had a small key with which I pretended to open the cupboard door.

Caleb, catching the spirit, eyes gleaming, recited, "When I'm very good . . . as good as good can be" every time he thought he should have a treat. Inserting the names of the goodies in Phil's stash, he'd say, "There's cherry twists and jelly beans for me, me, me."

Engaging our imaginations, Caleb and I created a great memory with that poem and my son's candy cupboard. The poem focused us on kindness and goodness in our daily interactions, because the secret of the cupboard isn't the key or the candy . . . the secret is in what *really* opens the cupboard door.

> JESUS, YOUR GOODNESS AND KINDNESS, IMPARTED TO ME,
> OPEN ETERNAL TREASURES TO WHICH YOU HOLD THE KEY.
> —CAROL KNAPP

Now when Jesus was born in Bethlehem of Judaea in the days of Herod the king, behold, there came wise men from the east. . . . And when they were come into the house, they saw the young child with Mary his mother, and fell down, and worshipped him: and when they had opened their treasures, they presented unto him gifts; gold, and frankincense, and myrrh.

—MATTHEW 2:1, 11

Today is the feast of the Epiphany, or Twelfth Night, when many Christians commemorate the visit to Bethlehem by the wise men, bearing presents for the Christ Child. Only Matthew records the coming of the Magi and their gifts of gold, frankincense and myrrh.

I read an article recently about the price of frankincense, which comes from the gum of a tree grown on the Arabian peninsula in Oman. Frankincense is used in one of the world's most expensive perfumes that sells for $220 an ounce. It is also an ingredient in cosmetics, anointing oils and some embalming fluids. Myrrh has similar properties.

The wise men's gifts were valuable and, according to legend, provided the wherewithal of the Holy Family's flight from King Herod into Egypt. We don't know the route that Mary, Joseph and Jesus traveled, their destination, the length of their stay, or who else helped them survive. The only thing of which we're certain is that God watched over them. No doubt they were frightened, worried and unsure about how they were going to survive in a strange land, but God provided. He always does to those who trust Him. That's good to remember in whatever trials we face in the new year ahead.

> TEACH US, LORD, TO TRUST YOU AND WAIT,
> YOUR TIMING'S PERFECT, NE'ER EARLY OR LATE.
>
> —FRED BAUER

Pride goes before destruction and haughtiness before a fall.
—PROVERBS 16:18 (TLB)

Years ago I made a list of things I wanted to ride, including a hot-air balloon, a snowmobile, an elephant, a camel, a toboggan, in-line skates, a surfboard, a go-cart, a wave runner, an alpine slide, a horse and buggy in New York City's Central Park and a helicopter. By my midfifties I'd done them all except the camel. Then I started a new list that included parasailing, a rickshaw and a train through the Paris-to-London Chunnel. I'm still dreaming about those. Just having the list makes me feel fit, fun and full of adventure.

Not too long ago my friends Wally and Shirley invited my friend Jack and me to tour downtown St. Petersburg, Florida (our neighboring town), on Segways, those funny-looking things on two wheels. You stand up and lean forward to go fast, and lean back to go slow or stop. A sensitive gyroscope senses your balancing act and keeps you moving.

Perfect, another interesting thing I can add to my list of fun things to ride, I thought. *This will be easy. I'm only sixty-one and they're all in their seventies. I'll run circles around them.*

Well, of the four of us, I was the only one who bumped into a lamp-post, swerved into the grass (three times), hit a big metal pole and knocked the Segway to the ground after screeching around in a sandy spot. My body wasn't hurt, but my brash, overconfident feelings sure were.

Lesson learned? Sometimes I need to slow down, obey the rules and take it easy in order to get the most out of life.

LORD, THANK YOU FOR ALL THE ADVENTURES WE CAN HAVE IN THIS GLORIOUS WORLD. HELP ME TO ENJOY THEM WISELY.
—PATRICIA LORENZ

THU
8

"Forget the former things; do not dwell on the past. See, I am doing a new thing! . . ."

—Isaiah 43:18–19 (NIV)

When I'm tempted to think that life has given me too many challenges, I remember one of my patients at the senior-care home where I nursed for seventeen years. Because of complications from diabetes, Mrs. Reimer had both of her legs amputated, yet she still maintained a joyous attitude toward life.

As a double amputee Mrs. Reimer had to learn to walk again. After I put on her prostheses, she'd take a few faltering steps with the aid of her walker. Then, returning to her bed, she'd sit back down and beam up at me. "Imagine, me at ninety learning to walk again. Now that's something!"

Instead of focusing on what she had lost, Mrs. Reimer made the most of what she still had. Often I'd find her reading a book (she loved biographies), working on a jigsaw puzzle or crocheting Christmas tree ornaments. "If I make one snowflake each day," she said, "I'll have more than three hundred to sell at the bazaar." And she did. Come Christmastime, some of her snowflakes will adorn my tree.

Mrs. Reimer showed me that when we view adversities as adventures, life becomes not only bearable but exciting.

Father, thank You for the gift of life and for this brand-new day. I want to make the most of it.   —Helen Grace Lescheid

FRI
9

Offer the sacrifices of righteousness, and put your trust in the Lord.

—Psalm 4:5

It was late. I sat in the dark at my computer, playing a mindless game while I tried to let the day's events settle. My son John came out of his room. He'd had a hard day and a long week battling irritability and anxiety. Now he wanted to talk. I girded myself for a long, trying conversation.

"Mom, I noticed that all of your Christmas presents were practical things," John began.

Taken off guard, I nodded. When did my eleven year old become observant? For years I've economized at Christmas by asking for wooden spoons, rubber scrapers, bath mats and other household essentials. Until now, none of the children had noticed.

"What would you want if we could afford something really nice?"

"Oh, I don't know," I replied casually but with an inner twinge. "I haven't thought about it for years."

"Well, what do you like to do besides take care of us?" John pursued.

I was silent, thinking. There isn't often room in my day for considering what I like to do. I searched my memory for what I'd enjoyed "pre-children."

"I like to read a lot. I like to visit art museums and go for walks in the woods," I began. "I like talking about books and eating Thai food with your father. I like having quiet time alone." A list of things I hadn't done for a long time poured out.

John said nothing. Then, "Are you sorry you had children, Mom?"

I turned, so he could see the fierce conviction in my eyes. "No, honey. Absolutely not. I wouldn't trade this for anything."

JESUS, EVEN WHEN A SACRIFICE IS MADE FREELY, IT'S NOT WITHOUT COST. DON'T LET ME TAKE YOURS FOR GRANTED. —JULIA ATTAWAY

I, even I, am he that comforteth you. . . .

—ISAIAH 51:12

SAT
10

I pointed my rental car eastward through the early morning clouds draping the San Francisco Bay Bridge. I was rushing out to a hospital in San Pablo to see my friend Van, who had collapsed from a stroke a few days before while waiting to board a cruise ship bound for New Zealand. His friend Daniel and nephew Gordon reported that he was in bad shape. I thought I might wait until they brought Van back to New York City, but a voice said, *No, you must go to him.*

What if he didn't know me? What if he was completely unresponsive? The mere thought of Van, one of my oldest and dearest friends, not even recognizing me was devastating; the thought that he might die, unthinkable.

I parked my car in the crowded hospital lot. Every step toward the entrance was an effort. I was afraid—afraid to face the worst. I wanted to turn back. *God, please help me do this.*

Van was alone when I got to his room. I spoke to him. No response. I leaned over and looked at his eyes. Closed. His mouth was open and his breathing ragged. My worst fears were coming true, and somewhere deep inside me a sob began to form, one I knew that I'd never be able to hold back. I slipped my hand around his. "Van . . ."

And I felt it, all the way up through my arm: Van's strong, hard grip. I felt it all the way to my heart. Then he pulled my hand to his lips and held it there for a long moment.

He didn't open his eyes or even move his head. He didn't speak. But he didn't need to.

Dear God, You guide us through the fog of our deepest emotions and give us clarity when all seems dark and hopeless. With You there is always comfort. —Edward Grinnan

---

Listen, O heavens, and I will speak;
hear, O earth, the words of my mouth.
—Deuteronomy 32:1 (NIV)

I had agreed to teach a group of teenagers at our church. I studied the curriculum and came to the first class with lots of material—all sorts of stuff I knew from twenty years of church work—and in return got plenty of blank stares. The next week, there was more of the same. And the next. By the fourth week, I'd had about enough of their attitude. "Don't you want to learn this?" I asked them.

"Sure we do," replied a quiet voice from the back. "But before you give us all your answers, wouldn't you like to hear our questions first?"

So I laid aside all those prepared notes and we talked. It was awkward the first time and only a little better the next. But I decided to give them as much time each week as I was asking they give me. Soon, I discovered we were digging into issues of faith—real issues, tough issues, *their* issues—and many I never would have imagined or predicted, even with twenty years of experience.

Oh, my expertise came in handy during those conversations—but mostly when I was willing to apply what I knew to the questions they were asking. In the end I guess the guy with all the answers needed to learn something too—how to ask the *right* questions.

GIVE ME EARS, GOD, TO REALLY LISTEN AND RESPOND IN LOVE. —JEFF JAPINGA

Editor's Note: This past year, when author Roberta Messner was searching the Internet for information on neurofibromatosis, she ran across something that really gave her pause. An article, written for those who, like Roberta, have the disorder, contained a startling statistic: The average life expectancy for people with NF is fifty-four years.

"I was going to turn fifty-four in September," says Roberta, "and as misleading as statistics can be, I couldn't stop thinking about that one." *One year until eternity? What if it really were so?*

So began an intensely personal quest as Roberta began to ask herself, "If I only had one year left on earth, how would I try to live?" Join her each month as she shares a different facet of her journey.

MON	
12	*Open my eyes, that I may behold Wonderful things. . . .*

—PSALM 119:18 (NAS)

A patient's wife came into my office at the Veterans Administration medical center where I work to show me a photograph a friend had recently taken. "Look, Roberta," she said excitedly, "you can see Jesus in the clouds." Pointing to various markings, she continued, "Here are His eyebrows, His mustache, the contour of His nose and chin." But try as I might, I

WITH ETERNITY IN VIEW

Looking for Jesus in Everything

couldn't detect anything but a blue sky with fluffy white clouds.

"Actually, I've had trouble seeing Jesus all day long," I lamented, reflecting on the morning's complete chaos. Before I even left for work at 7:00 AM, I'd already locked my keys inside my car and had to telephone a locksmith; chased after my sight- and hearing-impaired dog, which had taken off down the road; and spilled coffee on the front of my fresh-from-the-cleaners suit jacket. I was scheduled to give a presentation at an important medical staff meeting that afternoon, but I certainly didn't look—or feel—the part.

"Jesus hasn't had any trouble seeing you, Roberta," the woman answered gently, her eyes searching mine. "How I wish you could see Him too."

As the patient's wife left my office, I marveled at her startlingly simple trust. Her eyes were open to see Jesus everywhere, her faith so full of wonder. I wanted to be just like her, but I felt so very lost.

Without fanfare, I quietly prayed, offering myself anew to Jesus and vowing to look for Him in every person, place and situation. And you know what? I'm finding Him there.

PRECIOUS JESUS, HELP ME TO LOOK FOR YOU EVERY DAY ALL THE YEAR THROUGH.

—ROBERTA MESSNER

Out of my distress I called on the Lord;
the Lord answered me and set me free.

—PSALM 118:5 (RSV)

There were no words for the anger I felt as I stood in downtown Harare, watching children emerge from back alleys and storm drains. They came in waves, digging through trash bins, retrieving dirty bottles and cups. Soon the lady who brought tea and bread would be chugging up in her dilapidated car to fill the dirty bottles with morning tea.

God had beckoned me to Zimbabwe to write about the street children. But this was more than I could bear, and all my anger was focused in one direction—straight up to heaven.

I was armed with a writing pad, yet words couldn't describe the scene before me. My camera was strung over my shoulder, but film could never capture what I was seeing. Still, if I were going to make people understand what was going on in this AIDS-ravaged country, a photograph would be my most powerful tool.

My anger boiled as I grabbed my camera, pulled off the lens cover and flipped the On switch. "Okay, God, if You really think I have something to give, You take the picture!" I held the camera and clicked.

Back home I spread the freshly developed prints across the kitchen table. There it was: an AIDS child was looking straight into my eyes. It was the most powerful photo I had ever seen. In the years since, the face of that child has been in newspapers, on TV, in books and magazines. It's raised more money for kids in Africa than I can count. I'd like to take credit for the picture and be considered a great photographer, but I can't. It's God's photo, plain and simple.

FATHER, I CALLED OUT IN DISTRESS. YOU ANSWERED. WHAT MORE CAN I SAY?

—PAM KIDD

How can one be warm alone?

—ECCLESIASTES 4:11

It was freezing as I hurried across the parking lot to our weekly fellowship supper in the church activities center. As the last rays of the setting sun backlit an angry gray sky, a cold wind whipped across my face, turning my billowing coat into a sail. A winter storm was roaring in from the west Texas plains, and this was going to be a nasty night.

The fellowship hall was full and warm as I rushed in and sat down in the first available seat. Someone stuck out his hand and said, "Well, hello, preacher! You look a bit frozen."

Glancing up, I recognized John, our resident beekeeper. Still shivering, I asked, "John, how do bees keep warm on a night like this?"

"Well, it's simple," he began, sipping his coffee. "As a storm gathers, a colony of bees will stay in their hive bunched closely together and contract and vibrate their abdominal muscles in unison. This rhythmic motion stirs the air inside the hive and causes it to grow warmer. It's like a beating heart pumping warm blood through your body. On a cold night like this, bees are as toasty and warm as can be."

Gazing at the dozens of people inside the hall, drinking coffee and eating dessert, I recognized that God made humans to be a lot like bees. We need each other to keep warm. We depend upon the vibrant presence of friendship to transform a cold world into a place of comfort and cheer.

FATHER, THANK YOU FOR FAMILY AND FRIENDS WHO KEEP ME WARM AND ALIVE IN DIFFICULT TIMES. AMEN.

—SCOTT WALKER

19

THU
15

While we look not at the things which are seen, but at the things which are not seen. . . .

–II CORINTHIANS 4:18

Everything I saw indicated that my son Jeremy was heading in the wrong direction—again. Long-standing addictions resurfaced, along with risky living and foolish spending, and he had stopped taking medication for his bipolar disorder. He ignored the family and refused our phone calls.

Finally, I went to see him. The door of his apartment was unlocked, and I burst in. It was like looking into a corner of hell—Jeremy was in a rage, totally out of control. As he bellowed, "Get out!" I turned and left, defeated and almost without hope.

Outside his apartment distant church bells I'd never heard before softly chimed a familiar hymn: "Crown him with many crowns, the Lamb upon his throne. . . ." I forced myself to look up into the amazing blue sky and prayed. "Lord, I choose to believe You have a plan to redeem him."

It wasn't an easy prayer. I'm not certain I believed it. Day after day, month after month, as Jeremy's circumstances became worse and worse, I struggled not to let them control my thoughts. I remembered, instead, the clear chiming of the bells and tried to believe they rang for Jeremy's recovery.

Nearly a year later, Jeremy knelt at the altar as a small band of believers gathered around him. Bit by bit he moved into another dimension, physically and spiritually, leaving behind a lifestyle that had almost killed him. Before my eyes he became a man of integrity, purpose and righteousness.

I'd been given everything that I'd barely hoped for—and more.

FATHER, NO MATTER WHAT THE OUTWARD CIRCUMSTANCES, HELP ME LOOK TOWARD WHAT I CAN'T YET SEE.   —MARION BOND WEST

FRI

16

Here am I, and the children the Lord has given me. . . .
—ISAIAH 8:18 (NIV)

As an exercise in ego control, I sit down one day and list all the things I am terrible at. I write for an hour and sigh and realize I could be here for weeks.

I stare at the paper on which is written: *romance, carpentry, patience, hunting, plumbing, writing plays, appreciating ballet, appreciating rap, comprehending talk radio, flying a plane, filling out tax forms, being easygoing about laundry, all kinds of public confession, hiking, biking, dancing, prancing, courting, singing*—although, I realize happily, I'm an excellent bad hummer; I'm persistent and relentless to the point of driving my kids insane. In fact, my endless off-key nasal humming is what makes them roll their eyes and say, *Daaad!* more than anything else, which is a great sound when you think about it.

I get up from the table, grinning and thinking that, despite all the thousands of things I am terrible at, I'm the world champion at totally mortifying my kids, which doesn't seem an altogether bad thing to be good at. The further fact of the matter is that despite how much they complain and roll their eyes, I see the little half-smile they wear when they moan and whine, and that smile is everything to me.

No matter how crazy they make me with their demands and complaints and wet towels on the floor and Major League attitudes, no matter how dark I get about the sagging house and the mountain of bills and looming college tuitions, I always find myself humming happily at the very fact that God sent me three kids in miraculous skin boats from the sea of the stars. No man in the history of the universe ever got such a gift, so I had better hop to getting better at thanking the Lord of the Starfields.

DEAR LORD, THANK YOU, THANK YOU, THANK YOU. AMEN.   —BRIAN DOYLE

SAT 17

I will teach you by the hand of God. . . .
—JOB 27:11

People had casually suggested that we get our trees trimmed before winter, but we hadn't taken them seriously. One of the reasons we bought the house was because of the tall trees on the other side of our fences, and I loved looking at them, watching the seasons change just a few yards outside our windows.

Even when the storm started, I enjoyed watching the trees bend and move, though the yard was soon spattered with pine needles and the last of the dried leaves from the deciduous trees around the evergreens. We slept with our headboard up against one of the bedroom windows, but we weren't worried. It was such a joy to have weather again, after long years of the Los Angeles climate's sameness.

The crash woke me. My husband had gotten up earlier and was downstairs at his computer, but he just about flew up the stairs to where I was now sitting up in bed, trying to figure out what had happened. A long scrape across the glass above my head told us how narrowly the huge branch, which now filled our backyard, had missed breaking through into the house. Our fence lay broken under the bulk of the branch, and wood splinters had been driven into the rail around our back porch.

"Are you all right?" Keith was asking.

"I'm fine, as long as you don't count being foolish," I said. "We're getting the rest of the trees trimmed as soon as we can!"

The next time we got advice about storm preparedness, we were more than ready to listen.

HELP ME, GOD, TO RECOGNIZE SENSE EVEN WHEN I HAVEN'T HEARD IT BEFORE.

—RHODA BLECKER

SUN 18

All Scripture is God-breathed and is useful for teaching, rebuking, correcting and training in righteousness.
—II TIMOTHY 3:16 (NIV)

Last year I took an intensive workshop training teachers to tutor people who have great difficulty reading or writing. One day we observed our instructor Kay work with a thirty-five-year-old man who could only read at a second-grade level. The birth of his first child had motivated him to try to learn to read.

"We don't get many adult students," Kay told us. "Imagine how much courage it takes for people to admit they can't read." Kay asked if anyone could guess the three main reasons why adults will risk yet another humiliating experience of failure and seek instruction.

We surmised correctly that the need to read job applications or newspaper employment ads would prompt someone to try to learn to read. To our amazement, however, the reason most frequently given by adults seeking help is "to be able to read the Bible."

How often I take for granted my ability—and my freedom—to read God's Word. I know an Orthodox monk who traveled in the former Soviet Union during the years Christians were persecuted there. An elderly woman approached him and asked if he could give her a Bible. Anticipating such requests, he had brought Bibles with him and managed to give her one when his official guides weren't looking. Tears streaming down her face, she took the book from him and kissed it. Clutching it to her chest, she whispered, *"Spasiba, spasiba"* ("Thank you, thank you").

LORD, PLEASE REMIND ME NOT TO NEGLECT THE PRECIOUS GIFT OF YOUR WORD, BUT TO OPEN IT EACH DAY AND MAKE IT MY OWN.　　　　　—MARY BROWN

MON
19

And what does the Lord require of you?
To act justly and to love mercy and
to walk humbly with your God.
—MICAH 6:8 (NIV)

Our church's associate pastor asked me to work with him researching and writing a new sermon-drama. Pastor K.D. envisioned the hypothetical meeting of two of history's great reformers and preachers: Martin Luther King Jr. and Martin Luther. Pastor K.D., who would portray Dr. King, and I met several times to discuss the script. We planned to incorporate the writings of both men and portions of Dr. King's most famous speeches. We dug deeply into the impact of Dr. King's work, hoping the drama would not only educate our congregation but also pay tribute to Dr. King.

As Pastor K.D. and I huddled over books and notes in a coffee shop near the church, it occurred to me that the fact that we were collaborating on such a project was in itself a tribute to Dr. King. Back when he marched, there were many places where a white woman and a Black man wouldn't have been able to meet in public to work together. That realization shocked me but also showed me how far America had come in the last fifty years.

Would Dr. King say we're all the way there yet? I doubt it. But we've made a lot of progress. I read in one biography of Dr. King that after being shunned by some white neighborhood boys who had once been his playmates, young Martin told his mother, "One day I'm going to turn this world upside down." He did, and clearly the world is a much richer place because of it.

FATHER OF US ALL, STRENGTHEN MY COMMITMENT TO SEE EVERYONE I MEET AS A BROTHER OR SISTER, EQUALLY WONDERFUL IN YOUR EYES. —GINA BRIDGEMAN

I will praise thee, O Lord, with my whole heart. . . .
—PSALM 9:1

My hands clenched the arms of the dentist's chair. The drill whined, dredging the filling out of a tooth I'd broken the week before when I chomped down on a peanut. The anesthesia the dentist had needled into my gums kept the pain at bay, yet my muscles tensed, making my back ache.

Relax, I told myself firmly, *just relax.* The lecture didn't work.

Then I remembered what our minister had said the previous Sunday: "Praise God in all things."

Praise God for this? Well, it was worth a try.

God, I praise You for this dentist who is fixing my tooth. I praise You that this tooth didn't have to be pulled. I praise You for medicine that deadens pain. I praise You for this drill that is removing the old filling to make way for the new. Gradually my body relaxed.

At last the drilling stopped. The dentist patted my cheek and said, "The worst is over. Now we'll put in the new filling and you'll be on your way."

I praise You, God, for the gift of a fixed tooth!

F<small>ATHER, TODAY</small> I <small>WILL REACH OUT WITH THE MESSAGE OF</small> Y<small>OUR LOVE TO SOME-</small>
<small>ONE WHO IS AFRAID.</small> —M<small>ADGE</small> H<small>ARRAH</small>

Editor's Note: "I've always loved the passage about time in Ecclesiastes (3:1–11)," writes Marilyn Morgan King. "Lately, I've started asking myself questions about how the wisdom of these verses applies to my own life. Here's what I do: After asking my question, I sit in silent prayer, expecting an answer. And answers have come to me during this time of silence, from within me or from a loving Source beyond my limited human mind." Join Marilyn each month as she shares those answers with us.

WED
21

To every thing there is a season. . . .
—E<small>CCLESIASTES</small> 3:1

Koheleth—the Preacher—the author of Ecclesiastes, writes that there's "a time to every purpose under the heaven." And I ask myself, "So why do I so often feel as if I'm running a race against time—and losing?" As I hold this question in prayer, I see that the deeper question is, "How am I using the hours, minutes and seconds I have left?" Am I making time for. . .

A T<small>IME TO</small> E<small>VERY</small>
P<small>URPOSE</small>

rocking another newborn grandchild
in these aging arms
so well practiced in baby-rocking;

breathing in pink and coral sunsets,
white satin moons and
silent mountains
that take away my breath;

the simple things:
fixing a soup-and-fruit supper,
watering the plants,
sweeping the kitchen floor?

Saying "I love you"
to my husband, children and grandchildren;
"Good-bye" to old friends;

"Thank you" to mentors;
"I'm coming" to the
Mystery I call Beloved?

And the answer comes: *How much time? Only this God-given moment—only this eternal now.*

FATHER, MAY I HONOR THIS MOMENT, USING IT FOR WHAT I VALUE MOST, LIKE THE RAREST OF RAINBOWS, SO SOON GONE. —MARILYN MORGAN KING

And he has given them all kinds of skills, including the ability to design and embroider with blue, purple, and red wool. . . .
—EXODUS 35:35 (CEV)

We parked the car and walked toward the correctional facility and into the cold wind. The prison on the top of the hill was only a short distance, but the walk seemed long. *What in the world am I doing in this place?* I thought to myself. *How did we ever get inmates to crochet sweaters for the Guideposts Knit for Kids program?*

Inside the prison stern-looking correctional officers greeted us. Anne, the founder of Wings Ministries, one of Guideposts' outreach partners, returned their greeting. Anne's mission is to build bridges between children and their loved ones in prison. She didn't let the guards' demeanor bother her. She understood that their job was tough and that our safety was important to them.

A guard escorted us to the chapel to meet with inmates. We walked through the prison yard with its brick buildings, barbed wire fences and guards stationed at strategic locations. In the middle of the yard was a chapel, where the inmates were beginning to fill up the pews. Near the altar were more than a hundred sweaters crocheted by inmates. The colors of the sweaters—yellow, blue, orange, green, purple, pink—were a welcome contrast to the dull gray walls, the dim light and the faded blue prison uniforms.

"These sweaters allow us to give back to others," one of the inmates said. "These are for the kids," said another as he proudly showed us his sweaters.

I left the prison knowing that the Guideposts Knit for Kids program isn't just helping children around the world; it's doing wonderful things for everyone who's a part of it. And my walk down the hill to the car didn't seem as long as the walk up.

LORD, NO WALL IS THICK ENOUGH, NO HEART IS HARD ENOUGH TO KEEP OUT YOUR SPIRIT. —PABLO DIAZ

Editor's Note: For a copy of the Knit for Kids pattern, please visit our Web site at www.knitforkids.org or send a stamped, self-addressed envelope to Guideposts Knit for Kids, 39 Seminary Hill Road, Carmel, NY 10512.

Sing unto the Lord, bless his name: shew forth his salvation from day to day. . . . Give unto the Lord glory and strength.

—PSALM 96:2, 7

When I'm creeping along in the rush-hour crush of our Southern California freeways, I find it eases the frustration when a car with a fun or inspirational license plate pulls ahead of me. Recently I was cheered by MY KID'S INHERITANCE on the back of a classy convertible and the simple word BELIEVE on a dark green SUV. I'd like to have met the drivers of those two cars and found out the stories behind their plates.

The other day I pulled into a friend's driveway and parked behind her car. ADORATE DEUM, her license plate read at the top, followed by OMNES ANGELI EJUS at the bottom. "Translate and tell me about it," I asked her.

"Adore God . . . all His angels," she explained. "A few years ago I was studying Psalm 96, and this was part of the devotion in my prayer book. I believe in angels, and I decided that wherever I went, I wanted to encourage people to adore God, so I had a special-order license plate made."

"You sure blessed me," I replied. "How wonderful to declare the glory of God in such a practical way. I bet you get a lot of smiles."

ADORATE DEUM, I ADORE YOU, O GOD. DAY BY DAY, LET THIS BE MY SONG OF PRAISE. —FAY ANGUS

Forgive us our debts,
as we forgive our debtors.

—Matthew 6:12

Somewhere I read that when you feel like blaming some-one for some fault, you should look first to yourself to see how much of the fault might be yours. I suppose it's meant to be an exercise in for-giveness. Learning, as the Lord's Prayer puts it, to forgive others as I ask God to forgive me.

I didn't make much progress in this regard when we came back from our weekly trip to the supermarket, only to discover that the cashier had not put two items in our bag: the furniture polish and the stain stick for laundry. We had everything else, including the cookies I'd bought for the office, but no furniture polish or stain stick.

"Those are expensive things," I told my wife. "We shouldn't have paid for them if we didn't get them." I pulled out the long receipt and found that we'd been charged for both items. I waved it in fury.

"You can talk to them about it when we go back next week," Carol said, reasonably enough.

"But what proof do we have? Just a receipt. They'll never believe me." For the rest of the afternoon I fumed at the failure of people to do their jobs well. The sheer incompetence and laziness. The irresponsibility. Finally, I grudgingly recalled my spiritual goal about blaming. *Okay, Lord,* I said, *I for-give the cashier if You forgive me for getting so angry.* God and I left it at that.

Funny thing, though. The next day, when I lifted up the bag with the cookies for the office, it seemed heavier than usual. Guess what was inside?

WHEN I'M ABOUT TO BLAME SOMEONE, LORD, LET ME START CLOSE TO HOME FIRST.
—RICK HAMLIN

Let us not give up meeting together,
as some are in the habit of doing, but
let us encourage one another....

—Hebrews 10:25 (NIV)

After moving a few months ago, I started attending a new church nearby. I went every Sunday, singing the songs and listening to the sermon. I even took notes.

The only problem was that was all I did. I didn't join a Bible study, volunteer to hand out bulletins or play for the softball team. I usually arrived a few minutes late and left immediately after the service concluded, so I didn't get to know any of my fellow churchgoers.

Then one Sunday I ran into Rachael, a friend from college. She had been attending the church too. But unlike me, Rachael had gotten involved. She was attending a Bible study and had helped with registration for the upcoming retreat. She was part of the community.

Driving home from church that day, I finally understood that showing up on Sunday morning isn't enough. Having a relationship with God requires having relationships with His people, because it's through them that I will give and receive His love.

This past week I arrived early and met a few folks before the service started. Who knows? Maybe I'll even start handing out bulletins.

LORD, YOUR WORD COMPARES THE CHURCH TO A BODY. PLEASE SHOW ME THE PART I WAS MEANT TO PLAY IN IT.   —JOSHUA SUNDQUIST

MON
26

[God] comforts us in all our affliction so that we will be able to comfort those who are in any affliction with the comfort with which we ourselves are comforted by God.
—II CORINTHIANS 1:4 (NAS)

Last winter an ongoing problem with lower-back pain meant scheduling a series of medical appointments. Unfortunately, the appointments all seemed to fall on the coldest days of our Canadian winter, which meant bundling up against the cold.

With a sore back, hobbling into the doctor's office for each appointment was difficult enough without the added problem of removing mittens and parka and scarf and sweater and boots.

On one visit a frail elderly lady, her appointment over, grimaced with pain as she attempted to pull on her warm winter overshoes. In vain she bent down once, then twice. Noticing her predicament, I put aside my magazine and crossed the waiting room.

"Here, let me do that for you," I said quietly.

"Oh no!" she protested. "I couldn't let a stranger . . ."

"Of course you can," I replied, kneeling down in front of her and slipping her feet into her boots. "There, it's all done."

She looked down at me with a kind smile. "Thank you," she said. "It's my back, you know."

I knew.

LORD, I ALSO KNOW HOW DIFFICULT IT IS TO ACCEPT HELP. GIVE ME THE GRACE TO SET ASIDE MY PRIDE AND RECEIVE THE ASSISTANCE OFFERED BY THE PEOPLE YOU SEND AS CHANNELS OF COMFORT. —ALMA BARKMAN

Be careful for nothing; but in every thing by prayer and supplication with thanksgiving let your requests be made known unto God.
—PHILIPPIANS 4:6

"Mom, ready for dominoes?"

"When I finish," I say, quickly looking up from the computer. I read the prayer submitted to OurPrayer.org and click the Approve button so that it posts on the site. OurPrayer.org is a Guideposts Web site where I blog, edit inspiring stories and review prayers.

"Now?" Solomon taps the domino box on the computer table.

I nod. As a work-from-home mom, finding a happy balance between work and play is an ongoing challenge. The kettle whistles, and I pour myself a cup of chamomile tea and grab a juice box for Solomon. This time of day, while Henry naps, is what Solomon calls SMT: Special Mommy Time.

Solomon rests his chin on the table as we select our dominoes. One by one the tiles turn into a long snake of black dominoes and white dots. As Solomon thinks over his next move, my thoughts drift to a prayer that's submitted every day by the same OurPrayer member: "Dear God, thank You for today."

More than a decade ago, when I worked for a company that helped launch Web sites, we brainstormed the ways we thought the Internet would change the world. We spoke of advancements in entertainment and commerce; we never imagined people reaching out to each other online with love and support, one prayer at a time.

Sitting in a patch of sunlight with Solomon, I say a prayer of thanksgiving for the blessings in my life and for that special OurPrayer visitor who reminds me every day that today is a gift to cherish.

DEAR GOD, THANK YOU FOR TODAY. —SABRA CIANCANELLI

Editor's Note: Visit Sabra online at www.OurPrayer.org, a faith-filled community brimming with inspiring devotionals, firsthand accounts of the power of prayer, uplifting articles, a closer look at our *Daily Guideposts* contributors and much more.

WED
28

Let a righteous man strike me—it is a kindness;
let him rebuke me—it is oil on my head. . . .

—PSALM 141:5 (NIV)

It's been years since I've seen Rachel Rowe, but I still consider her my friend. I met her in Alabama while she and I were in an Army-sponsored technical writing/editing program. She was smart, quirky and could make a mean bowl of bean dip. But what I came to appreciate most about Rachel was that she was the kind of friend who had the courage to tell you when you were wrong.

I grew up in a family of sassy-tongued people. As a matter of pride and to protect myself, I developed my own tongue to a legendary sharpness. I was a word-slinger and I always had my weapon ready. I took pleasure in knowing that I could take out any bully, regardless of size, with just a few well-placed words.

One day I was offended by a man in the office where Rachel and I worked. I don't recollect what he said, but I do recall that he had embarrassed me in front of several people. Without batting an eye, I pulled out my weapon, took off the safety and let him have it right between the eyes. Just before I turned to walk away, I saw tears in his eyes.

A couple of days later Rachel came by my house to visit. I was happy to see her, and it didn't hurt that she'd brought a bag of tortilla chips and a bowl of bean dip. While we dipped and munched, she told me that what I had done wasn't kind; I'd used my gift of words for evil rather than for good.

Far more than for her winning ways with a bean, I admired Rachel for her honesty and courage, and for loving me enough to tell me the truth.

LORD, BLESS THOSE WHO HAVE THE COURAGE TO SPEAK TRUTH WITH LOVE. HELP ME TO BE NUMBERED AMONG THEM. —SHARON FOSTER

THU 29

My soul faints with longing for your salvation,
but I have put my hope in your word.
—PSALM 119:81 (NIV)

I'm still a relatively young man and yet it seems that I lose at least one friend every year. Four years ago Wayne died of throat cancer. Three years ago Basil died of injuries sustained in a car crash. Two years ago Steve died suddenly of a heart attack while traveling in Italy. And this past year Cynthia never recovered from a stroke that began on Thanksgiving.

On some days I miss them intensely. At other times I may go for a week without giving their lives and deaths much thought. How is that possible? *Survival*, I tell myself. In order to keep moving along with a modicum of emotional health, we simply have to ignore much of the death and sadness that we see or hear about every day.

When Cynthia was dying last winter, she told me to be hopeful.

"Hopeful for what?" I asked her one gloomy afternoon.

"For what will come," she said. "For what is greater."

I loved her. I loved her vision, and she was right. I have hope. Not a foolish, credulous hope, but a large one nonetheless. My hope is in the graciousness of the Father, Who will always comfort His children if they are willing to listen, in the love of the Son, Who knows what it feels like to suffer profoundly, and in the power of the Spirit, Who feeds our small hopes with the comfort of a mother and Who brings us faith that all things work together for good.

GRACIOUS GOD, SHOW ME YOUR LOVE WHEN I AM IN TROUBLE. TOUCH MY LIFE THROUGH THE LOVE OF OTHERS AND ALLOW ME TO DO THE SAME FOR THE GLORY OF YOUR FUTURE. AMEN. —JON SWEENEY

FRI 30

Present yourselves to God as those who have been brought from death to life, and present your members to God as instruments of righteousness.

—ROMANS 6:13 (NRSV)

I like to pray in different ways and in unusual places. Sometimes I try to incorporate movement and imagination into my prayers.

So when I feel helpless, confused or in need of comfort, I envision the Lord cradling me as He would cradle an infant. If I'm praying for my marriage, I picture Him walking with Charlie and me, arm in arm, or holding our hands as we all walk together. When I pray for someone who's ill, I imagine the Lord holding that person or raining a healing light down upon him or her. And when I pray for healing or forgiveness for myself, I throw my arms up into the air and ask Him to pour out His forgiveness and healing on me.

I was praying this way recently when it occurred to me that I might have it all backward. I'd opened my arms to the Lord, praying that He would pour His forgiveness and healing over me, but wasn't I missing a step? Shouldn't I be opening my arms to the Lord first to acknowledge and release the sin and the sickness I needed Him to forgive and heal? Only after I'd willingly relinquished these maladies of the soul and body to God, trusting that He would remove them, could I sincerely ask for the forgiveness and healing I sought.

JESUS, YOU KNOW MY FLAWS AND FRAILTIES. AS I PRAY IN YOUR NAME, GIVE ME THE COURAGE TO TRUST THEM TO YOUR HEALING SPIRIT. —MARCI ALBORGHETTI

SAT 31

His unchanging plan has always been to adopt us into his own family by bringing us to himself through Jesus Christ. . . .

—EPHESIANS 1:5 (NLT)

More than two hundred faces stared up at me from the cards on the table. Each represented a child in need of a sponsor. Thirty-five dollars a month could provide the child with a chance to go to school, have clean water and food, and learn about God's love.

"Do you sponsor a child?" my friend Jaycee asked when she noticed me looking at the cards.

"Well . . . no." I wanted to tell her how paralyzed I felt, looking at all the faces and having to choose just one.

"We sponsor a child from Zambia," she said. "Maybe if you sponsored one, too, we could visit them together."

"Okay," I said, still unsure. *But, Lord, how can I choose?*

Calmly, Jaycee asked me if I'd like to sponsor a boy or a girl.

"A girl," I said, thinking of my son Trace.

The man at the table was eager to assist us. Behind him were boxes filled with cards representing hundreds of children. Jaycee and I looked through the cards while people gathered around to help us search. Sometimes the country was right, but the child was a boy. Then someone found a girl from Africa, but not from Zambia.

Maybe I'm being too picky. Or maybe I shouldn't sponsor a child at all. Finally the man smiled and raised his hand. "Here she is," he said. "Her name is Falia."

The picture showed a petite girl with huge eyes and closely cropped hair. I paid, looking over the material as I started to walk away. Suddenly I stopped. "I can't believe this . . . Falia and I have the same birthday. What a strange coincidence!"

"Maybe it's not a coincidence," Jaycee said.

FATHER, BRING ALL THE WORLD'S CHILDREN INTO YOUR FAMILY.

—AMANDA BOROZINSKI

MY LIVING WORDS

1 _____

2 _____

3 _____

4

5

6

7

8

9

10

11

12

13

14

15

16

17

18

19

20

21

22

23

24

25

26

27

28

29

30

31

FEBRUARY

Heaven and earth shall pass away:
but my words shall not pass away.

—MARK 13:31

**SUN
1**

*And the pleasure of the Lord
shall prosper in His hand.*

—Isaiah 53:10 (NKJV)

Hugh Hudson's 1981 movie masterpiece *Chariots of Fire* tells the story of Eric Liddell, a runner in the 1924 Olympics who refuses to run on Sunday out of respect for God's Word.

Because of his refusal to run on Sunday, Eric is forced to run in a longer race, the 400 meter, for which he hasn't trained. But he flies like a rocket and breaks the tape in a thrilling victory.

What could inspire a man to such a feat? I wondered. I think the answer is in his conversation with his sister Jenny before the race. She thinks running is frivolous for a man who is going to become a missionary.

GOD SPEAKS
THROUGH OUR GIFTS

"God made me for a purpose," Eric explains. "He also made me fast. When I run, I feel His pleasure. To give it up would be to hold Him in contempt. To win is to honor Him."

Jenny is satisfied with his answer. Just before the race, she hands him a note on which she has written I Samuel 2:30 (RSV): "For those who honor me I will honor."

To do what God designed me to do is to feel His approval. When I'm writing on the chalkboard of my classroom, hoeing in my garden or fixing a student's car, I can feel God's pleasure flowing through my hands.

Everyone has gifts from God. To develop those gifts and to use them for others makes one a conduit for the power of God. You can almost hear Him say, "Well done, good and faithful servant."

HELP ME TO WIN THE RACE OF LIFE FOR YOUR HONOR, LORD.

—DANIEL SCHANTZ

**MON
2**

*You . . . are intimately acquainted
with all my ways.*

—Psalm 139:3 (NAS)

I stepped on the treadmill at the Y and attached my cell phone. Because I have relatives with drug and alcohol addictions, I believed it was my job to remain on the alert. That meant staying near the phone.

After working out, I glanced at the sauna. I'd never entered the steamy room, but that day I decided to put my phone inside a locker and go for it.

"How long do you stay in this thing?" I asked the woman sitting there.

She stretched her legs out on the wooden bench. "Twenty minutes. I love it."

I peeked anxiously through the door at the lockers. "You okay?" she said. "You look worried."

"Our family has a lot of . . . problems. I should be near my phone."

"What could you do if you heard bad news?" she asked.

When I didn't answer, she continued. "We've had problems too. Ten years ago, my babies and I lived in our car while my husband was in rehab."

"Really?" My skin tingled despite the heat.

"God never left me. One night, a restaurant manager realized we were hungry. He fed us."

"Is your husband sober now?"

"Yes."

"How did you fix him?"

"I didn't. Pain is a mighty fine teacher." She paused a moment. "Girlfriend," she said, "let go. Give it to God, unless you think you can do a better job."

GOD, FORGIVE ME FOR TRYING TO BE YOU. FOR TODAY, I RELEASE MYSELF AND MY FAMILY TO YOUR CARE. AND THANK YOU FOR SENDING AN ANGEL OF A WOMAN TO MEET ME IN THAT SAUNA.

—JULIE GARMON

You have been given fullness in Christ, who is the head over every power and authority.

—COLOSSIANS 2:10 (NIV)

My friend Joanna leads a girls' Bible study at our church. She tries to keep things light and uplifting, giving the dozen or so teenagers a brief respite from their daily stresses by studying God's Word.

When the class began, Joanna gave the girls an assignment. "At the next meeting, I want you to introduce yourself to the group." She wasn't looking for names and club affiliations, but for insight into how the girls saw themselves.

Joanna called me to talk about the assignment and asked me to do the exercise. She planned to read it to the girls at the start of the class to get the discussion moving. "Sure," I said. Certainly I knew myself well enough to write a few paragraphs.

"Who I Am; Ashley 101," I wrote quickly. Then nothing. I stared at the blank page in front of me, thinking of all the things I thought I might be expected to say. "I love Jesus. I am a Christian," I wrote. It was true, but somehow it felt forced. I scratched it out. Page after page lay crumpled around my bedroom. "Why is this so hard?" I said to no one in general and God in particular.

Then it dawned on me. I kept trying to make a list that had God as the first priority. It felt forced because He wasn't the first priority—He was so much more than that. He wasn't a bullet point on my list; He was the paper the list was written on, the foundation for everything I wanted to be and to do. Suddenly, writing about who I am and what I value became much easier.

LORD, HELP ME REMEMBER THAT YOU ARE IN EVERYTHING I DO, SAY, SEE AND EXPERIENCE. —ASHLEY JOHNSON

WED
4

"This happened so that the work of God might be displayed in his life. . . ."
—JOHN 9:3 (NIV)

"How are you?"

That familiar question makes me smile as I consider the possibility of giving a totally honest answer after living with cancer for the last two years.

Many times the question comes from a stranger, such as the waiter who introduces himself at our table in a restaurant. The answer is more about making him feel comfortable than about my current health. So I automatically say, "Fine, thanks," even when I'm not so fine.

When a good friend or a family member like my son-in-law asks, "How are you?" I sometimes go for the obvious, smart-alecky answer. "I have cancer," I say with a grin, "but otherwise, I'm great." To that, my son-in-law rolls his eyes and vows never to ask me that question again.

Many times the question comes from well-meaning people who care but don't need a lengthy description or a boring tale of woe. Last week at church, soon after I got home from yet another hospital stay, several people asked, "How are you?"

This is when the question challenges me the most. How do I give a current, appropriately honest answer? After all, when cancer enters a person's life, it changes how she is. I liken it to living within a picture frame with a persistent dark cloud on the horizon. But cancer also brings the odd gift of making today's sunshine preciously important, so that day I answered the question this way: "I'm good for today . . . and today that's good enough for me."

Next week or next month, the appropriately honest answer might be different, so I ask God's help in seeking the right words.

FATHER, I WANT THE ANSWER TO "HOW ARE YOU?" TO POINT BACK TO YOU. PLEASE GIVE ME WORDS THAT REFLECT MY FAITH.   —CAROL KUYKENDALL

THU
5

"Haven't I commanded you? Strength! Courage! Don't be timid; don't get discouraged. God, your God, is with you every step you take."
—JOSHUA 1:9 (MSG)

"What do you mean Joel doesn't know his colors? Of course he knows his colors!"

My voice was raised, and I sounded defensive; I was embarrassed by the outburst. I'd asked the school psychologist how our son had done on his kindergarten screening test, and she answered that he had done fine, but that she was surprised Joel didn't know his colors.

Soon I better understood our almost-five-year-old. When the psychologist related that an exasperated Joel had finally blurted out, "I can't tell you which circle is yellow until you tell me which one is red!" we realized that Joel is color-blind.

I shouldn't have been surprised. My wife Kathy's dad sees in shades of gray. Like Joel, I can identify color—maybe—if you give me the spectrum of colors from which I can choose. Because being color-blind made me feel inadequate, I had chosen not to share my difficulties, even with those closest to me.

That was twenty-five years ago, yet every time I open my suitcase, this story replays in my mind. Why? Because Kathy has to pack for me when I travel, so I can dress myself with coordinating colors of socks, trousers, jackets, shirts and ties. I wish there were little symbols sewn into my clothing, so I'd feel confident enough to pack my own bag. But until there are, I'm going to try to be grateful for the abilities I have and stop being discouraged or embarrassed by the ones I don't have.

LORD, WHEN I'M DISCOURAGED, REMIND ME THAT YOU ARE WITH ME EVERY STEP OF THE WAY, GIVING ME COURAGE AND STRENGTH. —TED NACE

When Paul saw them, he thanked God and took courage.
—ACTS 28:15 (NKJV)

Intimidated by the winter wind, I've been housebound for several days now. Cabin fever, my mother called it. But then this noon I phoned my brother Philip, clear across the country, hoping our conversation would follow its predictable pattern.

You see, every six months or so, when I'm feeling isolated and discouraged, I call him. We chat a few minutes and then I quietly say, "I need courage." *Courage.* The Latin core of the word is *cor* (heart).

Being a good listener and lifelong pal, Philip knows what I need. "I love you," he says, assuring me that I'm not a solitary individual but integrated into a larger family, brothers and sisters by birth and by faith. We talk awhile longer and finally he signs off with a challenge and command: "Courage!"

Our ritual is simple, but it works. I hang up the phone, feeling connected, spiritually enabled to heed my brother's *Sister, take heart!*

LORD, GIVE ME COURAGE. —EVELYN BENCE

Peter went up upon the housetop to pray. . . .
—ACTS 10:9

Have you ever tried to pray in a busy household, with one child dismantling the living room couch to make a fort, another practicing ukulele in an upstairs bedroom, your spouse banging pots in the kitchen and workers installing a boiler in the basement?

That's how it was for me the other day. I try to put in a few periods of quiet prayer each morning, but this time the obstacles looked overwhelming. What to do? I decided that the situation called for more than grousing; it needed a little "Yankee know-how," as we say here in New England.

I decided to scout the house for a solitary spot. There's another old New England saying that "the forest is the poor man's overcoat." In my case the stair landing became the poor man's prayer stall. I sat down, halfway between the chaos of the ground floor and the racket of the second floor, and positioned myself to look out a nearby window. I could see nothing but a line of scraggly firs. My perch was awkward, my back ached, Hawaiian melodies filtered down from above, assorted crashes rose from below, but I was finally alone.

Psalm 72:3 says, "The mountains shall bring peace to the people." I had found my mountain. It may have been cramped and manmade, but it was still my private retreat. So I bowed my head, giving thanks that even a stair landing in the midst of a noisy household could become a mountaintop, if the spirit was willing.

LORD, TEACH ME TO PRAY WHEREVER I AM, FOR YOU ARE EVERYWHERE AND LISTENING ALWAYS. —PHILIP ZALESKI

SUN
8

Meditate on these things; give yourself entirely to them. . . .
—I TIMOTHY 4:15 (NKJV)

Henry, my closest friend, served as Sunday school superintendent at our church. When Henry asked me to teach a class, my firm refusal was laced with guilt. *Me teach? The children deserve better than that.*

Then one Sunday, when I was hurrying down a hall in the church basement, I passed a darkened classroom and heard a muffled cry. I entered the barren room where a single lightbulb dangled from the ceiling. Two long tables filled the room, and a solitary window peeked down at the tables and out across the lawn. A little girl was huddled, weeping. I placed my hand on her shoulder. She glanced up, and between sobs she told me that her mother had died two weeks before. I hurried up the stairs to tell Henry I would try to teach.

Several Sundays later there was a knock on the classroom door before class began. I answered, and our assistant minister called me into the hall. "Oscar," he said, "always remember that the love you show these children on Sunday morning might be all the love they receive the entire week."

My mission was clear: I could share and I could listen with all my heart. The children showered me with attention, trust and love. Some remained after class to share their concerns. We needed each other.

CARING GOD, THANK YOU FOR USING MY EFFORTS TO STRENGTHEN AND ENCOURAGE YOUNG HEARTS TO STRENGTHEN AND ENCOURAGE ME. —OSCAR GREENE

MON 9

Don't you realize how kind, tolerant, and patient God is with you? . . .

—ROMANS 2:4 (NLT)

Today I was with my twenty-two-month-old grandson Brock, feeding him his lunch. Between bites, he asked me the same questions over and over. Bite of cheese. "Nana, where Mama?" Bite of turkey. "Nana, where Papa?" Bite of bread and butter. "Elmo? Elmo?"

The first two I could answer: "At work." The Elmo one I winged: "Yes, Elmo."

Brock took a drink of milk and the round began again. "Nana, where Mama?" "Nana, where Papa?" "Elmo? Elmo?"

I gave the same answers over and over and over. Our conversation took on a predictable rhythm.

I thought about Brock's incessant questions as I drove home and was suddenly reminded of someone else who tends to ask the same questions over and over—me. And the recipient of this repetitive babble? God.

Year after year I keep imploring, "Why don't You answer my prayers?" "Where are You when I hurt?" "Why must my family face this trial?" "Would it spoil some divine plan if You made me tall and thin, or at least let me keep off those eight pounds I keep relosing?"

And over and over the same answers come: *I hear you. Trust me. I love you just the way you are.*

If God tires or grows weary of my endlessly repeated questions, He never shows it. I guess patience is something God—and nanas—have in common.

OPEN MY EARS AND MY HEART, LORD, THAT I MIGHT HEAR AND BELIEVE YOUR PATIENT ANSWERS TO MY PERSISTENT PLEAS. —MARY LOU CARNEY

No, dear brothers, I am still not all I should be but I am bringing all my energies to bear on this one thing: Forgetting the past and looking forward to what lies ahead.

—PHILIPPIANS 3:13 (TLB)

Now that I'm in my sixties and working my way toward my nineties, when I hope I will finally be wise, I often ask myself, *Why am I here? Am I fulfilling God's purpose? Am I making a difference to the people who matter: my parents, children, grandchildren, friends and neighbors?*

When I get introspective like this, I rev up my action plan. I may not be wise yet, but I do know this: In order to feel good about myself, I have to give more of myself.

So I make plans to fly home to Illinois to visit my dad and stepmom. I promise myself to phone them more often, at least once a week. I listen to Hannah and Zachary, the two of my eight grandchildren who take piano lessons, play their lesson pieces for me on the phone. I organize a nature event, picnic, lunch or an arts-books-crafts fair for my neighborhood friends.

Am I making a difference? Yes, as long as I work at it every single day. You see, I've learned it takes work to make a difference.

LORD, YOU GAVE ME GIFTS WHEN I WAS BORN. HELP ME TO USE THEM EVERY DAY TO MAKE A DIFFERENCE IN THIS WORLD.   —PATRICIA LORENZ

"Oh, that I had the wings of a dove! I would fly away and be at rest."

—PSALM 55:6 (NIV)

Three days a week I'd drag myself into the gym, burdened by the weight of a full day's work and the commute from Manhattan to Newark, New Jersey. I'd take off my thick winter coat, and little by little the heaviness would fall away as I changed into my workout clothes. When I slipped on my white leather tumbling shoes, my back would straighten and the excitement would escape from the corners of my lips. I was ready to fly!

Flip City was a nonprofit trampoline and power-tumbling gym

located in one of the most dilapidated inner-city neighborhoods. But in the midst of poverty, decayed buildings and mural tributes to the dead, I found the one place where I felt the most alive.

The trampoline would lift me to the point of weightlessness as I soared above the world. I felt at home in the air, twisting and turning as if gravity were a curse that only applied to others. Although as an adult I stood out among the neighborhood children, in the gym we were all equal members of an exclusive club. We were the privileged few who knew what it felt like to fly. We were the fortunate ones who could lift our bodies toward the sky and experience the most intense form of freedom and euphoria.

Years have passed since I trained at Flip City, but I'll forever be grateful to a sport that not only propelled me toward the heavens, but also gave me and hundreds of inner-city children the confidence to reach for goals above and beyond the pull of gravity.

LORD, NO MATTER HOW EARTHBOUND MY BODY MAY BE, HELP MY SPIRIT TO SOAR.

—KAREN VALENTIN

THU 12

God looked over everything he had made; it was so good, so very good! . . .
—GENESIS 1:31 (MSG)

When I was a little girl, I loved coloring books more than anything. I'd choose a purple crayon for the leaves of a tree instead of the expected green, and my mother, a first-grade teacher, would smile and pronounce it perfect. "If leaves look purple to you, honey, then that's the color they are," she'd assure me. "Don't worry about what other people say."

But when I grew up and had my own home, I found myself moni-

WITH ETERNITY IN VIEW

Color Outside the Lines

toring the trends portrayed in glossy decorating magazines. Before long I was succumbing to them. *Better not paint the family room buttery yellow; hunter green is in this year. And use an antique Hoosier kitchen cabinet for a desk? What would the neighbors think?*

Then one day this year when I was out shopping, the craziest notion came to me: *Buy a coloring book and a big box of crayons.* Before long, I wasn't just coloring leaves purple; I was coloring outside the lines. And enjoying every minute of it! As I ignored the rigid rules of Coloring 101, I experienced a wonderful new freedom. Suddenly the world looked full of endless possibilities. When I nailed antique wooden shoe forms to a board to create a one-of-a-kind hat rack, I received compliments galore, a few of them even from the neighbors. Armed with newfound confidence, I retrieved that forgotten Hoosier cabinet from the garage, scooted a ladder-back chair up to its porcelain top and had the most serviceable desk ever. Its little drawers are ideal for housing pens and paper clips.

This year I'm celebrating both my Creator and my God-inspired creativity . . . and coloring outside the lines every step of the way.

THANK YOU, GOD, FOR THE WONDROUS WORLD YOU CREATED. HELP ME TO BE FEARLESS IN BEAUTIFYING MY LITTLE CORNER OF IT. —ROBERTA MESSNER

FRI
13

Give us this day our daily bread.
—MATTHEW 6:11

As a magazine editor I've interviewed any number of fascinating and inspirational people. I'll never forget the first time I met with Jim Stoval and his wife Crystal in New York City. As Crystal and I talked at a restaurant table, Jim entered the crowded room, navigated his way around tables and waiters, reached our table, and held out his hand. Later he asked the waiter if it was all right for him to play the grand piano he'd passed and then walked over, sat down and played a medley of show tunes to the delight of diners and staff. Jim is one of the most positive, focused and energetic people I've ever met. He's also blind.

In his twenties Jim was diagnosed with a degenerative eye disease. Instead of retreating into isolation and self-pity, he became a highly successful businessman, speaker and author, traveling around the world. Usually, Crystal or a colleague travels with him, but sometimes he'll go exploring on his own—no dog, no cane. Once he fell off a porch and down a ravine at a ski resort in Colorado. He climbed back up and never thought twice about it.

"How do you do it?" I asked him. "How do you go out into the world, all over the world, and face the unknown each day?"

Jim responded with a deep, rolling laugh. "Mary Ann," he said in his Oklahoma baritone, "that's why the prayer says, 'Give us *this* day our *daily* bread.'"

DEAR GOD, EVERY DAY, DAY BY DAY, YOUR BLESSINGS AND STRENGTH ARE AVAILABLE FOR ME TO CALL ON. THIS DAY, EVERY DAY, MY DAILY BREAD—I ASK FOR IT.

—MARY ANN O'ROARK

SAT 14

Beloved, let us love one another:
for love is of God. . . .
—I JOHN 4:7

I inherited my aunt's Bible. Lovingly worn, it falls open to her favorite passages. With her Bible in my hands, it's impossible not to think of my aunt and the many times she turned to it for strength: when my uncle was missing in action during World War II and later when she learned he was a prisoner of war; after the war, when they learned to make peace with their childlessness; and during my uncle's long illness, when my aunt prayed for him to let go and go to heaven.

After my uncle died, my aunt spent many years in poor health. She often slept with her Bible on her lap. During those last days she spoke through tears about how she longed for her Phil and how she couldn't wait to see him again.

The first time I opened my aunt's Bible, I was awestruck at the beautiful cards tucked in the pages, reminders of my great-grandfather, grandfather, great-uncle and uncle. Then, after having the Bible for almost a year, I found pressed deep in its pages a scrap of notebook paper folded into a tiny heart. It read:

Dearest husband,

I love you more than I will ever be able to express with pen and ink. You are my rock. My strength. My comfort. God bless you for your goodness.

I love you always and forever.

DEAR LORD, ON THIS VALENTINE'S DAY, REMIND ME THAT EVEN THOUGH LOVE ISN'T ALWAYS PERFECT OR EASY, ITS STRENGTH AND BEAUTY ARE EVERLASTING.

—SABRA CIANCANELLI

READER'S ROOM

At the end of the week, we had a terrible ice storm in Missouri. By Sunday we had lost our power. We were able to stay in our home because we had a gas range and a small gas stove for heat. This became a time to pray, meditate and thank God for His care. During the day I was able to read by the light reflected from the snow. And I drew on the Light of Christ to assure my heart of His presence. —*Carolyn Schemahorn, Joplin, Missouri*

SUN 15

Yet, O Lord, you are our Father.
We are the clay, you are the potter;
we are all the work of your hand.
—ISAIAH 64:8 (NIV)

Yesterday I had a busy day shopping, going from store to store and waiting in long lines at the registers. At one crowded store a group of teenagers stood in line behind me, talking loudly and acting silly. Annoyed, I'd turned my back on them.

In church today my pastor shared a story. It was about a man who had found a violin and reconditioned it. Expertly crafted by the master violin maker Stradivarius in the 1600s, it was known for its exquisite sound. When people found out the man was going to play it for the first time, a large crowd gathered. When he began, the crowd gasped in awe, not because of how beautifully he played; the crowd was in awe simply because they were hearing a violin made by a master.

The pastor paused, looking out at the congregation. "We should all do the same," he said. "When we see our husbands, our wives, our children, even people on the street, we should all be in awe, simply because of Who made them."

Yes, God has made us all—short, tall, young, old, quiet, loud, serious and silly. And tomorrow, while finishing up my to-do list, I plan to respond to the people around me with the reverence due those who have been lovingly and uniquely created by the consummate Master.

DIVINE CREATOR, KEEP ME EVER MINDFUL THAT WHEN I LOVE OTHERS, I AM LOVING YOU.
—MELODY BONNETTE

MON
16

Whom the Lord, and this people,
and all the men of Israel, choose, his
will I be, and with him will I abide.

−II SAMUEL 16:18

It was mild and clear last night, so my wife Julia took our three-year-old Stephen out to look at the moon. As she held him up so he could see over the wall that overlooks the Hudson River, he noticed the George Washington Bridge, its towers lit up for the holiday and glowing like crystal. "That's our bridge," Stephen said. "It used to be George Washington's, but he died. Now it's ours."

I don't think Stephen meant that we could change the bridge's name to the Attaway Bridge or that we could collect the tolls. He might have been a little hazy about when and by whom it was built, but somehow he grasped that its beauty—the French architect Le Corbusier called it "the most beautiful bridge in the world . . . the only seat of grace in the disordered city"—belongs to everyone who uses and enjoys it.

We call Washington "the father of our country." As its first and—with Abraham Lincoln—its greatest president, he gave an example that all who have succeeded him in office have tried to follow. And in doing so, he demonstrated that the presidency doesn't belong to any of its occupants, no matter how gifted and great. It belongs to all of us who help to choose its occupant and assist him or her in governing by our support and our criticism. It used to be Washington's, Lincoln's and Franklin D. Roosevelt's. But now, and always, it's ours.

LORD, REMIND ME TO KEEP OUR PRESIDENT IN MY PRAYERS NOT JUST ON PRESIDENTS' DAY BUT THROUGHOUT THE YEAR.   —ANDREW ATTAWAY

TUE
17

. . . A time to plant, and a time to
pluck up that which is planted.

−ECCLESIASTES 3:2

My husband Robert has taken up gardening in his retirement. At a recent gardeners' workshop, he learned that at our altitude in Colorado (7,800 feet), the growing season is only fifty days long! No wonder he can't get tomatoes or green peppers to ripen or irises to bloom.

So I ask in silent prayer, "What about those plantings that fail to grow?" As I wait, an answer seems to come from beyond:

A TIME TO EVERY PURPOSE

You sow seeds every day whether you know it or not.
Some plantings grow to be food for the soul:
the songs you sing aloud
or hum in silence;
the kind words you speak
to those with aching hearts;
the prayers that live within you.

Some plantings can crowd out the lettuce and the lilies:
weeds that plant themselves and settle in,
like hurtful words carelessly spoken.
These must be plucked up.

The planting and the plucking up
are two parts of one thing—
you are the sower; God is the grower.
The harvest is one whole and holy soul.

CREATOR GOD, I CONFESS THAT I SOW—AND REAP—BOTH JOY AND PAIN AS I WALK THROUGH LIFE. I TRUST THAT YOU CAN MAKE A THRIVING GARDEN OF MY PLANTINGS. —MARILYN MORGAN KING

WED 18

I will take the stony heart out of their flesh,
and will give them an heart of flesh.
—EZEKIEL 11:19

My right knee used to be one of my best knees. Not anymore. A year ago I was playing dek hockey when a very large young man fell on it, and my anterior cruciate ligament snapped like an old rubber band. I had surgery to replace the missing piece with a donation from a cadaver. (It's pretty bad when a dead guy's knee is in better shape than yours.)

Rehab was difficult. Tara, the physical therapist, was extraordinarily patient and encouraging, but she used the famous "we" voice found only in medicine: "Why don't *we* try to do some more reps and work it out more?" I found I could do many more leg extensions by visualizing that I was kicking her in the shin.

I learned a lot about myself during recovery—none of it good. I have the emotional maturity of a four-year-old, and that's probably unfair to most four-year-olds. I can't wait, even when waiting is best; I can't allow others to help, even if it means delaying my own recovery—which helps no one. Worse, I can be prickly and tense, especially to those I love.

There are times when I wonder whose knee ligament I received. The only thing I know about the donor is that he was male and under fifty, which makes his death all the more tragic. Yet here I sit a year later, virtually pain free, thanks to his family's generosity.

It's lucky I met the medical criteria for his donation: the right blood type, the right gender. I'm glad they didn't ask for the right attitude. Apparently I still have much, much more rehab to go.

LORD, THE KNEE MUSCLES HAVE BOUNCED BACK (THANK YOU!), BUT THE PUMPING RED MUSCLE IN MY CHEST HAS GROWN FLABBY. I NEED TO DO SOME MORE REPS AND WORK IT OUT MORE.   —MARK COLLINS

THU 19

"The Spirit of the Lord spoke through me; his word was on my tongue."

—II SAMUEL 23:2 (NIV)

When Ellie, a new coworker at the bookstore, told me that she used to be a counselor before she got laid off because of budget cuts, I patted her hand in sympathy. "This retail job must be a real comedown for you," I commented. If I'd expected her to agree with me, I was in for a surprise.

"Oh no," she said. "I come in contact with more hurting people in a day here than I did in my old job in a week."

"How on earth do you know that?" I asked. Most of the customers I met seemed confident and pulled together.

"Why, just yesterday," she said, "a lady came in looking for a book on divorce."

I remembered the woman vividly. She'd looked annoyed, I thought, so I'd passed her on to Ellie.

"Well, anyone looking for a book on divorce or grieving is obviously looking for help," I admitted, "but you make it sound like everyone can use help."

"I think that many of them can," Ellie said. "Do you remember that tall man who wanted a book on finances?"

I did remember him. He'd seemed so snappish that I'd kept right on shelving books while I let Ellie help him.

"He was facing bankruptcy," she said quietly. At my astonished look she said, "As I walk them to the right shelf, I try to say a kind word and then I listen carefully. And I ask God to help me say the right thing."

So I tried it. A man wanted a book on "neighbor law," and when he poured out his frustration about the child with a drum set who'd moved in above him, I briefly poured out my sympathy . . . and left both of us with a smile on our faces, for a change.

GOD, HELP ME TO HELP SOMEONE WITH A KIND WORD OR AN UNDERSTANDING EAR TODAY.   —LINDA NEUKRUG

FRI
20

"Let me tell you why you are here. You're here to be salt-seasoning that brings out the God-flavors of this earth. . . ."
—MATTHEW 5:13 (MSG)

Years ago I looked for a way to serve God on the front line. Some people told me the main thing was sharing the good news. Others said the best witness was to do things like visiting prisoners and feeding the hungry. Wanting to discover God's will for me, I dove into the Bible.

I was stunned to read that Jesus told His disciples to consider themselves blessed when "you're at the end of your rope," when "you've lost what is most dear" (Matthew 5:3–4, MSG), as if these tragedies were actually God's delivery vehicles for sending us His blessings.

Ridiculous! I'd already lost a lot and had been at the end of my rope! "Lord," I finally said, "just tell me straight: What good news do I have to share? Why am I even here?"

My eye caught Jesus' next sentence: "Let me tell you why you are here. You're here to be salt-seasoning that brings out the God-flavors of this earth."

My world changed. Maybe the best news I could bring was this: As I surrender my life to the Lord, He offers me the courage, honesty and willingness to face and walk through the most difficult problems with my eyes wide open! And for me, that's very good news.

LORD, YOUR BLESSINGS ARE GOOD NEWS INDEED WHEN IT COMES TO SPIRITUAL MATURITY, EVEN IF THEY SOMETIMES FEEL A LITTLE LIKE SANDPAPER. AMEN.

—KEITH MILLER

For in the day of trouble He will conceal me in His tabernacle; In the secret place of His tent He will hide me....
—PSALM 27:5 (NAS)

Gracie, the kitten who had been abandoned at our door when she weighed less than two pounds, had grown into a big, strong, beautiful cat, sleek with large amber eyes. But Gracie's little heart seemed to remain small, untrusting and afraid. The slightest noise or movement frightened her. She slept with my husband Gene and me, and would sit calmly with us in the evening. On her brave days she'd hop up on the kitchen counter when I was cooking.

Then my son Jeremy came to live with us for a few months. Gracie couldn't adjust. She fled each time he entered the room. When he left his shoes in the living room, she'd flatten her ears and creep away to hide.

I knew her hiding place—my bedroom closet. Often I'd follow her there and find her on a shelf, mostly hidden by hanging clothes, nestled down in a pair of my pajamas. Her bright eyes seemed to say, *I'm okay now. All is well. I'm safe in here.*

As I sat on the floor, talking softly to her one day, listening to her contented purr, I thought, *Gracie has a hiding place—a safe place to run to. Always.*

And so do you, Marion, came another thought. *So do you. I am your hiding place. Always.*

"I'M HIDING IN THEE. HIDING IN THEE, HIDING IN THEE, THOU BLEST ROCK OF AGES" (WILLIAM O. CUSHING, 1823–1902).   —MARION BOND WEST

SUN

22

Know therefore that the Lord your God is God; he is the faithful God, keeping his covenant of love to a thousand generations of those who love him and keep his commands.

—DEUTERONOMY 7:9 (NIV)

How do you describe being in a room with 450 people from ninety-seven different nations, all proclaiming that Jesus is the answer for the entire world? That was our experience last year, when my wife Rosie and I had the privilege of participating in the Triennial Council of World Vision in Singapore.

One of the highlights of the meeting was a service in which we sang a song of unity. As we sang, the song leader had us form a circle around the room. We began by standing and touching the shoulder of the person in front of us and then started to walk around the room. No one wanted to stop.

Rosie and I spent our mealtimes at tables with people from other countries rather than stay with the thirty-plus participants from the United States. We heard their stories as they shared their hearts, and enjoyed the unity of the worldwide body of Christ. I am so thankful that God is giving me a global perspective, making me grow past my old, smaller view of Who He is.

LORD, I PRAY THAT YOU WILL CONTINUE TO HELP MY VIEW OF YOUR BODY OF BELIEVERS AND MY KNOWLEDGE OF YOU TO GROW.   —DOLPHUS WEARY

MON

23

"From now on I will tell you of new things, of hidden things unknown to you."

—ISAIAH 48:6 (NIV)

At times I wondered why I'd brought our seven-year-old iMac along when we moved from California to New York. I'd already given away a newer desktop computer and was using my laptop for writing and accessing the Internet. The older iMac had been a giveaway from a company that went out of business, but I'd never used it much. Its software was outdated, its internal battery dead and its hard disk was wholly inadequate for today's programs.

Yet I was reluctant to junk something that I felt had never been given a chance to prove itself. So I did a little research. Using information and photographs from the Internet, I opened up the computer, replaced the battery, installed a new hard disk and loaded an upgraded operating system. And voilà! I now have an updated desktop computer that rivals my laptop.

I think of how much I'm like this old computer: aging, but ripe for new challenges. Recently I gained some great new insights through a men's Bible study I joined. God has provided me with a new prayer partner; we're praying for a spiritual revival. And I keep finding new ideas for my work. Even though I'm gray and past retirement age, the Master continues to update me. He seems to think I still have a lot of life left in me.

LORD JESUS, THANK YOU FOR SAVING ME, RENEWING ME, AND GIVING ME A LIFE THAT HAS PURPOSE AND MEANING. —HAROLD HOSTETLER

---

*If we confess our sins, he is faithful and just
to forgive us our sins, and to cleanse
us from all unrighteousness.*

—I JOHN 1:9

This morning I got it into my head to do some spring cleaning. It's not spring, of course, but I'm not above sending Christmas cards in June, and one year Elizabeth celebrated her ten-and-a-half birthday.

In the middle of washing down the tiles in the bathroom, I went to the kitchen to get some supplies and my eye fixed on the stepladder. Our apartment building was built in 1934, so the cupboards are high and deep. A stepladder is essential, not only for retrieving glasses and plates, but also as the official observation deck of the preschooler in the house. Three times a day a child perches there, watching, munching, "helping" as meals are prepared.

Needless to say, the stepladder gets grimy. It happens incrementally; I don't notice it right away. Then one day—like today—my eyes widen in disgust. *Time for that thing to have a bath!* I usually pop a couple of the children into bathing suits and hand them scrub brushes, but today I decided to tackle the task alone.

I like scrubbing the ladder. It's wet and messy, but it's also gratifying. I scrub, the gunk comes off and the ladder looks better. There's a rhythm to the scrubbing and a satisfying ratio of work to result. There are a lot of things in life I can't fix, but this one simple thing I can do.

As I replaced the stepladder in my kitchen, my thoughts turned from the ladder to myself. I muck things up pretty often and half the time I don't even notice until I need a good cleansing. Fortunately, Jesus left us a solution to that problem. I just have to be willing to see the grime, scrape it off and offer my apologies. Oh—and try hard not to let it reappear.

HOLY SPIRIT, GIVE ME THE GRACE TO SEE THE SINS I NEED TO CONFESS.

—JULIA ATTAWAY

WED
25

I will sacrifice unto thee with the voice of thanksgiving. . . .

—JONAH 2:9

My childhood friend Lynda and I shared many happy times, especially with food. We cooked together, using the same child's cookbook; licked the beaters and bowl when her mom decorated yet another cake; and snuck downstairs to the fridge and cookie jar during sleepovers. Staying for a midday meal always meant a three-course feast.

During a lunch in late winter, I had finished my casserole when I was served a dreamy banana-pudding-and-whipped-cream parfait with a cherry on top, in a tall glass like a vase. I was enchanted, until I noticed that Lynda had been served a saucer of plain red gelatin, with no whipped cream. Lynda noticed my bewilderment.

"I gave up desserts for Lent," she said simply.

"What's that?"

"You get ready for Easter by giving up something you like."

Unbelievable! My nine-year-old brain simply couldn't grasp self-sacrifice of that magnitude. During the next few weeks I kept a closer eye on Lynda and her lunch box. Sure enough: no cupcakes, no cookies, no brownies. She had made a simple promise, and she kept it.

Inspired by Lynda, I gave up bubble gum the following Lent and candy the year after that. It took me until high school even to try giving up desserts.

I practice Lenten self-denial with a deeper understanding these days, all begun by the cheerful resolve of a little girl who gave up her pudding.

LORD, THANK YOU FOR FRIENDS WHO DRAW US CLOSER TO YOU.

—GAIL THORELL SCHILLING

"Rejoice that your names are written in heaven."

—LUKE 10:20 (RSV)

Through circumstances we'll never know, my mother was separated from her own mother as a baby. I was given only two pieces of information regarding this missing side of my family: my grandmother's name and the "fact" that her father had said Leona could come home if she "left the brat behind." Consequently, I grew up with a fourth of my identity missing and conscious of a gaping hole in my sense of self.

I was fourteen when Mum happened to recognize her grandfather's name in a photograph at Fort Macleod in Alberta, Canada. Off and on over the years we researched him, looking to fill in the blanks. Bugle boy for the original Mounties in 1874, he was the youngest of the force, fifteen years old, and he went on to bring music to the prairies and become a major part of Canadian history. There was nothing in the archives to indicate, however, that Maj. Frederick Augustus Bagley was ever a man to turn his back on an infant.

The search did lead us to a brother and cousins for Mum, and last year I met my second cousin Doug for the first time. He showed me the flyleaf of a book I could only assume was our great-grandfather's Bible. In handwriting I'd come to recognize, Frederick had meticulously recorded the births of his six daughters and, to my wonder, Mum's.

With a rejoicing heart I stared at my great-grandfather's acknowledgment of her place in his life, the gaping hole of my missing self at last filled in. I was Wilbee, Slade, Goodfellow and now, proudly, Bagley.

DEAR LORD, I REJOICE THAT OUR NAMES ARE WRITTEN IN THE BOOK OF HEAVEN, A BIRTHRIGHT UNSURPASSED—COMPLETE AND ETERNAL IDENTITY IN YOU.

—BRENDA WILBEE

Let not your heart be troubled,
neither let it be afraid.

—JOHN 14:27

The icy wind bit my cheeks as I pulled the blue plastic sled, loaded down with hay, into the corral. I shooed my three horses and two mules away from me so I wouldn't get kicked while they fought over the hay. My mind buzzed with problems from work; I'm a lumber broker, and I sell truckloads of lumber to customers all over the United States.

Today I'd gotten a call from one of my Amish customers in Pennsylvania: "Rebecca, the wrong lumber is on the truck."

The mill—in Arkansas, 1,200 miles away—had misloaded the truck, but it was my responsibility to sell the lumber anyway. And I didn't know anyone else in Pennsylvania, much less anyone who wanted a whole truckload of lumber!

I tossed the hay into the last wooden feeder, and as I walked away, Little Girl, one of my mules, followed me. I slid the chain off the gate and felt Little Girl's warm breath on my neck. Then she gently placed her black fuzzy head on my shoulder. "I'm sorry, Little Girl." I turned around and stroked her face. "I was so caught up with my problems that I never even gave you a heart check."

It's my nightly routine to walk up to each horse and mule and wrap one arm over their withers (shoulders) and the other arm under their neck. I hold the hug, with my heart beating next to theirs, until they sigh.

I wrapped my arms around Little Girl. I held her for a moment, then she sighed as if she just unloaded all her problems. I sighed, too, and when I did, it was as if God were telling me, *Why don't you let Me wrap My arms around you? I'll take your troubles.*

"Okay, Lord," I said with a chuckle, "I might not know anyone in Pennsylvania, but You know everyone there."

LORD, THANK YOU FOR TEACHING ME TO DO HEART CHECKS WITH YOU.

—REBECCA ONDOV

*My heart and my flesh crieth
out for the living God.*

—PSALM 84:2

My local community choir is preparing to sing Johannes Brahms's *A German Requiem*. It's a stretch for us. The *Requiem* is a particularly tricky and taxing piece, but it's also one of the most rewarding of the choral masterworks.

At one rehearsal we focused on the fourth movement, "How Lovely Is Thy Dwelling Place." The text in that movement, largely from Psalm 84, testifies to our longing to be closer to God and the unbridled joy that drives us to sing His praise. That day, though, as we focused on technical issues, the words were just sounds, shapes for the pitches we were singing. Finally our director stopped us and declared, "My heart and soul cry out for joy unto the living God!"

We stared back at her. As a secular community choir, we didn't expect such announcements. It took a moment for us to realize she was speaking the words on the page. "I'm telling you that my heart and soul cry out for joy unto the living God. Did I get your attention?" Heads throughout the choir bobbed. "Now you tell me!"

We tentatively recited the lyrics. "Hold on. Think about it for a moment," she said and paused. "Now proclaim it!"

This time our tone was vibrant; the sound moved, the text was alive. "Again! In rhythm!" We chanted the words; the phrase swelled in intensity. "Now, on to *God*. Let's agree on how to pronounce that."

Chuckles rippled through the choir. Who couldn't pronounce *God*?

"It may seem unimportant, but if you all use the same vowel sound, it will sound like you are sharing a voice, singing with the same intent. Say *awe*." We did. "So put that *awe* in *God*. Now sing it!"

The joyful sound swelled and shimmered, and as the phrase ended, it sounded as though we were all calling out the same magnificent, awesome name: "God!"

LORD, HELP ME ALWAYS TO CALL ON YOUR NAME WITH AWE AND JOY.

—KJERSTIN WILLIAMS

1 _____

2 _____

3 _____

4 _____

5 _____

6 _____

7 _____

8 _____

9 _____

10 _____

11 _____

12 _____

13 _____

14 _____

15 _____

16 _____

17 _____

18 _____

19 _____

20 _____

21 _____

22 _____

23 _____

24 _____

25 _____

26 _____

27 _____

28 _____

MARCH

*For ever, O Lord, thy word
is settled in heaven.*

—PSALM 119:89

SUN
1

*Can you guide the stars season by season
and direct the Big and Little Dipper?*

—Job 38:32 (GNB)

It's four o'clock on Sunday morning, and I'm wakeful, feeling addled, anxious. *Lord, when I look back over my life, it seems so random, so accidental. I can't see the sense of it and the future is just as vague.*

I wander out to the kitchen, click on the coffeemaker and step out into the early morning darkness.

The air is wondrously crisp and clear. I stand there in my slippers, admiring an ebony sky strewn with diamonds and accented with a fingernail moon. Thin, Casper-the-Friendly-Ghost clouds drift slowly by, shuttering the stars off and on as they pass.

**G o d S p e a k s
t h r o u g h N a t u r e**

Lord, the universe seems so random, so accidental, as if You just took the stars in Your hand and hurled them into space. And yet there's order also. There are the Big Dipper and the Little Dipper, and up there is the stable North Star.

High in the heavens, some geese pass silently over the moon.

Lord, is it possible that my life is like the sky, with both order and disorder at the same time?

As I head back into the house, I think of a line by Alexander Pope I memorized in a college literature class. "All nature is but art, unknown to thee; all chance, direction which thou canst not see; all discord, harmony not understood."

In a few hours I'll be sitting in church, praising God. But here in this cathedral of creation, I'm reminded that I need not understand exactly how God works. It's enough for me to walk by faith and to enjoy the beauty of His random order.

Lord, You are my North Star in a world of mystery and disarray.

—Daniel Schantz

Editor's Note: Two years ago, Brigitte Weeks joined a Habitat for Humanity crew building houses in the New Orleans neighborhoods most devastated by Hurricane Katrina. For the next four days, Brigitte will take you with her as she learns how hope, like houses, can be rebuilt after the storm.

> *Be of good courage, and he shall*
> *strengthen your heart,*
> *all ye that hope in the Lord.*
> —PSALM 31:24

Devastation. It's a word we hear or read all the time about floods, wildfires, hurricanes, terrorism, accidents. But what does this word really mean? For me, it now means a rough grassy area stretching as far as the eye can see—just grass and weeds and, away in the corner, four brick steps leading nowhere. This empty field used to be the bustling Lower Ninth Ward in New Orleans. Visitors find it hard to believe.

A few days before, we had landed at Louis Armstrong Airport, thirteen people who barely knew one another, with no construction skills, full of energy to help build

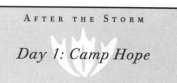

AFTER THE STORM

Day 1: Camp Hope

houses. What in the world did we think we could do in the face of this nothingness?

Our first stop was a school in St. Bernard's Parish, one of the areas worst hit by Hurricane Katrina. Years, not months, had passed since the storm, but the children were still scattered in nearby or faraway towns, the houses demolished with only a wall or part of a roof standing. The school had been partially repaired and was now a hostel for Habitat for Humanity volunteers, known simply as Camp Hope.

It felt like summer camp: the boys' dormitories on one side, the girls' on the other, lights out at ten and *no* talking. But we knew that it wasn't summer and we weren't teenagers anymore. So we unrolled our sleeping bags on the bunk beds made from rough two-by-fours, turned out the lights, and I prayed in the quiet dormitory:

LORD, GIVE ME THE STRENGTH TO BE USEFUL AND FULFILL THE PROMISE OF CAMP HOPE. —BRIGITTE WEEKS

TUE

3

Except the Lord build the house,
they labour in vain that build it. . . .

—PSALM 127:1

Out of the 26,900 homes in St. Bernard's Parish, fewer than half a dozen were left habitable after Hurricane Katrina. We were there to replace the concrete slab—all that was left of what had been home for Charles and his mother—with a simple, solid house, raised on breezeblock pillars, reinforced with steel ties and walled with concrete siding.

We worked all week on two neighboring houses. The few residents who'd returned came by every day to watch, chat and smile. They seemed almost bewildered by these New Yorkers climbing high on the rafters to

AFTER THE STORM

Day 2: To Work
Is to Pray

hammer in OSB (oriented strand board), then strips of tarpaper and then shingles. It was hot and scary up there, and the tar began to melt from the heat.

After two days of roof duty, I learned to caulk windows, which requires a steady hand and a well-placed ladder. A lot of the caulk ended up on me, but I got better with each window. Isabel, a software designer, developed a siding specialty, aligning each piece exactly straight and exactly level. Our leader Steve, a management consultant with a growing subspecialty in construction, ran the electric saw.

What brought us here? A desire to be useful, certainly; the challenge of something new; and for me, a long-standing passion for active prayer. I like to pray with my hands, so there I was, hammer in hand, banging in the six nails needed for each shingle. A black mark on my left thumb reminds me daily that the hammer didn't always meet the nail and that there's a house in St. Bernard's Parish that is truly a house of prayer.

LORD, WITH OUR MINDS, OUR HANDS AND, MOST OF ALL, OUR HEARTS, WE PRAY FOR ALL THOSE WHO ARE STRUGGLING WITH DISASTER AND LOSS.

—BRIGITTE WEEKS

WED 4

Like living stones be yourselves built into a spiritual house. . . .
—I Peter 2:5 (RSV)

"I want to talk about John," Steve, our team leader, had said as we swung out of the airport, crammed into a white minivan on our way to Camp Hope. "He's coming tomorrow by train, and he's not what you'd expect. You'll find he's different, but I think he'll be fine. I talked to him about what we plan to do, and he wants very much to help."

The next morning, having made a twenty-hour trip from New York City, John arrived. He was a tall man, hunched over in a mustard-colored sweater that he wore all week. He talked loudly and often about anything that came into his head, from movies of the 1950s to politicians he disliked. His memory appeared encyclopedic, but the monologues didn't always hang together. He mentioned health problems. But through it all, it was clear that he cared very much about being there and doing the work, helping to build.

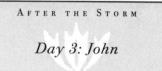

AFTER THE STORM

Day 3: John

That day we were putting on the first layer of roofing. John clumsily climbed the ladder. I watched anxiously as he staggered across the steep roof while calling cheerfully, "Throw me over that roll!" (tarpaper that was heavy enough to knock any of us off the roof).

"Hey, John, they need help across the street!" Steve called, rerouting John from the dangerous rooftop to hammering siding. No one wanted to hurt his feelings; the group had closed around him in a protective circle.

Only a few weeks after our return to New York City, we heard that John had died, possibly from complications of the epilepsy he kept so well hidden. There's a house on Caluda Lane in St. Bernard's Parish that stands as a monument to him and a chorus of prayer from New England to Washington, DC, that surrounded him on this last journey.

Lord, we ask for Your grace and the gift of eternal life for our team-mate John and for all who have died. —Brigitte Weeks

THU
5

As God's chosen people, holy and dearly loved, clothe yourselves with compassion, kindness, humility, gentleness and patience.

—Colossians 3:12 (NIV)

The walls on our house were up, the wiring done and the fiberglass bathroom unit, which came in one amazing piece, installed.

"What's next?" we asked Wayne, our Habitat site leader.

"Insulation," he said. "The truck is on its way."

Moments later, the battered pickup dropped off a pile of bales. They didn't look much like the fiberglass wool I was expecting. The bales were blue and soft. "What's that?" I asked as we began to unroll the sheets.

"Jeans," said Wayne cryptically.

"What do you mean, jeans?" I sputtered.

"It's insulation made from recycled designer jeans," he said. "Scraps from a manufacturing process."

I couldn't quite make the jump from name-brand clothes to bales of insulation, but there it was: cloth passed down from a luxury label to make this truly a designer home.

AFTER THE STORM

Day 4: Building with Blue Jeans

A group of local high school students, working on the site that day, picked up on Wayne's comment. Uniformly clad in blue jeans in varying states of disrepair, they pounced on the bales with gales of laughter.

"Can we put up the jeans?" they pleaded. Hammers and tacks were handed out and up went the former jeans to play a whole new role helping a New Orleans family to keep cool.

LORD, HELP US TO BE THOUGHTFUL AND CREATIVE IN OUR STEWARDSHIP OF THE WORLD AROUND US. —BRIGITTE WEEKS

FRI
6

Mine eyes are ever toward the Lord. . . .

—Psalm 25:15

My granddaughter Tirza recently turned one. During my daughter Kelly's pregnancy, I'd hoped for a brown-eyed girl. In my father's family the boys had brown eyes and the girls their mother's blue. I'd inherited my dad's darker eyes and passed them on to my daughter. I even purchased an elegant brown-eyed doll for Tirza before she was born and shared with the doll's designer my dream for a third-generation girl with chocolate eyes.

In the weeks after Tirza was born, I studied her eyes whenever I held her. They were a tantalizing mystery. While flirting with earth tones, that pesky blue wasn't giving in either. Finally Tirza's eyes cast their vote. Did brown win? Not exactly. But they sure weren't blue. They ended up slate gray with brown flecks. My wish hadn't been completely ignored!

Someday I'll tell Tirza the story of her grandma's thwarted dream. And I won't leave out the most important part: Brown, blue, green or gray, as long as they look to Jesus, the Lord of Life, her eyes are the right color.

JESUS, SON OF GOD, THE EYES THAT SEE AND LOVE YOU ARE BEAUTIFUL BEYOND TELLING.

—CAROL KNAPP

> *"I am the Lord your God, who teaches you what is best for you, who directs you in the way you should go."*
> —ISAIAH 48:17 (NIV)

Millie and I emerged from my apartment building into the bustling Manhattan morning. After three steps Millie crouched, dug in her paws and would go no farther, nipping at her leash. Across the street a garbage truck noisily hoisted a Dumpster into the air. Millie, my adorable ten-week-old golden retriever pup from rural Florida, cringed. She wanted no part of it. *Let's go back inside where it's safe and quiet,* her eyes pleaded.

Ten minutes of coaxing and tugging got her halfway up the block, where she promptly made a scurrying beeline back to the building, dodging the sounds of car horns, throbbing bus engines and the terrifying Dumpster being slammed back to earth.

Enter Winky, who belongs to a friend of mine. Winky is a wise dog who, like most New Yorkers, is completely acclimated to the urban cacophony around us. If I couldn't teach Millie to walk around the block, maybe Winky could.

We met Winky outside my building that afternoon. I had to drag Millie across the lobby and out the door, but the instant she spotted Winky, she perked up. Winky started up the street; Millie took a few steps after her, then put on the brakes. "C'mon, girl," I said.

Winky stopped and glanced over her shoulder. By now Millie was flat on the sidewalk, her puppy paws splayed, ears back, tongue hanging out, but I could see the two dogs' eyes meet. Winky waited, then turned. Millie looked up at me as if to say, *All right, I'll try.* An instant later she was right behind Winky, her legs pumping to keep up.

LORD, I STILL HAVE FEARFUL PUPPY MOMENTS, WHEN THIS WORLD YOU'VE GIVEN US SEEMS OVERWHELMING AND CONFUSING. YET YOU'RE ALWAYS THERE TO LEAD ME THROUGH.   —EDWARD GRINNAN

My times are in Your hand. . . .

—PSALM 31:15 (NAS)

My husband and I have an "atomic" clock and, like most modern-day objects I don't understand, I'm awed by how it works. Yet I do know that somehow, radio signals from the National Institute of Standards and Technology in Fort Collins, Colorado, are able to travel fifteen hundred miles to our home in Syracuse, New York, and automatically set our timepiece to official U.S. government time.

It was on a spring Sunday morning two years ago when my husband said, "I've been thinking . . . that clock's been on the mantel ever since we've gotten it, and I wonder if the TV set alongside might've affected it. Let's check."

Lawrence placed the clock on a windowsill, carefully facing it westward toward Fort Collins, so the radio waves from the National Institute could beam down and around the earth's curvature, right into our home.

But we were bewildered when the long hand on our clock's face suddenly started hiccupping forward. Then Lawrence laughed and said, "We forgot! Today begins daylight saving time. We're *supposed* to set our clocks an hour ahead."

LORD, IT'S NO WONDER THAT TO STAY ON TRACK WITH YOU, YOU TELL US TO "KEEP YOUR FACE TURNED TOWARD ME."   —ISABEL WOLSELEY

MON
9

Then someone came to him [Jesus] and said, "Teacher, what good deed must I do to have eternal life?"

—MATTHEW 19:16 (NRSV)

I was jet-lagged, sick and five thousand miles from home, riding a train in the dead of night through the mountains of eastern Croatia. I didn't know where I was and I barely knew where I was going—I had a piece of paper with the name of a small town where I was to get off the train and find its only hotel. There wouldn't be anyone there to meet me; my host, whom I'd never met, had been delayed by a snowstorm and wouldn't be there until at least the next day.

Each time the train slowed, I'd strain to see the name of the station. *No, not this stop.* Then, as we approached yet another station, I felt a tap on my shoulder. "Off here," said one of the men with whom I'd been sharing a compartment, pointing to the paper. And then, pointing to another man in the compartment who was also gathering up his belongings, he said simply, "Follow."

I followed the man to his car, whereupon I was driven wordlessly three kilometers through a blinding snowstorm to a small hotel. When I tried to pay him for his kindness, he pushed away the money. "You do," he said and then drove away.

Even now I can't forget those two words, *You do.* I guess I'll never really know what he meant, but here's what I think: So often I can't repay the goodness I receive from others. But I can give myself to others, in whatever way the day presents, just as others have given themselves to me. It's like paying graciousness forward rather than paying it back.

LET ALL THAT I AM AND EVERYTHING I DO BE MY PRAYER OF THANKS FOR THE THINGS YOU HAVE DONE FOR ME, GOD. —JEFF JAPINGA

TUE
10

In him was life, and that life was the light of men. The light shines in the darkness. . . .

—JOHN 1:4-5 (NIV)

The warm sun streamed into the kitchen, and the aroma from the pot of beef stew on the stove was pleasantly distracting. As I put labels on the tins of maple syrup we make and sell on our small farm, the radio announcer began the weather report, and the tranquility of my day vanished before the rapidly advancing cold front.

During sugaring season a farmer must constantly watch the weather. In order for the sap to run, the temperatures must rise above freezing during the daylight hours and then drop below freezing at night. The sap buckets must be empty if there is going to be a hard freeze or their side seams will split.

My husband Bill came in, and I told him that they were forecasting a deep freeze. "As soon as I get home from plowing, we need to gather the sap," he said, running out the door.

It was dark when we arrived at the sugar grove. We separated, each of us wading through two or three feet of snow and carrying a five-gallon bucket in each hand into which to pour the sap. Soon I couldn't see Bill, but I sure could hear him. He was frustrated trying to replace the buckets on the small hooks that hung from the spouts in the trees. "Are you having trouble seeing what you're doing, Patti?" I heard from the distance.

I smiled as I clicked the side button on my cell phone, using the glow from the dial to see the hook and the hole in the bucket. *Thank You, Lord for modern technology.* "I'm doing just fine, Bill! I have a little divine light helping me."

EVEN IN THE DARKEST MOMENTS OF LIFE, LORD, THE LIGHT OF FAITH ALLOWS ME TO SEE WHAT I NEED TO DO TO ACCOMPLISH YOUR WILL. —PATRICIA PUSEY

Editor's Note: We invite you to join us a month from today, on April 10, as we pray for all the needs of our Guideposts family at our thirty-ninth annual Guideposts Good Friday Day of Prayer. Send your prayer requests to Good Friday Day of Prayer, 66 E. Main St., Pawling, NY 12564.

WED
11

"For we were born but yesterday and know so little. Our days on earth are as transient as a shadow."

—JOB 8:9 (NLT)

Whenever someone in the neighborhood or in our church passed away when I was growing up, Mother would take her yellow bowl down from the kitchen shelf and get to work on her famous potato salad. But that wasn't all. "Don't forget the viewing tonight for Mr. Tow," she'd call to us girls as we soared high in the air on our backyard swings.

"We already took them potato salad and a pie," I'd grumble. "Isn't that enough?"

That always prompted a speech from Mother on *empathy*. The strange-sounding word meant "feeling another's hurt in your heart."

Empathy also meant going to the funeral parlor, where sweet-smelling roses made my head hurt. Mother would march us up to the circle of mourners at the casket and

WITH ETERNITY IN VIEW

Always Show Empathy

tap my shoulder, the signal that it was time for me, the oldest, to say, "We're very sorry about your loss."

When I got out on my own, I shed the funeral-home ritual like a coat that had become too small. When someone I knew lost a loved one, I consulted a greeting card company or ordered a bouquet of flowers instead.

Today, while sorting through some of my father's old papers, I thought back to the time when he passed away. Visitation was from 11:00 AM until 1:00 PM in the middle of the week. "No one will show up," I told my siblings. "People would have to leave work."

But I was wrong. When I entered the funeral home, my heart heavy with grief, the sight took my breath away. The place was filled with neighbors, church friends and work colleagues who had put inconvenience and personal preference aside to communicate empathy.

THANK YOU, LORD, FOR THE PRIVILEGE OF SHARING IN A FRIEND'S SORROW.

—ROBERTA MESSNER

THU 12

For my thoughts are not your thoughts, neither are your ways my ways, saith the Lord.

—ISAIAH 55:8

My computer is broken, and it's been driving me crazy. I have mounds of freelance work to do, and until a new motherboard arrives, there's absolutely nothing I can do about it.

I feel helpless and I don't like it. The other night, after talking to the computer support person for the third time, I was so on edge that all I wanted was to curl up, very quiet and still and alone, and wait until things got better—which, when you have a husband who's just returned from a three-day business trip and five children, isn't in the realm of possibility. *Perhaps God doesn't see the problem the way I do. He must have some reason for letting me slog through this massive inconvenience,* I thought. I sat glumly for a while and tried to figure out what that purpose could be. Nothing came to mind.

Before bed, I said to my husband Andrew, "I feel so frazzled that I'm using all my energy to stay calm. At this point anything—even help—would be too much."

Andrew looked up from his book, surprised. "I feel like that when I'm upset too. But most of the time you don't understand it because you're so practical. You usually try to get me to think of solutions."

I looked at Andrew. It's true: I'm a problem-solver. I rarely get to this level of frustration because I'm good at keeping a constructive attitude. But I'd never figured out why my husband withdrew so much when he was stressed. "You reach this point a lot faster than I do," I said.

"Yes," Andrew replied quietly.

I climbed into bed and curled up, still wanting to be alone. I didn't know what I was going to do without the computer. But if I had to make a choice, I'd rather have more insight into my spouse than a new motherboard.

LORD, YOUR WAYS REALLY ARE DIFFERENT FROM MY WAYS. AND IT'S A GOOD THING TOO! —JULIA ATTAWAY

READER'S ROOM

A morning fog wraps the woods in a soft halo, early light coming through a cotton-candy scrim. I walk beneath a pewter-bowl sky and a silver-dollar sun. Across the frost-browned pasture the curtain of white recedes, revealing two horses, the feeding longhorns, a crow on the wing, the slowly emerging shape of a live oak tree and beyond, a clear little creek flowing on its unhurried way to the sea. I stand in solitude, thankfully seeing as far as I am allowed.

—Jack Brewer, Hockley, Texas

FRI 13

One thing I know, that, whereas I was blind, now I see.

—JOHN 9:25

One of my favorite authors is the late Robert Penn Warren. A writer of fiction, poetry and literary criticism, he was awarded three Pulitzer prizes and was selected to be Poet Laureate of the United States.

Recently I learned that when Robert was in high school, he dreamed of attending the United States Naval Academy and becoming a career naval officer. Accepted by the academy, he was elated and spent his senior year of high school preparing mentally and physically for the challenge. Several months before graduation, Robert was playing with his younger brother, who threw a lump of coal at him. The jagged coal hit Robert in the eye, permanently limiting his vision and shattering his dreams of attending the academy.

Attending Vanderbilt University the next year, Robert floundered for direction and a new ambition. Always an avid reader, he was naturally attracted to literature and soon began to write. Gradually his talent emerged, and Robert's life turned in a direction he had never considered. The blinding of an eye had created a new vision.

We can be sure that a God of infinite love never causes our tragedies and losses. But God is always the God of another chance. God is faithful to create order out of chaos, goodness out of tragedy, resurrection from our most agonizing crucifixions.

FATHER, WHEN THE BRIGHTNESS OF MY VISION DIMS, HELP ME TO TRUST THAT YOU WILL RESTORE MY SIGHT AND CAUSE ME TO DREAM AGAIN. AMEN. —SCOTT WALKER

SAT 14

Find a good spouse, you find a good life— and even more: the favor of God!

—PROVERBS 18:22 (MSG)

Like most couples, Wayne and I have not had the perfect marriage. At one point we separated for nearly eighteen months before deciding that just wasn't the solution. Once we reunited, though, it wasn't smooth sailing. Old resentments surfaced, and I struggled with letting go of the pain from the past. One weekend I felt I needed to get away, and visiting my parents was the perfect excuse.

When I arrived, my mother insisted on picking up a bucket of her favorite chicken for dinner. For some reason she decided to drive. I climbed in the car with her, and she said, "Look behind me. Is anyone coming?"

I twisted around and checked. "You're clear."

"Great." She revved up the engine, and we shot out of the driveway and onto the street.

"Mom," I asked, suddenly suspicious, "can't you look behind you?"

"Good grief, no. I've had a crick in my neck for nearly twenty years." She proceeded to show me the elaborate way she twisted the rearview mirror to check for traffic behind her. I couldn't keep from smiling and joked with her about it.

The next day, as I was heading home, it struck me that God was speaking to me through my mother. She looked forward, not back. God seemed to be asking me to do the same: Concentrate on the present, look with faith toward the future and release the pain of the past.

LORD, I'M GRATEFUL FOR THE MIRACLES YOU'VE WORKED IN MY MARRIAGE, FOR THE HUSBAND YOU GAVE ME AND FOR ALL THE YEARS WE'VE SHARED TOGETHER— THE GOOD WITH THE BAD. MAY WE BOTH LOOK TO YOU AS WE STEP TOWARD THE FUTURE.   —DEBBIE MACOMBER

"I tell you the truth, unless you change and become like little children, you will never enter the kingdom of heaven."

—MATTHEW 18:3 (NIV)

Last Sunday I attended church with my friend Lurlene. By the time we arrived, the sanctuary was almost full. "We like to leave the back pews for the families with little children," Lurlene said as she steered me toward the front of the church.

I glanced into the rows as we passed. Young mothers and khaki-clad fathers sat with children between them. Small quiet toys were on the floor, and little hands were already busy scribbling on scraps of paper.

After the opening Scripture and hymns, the pastor moved on to the prayer. It was a long and sincere prayer, starting with the missionaries and moving on to the concerns of the church, including supplications for the well-being of several local women who were expecting.

At the end of his prayer, the pastor invited the congregation to join in the prayer that unites all Christians: "Our Father, Who art in heaven . . ."

The mature voices droned out a subdued recitation of the familiar prayer. But coming from the back rows were smaller and brighter voices. "Our Father, Who art in 'eaven, hawoed be thy name." Word for word, the children offered the Lord's Prayer, a bright descant to our more plodding, predictable rendition.

I listened to the children and thought about what they were saying. *Our Father.* Already they were learning that they had not only an earthly father but also a heavenly one.

My mother used to say that "God has no grandchildren, only children." I thought about that as I listened to the final strains of those little voices. And I was pretty sure that the tiniest seekers in the building were also those closest to their Father.

THANK YOU, GOD, FOR CHILDREN. EVEN AS WE TEACH THEM, MAY WE BE OPEN TO THE THINGS THEY CAN TEACH US: INNOCENCE, SIMPLICITY AND ABSOLUTE TRUST.

—MARY LOU CARNEY

MON
16

Be still before the Lord and wait patiently for him. . . .
—PSALM 37:7 (NIV)

Two weeks ago I was going to a job interview when I realized I'd forgotten to put on a belt. I rushed into a clothing store and picked up a new one, then found myself stuck in an incredibly long checkout line. As I stood there waiting, I gritted my teeth, convinced I would be late for my interview. *This line is ridiculous! Why is everyone so slow?*

Finally I remembered to pray, and the anxieties racing through my mind slowed immediately. With my worries quieted, I found myself hearing the discussion at the front of the line.

"Are you sure? Can you check again?" a customer was asking.

"I've already checked twice for you and asked my manager. There is no match for that shoe," said the cashier. "Could you move, please? You're holding up the line."

The customer sighed, starting to walk away. "But what will you do with just a single shoe?" he asked.

"Throw it away probably," the cashier said.

"Excuse me," I said. "Is that shoe a left or a right?"

"A right," said the cashier.

"What size is it?"

"It's a ten."

"That's my size!" I said. "I'll buy it."

As an amputee, I usually have to buy a pair of shoes and throw one away, but that day I got a single shoe for just $2.12—all because I slowed down long enough to see a gift God had put in front of me. And as a bonus, I made it to the interview on time and got the job!

LORD, HELP ME SLOW DOWN LONG ENOUGH TO RECEIVE YOUR BLESSINGS.

—JOSHUA SUNDQUIST

TUE
17

We also rejoice in our sufferings, because we know that suffering produces perseverance; perseverance, character; and character, hope.

—ROMANS 5:3–4 (NIV)

On a cold day in New Jersey, my then seven-year-old daughter Lanea and I piled out of our car just in time for the St. Patrick's Day parade. The air made frost of our breath, and I was glad that she was dressed warmly.

She was wearing a navy blue sweat suit and a big polka-dot bow atop her head and another huge bow with white dots perched on her behind. Her hair was in a large fluffy ponytail, and she carried a baton in her hand. She was making her marching-band debut with the twirling team in the parade.

It took a lot of courage for Lanea to be there that day. She couldn't throw the baton high in the air without dropping it. Most of the other girls, who had been twirling longer, could step higher, twirl in more complicated patterns and never forgot to smile. Lanea, frustrated, didn't smile a lot at practices. After each practice I kept waiting for the words, "Mommy, I don't want to do it anymore." My daughter didn't like doing things that didn't come naturally; she didn't like not automatically being one of the best.

The twirlers began their way down the street, followed by the Fort Monmouth military color guard. *Lord, just let her make it through the parade without crying,* I prayed from the sidewalk.

Lanea flashed her little-girl smile at the waving crowd. I held my breath as she threw her baton in the air while high-stepping and executing complicated dance steps.

As the parade ended, Lanea and I hugged, delighted that she had made it to the end of the route. We added screams to our hugs when we learned that Lanea, the least likely to succeed, had won "the smile award" for her dazzling smile and apparently effortless performance!

GOD, WHEN THE ODDS ARE AGAINST ME, HELP ME TO GO THE DISTANCE.

—SHARON FOSTER

Thou hast put gladness in my heart. . . .

—PSALM 4:7

Panda is a purebred cocker spaniel. She got her name because her black-and-white markings resemble those of the winsome bear. When my son took a job in Colorado, I inherited Panda. She has floppy ears that tend to get infections and a sensitive digestive system that calls for careful regulation of what she eats. She's loyal and affectionate, but she's a high-maintenance dog.

The pet store had a wide selection of books on the care of cocker spaniels. As I thumbed through one, then another, a young man came to the shelves and reached for a magazine. He grinned and said, "You have a cocker? I've had my Sandy since she was a puppy." That's all it took to get us talking. He had some great tips for Panda: Use an antibacterial wash for her ears and, "Too bad, but absolutely no table scraps." He handed me a dog-care manual. "This is the book I'd recommend. It covers just about everything. Good luck!" He looked at his watch and quickened his step as he walked to the cashier.

Hmm, $16.95, I thought as I looked at the book. Expenses had been heavy that month, with a hefty vet bill for Panda. *Oh well, I really do need this,* I decided and added it to the sack of dog food in my cart. "So *you're* the lady," the cashier said as she separated the book from my supplies. "The tall blond guy paid for this. He said to tell you it was a gift to help you take good care of your cocker!"

I looked around, but he'd gone. "Wow," I said, "I didn't even know him! How kind."

She nodded, "Yeah, made your day, eh? Made my day too. Here." She scooped up several small bags of dog treats. "These are freebies."

THANK YOU, LORD, FOR THE JOY OF SWEET SURPRISES FROM THE GENEROUS HEARTS OF STRANGERS.   —FAY ANGUS

In the process of time it came to pass. . . .

—GENESIS 4:3 (NKJV)

My Christmas cactus lives in matted soil near a cold window, bright with morning light. I give it sips of water, dust its flat leaves and basically leave it alone. Then once a year it rewards me with exotic, sunrise-pink blossoms, which create fiesta color against the drab winter sky. The wonder and surprise never fail—mostly because I never know when it will bloom. *Christmas cactus* is a misnomer, for sure. By the end of Advent, this cactus had only three blossoms. Today, it has a dozen.

No, my cactus doesn't bloom on a schedule or according to a calendar, and neither did I. My friends' children were in fourth grade by the time I had my first baby; I earned my teaching credentials at fifty. Being on a different timetable from that of my friends and colleagues hasn't made a particle of difference.

So I think of my students who need an extra semester or two to make up gaps leftover from high school; many students in their forties are just now hitting stride. When they fret, "Oh, I've been out of school for five years," I tell them the story a first-grade teacher used to reassure her slower readers: "Look at the apples on the tree. Some are red. Some are red and green. Some are green. All ripen at different times, yet each apple is delicious. One isn't any better than another."

My Christmas cactus thrills me, even when it blooms in March. I think God is thrilled, too, when we use our talents, no matter what our season in life.

ETERNAL FATHER, THANK YOU FOR THE GLIMPSES OF ETERNITY IN OUR TIME-BOUND LIVES. —GAIL THORELL SCHILLING

The Lord God took the man and put him in the Garden of Eden to work it and take care of it.

—GENESIS 2:15 (NIV)

Human life began in a garden; in the Song of Solomon, two people fall in love in a garden; Jesus was buried and rose again from a tomb in a garden.

Life, love, death and rebirth—all in a garden; to this my wife would say, "Of course." She'll retire from teaching next spring and work in our garden during the week. Imagine that: paradise all week, not just on weekends! She'll harvest our garden next fall, until the first deep frost covers our crops and postpones paradise until the following spring. My wife doesn't need Bible references to know that a garden is good. The blessings of a well-tended one grow every day.

Last spring Rob and Paula, who own a ranch near us, gave us straw to use for garden mulch. In return I brought them some tomatoes in August. As a result of that visit, Rob and Paula and their youngest daughter came to church with us in September. The connection between their mulch and our tomatoes may not be direct, but it is very real. The connection between their generosity, our gratitude and worshipping God together may not be direct either, but it is just as real.

DEAR GOD, I'M SO GRATEFUL TO LIVE IN THE GREAT GARDEN YOU CREATED FOR US. HELP ME TO WORK IT AND TAKE CARE OF IT EVERY DAY, EVERY YEAR.

—TIM WILLIAMS

And the Lord God said, "It isn't good for man to be alone. . . ."

—GENESIS 2:18 (TLB)

My daughter Maria and I decided to walk in the Komen Race for the Cure with our church's team. All over the United States these races raise money for breast cancer research, screening and education. When we picked up my new friend Karen, I was surprised by what she was wearing: a pink shirt, signifying that she is a breast cancer survivor. "Oh, I didn't know," I stammered.

"That's okay," Karen said. "I'm three years' cancer free and feeling great!"

Karen seemed excited to get to the race, and when we arrived I understood why. The crowd was filled with pink shirts. The survivors received special gift bags and pink hats studded with rhinestones, then snacked on fresh fruit at linen-covered tables in the Pink Hat Café. Live music, laughter and loud voices created a party atmosphere. Later we cheered as Karen crossed the finish line in the Survivors' Race, arm in arm with other women in pink shirts.

Fighting any difficulty alone can't be what God intended for us. There's power when we unite; for one thing, thirty-seven thousand people raised two million dollars for the cause that day. But beyond that, these survivors showed everyone the power of God's spirit in His human creation. Through even the worst circumstances, He helps us hold each other up, strengthen one another and celebrate one more day of living for the gift that it is.

THANK YOU, LORD, FOR YOUR SPIRIT THAT BRINGS US TOGETHER AND STRENGTHENS US FOR THE TOUGH BATTLES WE FACE. —GINA BRIDGEMAN

When Jesus had thus said, he was troubled in spirit, and testified, and said, Verily, verily, I say unto you, that one of you shall betray me.

—JOHN 13:21

Last year during Lent, our church did a tableau of the Last Supper. Twelve of us depicted the disciples, and another member portrayed Jesus. He was the only one at the table who didn't speak.

I played Philip, whose hometown was Bethsaida in Galilee. He had heard John the Baptist preaching in Bethany, and it was there that Jesus recruited him. Philip immediately recommended his good friend Nathanael, who was not, at first, excited by the idea. But he came around. Philip, you may remember, was present at the feeding of the five thousand, and he wanted to know where they would find the wherewithal to buy bread for the throng.

"Little did I know," I told the audience, "that Andrew was already bringing a lad and his lunch to Jesus." Following the miracle, Philip saw to it that the Greeks in the crowd were given an audience with Jesus.

At the conclusion of my monologue, reacting to Jesus' prediction that one of His disciples would betray Him, I asked, "Does the traitor not know that in betraying Jesus, he is also betraying God? That in conspiring against Jesus, he is conspiring against God? How can any of our number be so blind? Can it be Philip? Is it I?"

People who fall short of Christ's high calling—and that includes us all—betray Him every day. We don't need to ask, "Is it I?" We know the answer. Thank God for His forgiving grace. It allows us to begin each day with a clean slate and the peace that comes from knowing He understands.

FORGIVE US, DEAR LORD, WHEN YOU WE BETRAY.
HELP US REFLECT YOUR LOVE EVERY DAY.

—FRED BAUER

Cast thy bread upon the waters:
for thou shalt find it after many days.

—ECCLESIASTES 11:1

Bring up hard times in our family and before long we'll be talking about my Uncle Bill. Alcoholism ravaged his life and left him broken and penniless. We prayed and fasted for him and tried to let him know we cared. Then we got good news: He had discovered Alcoholics Anonymous; he was reaching out to help others; he was on his way back.

David and I were newly married and living on less than a shoestring, but when we learned that Uncle Bill had managed to find work as an investment adviser, we saw a chance to help him out a bit. David contacted him, offering to be one of his first clients. We figured we could manage to invest fifty dollars a month. It was a difficult commitment. We really needed that extra money.

Over the next few years Uncle Bill rebuilt his life; he simply served others. The transition was amazing, and I'll have to admit that we felt pretty good about doing our part to help Uncle Bill get by. Then, without warning, cancer came, and he was gone.

Some months later a man from Uncle Bill's investment company called. "You might want to transfer your account over to someone in the Nashville market," he said. There was a pause, and then he cleared his throat and added, "But I have to warn you . . . I've never seen anything quite like this before . . . you can't expect it to continue."

"What do you mean?"

"Well, it seems that your investment adviser was putting his fees back into your account . . . and that's unheard of in this business."

FATHER, LIKE MY UNCLE BILL, THE WAY YOU DO BUSINESS IS UNHEARD OF IN THIS CRAZY WORLD.   —PAM KIDD

Blessed be the Lord, who daily loadeth us with benefits, even the God of our salvation. . . .
                                                        —PSALM 68:19

Last month I shooed my children into the van and drove around the block. After a couple of circuits, I told them they were about to witness history: The odometer would be registering two hundred thousand miles.

They were less than impressed. "Does that mean we can buy a new car now?" Hope asked.

It's a fair question, because the van is in less than fair shape. The Check Engine light is on permanently; sometimes it flashes three dots . . . three dashes . . . three dots. (Where's that owner's manual?) The rain gutter is loose—at high speeds it beats out a rhythm reminiscent of early Bob Marley.

Which got me thinking: Chances are that the odometer is not accurate—see above—but it's still an achievement, right? Since my van was born, we've had three presidents. Two of my three children were born, too, as were millions of other kids. People were married, divorced, lost jobs, found five dollars in the lint tray, got sick, got better, played pinochle or hearts, or had their hearts broken.

It's funny how we celebrate arbitrary dates but rarely celebrate the fantastically wonderful mundane of today, of this afternoon, of now. Your youngest can read and write—do you have any idea what a gift that is? The roof will stay on your house through the next storm because of the good work of a carpenter you've never met. Tonight a four-year-old and a soldier in Iraq and a surgical nurse and a truck driver and your cousin Vinnie will say a prayer, and it will be answered. And my van will start, I think, and I will be thrilled as I inch my way through traffic toward home—a little cold, limping toward the next ordinary extraordinary milestone, listening hard to a Bob Marley song called "Redemption."

LORD, KEEP ME FROM OVERLOOKING THE DAILY, UNSPECTACULAR BLESSINGS ALL AROUND ME. NOW, ABOUT THAT NEW CAR. . . . —MARK COLLINS

WED
25

*"Incline your ear and come to Me.
Listen, that you may live. . . ."*

—ISAIAH 55:3 (NAS)

Every year I visit our provincial agricultural fair, held during spring break. I can usually count on taking some interesting photos—city kids encountering their first cow or horse or chicken, a little girl cuddling a lamb, or a boy proudly exhibiting his rabbit.

But the highlight of the fair for me is the horse competition. My heart always beats a little faster when I hear the hoofbeats of the Clydesdales in an eight-horse hitch, their harness gleaming, their feet in rhythm as they enter the arena. I marvel how their driver, his feet braced against the front of the wagon, skillfully handles eight reins at once, expertly maneuvering his team around the show ring.

Just prior to the competition, the announcer appeals to the crowd to be as quiet as possible and to listen as each driver gives commands to his two lead horses way out in front. Despite their massive size and strength, they obey his voice, flicking their ears backward to hear his every word as they lead the rest of the team through their paces.

Conflicting sounds easily distract me, so I find it amazing that regardless of how many teams are in the show ring at the same time, the lead horses of each team listen only to the commands of their own driver.

LORD, MAY THE INTRUSION OF OTHER VOICES NOT INTERFERE WITH MY OBEDIENCE TO YOU.
  —ALMA BARKMAN

*. . . A time to break down,
and a time to build up.*

—ECCLESIASTES 3:3

When my brother Don was a boy, he loved to build fragile model airplanes with balsa wood and tissue paper. One day, when family friends were visiting from Wisconsin, the adults noticed that their little boy Bobby, who had gone to play in another room, was ominously silent. Don found the toddler qui-

A TIME TO EVERY
PURPOSE

etly breaking all of the carefully glued pieces of an airplane he had worked on for weeks. My brother burst into tears, but the damage was done and there was no remedy.

Don began saving his allowance. Finally, he bought an even more elaborate airplane kit, and within a couple of weeks he had created his best model airplane yet.

Like Koheleth, I tend to believe that everything happens for a purpose. So my prayer question today is, "Where is the purpose in such painful incidents?"

*Sometimes a run-down house has to be razed,
so a better-built home can take its place.*

*Remember the boy who broke your heart in junior high?
You thought you'd surely die!
Now at the other end of life you have true love,
and it's so much more
than cotton-candy words, hand-holding walks
and kisses after dances.
It's sharing common interests;
listening with the heart
and knowing you can trust each other.*

*Still I must speak a hard truth to you:
Most things break, my dear.
But here's the reason:*

*The new can come forth
only when the old is out of the way.*

HOLY SPIRIT, TEACH ME TO TEAR DOWN WHAT NO LONGER SERVES. THEN, WITH
FREE AND EMPTY HANDS, I'LL BUILD A FRESH NEW START.

—MARILYN MORGAN KING

Listen to Me. . . .

—ISAIAH 49:1 (NAS)

I've never been a good listener; I have so much to say
that listening is difficult. But I'd been making it a point
to learn to listen. On my early morning walks praying and silently singing
hymns to God came naturally. But listening for His voice remained hard.

One early spring morning I'd walked off my street onto a much
busier and larger road. With all the new subdivisions going up, the traffic had become heavy. I'd learned to watch for trucks turning into the left
lane where I walked. When I saw one, I always moved quickly into the
weeds at the side of the road. I was thinking of the song, "We Are
Standing on Holy Ground," when God suddenly seemed to talk to me.

Listen, Marion!

I stopped my silent hymn-singing and in my mind's eye I saw my
two girls jumping rope in our driveway when they were very small. One
of my daughters and I turned the ends of the rope while my other daughter jumped high over it. I even remembered the song we sang: "Down in
the meadow where the green grass grows . . ."

No, Marion. Listen. Jump! Jump!

Just then a logging truck loaded high with tall stripped pine trees
came speeding around the corner. A piece of pine about three feet long
and as big around as a basketball rolled toward me. When it was inches
from me, I jumped up in the air, lifting both feet at the same time. The
heavy piece of pine barely sailed underneath my drawn-up knees.

MY FATHER, I PRAISE YOU FOR THE TRUTH IN THE HYMN "IN THE GARDEN"
BY C. AUSTIN MILES: "AND HE WALKS WITH ME, AND HE TALKS WITH ME."

—MARION BOND WEST

*Whether you turn to the right or to the left,
your ears will hear a voice behind you,
saying, "This is the way; walk in it."*
—Isaiah 30:21 (NIV)

Our family has three cats in a small house. They are all females, and as any vet will tell you, females are the alpha cats. That's why Rocky never had a chance.

Rocky arrived unannounced on our side porch last spring. She was clearly a kitten on her own, probably kicked out of her mother's home in the loft of a nearby barn. The children quickly took food out to her and named her. "She must be a fighter," my son Joseph reasoned, "if she survived our woods."

"She's adorable!" my daughter Sarah said. "And she needs us," added Joseph. So we took her to the vet. He said that she had a spoonful of ear mites, easily removed, and gave her the shots every kitten needs to be healthy.

Then we took her home and introduced her to the other cats. But as I said, she didn't have a chance; a male would have known his place in an instant.

Home should be the place where you are safe and loved. We tried to be home to Rocky. But our other three cats wouldn't cooperate! By the end of the week, it became clear that the best place for Rocky would be in another home, where she could be the alpha cat. And in the home we found for her, an elderly neighbor desperately needed some additional love in the house.

I've lived in many houses and I've been blessed that each of them was also a home. A home doesn't have to be large or well furnished; it only has to be a warm place where you are safe and loved.

HEAVENLY FATHER, MAKE ME GRATEFUL FOR YOUR SURPRISES. HELP ME TO SEE THE UNEXPECTED EVENTS OF LIFE AS YOU STOP BY. —JON SWEENEY

SUN
29

Now hope that is seen is not hope. For who hopes for what he sees? But if we hope for what we do not see, we wait for it with patience.

—ROMANS 8:24–25 (RSV)

I was ambling to church this morning when two boys zoomed by on their scooters. The older one said, "So what color is my helmet?" and the little one said, "It's the color of fire at the end of the fire." I nearly fainted with delight and shuffled faster to try to catch the rest, but the boys had sailed away, their talk trailing behind them like shards of smoke.

I spent the rest of the day chewing on that remark, turning it in my mind like a prism, this way and that, tasting the way a fire roars and peaks and fades, flaring and glaring; the way everything rages and subsides; the way when things look to be coldest and deadest, they're not; the way there's always heat in the heart; the way that, no matter how dark and low and empty and shriveled and exhausted we are, there's always a fire ready to bloom. Isn't that an extraordinary gift, one of the umpteen million we don't think about enough?

Hope is a seed, and there are more seeds than we could ever count. How no matter how cold and dead Old Man Hope looks to be, he always pops up for the next round of the fight. You have to admire Old Man Hope, I conclude at the end of the day, sitting by the fire, watching it rumble and crumble. That hope is one *tough* bird.

DEAR LORD, FOR ALL THOSE TINY MOMENTS WHEN HOPE LOOKS LAID OUT COLD, AND SUDDENLY OLD MAN HOPE POPS UP AGAIN, THANK YOU.   —BRIAN DOYLE

MON
30

"But when you do a kindness to someone, do it secretly. . . ."

—MATTHEW 6:3 (TLB)

Let me introduce you to my colleague Colleen Hughes, the editor-in-chief of *Angels on Earth* magazine. In the years I've worked at Guideposts, I've always known her as one of those good office friends you can talk to about anything—anything. She's sympathetic, thoughtful, generous, and she can make you laugh when it's just what you need.

One day, this spring, I was trying to think of something nice to do for her. (I couldn't begin to pay her back for all her kindnesses to me.) On Monday, on the way to work, I passed a flower shop with the most brilliant display of daffodils. *That's it!* I thought. I bought a couple of dozen, and early in the morning before anyone else got to work, I put them in a vase in her office. No note; just those buttery daffodils. Maybe, at last, I'd outgive her.

At 9:45 that morning, we gathered as usual in the conference room for Guideposts Prayer Fellowship. We were reviewing letters from readers and bringing up their prayer requests, when Colleen said, "I'd like to thank God for my flower angel today."

I've heard it said that a gift given in secret has extra value for the giver. I'll have to admit that being called an angel was more reward than I'd ever expected. Okay, so when Colleen reads this, the secret will be out. But in the meantime, I hope she's looking at all the angels in her life who are desperately trying to outgive her in ways they'll never reveal.

LET ME NEVER BE WEARY, LORD, OF GIVING.   —RICK HAMLIN

TUE
31

"Oh, that their hearts would be inclined to fear me. . . ."
—DEUTERONOMY 5:29 (NIV)

I had been attending a meeting in Seattle and got up early to catch a 6:00 AM flight to Pittsburgh. There I was picked up at the airport and driven two hours through the West Virginia hills to a place called Philippi for a rural Christian community development conference.

At one of the sessions, a young man stood up. He said he was a basketball coach. "I want to introduce you to twelve thirteen-year-old girls who have just won the national basketball championship for their age group." I sat up and listened as he continued. "We have been working with these girls as a church since they were ten years old. Our number one goal is not basketball but to teach them the fear of the Lord."

How wonderful, I thought, *that someone is investing in the lives of these girls, teaching them the Word of God, encouraging their walk, giving them consistent discipline and challenging them to achieve team goals.* After the presentation, I went up to thank the coach and greet the girls and to let them know what I'd learned.

These girls had come from many different backgrounds, some from broken homes and single-parent families, and society's message to many of them was that they were worthless. Yet someone had been teaching them that they were special in God's eyes. As I looked into their faces, I could see that they were.

LORD, ENCOURAGE THOSE WHO WORK WITH YOUTH TO INSPIRE THEM WITH YOUR WORD AND TEACH THEM THE VALUE OF DISCIPLINE. —DOLPHUS WEARY

MY LIVING WORDS

1 _____

2 _____

3 _____

4 _____

5 _____

6 _____

7 _____

8 _____

9 _____

10 _____

11 _____

12

13

14

15

16

17

18

19

20

21

22

23

24

25

26

27

28

29

30

31

APRIL

Let thy mercies come also unto me,
O Lord, even thy salvation,
according to thy word.

—PSALM 119:41

If someone has done you wrong,
do not repay him with a wrong. . . .

—ROMANS 12:17 (GNB)

I'm not a vengeful person, but there are limits to my patience. I was in a hurry to buy some shoes before we left for a holiday trip. The store parking lot was packed with holiday traffic, and I joined a train of cars that was cruising the rows, looking for a parking spot. Rain was falling in bursts.

After what seemed like hours, I spotted two parking spaces near the entrance. I was behind a young man in a red sports car. *He'll take one of those spaces and I can have the other,* I thought. Instead, the young man pulled in diagonally, taking both spaces. He hopped out and dashed into the store.

GOD SPEAKS
THROUGH CONSCIENCE

My face turned crimson at his selfishness, and again I began cruising for a parking space. At last I found one, far from the store. The rain had stopped, and as I headed for the store, I gathered up a half-dozen carts that were blocking spaces and pushed them up toward the store.

As I neared the entrance, I passed by the red sports car, and suddenly I had an idea where I might put those carts so as to restore the scales of justice. Never mind what I did, let's just say that my decision was satisfying and I had no regrets.

At least not until bedtime, when I lay there wondering, *What if that young man was in a hurry to buy medicine for his dying grandmother?*

Or not, my conscience reminded me.

My conscience and I will try to be better in the future.

THANK YOU, GOD, FOR MY CONSCIENCE, WHICH CONTINUES TO SPEAK EVEN WHEN I IGNORE IT. —DANIEL SCHANTZ

He determines the number of the stars and calls
them each by name. Great is our Lord. . . .

—PSALM 147:4-5 (NIV)

At the restaurant where I like to eat breakfast, the waitresses have stars on their aprons to tell you how many years they've been dishing up oatmeal and toting plates of bacon and eggs for their clientele. Some wear three or four stars; this morning my waitress Trina boasted six stars.

As I left, filled with biscuits and gravy just like my mother used to make, I saw a young woman coming out of the kitchen. She couldn't have been much out of her teens. She was wearing the brown apron of a waitress, and I checked for the brightly embroidered stars. Where they would have been were two words in bold script: *Rising Star.* Not *Beginner* or *Trainee.* Not *New* or *Inexperienced.* Not *Good-Luck-with-Getting-Your-Order-Right. Rising Star,* an affirmation of what they were expecting her to become: competent, efficient, outstanding.

I left the restaurant determined to give everyone the benefit of believing they can accomplish great things. Everyone—even me!

FATHER, I WANT TO BE A SHINING STAR FOR YOU, RISING TO EVERY OPPORTUNITY YOU SEND MY WAY! —MARY LOU CARNEY

Take hold of the eternal life to which you were called. . . .
—I TIMOTHY 6:12 (RSV)

Millie, my golden retriever puppy, is asleep on her bed in front of a woodstove on a chilly spring night, totally tired as only a busy puppy can be. Earlier in the day she had her first visit to my office. Then it was into the Jeep for the three-hour ride to our house in western Massachusetts, Millie's first visit there too. She was a little carsick on the way up, and the look on her face when we finally parked in the driveway was like someone who had just gotten off a wild amusement-park ride. As soon as she hit the ground, though, she was off like a shot, tearing down the hill out back, right for the woods.

"Millie!" I yelled.

Coyotes, bears, mountain lions . . . skunks!

"Millie!"

All the books say not to run after a puppy; they like being chased. Stay still and call them. I immediately ran after her.

"Millie!"

She made a sharp right turn into a neighbor's yard and raced around to the back porch where she encountered a black Lab named Simon through the kitchen window. Simon came out, and they played and chased for the next hour until they both dropped from exhaustion. I gave Millie some extra treats with dinner that night, and now, here she was, snoring gently by the stove, as oblivious to the world as can be.

And all at once I want to freeze everything in time—this moment, this day, Millie's gentle breathing, this incredible feeling of peace and contentment that has swept over me. I want to grab that feeling and hold it so tight I will always remember what this moment feels like. I don't want time ever to move again because I would be perfectly happy living in this moment forever.

THANK YOU, GOD. THANK YOU FOR THESE INCREDIBLE MOMENTS OF BLISS AND GRACE, THESE LITTLE GLIMPSES, IT WOULD SEEM, OF HEAVEN ITSELF.

—EDWARD GRINNAN

Editor's Note: "Living the Word," says Elizabeth (Tib) Sherrill, "is literally what our church does at this time each year. We have daily services built around the biblical account of this most important week in the Christian calendar." The readings are always the same, but "the miracle of the Bible is that they say new things to us each time." In "Living the Word in Holy Week—and Beyond," Tib shares the verses that have special meaning for her this year.

SATURDAY BEFORE PALM SUNDAY	LIVING THE WORD IN HOLY WEEK—AND BEYOND

SAT
4

And they were in the way going up to Jerusalem; and Jesus went before them . . . and as they followed, they were afraid. . . .
—MARK 10:32

They had reason to be afraid, these disciples following their stubborn leader into the stronghold of His enemies. To me this reluctant trip represents the journeys in my own life that I don't want to take.

One of them was to the nursing home in Sudbury, Massachusetts, where my elderly mother was dying. I'd made the five-hour drive from

New York many times, but this one, I knew, would be the last. Our son had brought two-year-old Lindsay up from Florida, so I could show Mother her great-granddaughter. "Before she dies" were words we didn't say.

In Mother's room Lindsay sat very quietly on my lap. I'd worried that the sights and smells of a nursing home might be frightening for her or that Mother's beautifully wrinkled face might seem forbidding.

After perhaps half an hour, Lindsay began to squirm. "She's sat about as long as a two-year-old can," I apologized to Mother.

I set Lindsay down and took her hand to lead her to the door. She pulled free and ran straight to where her great-grandmother sat bent in her wheelchair. Reaching up a tiny hand, she stroked Mother's cheek. Again and again, that gentle stroking. Mother's eyes opened, blue as the little girl's, and the two smiled at each other.

Watching, it seemed to me that Jesus was showing me Mother as He saw her—not an old and ailing woman, but a wide-eyed young girl at the beginning of life.

This vision of Mother has stayed with me through all the years since: Jesus' gift delivered by a child on the journey I didn't want to take.

"Jesus went before them." As He goes before each of us down every fearsome road.

HELP ME FOLLOW YOUR STEPS, LORD JESUS, INTO EACH MOMENTOUS DAY OF THIS HOLY WEEK.   —ELIZABETH SHERRILL

PALM SUNDAY   LIVING THE WORD IN HOLY WEEK—AND BEYOND

SUN
5

"The Lord has need of it. . . ."
—MARK 11:3 (RSV)

It's the day of the grand entry into Jerusalem! Jesus had come to the city many times, an itinerant rabbi arriving on foot, one visitor among thousands. This was to be a different kind of arrival, a ceremonial one in fulfillment of ancient prophecy.

And for it, Jesus needed a donkey. Go to the next village, He tells two of His disciples, untie the donkey you'll find at a certain spot and bring it here. If challenged—certainly this will look like a brazen theft of a valuable animal—you are to say, "The Lord has need of it." Those few words will be enough.

They were enough for me, too, when I was given the job of raising money to buy books for the school in Uganda where I was teaching. Asking for money was something I'd always dreaded doing. I rehearsed a little speech outlining good reasons to give, but as I made the rounds of businesses in Kampala, I heard the apology in my voice, the expectation of refusal.

Then one day, when I'd come back to the house exhausted with a single pledge for the day's effort, my husband John asked me a question. "Do you think," he said, "that God wants the kids to have these books?"

I didn't say the words "The Lord has need of it" aloud, as I resumed my rounds of the business district on the next day. They were in the excitement, the hope, the authority I felt as one commissioned not by the trustees of a school, but by God, to do His will in this particular small corner of His world. In two days I raised not only enough for books, but for a year's supply of pencils!

REMIND ME TO ASK OF EVERY UNDERTAKING, "LORD JESUS, DO YOU HAVE NEED OF THIS?" —ELIZABETH SHERRILL

MONDAY OF HOLY WEEK	LIVING THE WORD IN HOLY WEEK—AND BEYOND

MON
6

"*Give to Caesar what is Caesar's and to God what is God's.*"
—MARK 12:17 (NIV)

Alarmed by the cheering crowds that greeted Jesus' entry into Jerusalem, His enemies tried to trap Him into making some statement that would land Him in trouble with the Roman overlords. A particularly cunning question, they thought, concerned taxes: Should a faithful Jew pay them to a pagan government?

"Give to Caesar what is Caesar's," Jesus answered. *What are the things that belong to Caesar today,* I wondered.

Two years ago I visited the concentration camp where in 1945 Dietrich Bonhoeffer was executed on personal orders from the Caesar of his day, Adolf Hitler. But that was not Dietrich's first encounter with the life-and-death powers of the state. In 1917 his beloved older brother, eighteen-year-old Walter, had been summoned by "Caesar"—*Kaiser* in German—to serve in the trenches of World War I. Dietrich and his mother went to the train station in Berlin to see Walter off. Though he was only eleven, Dietrich never forgot the words his mother called out as the train gathered speed. "Remember, Walter, it's only miles that separate us!"

Walter was killed two weeks later, one small statistic in the hideous slaughter, one life demanded by the Caesar of that time and place.

Whenever we live, whatever land we live in, "Caesar" seems to have all the power. He *does* have power, Dietrich would agree. If we disobey him, it may cost our lives, as Dietrich knew when he said *no* to Hitler. But our earthly existence—and our taxes—are the only things that belong to Caesar.

The rest—the love, the faith, the closeness no miles or death can destroy—these things belong to God, safe in His keeping forever.

LORD JESUS, GIVE ME THE FAITH THAT SEES DIETRICH AND WALTER AND THEIR MOTHER REJOICING TODAY IN THE KINGDOM THAT MAKES CAESAR'S WORLD LOOK VERY, VERY SMALL.   —ELIZABETH SHERRILL

TUESDAY OF HOLY WEEK	LIVING THE WORD IN HOLY WEEK—AND BEYOND

TUE
7

"He is not the God of the dead, but of the living, for to him all are alive."
—LUKE 20:38 (NIV)

It was another of the challenges hurled at Jesus during this tumultuous week, this one from members of a sect that taught that the grave was final. Listening to Jesus' answer, I remembered my friend Marge, grieving the loss of a stillborn son. It was her two-year-old son Andrew, though, that she'd worried about.

Andrew had looked forward as much as his parents to the birth of the baby they'd named Aidan, even placing a favorite terrycloth dog in the waiting crib. "He was so excited about having a brother—talked all the time about what he and Aidan would do together."

When told that his brother had gone to live in heaven, Andrew showed no reaction. "We didn't know whether he was bottling up his feelings or whether the shock had simply numbed him." As days passed, Marge worried that this emotional distance might become permanent. Hoping to rouse some response from him, she bought Andrew the big red balloon he'd been begging for.

"We'd barely left the store when it got away from him." Ordinarily he would have bawled, Marge told me. She would have been glad even for that, happy for any kind of reaction. "Nothing. Not a peep. He just stood staring solemnly as it sailed off into the sky, as though he couldn't feel anything anymore."

Andrew didn't say a word about the lost balloon, not until his dad got home from work that night. Then the little boy rushed to him. "Daddy," he said, "I gave Aidan a balloon!"

To God and to Andrew, I thought, *Aidan is most definitely alive.*

LORD JESUS, GIVE ME THE FAITH OF A CHILD.   —ELIZABETH SHERRILL

WEDNESDAY OF HOLY WEEK   LIVING THE WORD IN HOLY WEEK—AND BEYOND

WED 8

> *"If you hold anything against anyone, forgive him, so that your Father in heaven may forgive you your sins."*
> —MARK 11:25 (NIV)

Knowing that His death was near, Jesus spent the precious days teaching the crowds that followed Him. Especially important, He stressed, was learning to forgive.

For me Jesus' words brought back a long-ago phone call. At eighty-two and in poor health, my mother-in-law was calling from Louisville, Kentucky, "to set right anything wrong between us." The best-organized person I've ever known, I realized that she was preparing for death with her usual efficiency. There'd been times, she went on, when she'd been impatient, judgmental, unkind.

"I'm asking you now, Tib, to forgive me."

And I, touched by this gesture from a proud and accomplished woman, blurted out, "Why, there's nothing to forgive! You've been the best mother-in-law in the world!"

For the most part, this was true: She'd been generous, caring, supportive. Inevitably, over the course of thirty years, there'd been friction between her disciplined lifestyle and my less-so one. Some episodes still rankled, like the time a traffic jam made us half an hour late for dinner at her home. We arrived to find the others eating.

Embarrassed to admit I remembered anything so petty, I assured her again that all was well between us. Mother Sherrill's request was made with seriousness and integrity. And I took the easy, self-protective, socially graceful way out: *There's nothing to forgive.*

But there is, of course, in any long-term human relationship. To forgive, I understood too late for what could have been the closest moment ever for the two of us, means being truthful about the damage so that the forgiveness, too, will be true.

LORD JESUS, YOU REVEALED THE SERIOUSNESS OF SIN BY GOING TO THE CROSS. HELP ME IN THE HARD WORK OF FORGIVENESS.   —ELIZABETH SHERRILL

| MAUNDY THURSDAY | LIVING THE WORD IN HOLY WEEK—AND BEYOND |

THU
9

"Love one another as I have loved you."
—JOHN 15:12 (RSV)

Maundy (Commandment) Thursday takes its name from the charge Jesus gave His disciples at their final meal together: "A new commandment I give to you, that you love one another." To demonstrate what this meant, He poured water into a basin, knelt and washed His disciples' feet, a chore usually reserved for the lowliest slave.

Hearing the passage read out loud, I recalled a Maundy Thursday service on Cape Cod that included a foot-washing ritual. Fifteen chairs were lined up in front of the altar, a towel and a basin of water at each one. Everyone, the minister instructed, was to wash someone's feet and to have his or her own washed. "If there's anyone here," he added, "who's wronged you in any way, that's the person whose feet you should wash."

I was glad this didn't affect me; the only person I knew here was my friend Elaine, who'd brought me. I washed the bony feet of an older man who seemed as glad as I when the little symbolic act was over.

Then it was my turn to sit. And from the back of the church someone all but ran straight to me. It was Elaine. As she washed my feet, I was astonished to see tears falling into the basin. Yesterday I'd remembered a time when I needed to forgive; now I was the offender! When? How?

Back at Elaine's house, it came out: an old resentment over a remark I couldn't even remember making. Apparently I'd said (about a clothing drive for Africa), "Until you've lived in a Third World country, you can't imagine how little people have."

"You've been to so many places," my friend said, tears coming again. "I'd love to travel, but because I haven't, you think I don't know anything."

It was my turn to cry—for the pain caused by my heedless remark. I apologized, Elaine forgave me, and our friendship has been deeper, stronger, more joyous ever since.

LORD JESUS, TEACH ME TO LOVE.   —ELIZABETH SHERRILL

GOOD FRIDAY   LIVING THE WORD IN HOLY WEEK—AND BEYOND

FRI
10

"My God, my God, why have you forsaken me?"

—MARK 15:34 (NIV)

At our church from noon to 3:00 PM today, we recall the Seven Last Words of Jesus, spoken from the Cross. Of them all, the one I can hardly bear to hear is this cry of abandonment from the Son whose trust in the Father has been absolute.

Bible students believe that Jesus, Who knew the Scriptures so well, was in His agony reciting Psalm 22, which opens with this fearful outcry. How uncannily the lines, written hundreds of years earlier, describe His suffering! "They have pierced my hands and my feet" (Psalm 22:16, NIV).

The congregation kneels as we read the Psalm aloud: "They divide my garments among them and cast lots for my clothing" (Psalm 22:18, NIV). And once more the familiar marvel of the Living Word repeats itself; lines I've read a thousand times light up with new meaning. This time it's the final verses of the Psalm: "Future generations will be told about the Lord. They will proclaim his righteousness to a people yet unborn—for he has done it" (Psalm 22:30–31, NIV).

We are that future generation, those people not to be born for two thousand years. We *have* been told about Him, we know that "he has done it"—suffered death in order to rise with the promise of everlasting life. We know how the story ends.

Our friends Mark and Penny are such passionate partisans of the football team the Dallas Cowboys that they can't bear the suspense of awaiting the final score. Rather than watch the games, they record them. Then, when they know how it has turned out, they can enjoy the plays, the tackles, the passes that brought it about.

We can bear that grief-stricken cry from the Cross. We know how it turns out.

LORD JESUS, HELP ME ENDURE THE DARK TIMES IN MY OWN LIFE IN THE KNOWL-
EDGE THAT DEFEAT IS NOT THE END OF THE STORY. —ELIZABETH SHERRILL

Editor's Note: We invite you to join us in prayer today as we observe our annual Good Friday Day of Prayer. Guideposts Prayer Ministry prays daily for each of the prayer requests we receive by name and need. Join us at www.OurPrayer.org and learn how you can request prayer, volunteer to pray for others or contribute to support our ministry.

HOLY SATURDAY LIVING THE WORD IN HOLY WEEK—AND BEYOND

SAT
11

Christ . . . went and preached to the spirits in prison.
—I PETER 3:18–19 (RSV)

There's no service at our church today; it's a time for quiet meditation. The sanctuary is dark and bare, stripped of hangings, vessels—everything bright and colorful. On the altar a wooden cross is draped in black.

In the silence I reflect on a world whose Light has gone out. Jesus shrouded and motionless in the tomb.

It's an image I don't want to linger on. I'm relieved when the sanctuary lights are switched on, and people begin carrying in pots of tulips, lilies, hyacinths and daffodils for tomorrow's great celebration. I leave to get mint jelly for our Easter dinner. *After all*, I think, *this is essentially just a day of preparation for the great event.*

I thought so, that is, until last year, when I made my first trip to Russia for a seminar on the Orthodox Church. In icons, those images that are not paintings but "windows into heaven," I recognized familiar scenes of Jesus' life—His baptism by John, the raising of Lazarus, the Crucifixion. But what episode was this? In every church a prominent icon showed Jesus, robes flying, striding into a dark opening in the earth. Graves are opening as He seizes the hands stretched out to Him, drawing lost souls from the depths of hell.

Jesus, on this day, inert and passive in the tomb? Not in the Orthodox tradition! Here is an avenging Savior, confronting the forces that corrupt and imprison His creatures. Gazing at the drama depicted in these icons, I thought of the phrase in the Apostles' Creed that I've said so often and reflected on so little: "He descended into hell." Here, Holy Saturday celebrates the Savior Who has endured the worst that Satan can do and now descends to free the captives of a defeated enemy.

FREE ME, TOO, LORD, ON THIS HOLY DAY AND EVERY DAY, FROM THE SIN THAT ENTRAPS.
—ELIZABETH SHERRILL

| EASTER | LIVING THE WORD IN HOLY WEEK—AND BEYOND |

"He is not here; he has risen! . . ."

—LUKE 24:6 (NIV)

"He is not here," the angels told the little group of grieving women who came to the tomb that first Easter morning. "He has risen!" This is what angels, in their myriad shapes, tell us still, not only on this Easter, but every day.

For me, one of those angels is a handsome conifer, the only large tree in our yard. My husband John and I were new homeowners, not sure of how to care for the lawn and shrubs. But whatever our failures, the tree towered above them, drawing the eye away from weeds and bare spots.

That's why we were distressed when that fall some brown patches appeared among the dark green needles. We mulched the tree, fed it, watered it, talked to it. Nothing stopped the withering of the needles. They dropped from branch after branch until of our lovely tree only a great gaunt skeleton remained etched against the November sky.

To leave the dead tree there was just too sad. Dangerous, too, we worried. What if it fell against the house! All winter we debated whether to cut it down ourselves (too big) or to hire a tree service (too expensive).

It was in April that the first pale green fuzz appeared on the highest branches, then lower down, swelling, spreading, darkening, clothing every branch with glorious new growth. Our tree, we learned that year, was not an evergreen, but a larch—an unusual conifer that sheds its needles in the fall only to replace them in the spring, brighter, more bountiful than ever.

Today the tree is twice the height and width it was when we moved here. Autumn and spring, for forty-nine years it has played out this little drama of death and resurrection. For forty-nine years it has repeated the angels' joyful shout: "He has risen!"

R ISEN L ORD, WITH EVERY OUTWARD SIGN OF LOSS OR DEATH, GIVE ME EYES TO SEE THE E ASTER MIRACLE DEEP WITHIN. —E LIZABETH S HERRILL

| E A S T E R M O N D A Y | L IVING THE W ORD IN H OLY W EEK —AND B EYOND |

"I am going fishing." . . .
—J OHN 21:3 (RSV)

It's the day after Easter. Yesterday at church there were flowers, triumphant hymns, shouts of "Hallelujah!" Today comes as a letdown. Time to go back to work. How I'd like to prolong the splendor of Easter!

One year I tried. There's a retreat house forty miles north of us where I was sure I could maintain the Easter spirit. I drove up there that Monday, took my suitcase to the room assigned to me and went into the chapel to try to recapture the exaltation of the day before.

And all I could think about were the half-done projects on my desk and the car inspection due that week. I stayed on in that serene setting for two days. There were worship services, silence, beauty. But on my mind were only unwritten letters and the torn lampshade that needed replacing. By Wednesday I was back at my desk. There were forty-three new e-mails waiting and the phone never stopped ringing and the plumber who was going to work on the sink couldn't come. And it was there, in the workaday world, that I was overwhelmed with the sense of Jesus' risen presence. "Where've you been?" I could almost hear Him say. "I've been waiting here for you."

The apostle Peter was wiser than I. After the awestruck reunion with his resurrected Lord in the room with the locked door, Peter did not linger in that sacred space. He did not run again to the empty tomb, trying to recapture that moment of moments. A fisherman, he went back to his job of fishing. And there is where Jesus waited for him, preparing a meal on the lakeside for the hungry laborers before sending them out to carry the Easter message to the world.

RISEN LORD, SHOW ME THE DIFFERENCE YOUR RESURRECTION MAKES, TODAY AND EVERY DAY. —ELIZABETH SHERRILL

"You are to judge your neighbor fairly."
—LEVITICUS 19:15 (NAS)

There's an old joke that says, "If the doctor tells you that you only have six months to live, join your homeowners' association. It will be the longest six months of your life."

I only wish that I had heard that joke before I joined the board where I lived. I faced the first meeting with eager anticipation and the following meetings with dread. By the end of the third meeting—to decide if potted plants on the balconies had to be in pots under twenty-four inches or thirty-six inches—I was ready to jump off a balcony. Instead, I silently invented nicknames for the other participants.

There was Dina, the "Detail Woman," who would wave a copy of the rules and regulations as she let us know about every tiny loophole in whatever we were discussing; "Lucy Late," who dashed in halfway through and insisted on a recap of every topic; and Bruce, the "Big-Picture Guy," who kept saying, "We're not seeing the big picture here!"

After the meeting droned to a close, Julie, a longtime neighbor, walked alongside me as we left the meeting room. "That was dull as a butter knife," I commented.

"You made your feelings pretty obvious," she told me.

Stung, I stopped in my tracks. "But I didn't say a word!" I protested.

"No," she agreed. "You just rolled your eyes, sighed a lot and drummed your fingers on the table." More kindly, Julie continued, "Long ago I realized that these meetings would never be entertaining. But they *are* necessary. So if I'm going to participate, I need to be there, body and soul."

I had to admit that Julie had a point. And while the meetings never became interesting, I did learn that I could respectfully listen as we took care of the necessary business of living in a neighborly way.

GOD, SOMETIMES MY SILENCE CAN SPEAK MORE SHARPLY THAN MY WORDS. HELP ME LISTEN TO EVERYONE RESPECTFULLY. —LINDA NEUKRUG

I will sing a new song to thee, O God. . . .

—PSALM 144:9 (RSV)

Last year I learned that a friend from my youth group in Arizona lived near me in the Pacific Northwest. I hadn't seen her for more than thirty-five years, and so it was an adventure to meet her again.

"Hey, you played clarinet, didn't you?" asked Rachel over coffee.

"Yes."

"You read music, right?"

"Yes."

"Want to join my church's handbell choir?"

Was she kidding?

Turns out, Rachel goes to a little church in the country, an old-fashioned one with a steeple and bell and high front steps—and a swarm of people so busy with local relief work that I get dizzy with the excitement. I drive out to this oasis every Wednesday night for a home-cooked, two-dollar supper, and hear stories of refugee support, food bank collections and raffles for missionaries. Then a dozen of us climb creaky stairs (too steep) to the belfry (too hot), where Rachel conducts our practice, the highlight of my week.

I love the lifting of my arms, the snapping of my wrists, the clear pure note sounding in with others in perfect harmony. A friend said, "How very Currier-and-Ives of you." Perhaps, but I think the truth lies closer to the fact that my heart and soul are alive to God's work and I am able to sing a new song with an old friend, in harmony with people who share God's love and blessings.

BLESS THE WORK OF THIS LITTLE COUNTRY CHURCH, LORD, AS THEY FEED THE HUNGRY AND SHELTER THE DISPOSSESSED—AND ALLOW ME TO SHARE THE JOY OF "SINGING A NEW SONG" TO YOU IN WORSHIP AND PRAISE. —BRENDA WILBEE

"Wisdom is with the aged, and understanding in length of days."
—JOB 12:12 (RSV)

Finally I was cleaning out the back—way back—of my bedroom closet. I pulled out a flattened tennis shoe (only one—why on earth had I kept it?), a bag of yarn I'd used years ago for needlepoint, a clump of yellowing dry-cleaner bags. As dust filtered through the air, I was already ready to quit. But there was one more item, something flat, along the wall.

I pulled it out, a framed picture. I wiped off the dust with a crumpled sock. It was a picture I remembered seeing as a little girl in my Grandmother Paisley's house in Steubenville, Ohio. Later my mother kept it in our home displayed in an upstairs bedroom. It was a picture of Jesus on His knees in a garden in prayer, gazing upward. As a child and teenager, I'd loved it; as a cynical adult, I'd rolled my eyes and dismissed it as sentimental and irrelevant.

Had my grandmother cared enough to cut this from the pages of a book or magazine and put it in a frame? I pushed open the tabs at the back of the frame and pulled out the cardboard. Yes, that's what it was— an illustration or reproduction, probably from some kind of Easter devotional book. On the back I read this blurb in flowing type: "The risen Christ brought inspiration, joy and cheer to His disciples. To all who follow Him in simple faith, He does the same today."

Tears stung my eyes. In an instant all intellectual fussiness and self-important judgment was gone, the purity and profundity in this simple statement rang true across the ages. An iconic picture cut out and framed by my beloved grandmother probably seventy-five years ago now glowed with astonishing new life.

I copied the words, reassembled the picture in its frame, pasted the words on the back of the picture and recorded them in my journal—and in my heart.

Lord, thank You for the simple faith in the risen Christ that brings inspiration, joy and cheer—yesterday, today and tomorrow.

—Mary Ann O'Roark

Ye shall seek me, and find me, when ye shall search for me with all your heart.

—Jeremiah 29:13

On the Friday after Easter, my colleague Ptolemy and I made a trip to the Abbey of Gethsemani outside Louisville, Kentucky. The place has been a spiritual landmark for me because of the writings of its most famous resident, Thomas Merton. A gifted poet and author, he entered the monastery in his twenties to devote himself to a life of prayer, teaching and study. Here he wrote his autobiography *The Seven Storey Mountain,* and it inspired me in my own spiritual search. But somehow a visit to the place where he lived was less than inspiring. Yes, we could see the sanctuary where he worshipped and the garden where he walked. In the bookstore we even spoke to one of the brothers who knew him. But I didn't feel as if I was meeting Merton.

"Go for a walk in the hills," a brother urged us, giving us a map. Ptolemy and I set off along the trail, trudging across fresh-mown pasture, winding through wooded hills, pausing at a sculpture garden, climbing a mountain where there was supposed to be a view of the abbey (hard to see through the trees). For a moment we got lost, and I worried that I'd brought Ptolemy on a wild-goose chase. He was good-natured, but I was fretting. It was getting late, and we needed to get back to Louisville. Then we came out of the woods onto a dirt lane leading to a meadow with a rusty old tractor, a red barn and a rough-hewn cross.

That's when I met Merton . . . in that humble scene before me. I was reminded of how faith can transform the things of everyday life and how when you follow an unknown path—searching, trusting—God will lead you somewhere.

GOD, I KNOW THAT IN MY SEEKING, HOWEVER LOST I FEEL, YOU ARE THERE.

—RICK HAMLIN

Pray for one another. . . .

—JAMES 5:16 (NAS)

I was shopping one Saturday this year at an estate sale when a petite blonde woman touched my elbow. "Aren't you Roberta?" she asked somewhat shyly. "I believe you spoke to our women's group at church some time back. You talked about prayer."

As I tried to recall the event, words spilled from her. "I could sure use some of that prayer right now. I'm having brain surgery on Tuesday." She hesitated for a moment as the two of us looked at a white chippy-painted chair. Rubbing her fingers along the chair's rough surface, she asked, "Could you pray for me?"

Worry creased her features, and I knew what she really needed was prayer right then. *But here on the porch of this old brick home, Lord? In the midst of all these people?* I didn't know her name and I was too embarrassed to ask.

I motioned to her to follow me to a corner of the porch where there were no shoppers. The two of us leaned against the wobbly porch railing and I took her hand. "How about us talking to the Lord about it right here?" I quietly suggested.

WITH ETERNITY IN VIEW

Pray on the Spot

As I closed my eyes and squeezed her fingers, I shut out the world. I asked God to watch over her every step of the way. "Be with the neurosurgeon, the nurses, everyone who takes care of her," I prayed. Three days later the woman's sister telephoned to tell me that the surgery had been a complete success and a full recovery was expected.

Now, when people ask me to pray *for* them, I ask if they would like me to pray *with* them. More often than not, the person is enormously relieved and the two of us enjoy a new bond as prayer partners.

THANK YOU, LORD JESUS, FOR THE PRIVILEGE OF PRAYING WITH YOUR CHILDREN.

—ROBERTA MESSNER

Spring was buzzing. Oh, how I longed to dive into my flower garden and begin planting marigold seeds and tulip bulbs. But surgery must take first priority. So here I lie in bed with spring just outside my door, resting, healing, praying and recuperating. God is near, though; I feel His presence in each card I receive, each prayer prayed for me, and in the teenagers from church who agreed to plant my seeds and bulbs. With His help, I've bloomed quite beautifully.　　　—*Linda Grazulis, Cuyahoga Falls, Ohio*

SUN
19

. . . For the gift bestowed upon us by the means of many persons thanks may be given. . . .

–II Corinthians 1:11

　　It was a wonderful Easter. Morning worship at our son Patrick's church in Texas featured an excellent choir and inspiring sermon. Our daughter-in-law Patricia prepared a veritable feast for dinner. Our traditional family egg hunt—held indoors because of spring snowflakes—ended with only two children in tears, and they were soon comforted.

　　Then my husband Don said, "We need to head home, so we can stop in Amarillo and get Penney's Easter surprise."

　　I looked at Don, then at my smiling children and grandchildren. My heart dropped to my toes. Without thinking I blurted out, "Not a dog! It better not be a dog! The last thing I want or need is something else to take care of."

　　Shock, hurt and dismay registered on every face. I tried to backtrack but, of course, I couldn't undo the damage. Finally Don said, "Will you at least look at her?"

　　I agreed, and Patrick found an old cat carrier for us, "just in case." You can guess what happened: I met a fat, wiggly ball of fur and promptly fell in love with Tarby, a golden chow.

　　Is she something else to care for? Oh yes. She has to be fed, watered, groomed, walked and trained. Is she worth it? Absolutely. Her wagging tail and yips of "hello" never fail to lift my spirits. She's always ready to walk along with me or sit silently beside me. If I go away, whether for an hour or a week, she joyously welcomes me home.

The gift I didn't want turned out to be the next-to-best Easter surprise ever.

GRACIOUS GOD, THANK YOU FOR GIVING ALL OF US THE MOST PRECIOUS EASTER GIFT OF ALL IN THE RESURRECTION OF YOUR ONLY SON, JESUS THE CHRIST.

—PENNEY SCHWAB

Hear counsel, and receive instruction,
that thou mayest be wise in thy latter end.

—PROVERBS 19:20

I looked across the restaurant table at my daughter Kristal as we dug into our first breakfast alone together in . . . how many years? Since she was in high school? Now she was married, with two little boys, and we had lived on opposite sides of the country for eight years. My wife Carol and I had moved to California the same year Kristal got married. Now we were back in New York, living only a few miles from her.

"Dad, could we go to breakfast like we used to?" she'd asked me one day when she and the boys were visiting.

From the time they were little girls, I'd taken each of our daughters to a restaurant regularly for "breakfast with Daddy." More recently, our older daughter Laurel and I had gone out to breakfast occasionally when she lived near us in California.

Now, Kristal wanted to discuss the plot and characters of the novel she was writing. She'd experienced a renewal of faith a couple of years earlier, and she wanted my advice on some spiritual aspects of the story. Breakfast seemed an ideal time to talk without interruption.

We ordered coffee and discussed how a reader might identify with each of the novel's main characters. In minutes Kristal began to see things she hadn't considered, and after breakfast she headed home with new enthusiasm. "We need to do this again," she suggested.

"Yes," I agreed. And since Laurel had moved east with us, there was another breakfast I needed to schedule.

WHAT A JOY IT IS TO HAVE DAUGHTERS WHO STILL SEEK DAD'S ADVICE. FATHER, THANK YOU FOR THE WISDOM YOU'VE GIVEN THAT I CAN SHARE WITH THEM.

—HAROLD HOSTETLER

TUE
21

How good and how pleasant it is for brethren to dwell together in unity!
—PSALM 133:1

I was sitting at the meeting of our committee at the Valley Interfaith Council when word came to us that someone had spray-painted swastikas on a local synagogue. We were appalled but not shocked. There had been incidents before, though not in the past few months. The other Jewish committee members and I exchanged sorrowful glances and began to discuss whether we should cut the meeting short to go over to the synagogue and help clean up the vandalism.

One of the ministers on the committee got up and went straight for the phone. He called his church office, and said, "Mary, start calling our congregation. We're going to need them to help with cleanup over at the synagogue. Thanks."

He hung up the phone and sat down at the table again.

I said hesitantly, "Someone from your church couldn't have been responsible for the spray painting."

"I don't think so," he said.

"Then why—" asked another of the Jewish committee members.

He smiled at us. "This isn't just a Jewish problem," he said, "it's our community's problem. Is there anything else on the agenda? If not, let's all go over to the synagogue."

Nothing in any previous work on the interfaith council had showed me so clearly that people of goodwill do not have to share a faith to stand together.

PLEASE HELP ME TO SHOW GENEROSITY TO EVERYONE, LORD, ACCORDING TO THE EXAMPLE YOU HAVE SHOWN ME THROUGH OTHER PEOPLE.   —RHODA BLECKER

WED 22

"Rule over the fish of the sea and the birds of the air and over every living creature that moves on the ground."

—Genesis 1:28 (NIV)

I watched my three-year-old granddaughter Karis make friends with a ladybug this afternoon on our way home from a walk around the neighborhood.

"A ladybug!" she squealed with delight when she spotted the bright red beetle crawling curbside at her feet. She squatted down, resting her chin on her knees, and placed her hand in front of the ladybug, which crawled right onto it, as if that's exactly what the tiny bug wanted to do.

"Oh, cute!" Karis cooed as she brought her hand to her face, so she and the ladybug could see eye to eye. She then stood up and began moving her hands, one in front of the other, so the ladybug could keep crawling forward, getting nowhere.

"Are you all right?" she asked her new little friend. "Do you need to find your mommy and daddy?" We slowly walked a few more steps. Then Karis looked up. "The ladybug likes me," she announced with confidence.

I thought about all I read and heard urging us to care for our planet: how to "re" everything. Recycle, reuse, repurpose, save energy, conserve resources, go green. All good stuff, but I confess that I sometimes get too lazy to make the simple sacrifices.

But watching Karis tenderly care for one of the smallest of God's creatures gave me plenty of motivation to take better care of all God has given us, so the next generation and all the generations that follow can still make friends with ladybugs.

Father, You have given us the responsibility to care for Your creation. Thank You for sprinkling our days with motivation.

—Carol Kuykendall

THU 23

Train up a child in the way he should go. . . .

—Proverbs 22:6

"Let's climb Arthur's Seat today," said my son John, as my family and I ate breakfast in our Edinburgh hotel.

Arthur's Seat, John explained, was a popular tourist destination in Scotland, the remains of an extinct volcano towering eight hundred feet over the city center.

An hour later we arrived at the base of the peak, our necks craned to follow the winding route to the summit. Scores of people were climbing up and down the path; it looked to be an easy ascent. I was happy to be at this lovely spot, ready to conquer the heights.

As soon as we started, though, I felt a twinge in my right ankle. My heart sinking, I sat down on a nearby rock. It was my old Achilles tendon injury acting up. I had damaged it years ago while exercising and ever since then the ankle had required gingerly treatment to avoid a rupture. Right away I realized that climbing was out of the question. I looked at my family, my voice filled with disappointment—and a dash of self-pity—and said, "Sorry, kids, I'm grounded. It's the ankle again."

I had expected howls of protest or at least some looks of disappointment to match my own. Instead, John said, "That's okay, Dad. You sit here and enjoy the sunshine," and little Andy added, "Sure, Dad. We'll climb Arthur's Seat for you!"

"Okay," I said. "Give me a wave when you get to the top and I'll wave back." And, don't you know, that wave was worth all the successful ascents in the world.

LORD, HELP ME TO FIND REJOICING, NOT REGRET, IN THE KNOWLEDGE THAT WHEN I MUST STAY BEHIND, MY CHILDREN CAN MARCH FORWARD.   —PHILIP ZALESKI

A time to weep, and a time to laugh. . . .
—ECCLESIASTES 3:4

When our son Paul was seventeen, he was in a tragic car accident. His girlfriend was killed, and Paul spent several days in a coma in the ICU.

When Paul came home from the hospital, we put him in the bedroom nearest to ours, so I could check on him during the night.

A TIME TO EVERY PURPOSE

Night after night, I heard him weeping. Sometimes I went to him several times a night to comfort him until he finally went back to sleep. Then an hour or so later, he'd be crying again. It wasn't the physical pain that caused his tears; it was the emotional pain.

So today I ask of the One Who knows, "Do injury and grief serve any good purpose in our lives?"

The answer is kind and gentle.

The heart that hurts cries out for comfort.
A door swings open and the Spirit enters,
speaking soothing words: "I heard your cry, my child,
and I have come to comfort you."

The Spirit holds the broken one; the pain drains out
and the aching heart, grown hard to keep the grief away,
slowly softens and learns to love again.
Compassion, you see, is the gift of pain.

Though I'm sure Paul will always carry some of that deep sorrow, his heart eventually healed and he went on with life, fell in love again and married, becoming the father of eight children. And a most loving and compassionate father he is.

GENTLE SPIRIT, I ASK YOUR COMFORT FOR ALL WHO WEEP THIS NIGHT. SOFTEN THEIR HEARTS AND TEACH THEM COMPASSION. IN YOUR HOLY NAME I PRAY, AMEN.

—MARILYN MORGAN KING

And the Lord God formed man of the dust
of the ground, and breathed into his nostrils the
breath of life; and man became a living soul.

—GENESIS 2:7

For our nine-year-old Mary and the other children at her ballet school, late April means Spring Performance. Since the week after Christmas, they've been preparing, learning the choreography and rehearsing, in addition to their regular schedule of classes.

Mary thrives in the ballet world. The more she dances, the more her enthusiasm grows. If I'm a few minutes late picking her up after class, I find her sitting in a studio doorway, watching the older children go through their routines. When she catches sight of me, she puts her bag over her shoulder, exchanges a few giggles with her friends, and dances out the studio door and across West 68th Street, then down Broadway to the subway station, barely pausing long enough to pick up a snack along the way.

She's been taking ballet for more than half of her life, and she's worked hard, growing stronger and more flexible every year. More than anyone in our family, Mary is at home in her body.

This year, my body and I haven't been on quite such good terms. My doctor tells me that the weight I've been carrying around most of my life is taking its toll, and I've been seeing a nutritionist for some help in slimming down. For the past three months, I've bidden a reluctant farewell to muffins, doughnuts and cookies, and have struggled to give my affections to salad, yogurt and fresh fruit. So far, it's been working: My clothes are getting looser, and I'm about ready for a new and smaller belt.

I've got a ways to go, but by next year's Spring Performance, I want to be able to dance down the street with Mary without huffing and puffing, with a slimmer physique and a much lighter heart.

LORD, HELP ME TO BE A GOOD STEWARD OF THE LIFE AND THE BODY YOU'VE GIVEN ME.   —ANDREW ATTAWAY

And ye shall seek me, and find me, when ye shall search for me with all your heart.

—JEREMIAH 29:13

One morning I was teaching my Sunday school class of fifth- and sixth-graders the story of Jonathan and David's friendship. I explained how David was running for his life from Jonathan's father King Saul, and how Jonathan could have chosen to help his father kill David and possibly have become king someday. Instead, he decided to help David because of their great friendship.

A boy's hand shot up. "Just like in *Talladega Nights,*" he said. Everybody laughed, because a raucous Will Ferrell comedy isn't typically what we discuss in Sunday school. But when I asked the boy to explain what he meant because I hadn't seen the movie, its story of friendship did sound familiar, even if the setting had shifted from ancient Israel to NASCAR. More importantly, this boy had made a connection, finding a God-message amid the laughter of a film comedy.

I often complain that God is absent from the things of this world, but maybe I'm the one leaving Him out. I don't expect to find God in everything I see or read, but maybe I'm tuning out too quickly and missing what is there. Later that same morning, I learned that some friends are taking an adult Sunday school class based on the early 1960s TV show *The Twilight Zone.* I guess you never know where you might find a God-message until you start looking.

HELP ME FIND YOU IN THE UNEXPECTED PLACES, LORD, AND TO USE THOSE MOMENTS TO HELP OTHERS FIND YOU AS WELL.   —GINA BRIDGEMAN

I the Lord search the heart . . . even to give every man according to his ways, and according to the fruit of his doings.

—JEREMIAH 17:10

My son was driving me and two of my daughter Tamara's children to their home where I was going to spend "grandma time." Somewhere along the way I began handing out saltwater taffy to Caleb, five, and Ruby, four, in the backseat. The problem was I only passed them the flavors I didn't like. They got blueberry and licorice and raspberry; I got cinnamon and peppermint and chocolate. They didn't know the difference, but I did.

I began to wonder, *Is it really sharing if I'm giving something I don't want? Shouldn't I have a stake in it for it to be true sharing?*

We arrived at Tamara's, where every night Ruby and I read a book about what love is. One page said, "Love is sharing your umbrella in the rain."

There was no precipitation in Alaska's forecast the evening Tamara walked into Ruby's bedroom and rained M&Ms, my favorite candy, in my lap. Ruby was on red alert. Holding out her small hand, she announced, "Don't you know love is sharing?"

I parted with my M&Ms that night to a gleeful voice inside me that said, "Now *this* is sharing."

GOD, SUPREME GIVER, PREPARE ME FOR BOUNTIFUL GIVING BY FIRST KEEPING ME GENEROUS IN THE SMALL STUFF.   —CAROL KNAPP

"Let me give you a new command: Love one another. In the same way I loved you, you love one another. This is how everyone will recognize that you are my disciples—when they see the love you have for each other."

—JOHN 13:34-35 (MSG)

I felt angry one day, listening to theologians poking fun at people who believe that every word in the Bible is true and to those who look down their noses at the scholars. Both sides seemed angry and sarcastic.

The next morning I happened to read the new commandment Jesus gave His disciples before He left them. I felt pretty smug for about thirty seconds. Then it hit me: I didn't feel love for any of the combatants I'd heard arguing the day before.

Squirming, I turned to James 5:16 (MSG): "Confess your sins to each other and pray for each other so you can live together, whole and healed." My discomfort grew. I saw that there can never be reconciliation until I confess my sins against those who differ from me. If I can't stop angrily judging others, people will know I'm not Jesus' disciple. And I won't be able to show others the amazing life of love He brought us all.

LORD, TEACH ME HOW TO LOVE PEOPLE, EVEN IF THEY NEVER AGREE WITH ME. AMEN.

—KEITH MILLER

"He will yet fill your mouth with laughter...."

—JOB 8:21 (RSV)

Some years ago we entertained someone in our home who had experienced one of those life-after-death episodes. While others demanded specifics ("How does heaven look?" "Do you see people you know?"), my son Brock's question was different: "Does God have a sense of humor?" he asked hopefully. I understood perfectly where Brock was coming from. If God doesn't have a sense of humor, most of us are in big trouble.

But something tells me we're safe. After all, God made giraffes and teenagers and avocado seeds. Each had to be created with a chuckle of mischievous delight. And think about what nice pencil holders ears make, and how ugly ducklings and even uglier caterpillars are born to soar on magnificent wings.

Brock, however, was thinking of something else. Religion in the South sometimes takes on a harsh tone. Some see God as a hard disciplinarian, intent on separating the worthy from the unworthy. A few weeks earlier, in the throes of a painful divorce, Brock had received an angry letter from someone who fancied himself as a sort of heavenly judge.

Believing that God is like a good Father, I have to disagree with that unhappy letter writer. The fathers I know laugh a lot when they are with their children. They love hearing their stories. They pick them up when they fall. No matter what kind of mistakes their children make, fathers love them just the same.

So I wasn't surprised when our guest looked straight at Brock and said, "God pulls for us. He suffers with us. And you can bet that when we laugh, He laughs with us!"

FATHER, LAUGH WITH US AS OFTEN AS YOU CAN.   —PAM KIDD

Jesus replied, "If anyone loves me, he will obey my teaching. My Father will love him, and we will come to him and make our home with him."

—JOHN 14:23 (NIV)

Weeks before my wedding day, my little apartment went through some major modifications. I emptied a large closet and several dresser drawers to make room for my husband-to-be. I filled numerous garbage bags with old clothes, useless trinkets, broken electronics and countless other things I no longer used. I took down the framed black-and-white photos I'd taken in college, along with the paintings, clocks and decorative mirrors. I wiped my refrigerator clean of every magnet, from Paris to California, and stored them in a little tin can. I even changed the bed linen from a colorful print to plain white. I wanted an empty canvas.

Every corner, every wall was now free from the person I was. In less than a month, the life that had been mine alone would be shared with someone else. After our vows I wanted us to build together: Pick the colors, hang new paintings, fill picture frames with photos of *our* experiences and adventures.

As I sat in my living room, surrounded by the clean white walls, I wondered, *Did I go through this much trouble when I asked God to share my life?* I closed my eyes and prayed that He felt just as welcome and at home in my heart as my future husband would be in our little New York City apartment.

LORD, AS OUR FAMILY GROWS, MAKE OUR HEARTS YOUR DWELLING PLACE.

—KAREN VALENTIN

MY LIVING WORDS

1

2

3

4

5

6

7

8

9

10

11

12

13

14

15

16

17

18

19

20

21

22

23

24

25

26

27

28

29

30

MAY

*Thou art my hiding place
and my shield:
I hope in thy word.*
—PSALM 119:114

FRI 1

*Let the righteous smite me,
it shall be a kindness. . . .*

—PSALM 141:5

As a college teacher I live in dread of student evaluations. It's not because I get bad reviews, and it's certainly not because I feel I'm above criticism. It's just that I always forget the nice things they say and never forget the bad things. I have a tendency to beat myself up as it is, and when students add their own whacks, I reel from them. But after I work through the shock and grief of student invective, I find some nuggets of gold.

Criticism is necessary, I think, because we cannot see ourselves clearly. "Who can understand his errors," David acknowledged in Psalm 19:12 (NKJV). My critics are like mirrors that show me where I'm presentable and where I have egg on my face. Every criticism may contain some candle glow of truth that will help me make a good class better.

GOD SPEAKS
THROUGH CRITICISM

The most important thing I've learned from evaluations is the need to be a gentleman when I criticize others. When I have to correct a student or a staff member, I need to be as gentle and careful as a brain surgeon. After all, I'm dealing with students who may already be on the verge of dropping out of school.

Ironically, when I "speak to the rock," instead of "striking the rock," as Moses did, I get much better results.

LORD, CORRECT ME WHEN I'M WRONG, BUT PLEASE BE GENTLE WITH ME.

—DANIEL SCHANTZ

Editor's Note: Take a few moments to look back at what you've written in the journal pages "My Living Words," and let us know what you've been hearing in your spiritual journey this year. Send your letter to *Daily Guideposts* Reader's Room, Guideposts Books, 16 E. 34th St., New York, NY 10016. We'll share some of what you tell us in a future edition of *Daily Guideposts*.

SAT 2

"And I pray that you and all God's holy people will have the power to understand the greatness of Christ's love . . . how wide and how long and how high and how deep that love is."

—Ephesians 3:18 (EB)

Our grandsons were settled in the church nursery with their babysitters. The rest of my family, minus my wife Kathy, slipped into two pews just minutes before the chords of the processional began. My sister-in-law Bunny was marrying her beloved Don in the very church where they had met. We were excited for them, yet I was apprehensive: Bunny was adamant that my eighty-seven-year-old father-in-law was going to walk her down the aisle and give her away. Earlier, as Kathy helped her dad into his tux, I had heard their conversation.

"What am I getting all dressed up for?"

"Today's such a special day, Dad. Today, Bunny's getting married to Don."

"I don't think I ever met him."

"Oh yes, Dad. He's such a nice man, and he treats Bunny so wonderfully. You'll remember him when you see him."

You see, in addition to the effects of a debilitating stroke six years ago, my father-in-law has Alzheimer's disease. Pastor Scott knows this, so I knew any hiccups would be handled with gentleness and compassion.

Bunny held her father's hand as he was pushed down the aisle in his wheelchair by Kathy's twin brother Ken. When Pastor Scott asked, "Who gives this woman to be married to this man?" there was silence.

Dad began to weep. Ken was about to lean down to prompt his father when Dad composed himself, then proudly and tearfully announced, "I do."

For three days Dad remembered everything about the wedding, the reception and even his dance with Bunny as she swished him and the wheelchair around the dance floor to the song "In the Mood."

Thank You for Dad, Lord, and for the loving miracle You lavished on us through him.

—Ted Nace

SUN 3

"You shall love the Lord your God with all your heart, and with all your soul, and with all your might."

—Deuteronomy 6:5 (RSV)

Last Sunday after church, I heard a friend say that he had "half a mind" to go back to college. I told him, "You'll need more than that to get enrolled, go to classes and do the studying it will require." He laughed.

But it's true. I think I first heard such advice from Norman Vincent Peale, who hired me as *Guideposts* magazine managing editor many, many moons ago. I forget what the subject was, probably an article I was contemplating. Dr. Peale's response to my lack of commitment was, "Nothing worthwhile is ever accomplished with half a mind, half a heart or half a will." And, of course, he was right.

I'm reminded of what Jesus had to say about lukewarm faith in Revelation 3:16 (RSV): "Because you are lukewarm, and neither cold nor hot, I will spew you out of my mouth." Now there's a powerful verb you don't hear much anymore. I thought *spew* meant "to spit," but it really means "to vomit." Apparently, Jesus wanted His followers to know how revolting He found lukewarm commitment. Or maybe that half a faith is no faith at all.

FILL US WITH PASSION, LORD, PASSION TO DO YOUR WORK,
TO LOVE AND SERVE YOU DAILY—AND NEVER SHIRK.

—FRED BAUER

MON 4

But even so, you have done right in helping me in my present difficulty.

—Philippians 4:14 (TLB)

A savage tornado hit Greensburg, Kansas, a couple of years ago. Almost every house and business was destroyed, power and water supplies were cut, and most of the 1,500 residents were left homeless.

People and churches from all over the country responded quickly and with overwhelming generosity. Teams of workers, supplies and cleanup equipment poured into the area. My husband Don and I wanted to help, but we were uncertain what to do. We prayed, of course, and sent a donation to the disaster fund. But I wanted to do something more.

My uncertainty lasted until I heard the Greensburg disaster report at a church conference. The bishop and the on-site response team reported on the progress of the recovery. He asked us to take home three images:

1. Scripture, because God's Word shapes our lives and leads our hearts to respond with Christ's love.
2. Church connection, because in three short weeks an amazing amount of money for rebuilding had poured in from churches all over the world.
3. A toothbrush, to remind us to give with our heads as well as our hearts. Greensburg received 1,400 toothbrushes per resident and so much clothing that storage was a major problem.

On-site responders who can offer real assistance and comfort are essential in helping people recover from any disaster. But money and prayers for those who have experienced loss and those who aid rebuilding are valuable gifts too.

COMPASSIONATE JESUS, TEACH ME TO GIVE GENEROUSLY, THOUGHTFULLY AND WITH COMPASSION.   —PENNEY SCHWAB

TUE
5

The bird also has found a house. . . .
—PSALM 84:3 (NAS)

One year our son Brent in Toronto gave me an unusual birdhouse. Red bricks were painted on the sides and chimney; white shutters set off windows complete with yellow painted curtains; flowering shrubs "grew" along the foundation; and a little picket fence had been built out front.

In my mind's eye I could see a feathered singer perched on that picket fence, but the birdhouse was so beautifully painted that I was reluctant to expose it to the elements. For several years it sat as a conversation piece in our living room, but deep down I knew that wasn't where it belonged. This spring I finally asked my husband Leo to hang the birdhouse in the big apple tree in our front yard, facing the picture window so I could still see it.

No birds came.

Then one morning I asked God to direct some tenants to the birdhouse. I had no sooner completed my prayers than I heard the familiar song of a wren. And there it was, perched on the little picket fence just as I had imagined, telling the whole wide world that it had just laid claim to the prettiest birdhouse in the neighborhood.

LORD, YOU DIDN'T MAKE ME JUST TO SIT ON THE SHELF. PUT ME WHERE I TRULY BELONG, SO I CAN BE OF GREATER SERVICE TO YOU. —ALMA BARKMAN

For whether we live, we live unto the Lord; and whether we die, we die unto the Lord: whether we live therefore, or die, we are the Lord's.

—ROMANS 14:8

Recently I've dealt with the loss of several loved ones. I include in that tearful list my beloved cocker spaniel Sally Browne, who went to her reward at age sixteen. She died in my arms on a beautiful May morning when once she would have streaked through the woods out back, flaxen ears flying and tongue lolling out, chasing some enthralling scent no mere human could hope to apprehend. Those years had long since passed for Sally and finally, that May morning, I brought her to her vet's. As her life slipped away, I felt the warmth and weight of her body fully against me. The vet put a stethoscope to her chest and whispered, "She's gone."

Gone is a hard concept. Gone is a full stop. Every part of us rebels against it. When I think of my friend Van, whom I also lost, I'm tempted to think of a great emptiness where his presence once was. I knew him much better than I knew most people, and he me. To lose him was incomprehensible, as if I'd lost a part of myself.

Yet loss *is* comprehensible, but only through the presence of God in my life, Who gives both life and death. To accept death, to accept loss, is to move past my pain and embrace God, trusting in His perfect love and comfort. Only He can bridge that cold gulf between loss and life, and help me forge pain into acceptance. It's only then that I can focus not on the one who died, but on the one who lived.

As I move closer to You, Lord, help me find the Presence that will never fade or die and is there for Van and Sally and all who have gone ahead.

—Edward Grinnan

THU
7

O Lord, You are my God; I will exalt You, I will praise Your name; for You have done wonderful things....

—Isaiah 25:1 (NRSV)

I walk every day. When I have a lot on my mind, these walks can become intense. I've been told that friends regularly pass me in their cars, waving like NASCAR signalers, and I don't even notice.

Lately, I've been battling my self-absorption by mixing a little conversation with God into my daily exercise. Since my purpose is to be less focused on myself, I pray for others.

If I see a gorgeous, well-tended garden, I thank God for the people in that house and pray for their continued success.

When someone in a car passes too close to me or speeds by, instead of getting furious, I ask God to keep the driver and everyone he or she encounters safe.

If I see a Coast Guard ship or one of the submarines from the base downriver traveling out to sea, I pray for the safety of the cadets or the submariners.

When I pass the houses of those I know who oppose me on issues like school spending or the homeless shelter in our city, I ask God to keep them well.

If I see a work crew painting a house or mowing a lawn, I pray that their work will go well and that their skin will be safe from the sun.

As I pass the local college, I ask God to help the young people and their professors lead us to a better tomorrow.

When I see some nurses from our city's hospital power-walking along on their break, I pray for their continued strength, health and gentleness.

And suddenly my walk is over!

It's amazing how many people I can put in my prayers ... especially when I'm not thinking about myself.

LORD, HELP ME TO BE SELFLESS IN MY PRAYERS.

—Marci Alborghetti

So faith, hope, love abide, these three;
but the greatest of these is love.

—I Corinthians 13:13 (RSV)

My old boss used to say to his employees, "We all get along like a family!" And I thought to myself, *Do you know any families?* Families are sometimes a mixed blessing, and my two oldest daughters are prime examples. Yes, Faith and Hope get along splendidly— until they don't. After one particularly bruising encounter, I separated the combatants and suggested that they tackle homework instead of each other. I knew Faith had a speech due for her high school English class, and this is what she wrote—the most unexpected, most unmixed blessing of all:

> My sister Hope and I are close in age, but we're different in some ways—Hope likes different music than I do. She also dresses much "cooler" than I do. Plus, she can make me laugh more than anyone I know. She can also make me feel better more than anyone else. In some ways, Hope and I are opposites. While I can be uptight and critical, Hope can always be happy-go-lucky.
>
> I'm making a tribute to Hope because I could not live without her. She is my other half, as clichéd as that sounds. I guess you could say, "There is no faith without hope," which applies not only to my sister and me, but to life.
>
> Emily Dickinson wrote:
> "Hope" is the thing with feathers—
> That perches in the soul—
> And sings the tune without the words—
> And never stops—at all—
>
> I couldn't have said it better myself.

Neither could I.

LORD, THANK YOU FOR USING FAITH TO REMIND ME THAT "GETTING ALONG LIKE A FAMILY" ISN'T MEANT TO BE PERFECTLY HARMONIOUS OR PERFECTLY CALM—OR PERFECT. IT'S MEANT TO BE THE THING WITH FEATHERS THAT SINGS THE TUNE WITHOUT WORDS AND NEVER STOPS AT ALL. —MARK COLLINS

<table><tr><td>SAT
9</td><td>Encourage one another and
build each other up. . . .
—I Thessalonians 5:11 (NIV)</td></tr></table>

One May evening a few years ago, the phone rang. It was our daughter Danita, who is a pediatrician in Natchez, Mississippi. She said to her mother, "I just got the news about my cousin's heart attack and it bothers me. She's only a few years older than I am; she has a weight problem and so do I. I'm going to work to do something about my weight. Please pray, because I know it's going to be a long, hard process." Rosie assured Danita that we would pray with her and encourage her.

Danita joined a program and began to exercise, and by the next year, she had lost 112 pounds! We marveled at her determination, and she's been an awesome encouragement to friends, relatives, coworkers, patients and also to us. Rosie was inspired to lose twenty-five pounds, and I've begun to walk more and eat more carefully.

The lesson we've learned from Danita is not just about losing weight; it's about discipline and faithfulness and being consistent in all that we do.

LORD, YOU ARE THE FAITHFUL ONE. THANK YOU FOR USING OUR DAUGHTER TO ENCOURAGE US. —DOLPHUS WEARY

<table><tr><td>SUN
10</td><td>Behold, thy mother. . . .
—Mark 3:32</td></tr></table>

When I was a little girl, the Saturday before Mother's Day always included a trip to the florist. There we would pick up white cardboard boxes. Inside were carnations—a white one for Grandma and red ones for my mother, my sister and me. "This is to honor your mother," Grandma would say as she pinned the bright flower to my dress before we left for church on Sunday. "Red says that your mama is alive. White means she's already gone on to heaven." She touched her own pale flower tenderly.

It was Anna M. Jarvis of Philadelphia who—almost a hundred years ago—began a letter-writing campaign to a variety of influential people, which eventually resulted in establishing Mother's Day as a national holiday. It was Anna, too, who championed the wearing of carnations. Her own dear mother had loved white carnations, and Anna thought that the flower represented the purity of motherly love. Later, red carnations were added for those whose mothers were living.

I don't see red and white corsages on Mother's Day anymore. But this year I think I'll go back to that tradition—with a bit of a change. I'll wear a white *and* red carnation. White to show that my mother "has gone on to heaven," but red to show that she's very much alive there!

UNLIKE EVEN THE FAIREST FLOWER, LORD, A MOTHER'S LOVE NEVER DIES. THANK YOU, THANK YOU, THANK YOU!　　　　　　　　　　　—MARY LOU CARNEY

And great multitudes were gathered together to Him . . . and . . . He spoke many things to them in parables. . . .
—MATTHEW 13:2–3 (NKJV)

Today I visited a university library, searching for a small book. More than fifty years had passed since someone had last borrowed the book and read its yellowed pages. When I found it, I moved to a soft corner chair and began to read. A beautiful story unfolded, and I was mesmerized by the author's words. Several hours later I put the book back on the shelf, my life enriched by the encounter.

As I left the quiet library and ambled into a bright spring afternoon, I felt sad that this little leather book now sat alone, helpless to tell its story unless someone found it, dusted it off and read its pages. Would it be another half century before a student stumbled across this treasure?

Unlike that book, I have the opportunity to tell my story anytime I desire. I don't have to wait for someone to pull me off a shelf in order to relate the truths that I've discovered, the adventures I've experienced, the passions that enthrall me and the laughter that rolls within. I can speak at will; I can write; I can share my thoughts; I can tell my story.

Today I have a choice: to be a closed book on a remote shelf or to share my life with others. Telling one's story is a wonderful way to love another person. And that's why Jesus was a master storyteller.

FATHER, GIVE ME THE COURAGE TO BELIEVE THAT MY STORY IS A GIFT THAT OTHERS WILL TREASURE. AMEN.　　　　　　　　　　　—SCOTT WALKER

READER'S ROOM

Our daughter was trying to teach our six-year-old grandson not to hit his three-and-a-half-year-old sister. "Use your words, not your hands! Tell her, 'I don't like it when you interrupt my game.' Can you use your words?"

Our grandson took this all in, nodded and said, "And then can I hit her?"

I had to smile as I heard this story, remembering the many times I've "used my words" with God and then asked, "And then can I do it my way?" —*Janet Markoff, Hamilton, Ohio*

TUE
12

The heavens are telling the glory of God; they are a marvelous display of his craftsmanship.

—Psalm 19:1 (TLB)

I love colors: wild, vibrant colors; bold colors. Like the Florida sunsets that are so alive with reds, oranges, pinks, and shades of blue and violet that you can hardly believe the magnificence.

My favorite colors are lime green and royal blue. Probably half of my clothes contain one or both of them. My toenails are always painted lime green to match my shirts, shorts and Capri pants. My bathroom is filled with eight small, round throw rugs, four in each color, plus green and blue towels and fourteen glass jars I hand-painted to decorate one wall.

I was once at a retreat center south of Minneapolis, where the entire front of the chapel was ceiling-to-floor windows, and the lime green trees and bushes in the foreground of a dynamite blue sky and a blue lake a shade lighter nearly gave me goose bumps. When I'm doing water aerobics every morning, the robin's-egg-blue sky dotted with giant whiter-than-white clouds amazes me with its beauty.

Over the years I've learned that whenever I'm feeling tired, depressed, overworked, lonely or sad, all I have to do is go outside and find some color. Where will I go? To the Gulf of Mexico, with gorgeous, soft tan sand, dark blue waves dotted with stunning whitecaps. To the botanical garden, where the flowers compete with the colors of the umbrella tables and mosaic lounge chairs. Perhaps I'll jump in my little fire-engine-red car and drive to Turtle Park, where so many shades of green defy the imagination.

Spirits lifted, colors sorted, smiles returned, I head home, thankful for the colors of my life.

HEAVENLY FATHER, KEEP ME MINDFUL THAT ALL COLOR COMES FROM YOU. THANK YOU FOR THE GIFTS OF COLOR AND SIGHT. —PATRICIA LORENZ

We are troubled on every side, yet not distressed. . . .
—II CORINTHIANS 4:8

I was on a new job as a reporter for a small-town newspaper, and my adrenaline flowed as fast as the copy as my deadline drew near. Keyboards chattered, the radio blared, the police scanner crackled, staff members raised their voices. Beneath the racket I could hear the presses in the backroom thundering like a train, printing the back sections. Next up, the front section and my story—and my contact hadn't answered the phone.

"He doesn't answer. What am I going to do?" I asked no one in particular.

"Hey, forty-five minutes till press time, Gail." My seasoned editor-in-chief smiled and strolled past as though on a tropical beach.

How can he be so calm?

There was still no answer to my calls. I slammed down the phone and suddenly felt hands on my shoulders: Charlie, the sixtysomething news editor, stood behind me, smiling, in his trademark suspenders. He pulled up a chair and settled in as though we had nothing to do for hours.

"Let me tell you a story. When I was about your age, I worked in the Air Force for a department testing new aircraft. One time an engine caught fire at thirty thousand feet. The pilot radioed me.

"'Help! Help!' he yelled. 'The wing's on fire! I've got to put out the fire!'

"I rushed to my commander. He snatched the radio and thundered, 'Roger. First land the plane!' Then he broke contact."

Charlie smiled and patted my now relaxed shoulders. "So when there's not a thing you can do, save your energy. First, land the plane."

I made my phone call, finally reached my contact person and wrote my story—calmly, and in time.

LORD OF HEAVEN AND EARTH, EVEN WHEN I'M NOT IN CONTROL, I KNOW THAT YOU ARE. —GAIL THORELL SCHILLING

Do not let any unwholesome talk come out of your mouths, but only what is helpful for building others up according to their needs, that it may benefit those who listen.
—EPHESIANS 4:29 (NIV)

When I don't like something, I want people to know about it, and I generally won't stop complaining until everyone else is unhappy. But a few months ago this habit nearly caused a disaster.

I had been asked to speak at a high school by its PTA president. On the day of my talk, I arrived early and ate lunch at a restaurant a few blocks away. The food was good, but the restaurant had some of the ugliest decorations I had ever seen. Naturally I couldn't wait to tell someone about it.

When I arrived at the school, the PTA president escorted me backstage and waited with me while the students filled the auditorium. I thought that as a resident of the area, she would appreciate my observations about the restaurant's decor. But before I could bring up the subject, she asked if I was familiar with the restaurant.

"Yes, I ate there today," I said, delighted to have found the perfect opportunity to unleash my tirade. "And actually—"

"My husband and I own it," she said.

I was dumbfounded. "Oh . . . I, uh, well . . . that's terrific," I stammered.

I wondered how many times my careless complaining had offended others . . . and resolved to keep my criticism to myself.

And that PTA president? She asked me to come back again next year.

LORD, HELP ME TO CHOOSE MY WORDS CAREFULLY TO ENCOURAGE, NOT DISPARAGE. —JOSHUA SUNDQUIST

FRI
15

*Now I know in part; but then shall
I know even as also I am known.*

—I CORINTHIANS 13:12

Andrew and I were chatting in the kitchen after our children were in bed. "I was just in the bathroom," I reported, "and I noticed the bathroom tissue was on the wrong way. At first I was irritated, but then I realized that somebody had replaced it without being asked. Amazing!"

Andrew laughed and then suddenly grew suspicious. "Um, which way, exactly, is the right way?" he asked. I paused, stunned. Fourteen years of marriage, and he didn't know? How could this be? Knowing how your spouse likes the bathroom tissue is as fundamental as knowing if she prefers her peanut butter crunchy or creamy.

I girded myself. "The paper comes out underneath."

Andrew exhaled. "Oh good!" he replied. "It tears when you pull it over the top."

Another day, another crisis resolved. Not all of our marital issues are this easily addressed, of course. But a lot of them share something with our bathroom tissue conversation. One of us says something that causes the other to wonder, *Who is this stranger who has suddenly taken the place of my spouse? How can it be that we've been together so long, yet sometimes know so little about each other?*

Perhaps familiarity breeds assumptions. Although I do know a lot about Andrew, I tend to assume I know everything. Then when he acts differently from what I anticipated, I'm startled or shocked or angry.

But there's more to my husband than I can either absorb or imagine. He is, after all, created in the image and likeness of God. Our married life goes easier when I remember that little fact and harder when I forget it.

LORD, YOU KNOW ME BETTER THAN I CAN IMAGINE. DON'T LET ME ASSUME I KNOW YOU AS WELL AS I EITHER CAN OR OUGHT.   —JULIA ATTAWAY

SAT 16

The Lord will be your everlasting light. . . .
—Isaiah 60:20 (NKJV)

Last week I noted a headline in the *Washington Post*: Fond Memory: The Short Life of the Floppy. The "Appreciation" essay, written like a eulogy, referred to the 3.5-inch-square disks that we used to slip into our computers to store information. "Floppy's gone," the writer said, as if the plastic object were a person.

The "death" wasn't exactly news to me, but the "obituary" churned up a fear of obsolescence. My five-year-old laptop has been declared no longer supportable. What's next? I remembered the demise of slide projectors, cassette tapes, VCRs—gadgets and machines that I used to rely on before technology advanced and marketers introduced something new. *If old means out—no longer relevant or useful—what can I depend on tomorrow? Next year?*

The question, almost a prayer, lingered. And then yesterday morning I received an eight-line "God Poem" from my niece's eight-year-old son Dylan. His first lines seemed unremarkable: "God is righteousness. God is love." But I couldn't stop staring at his finale: "God is not that old."

What? God is ancient! On the other hand . . . Dylan's paradoxical statement prompted me to open a concordance, where I was reminded of God and His everlasting—never obsolete—righteousness (Psalm 119:142), kingship (Jeremiah 10:10), strength (Isaiah 26:4), and love (Jeremiah 31:3), which means that today I'm confidently relying on God's everlasting arms (Deuteronomy 33:27).

Dear Dylan, may I suggest a new title for your poem? Try "The Long Life of God."

MY EVERLASTING GOD, DON'T LET ME FORGET THAT I CAN DEPEND ON YOU. AMEN.
—EVELYN BENCE

SUN 17

"I led them with cords of human kindness, with ties of love. . . ."
—Hosea 11:4 (NIV)

A tumor was growing inside my mouth and the only thing that relieved the pain was to hold ice on it. Round cubes from a fast-food place were fine, but crushed ice from a nearby restaurant was the absolute best.

I feel ridiculous that my life has been reduced to ice, Lord, I prayed that Sunday morning. After church I headed to my brother Robert's house for a family gathering. *Their refrigerator makes those big ice cubes,* I remembered. *What I would give for some crushed ice.* But the restaurant was closed on Sundays.

WITH ETERNITY IN VIEW

Make Time for Small Pleasures

When I arrived at Robert's house, I noticed a white Styrofoam cooler on a small table. "A surprise for you, Aunt Roberta," my nephew Alex said. He wrapped an arm around my shoulders and pulled me close. "I know how you like that crushed ice, so I went to the school where I teach to get some for you. We have to make time for small pleasures, you know."

That simple gesture transformed my entire day. As I finished up laundry in anticipation of the workweek, I remembered how soothing that soft crushed ice felt in my mouth. "I wonder what simple pleasures I can create for others, Lord," I prayed.

Come Monday morning, I found I wasn't filled with the usual new-week dread. I'd stocked a baggie with several packets of mint tea for Barbara to enjoy on her breaks, given some of my heart-shaped notepad for Carolyn to use at her desk. Small pleasures all that I was passing along to someone else.

THANK YOU, LORD, FOR YOUR GIFTS LARGE AND SMALL. HELP ME TO SHARE THEM WITH OTHERS.

—ROBERTA MESSNER

"*Search from the book of the Lord, and read. . . .*"
—ISAIAH 34:16 (NKJV)

When Charlotte, the devoted leader of our church's Monday-evening Bible study, died, her husband asked my friend Frank and me to serve in her place. We were hesitant; our knowledge of Scripture was limited to listening to the readings from the lectern on Sunday mornings. But eventually we agreed.

At first we stuck with the Sunday-morning Gospel readings and we quoted our pastor's sermons. But soon our group was studying Genesis.

There we learned from the patriarchs that faith made things possible but not easy. We continued with Exodus, and we learned that Moses refused to lead the people five times because he felt unworthy. Later, we enjoyed Ruth, First and Second Kings, Esther, and Isaiah.

Our last two years were spent studying the Gospel according to Luke. We learned that the Gospel was carefully written and was the easiest Gospel to read. And we learned that Jesus needed human friendships and that He never refused an invitation to dine.

As we listened to Scripture and to each other, we became a family, sharing the heartbreak and the joys of our lives. And we began to see that God doesn't select those who are ready; He makes ready those He selects. Ordinary people can—and do—change the world each day.

TEACHER, THANK YOU FOR GATHERING US TO STUDY YOUR WORD. HELP ME TO LIVE IT AND SHARE IT WITH OTHERS.

—OSCAR GREENE

TUE 19

The patient in spirit is better than the proud in spirit.

—ECCLESIASTES 7:8

Ruby is my Eskimo granddaughter, welcomed to our daughter Tamara's family when she was two days old. Now she is a grinning, bright-eyed four-year-old who says she is "Eksimo."

One day, while working with Ruby and her siblings on the subject of patience, I grouped the letters in the word *patient* and converted it to a singsong chant. *"PA-TI-ENT,"* I called. "What does that spell?"

Ruby enthusiastically shouted, "Patient!"

"What does *patient* mean?" I asked.

In her best four-year-old pronunciation she explained, "It means waiting without *cwying.*"

Ruby wasn't satisfied just to know the definition; she wanted to learn to spell the word. She practiced over and over. Her tongue continually stumbled and tripped, but she stayed with it. "PI."

"No, it's PATI," I corrected.

"PATIENP."

"Not quite. It's ENT."

"PATAENT."

"Oh, you're close. Remember, PATI."

Ruby tried once more, heard herself make a mistake, good-naturedly proclaimed, "I messed up again," and started over.

The day came when she got it right and we whooped it up. She may not remember her achievement down the line, but I'll never forget the day I watched my Eskimo granddaughter patiently work to spell *patient.*

DEAR GOD, SPELLING AND DEFINITIONS ARE FINE, BUT WHEN IT COMES TO YOUR WORD, THE MEANING IS IN THE BEING AND THE DOING.   —CAROL KNAPP

"But its leaves will be green,
And it will not be anxious. . . ."

—JEREMIAH 17:8 (NAS)

Thomas, our youngest, had forgotten my birthday. It was so unlike him. He was not quite sixteen when I turned forty-seven. Sure, he'd said "Happy birthday," but there was no homemade card or even a hug. Maybe he was too busy for his old mom.

On the day after my birthday, I woke up and lay in bed for a few minutes, remembering the births of our children. My mind moved on to the difficult teenage years of our two daughters, now in their twenties. *Thomas' time is coming. How will I deal with that? His rebellion has probably started. See, I'm not important to him anymore.*

Minutes later I heard, "Mom, can you come here?" I slid into my slippers and plodded to the kitchen.

Thomas had gotten up early, clipped roses from the yard, put them in a vase, toasted and buttered me a bagel just the way I like it, and poured my orange juice. He even put out strawberry jelly and a spoon.

"Happy birthday, Mom. Sorry I forgot yesterday." He'd passed me in height over the last year, but he still gave me one of his best little-boy hugs.

"You're going to make a mighty fine husband," I said. Then I glanced out the open window and spotted the wild dogwood in full bloom. I heard the birds singing. They'd been at it since daybreak, but somehow I'd missed them.

GOD, NO MATTER WHAT THE SEASON, YOU SEND GLIMPSES OF HEAVEN.

—JULIE GARMON

THU 21

While he blessed them, he was parted from them, and carried up into heaven.

—LUKE 24:51

Recently I saw a painting of Jesus' Ascension from the fourteenth century. A cluster of men stands, staring up at a small white cloud from which dangle two legs and two sandal-clad feet. In a moment, we understand, these, too, will disappear.

I felt a little envious of that long-ago artist. *Ascending* was an easier concept on an unmoving earth in the center of the heavenly spheres. But as I let the Word live in me today, what does this verse say to me?

Certainly, that at a particular time the physical appearances of the resurrected Jesus—in Jerusalem, in Galilee, en route to Emmaus—ceased to occur. *How sad,* I thought, looking at those upturned faces gazing grief-stricken at their rapidly disappearing Lord. *How wonderful if there'd been no Ascension and we could still see Him, hear Him, touch Him!*

Then, across the years, a scene sprang up before me. I saw a mob of shrieking teenage girls behind a police barrier, hands outstretched, shoving, straining to touch the slender young man walking past. Though far back in the crowd, I was yelling, too, caught up in the hysteria, struggling to get even a few inches closer to him.

I looked again at that painting. *If Frank Sinatra,* I thought, *could set thousands of us trampling one another to get close, what would Jesus' continued physical presence on earth have brought about?* How discreet those post-Resurrection appearances were! To a single person here, a little group there, disappearing as swiftly as He came, remaining in His bodily form only long enough to leave chosen witnesses before entering into a larger kind of existence.

No longer, now, a limited physical being, occupying a specific space at a specific time, but a presence everywhere at once, as close as a prayer.

ASCENDED LORD, I REACH OUT TO TOUCH YOU NOW! —ELIZABETH SHERRILL

FRI
22

*"There is rejoicing in the presence of the angels
of God over one sinner who repents."*

—Luke 15:10 (NIV)

Our daughter Jody asked me to watch her cat Jake-O over the weekend while she was out of town. I didn't mind, although Jake-O was spoiled and fussy. From the moment Jody left him with me, he either hissed at me or hid beneath the sofa.

My day brightened when my husband Wayne, who'd been out of town, arrived home early. I rushed outside to greet him and in my excitement left the front door open. Seeing his opportunity, Jake-O, who'd never been outside and had been declawed, shot out the door and into the woods.

Wayne and I searched for hours. We offered a reward for anyone who would return him to us. But by the end of the day, we'd given up hope.

That night all I could think about was poor Jake-O. In a strange environment he'd be unable to find his way back to the house. Without claws he had no way to protect himself and some forest creature was sure to kill him. As I lay in bed, sick at heart, I prayed that the angels would watch over him.

Eventually I fell asleep, but my dreams were filled with Jake-O. I woke to the faint and distant cry of a . . . *Could it be a cat?* Disoriented, I raced down the hallway. Sure enough, it was Jake-O. He was on the second-story windowsill, peering at me through the glass.

Wayne joined me, and we both marveled at how Jake-O had gotten up so high. Jokingly, Wayne suggested that perhaps an angel had planted him there. I remembered my prayer and smiled.

"You know, sweetheart, you just might be right."

Lord, thank You for caring about those who are lost and for rejoicing when one of them is found, even if it's a fussy cat named Jake-O.

—Debbie Macomber

SAT
23

*"The Mighty One has done great things for me—
holy is his name. His mercy extends to those
who fear him, from generation to generation."*

—LUKE 1:49–50 (NIV)

My father lives in Utah. Though we communicate by e-mail and phone, we rarely see each other. This past May he came to North Carolina to celebrate my son Chase's graduation from the voice program at North Carolina School of the Arts. We were all excited, and it was a special treat for my father, who once also sang regularly. Both my birthday and my father's are in May, and we wanted to celebrate his birthday while he was visiting. But in the flurry of activity, there was no time.

As part of the graduation festivities, Chase had a solo vocal recital. While he stood on stage, my father and my daughter Lanea sat next to me in the audience. It was extraordinary to think of the generations of love and blessings in that hall—to think that my father, who had sung the role of Sportin' Life in a college production of *Porgy and Bess*, now sat some fifty years later listening to his grandson sing the same music.

As we stood in the lobby after the concert, Chase's voice teacher called my father over. He and Chase were surrounded by at least fifty other opera students. Then they and the other vocal coaches began to sing in celebration of my father's birthday. The song was breathtaking, heavenly; no party and no cake could have been sweeter.

THANK YOU, LORD, FOR BLESSINGS THAT EXTEND FOR GENERATIONS.

—SHARON FOSTER

SUN
24

*Those God foreknew he also predestined to be
conformed to the likeness of his Son. . . .*

—ROMANS 8:29 (NIV)

My roommate Kathleen was in the car with her brother and his family, including her five-year-old niece Bright. They'd just come from church, where the minister had preached on imitating the qualities of Jesus.

The car radio played oldies music as the family cruised along on their way to lunch. When they stopped at a red light, Kathleen's sister-in-law caught sight of a woman in oversized curlers, bright red lipstick and white-and-purple sunglasses in the car beside her. Unable to help herself, she burst out in giggles, then alerted the rest of the family to the spectacle next to them.

From the backseat a little voice piped up. "Mommy," scolded five-year-old Bright, "we are supposed to be Christlike. That is not very Christlike."

Bright's dad struggled to compose himself as he looked at his wife. "Yeah, Mommy," he said, "Christlike."

A point had been made, by a preschooler, no less: The words we hear in church shouldn't be left behind the minute we step out of it. They're meant to follow us into our daily journeys—unto the ends of the earth or to the local Mexican restaurant.

LORD, THANK YOU FOR THE LESSONS CHILDREN REMIND US OF EACH DAY.

—ASHLEY JOHNSON

The righteous shall be in everlasting remembrance.
—PSALM 112:6

Who's buried in Grant's Tomb? It's a bit of a one-line joke, but in all the years I've lived close to Grant's Tomb, and for all the times I've driven past it on its bluff overlooking the Hudson River, and even when the boys were in nursery school right next door, I'd never visited it. Neither had my wife. So on Memorial Day last year, after paying bills, doing some gardening and feeling generally grateful to have a day to catch up, we set off on our expedition.

"Better get some gas first," Carol said, noticing the gauge.

"Should we stop at the market on the way?"

By the time we got to Grant's Tomb and parked the car, it was 5:00 PM. "I wonder when it closes," I said, worried. We marched up the wide marble steps beneath the flags and bunting, and I pushed the door. Locked. I put my hands up to the glass and peered inside. Closes at 5:00 PM, said the sign.

All at once I felt foolish and selfish. Here was a chance to do what Memorial Day was set aside for, and we'd missed it through our own busyness. Yes, catch-up days are a blessing, but isn't it good to remember just what a holiday is for? I sank down on the steps, disappointed and irritated with myself.

Just then the door opened and a park ranger stepped out. "Would you like to come inside for a minute?" he asked.

Would we ever!

I can now tell you on full authority who's buried in Grant's Tomb: Gen. Ulysses S. Grant and his wife Julia. Next year I'll go back earlier, so I can tell you what else is to be found inside.

I SHALL NOT FORGET, LORD, THE HEROES OF THE PAST.   —RICK HAMLIN

"Your eye is the lamp of your body. . . ."
                                              —LUKE 11:34 (NIV)

When my son Henry was born, I gazed at him for hours, noticing every detail. We both had dark hair and dark eyes, but Henry looked different.

"Now, who does he look like?" my mother asked, peering down at him in his pink-and-blue-striped blanket.

"I don't know," I said.

"He looks so familiar," she said.

A few weeks later, when my sister was visiting, she looked down into the bassinet and said, "Wow! Those dark eyes—he looks just like you-know-who."

"Who?" I asked.

"Dad," my sister said.

"He doesn't!" I said almost as a reflex. My father lives abroad; he's been absent most of my life, but as a child I had always hoped we'd be closer when I got older.

I suppose I figured that when I had children of my own, I'd understand our relationship. Instead, when I had my first child, Solomon, the love I felt for him confused me more. Curling beside him, reading him stories, I wondered how my father could have willingly opted out of so much of my life.

A few days after my sister's remark, Henry looked at me longingly. Gazing into the depths of his dark eyes, I thought, *What would happen if I extended the same acceptance and unconditional love that I give to this brand-new baby of mine to my father, looking at him with the same loving eyes?*

DEAR LORD, HELP ME TO REMEMBER THAT MY RELATIONSHIPS ARE WHAT I MAKE OF THEM.

—SABRA CIANCANELLI

WED 27

A time to mourn, and a time to dance.

—ECCLESIASTES 3:4

I was napping when the phone rang. "I've got bad news," said my brother. "When I stopped to see Mother, I found her on the floor. She'd apparently fallen and hit her head on a table corner. She's dead."

Mother was seventy-six, in reasonable health and still living comfortably alone. My brother, a doctor, made a point of stopping to check on her every day at noon. On this day she was suddenly gone. No chance for

A TIME TO EVERY PURPOSE

a last hug, an expression of appreciation or a regretful good-bye.

I missed her most painfully whenever something good happened. My first thought was *Oh, Mother will be so pleased!* But I couldn't tell her. She was gone, leaving a huge space in my life.

So I have learned something about mourning, and my bigger question is, "How does a grieving person move from mourning to dancing?" The Voice within replies:

> *I feel your pain and grief, my child,*
> *for death has walked before Me too.*
> *It takes away your loved ones*
> *to where you cannot follow.*
> *But you can choose to dwell*
> *in loving moments lived,*
> *or cling to sorrow and live a broken life.*

You can choose to cling to your loss
or you can learn to dance again.

O HOLY ONE, COMFORT ALL WHO GRIEVE TODAY. HOLD THEM CLOSE TILL THEY
CAN ONCE AGAIN MAKE THE CHOICE FOR LIFE. THEN LET THE DANCE BEGIN!

—MARILYN MORGAN KING

Continue to live in him, rooted and built up in him,
strengthened in the faith as you were taught,
and overflowing with thankfulness.

—COLOSSIANS 2:6 (NIV)

Early one evening I walked outside to check on the progress of my orchid cactus, a plant that only blooms at night. It was full of buds, so I'd been checking on it every evening, anticipating some beautiful flowers.

I sat down on the bench on my patio and observed my plant. I counted about thirty tightly closed buds. *Just a few more days until it blooms,* I thought. I looked out across the yard to the pond. A white egret loped along the bank, its spindly legs barely causing a ripple in the water. A mama duck quietly swam past with her baby ducklings in single file behind her. An owl hooted in the distance, stirring up a chorus of katydids.

Lord, I prayed, *thank You for this hot, humid evening with its nighttime serenade. Thank You for the ducks and the egret and the blue heron that sits on the No Fishing sign in the pond. Thank You for this huge live oak tree here in my yard that gives the squirrels and birds a place to play and nest. Thank You, Lord, for this perfect moment with You.*

I looked over at my plant. I noticed one unusually large bud. *And for this most precious bud about to bloom, I especially thank You, Lord.*

As if on cue, the bud popped wide open, releasing all of its slender petals to form a magnificent white flower. There, right in front of me, while I thanked God, He, in His most glorious way, replied, *"You're welcome."*

LORD GOD OF ALL CREATION, I AM FULL TO OVERFLOWING WITH YOUR LOVE.

—MELODY BONNETTE

For thou, even thou only, knowest the
hearts of all the children of men.

–I KINGS 8:39

My husband Keith had been diagnosed with prostate cancer and I was terrified. Surgery was scheduled, though of course not nearly soon enough, and I wasn't at all sure how I could cope with the stress. At the monastery where we go on retreat, the nuns prayed for Keith every day.

One of my friends in another city, more than a thousand miles away, had gone through the same thing with her husband. He had been cancer free for five months, so I asked her for advice. "No matter what, have someone sit with you through the surgery," she suggested. "It can take hours and you mustn't be alone."

But I couldn't ask. All my good friends were back in Los Angeles, and I didn't want to be a burden on new acquaintances. And while the nuns were only two hours away, they were always very busy.

The day of the surgery finally arrived. When we got to the hospital, one of the women from our congregation was already there. She sat with us during the check-in process and stayed with me while they took Keith to pre-op. She came with me when I was allowed to wait with him in the ready room. While we were sitting there, Mother Catarina from the monastery showed up. She said she would stay with me at home that night, since I would have to leave Keith at the hospital. When they moved Keith to the operating room, the three of us went down to the lobby to wait and found the rabbi and six other women from the congregation already there.

I hadn't had to ask; God had seen my need and provided for me in abundance.

DEAR LORD, YOUR BLESSINGS OVERWHELM ME—ESPECIALLY THE ONES I DON'T
HAVE THE COURAGE TO ASK FOR.   —RHODA BLECKER

He shall make amends for the harm. . . .

—LEVITICUS 5:16

Cooking has never been a pleasure for me, and it was especially stressful when my four children were small. I sometimes dream that we're all young again and that I'm in the kitchen, happy and content.

Recently, Jeremy, one of my twin sons, came to live with my husband Gene and me for a short time. Jeremy had made some stunning changes in his life, which had been marked by addictive behavior fueled by refusing to take medication for his bipolar disorder. Now we were seeing an amazing new young man emerge.

One spring Saturday afternoon as Jeremy trimmed our hedges, I made supper for a friend who'd had surgery. Pot roast, asparagus casserole and banana pudding were on the menu. As I layered a large bowl with vanilla wafers, Jeremy came through the back door, hot and tired. He leaned on the kitchen counter, poured himself a glass of iced tea and smiled. "Wow, Mom," he said, "banana pudding—my all-time favorite!"

"It's not for us," I answered without looking up. "I'm making it for a friend at church."

There was silence, and our eyes met. I had to look way up at him now, but the years unexpectedly rolled back and I saw myself staring down at a small redheaded boy and saying, "No!" to cookies or punch or whatever he asked for.

As Jeremy went into the living room, an inaudible voice suggested, *It's never too late, Marion.* I made a miniature banana pudding in a custard dish, and a burst of joy filled my heart and, it seemed, the entire kitchen.

In the living room I presented the pudding to Jeremy. "For me?" he asked. "For me? Thanks, Mom!"

SHOW ME MORE WAYS, LORD, TO MAKE THOSE I LOVE HAPPY.

—MARION BOND WEST

When the day of Pentecost had come,
they were all together in one place.

—ACTS 2:1 (RSV)

Today, on Pentecost Sunday, we read the account in Acts of the once confused and frightened followers of Jesus empowered by the Holy Spirit to preach, heal and carry the glad news of His salvation to the ends of the earth.

But Pentecost is not just a Sunday. Today ends the fifty-day Easter season; tomorrow begins the six-month season after Pentecost, the longest in the year and, for me, the most challenging, because after Pentecost the story is open-ended. After Pentecost the story is still being written. For the next twenty-six weeks the Word asks what *I* am doing with the Spirit's gift.

I'm uncomfortable with this second half of the year. Me, carry the sacred story forward? Me, become Jesus' hands and feet and voice? How can I? How would I know His will? How would I find the strength?

By coming together, the Word tells me on Pentecost, with other believers. This is the birthday of the church, that great Body assembled "from every nation, from all tribes and peoples and tongues" (Revelation 7:9, RSV). Today I'm going to renew my commitment to church attendance and to joining with fellow believers wherever I can. It is when we gather *all together in one place* that the Spirit gives us wisdom and power. It's from that place that He sends us out, as He sent the disciples on this day, to carry His blessings to the world.

HOLY SPIRIT, DRAW US TOGETHER, THAT WHEN WE GO EACH TO OUR OWN ASSIGNMENT, WE MAY GO IN THE STRENGTH THAT COMES ONLY FROM YOU.

—ELIZABETH SHERRILL

MY LIVING WORDS

1
2
3
4
5
6
7
8
9
10
11
12
13
14
15

16

17

18

19

20

21

22

23

24

25

26

27

28

29

30

31

JUNE

For the word of the Lord is right;
and all his works are done in truth.

—PSALM 33:4

MON
1

He does not delight in the strength of the horse. . . . The Lord takes pleasure in those who fear Him. . . .

—Psalm 147:10–11 (NKJV)

I was reading a children's story to my granddaughter Hannah. It's a true story of a grandfather in Sweden who loved to ride his bike. When he heard about a thousand-mile bike race, he wanted to enter it, so he applied but was refused because of his age.

Not one to take *no* for an answer, Grandpa rode six hundred miles to the site of the race, and when the gun went off, Grandpa went into action. It was a classic tale of the tortoise and the hare. Young riders underestimated Grandpa's discipline and, in the end, Grandpa crossed the finish line ahead of everyone else.

GOD SPEAKS
THROUGH CHILDREN

Since I'm also a grandfather who rides a bike, I was thrilled with the story. The thought of putting all those cocky young guys in their place was a tonic for my spirits.

So I asked my granddaughter, "What did you think of that story?"

She looked at me coldly and said, "Grandpa was disobedient."

My face fell. Somehow I had missed that point. In my admiration for the gutsy old man, I'd forgotten that he had disobeyed the judges. Officially, he wasn't even in the race, and he didn't receive a trophy, only some fame.

In these days of sports cheating and business scams, Hannah reminded me that winning doesn't mean a thing if I don't play by the rules. It takes more than talent and hard work to make a champion; it also takes integrity.

THANK YOU, LORD, FOR THE WISDOM OF CHILDREN, WHO SEE RIGHT THROUGH US.
—Daniel Schantz

Then shalt thou call, and the Lord
shall answer; thou shalt cry, and
he shall say, Here I am. . . .

—Isaiah 58:9

Yesterday I stood in a shopping mall dressing room, forcing myself to try on bathing suits to replace my dilapidated tank suit that had finally disintegrated. How had my once-girlish figure gone from lithesome to lumbering so fast?

Trying to wriggle out of a spandex suit for a "mature figure," I bounced against the wall, and someone in the next dressing room asked if I was okay. *I'm not okay,* I wanted to wail. *I'm older, heavier, and way more insecure and scared than I ever thought I'd be at this stage of my life.*

I left the store without buying anything, feeling sad and upset. But then, as I looked at the sun glinting off a runaway balloon soaring over the parking lot, a conversation went back and forth in my head.

"I'm older," a woeful voice said.

Another voice answered right back, *Yup, you are.*

"I don't know what the future will bring."

Nobody does.

"My health could fail."

It might.

"I'll run out of energy."

Could happen.

"I can't stand to live with this anxiety."

Don't have to.

"But I'm stuck! I'll always be inadequate and anxious!"

No, you won't. You can change. You can accept that life changes and trust that I'll always be present to help you.

Me whining, the "other voice" answering. The voice of God.

Dear God, help me to be aware that You're always "talking back to me." And help me actually to listen.

—Mary Ann O'Roark

If any one imagines that he knows something,
he does not yet know as he ought to know.
—I Corinthians 8:2 (RSV)

The morning began with my now daily trip to the ICU, where my quadriplegic sister tries to fight off pneumonia with a ventilator and her own iron will. (If the image of a woman who can move only her elbows seems beyond tragic, add a respirator and take away her speech. The lexicon has no words for this. I checked.)

Needless to say, I've had better mornings.

Which is worse: helplessness or rage? The former hurts, but the latter sticks. In my family's case you'd think years of practice would give us an edge; we've had plenty of dress rehearsals for her death. If the average person spends two years of life waiting in lines, then my family has spent four decades waiting in drab-colored rooms with big windows and industrial carpet, waiting for visiting hours or blood tests or surgeons or answers or miracles. Mostly miracles.

And I've spent twice that time in church—an eternity, really—waiting and praying for miracles and answers.

On days like today, sitting bumper to bumper on the Parkway East on my (late) way to work, prayer seems like an ill-timed joke, and God reminds me of a careless absentee landlord who's put me up in a windowless coldwater flat with no heat and no chance at subletting—except maybe to my sister, who'd welcome the change.

Somewhere near the Squirrel Hill exit, I remember a line from *The Book of Common Prayer*: "Lord, save us from the presumption of coming to this table for solace only, and not for strength; for pardon only, and not for renewal." And I'd add another:

Lord, save me from the presumption of knowing what's best; save me from the presumption of knowing what's worst. Save me from the presumption of knowing. —Mark Collins

God does not show favoritism.

—ROMANS 2:11 (NIV)

I went back to New York City for a long-awaited visit to see my sister and her two young sons. There'd been no direct flight, I had to wait in an overcrowded airport and now the plane had been circling for an hour. "To add insult to injury," I jotted down in a letter I'd already begun to a friend back home, "the first-class flyers were given free food and drink while we waited like cattle—" I stopped writing midsentence, for finally the plane was about to land. As the first-class passengers were effusively thanked for their patience, I bristled at the quick good-bye from the flight attendants.

During my visit all this was put on hold but not forgotten. *Maybe I'll write a letter to the airline when I get home,* I thought.

Then, coming back from my nephew's soccer game, I overheard him talking to my sister. Instead of reviewing his winning moves, he sounded upset. "Mom," he said, "why did Aunt Linda go to *two* of Adam's soccer games and only *one* of mine?"

Uh-oh, I thought, *sibling rivalry rears its ugly head.*

My sister sounded amused when she answered, "That's because you only had *one* soccer game."

"Oh," was all he said.

I never let on that I'd heard that silly conversation, but I knew that God had directed its message just to me. Instead of focusing on my winning week (great times with my adorable and funny nephews, good food, good talk), I was moping because I hadn't gotten an effusive farewell from some probably exhausted airline personnel.

"What are you laughing at?" my nephew asked as he skipped over to me.

"Just myself," I told him honestly. "Just myself."

GOD, AM I UPSET BECAUSE MY SISTER GOT FIFTY CHEERIOS IN HER BOWL AND I GOT ONLY FORTY-SEVEN? JUST FOR TODAY, LET ME STOP COUNTING AND BE THANKFUL FOR WHAT I HAVE!

—LINDA NEUKRUG

Praise the Lord, I tell myself, and never forget the good things he does for me.

—PSALM 103:2 (NLT)

I think I know why those of us who are older than forty are better at remembering things that happened years ago than what we did yesterday. When we're born, our brains are like brand-new computers—still empty but with lots of storage potential. What we put in first are the basics we need for living: eating, talking, seeing. Next comes what we learn in school and so on. Over the years nonessentials have sneaked in and hogged quality space without my knowing it. That is, until a "senior moment" happens. These I excuse with, "I've had a lot on my mind recently."

So what are those lot-on-my-mind things that use up my brain bytes? (In computerese, a byte is a single letter, digit or space.) I waste valuable storage by keeping bits of trivia that should be deleted.

For example, what's the use of my being able to pull up my childhood phone number when I can't pull up what it was I came into the room for? Or recalling words to the 1940s hit song "Mairzy Doats" when I forget the name of someone I met five minutes ago? Or that bread once cost a dime when I can't remember to buy a loaf when I'm at the store? Well, the list goes on and on. It's no wonder I recall stuff that happened eons ago but not recent items of importance. It's because there's not enough space left.

It makes me wish that the Lord would insert a disk into my mental computer that would automatically keep out worthless clutter. Or, even better, that God would add a gigabyte (a gigabyte is a billion bytes) to my remembrance capacity.

NEVER LET ME FORGET, LORD, YOUR LOVE, MERCY AND FORGIVENESS. EVERYTHING ELSE PALES IN COMPARISON!   —ISABEL WOLSELEY

SAT

6

Cast thy burden upon the Lord, and he shall sustain thee. . . .

—PSALM 55:22

This is the part of parenting I'm not good at: waiting for my teenager to come home from a party on a Saturday night. I was good at soothing hurts and listening to those preteen woes, but I'm not good at waiting. It's nearly eleven o'clock, Ross's curfew time, so he should be home soon. Sitting upright in the reclining chair in the family room, I'm trying to distract myself by watching TV. A news promo says there's been a bad accident but doesn't say where. I know Ross is a good driver, careful and smart about all that he does. Besides, I can't do anything sitting here at home.

Suddenly I'm reminded of something my friend Nancy said the other day as we talked about our children. When I asked why she seemed unfazed by their problems, she said, "I guess I just don't pay attention to things I have no control over."

Tonight, that thought keeps echoing in my mind. Isn't that really the source of my anxiety? Paying too much attention to something I should be letting God pay attention to, trying to control what only God can control?

I finally realize that all I can do is turn to God and say, "Here, You do it. I can't manage this."

His response? *Then don't. I will.*

Watch over him, Lord, I pray. *Take away my fear.*

And I keep praying until I hear Ross's key in the door.

LORD, HELP ME RECOGNIZE THOSE TIMES WHEN I CAN DO NOTHING BUT TURN TO YOU.

—GINA BRIDGEMAN

SUN

7

"Wisdom is proved right by her actions."

—MATTHEW 11:19 (NIV)

"How about celebrating your fortieth wedding anniversary with an outdoor party on Sunday afternoon?" one of our daughters enthusiastically proposed as we sat outside on our patio, enjoying a near-perfect June evening.

It sounded like a pretty good idea, except for one small detail. "Sunday is only four days away," I reminded her, "and important anniversary celebrations are usually planned months in advance."

"Let's be spontaneous!" she answered.

I usually like spontaneous, especially when it comes to entertaining. The more spontaneous, the less the expectation. If you invite people to dinner at the last minute, they expect an informal evening of easy food. If you send out an invitation weeks in advance, the expectation goes way up.

But something deeper stirred inside me. My husband Lynn and I had both been battling cancer over the last two years, which left our family with an unspoken commitment to make the most of every opportunity to celebrate our blessings.

"The flowers in the garden look great right now," my daughter continued, "and the forecast is good through the weekend. So why not?"

I had no good answer, so she conferred with her brother and sister, and together they composed an e-mail that they sent to forty people, asking them to come to a "Spontaneous Sunset Celebration" with this explanation: "In these last two years, we've learned the importance of spontaneous celebrations. So we hope you can join us for a time of gratitude on our parents' fortieth wedding anniversary." Then they planned and shopped and made some great food, and on a spectacular Sunday afternoon thirty-eight friends showed up for a glorious celebration.

We're still savoring the memory of the party, not only the special time spent with family and friends, but also the reminder that God greatly blesses our celebrations of His goodness.

LORD, MAY I ALWAYS RESPOND TO YOUR NUDGES WITH SPONTANEITY AND A SPIRIT OF TRUST. —CAROL KUYKENDALL

Whosoever is of a willing heart, let him bring . . . an offering of the Lord; gold, and silver, and brass.

—EXODUS 35:5

The early light danced across the living room where I sat checking e-mail on my laptop. I was deleting the usual pile of junk mail, when a note from a *Guideposts* reader appeared on the screen. The sender had read my story about our project with AIDS orphans in Zimbabwe. "Would you accept a piece of jewelry to sell for Village Hope?" she asked.

"Of course," I e-mailed back.

A few days later a small package arrived. I opened it and unwrapped a long roll of plastic. A small metal object rolled out onto the counter and I picked it up. The unmistakable sparkle of diamonds startled me.

The ring I held was lovely. It was white gold, bedecked with more than a carat of diamonds. The donor had even included a professional appraisal that told me the ring could easily fetch enough money to pay school fees and more for the sixteen children who lived at Village Hope. During the next few days, as I shopped the ring among church members and friends, the response was always the same: "How can anybody be that generous?"

Before long a dear man offered to buy the ring for an amount that exceeded the appraisal. "It's not just a ring," he explained, "it's a story. The woman who sent it gave with abandon. She trusted without seeing. Every time I see it on my wife's hand, I'll say to myself, 'I want to live that way too.'"

F ATHER, LET MY ACTIONS TELL Y OUR STORY WITH GENEROSITY THAT SURPRISES AND WITH KIND ACTS THAT SPARKLE. —P AM K IDD

TUE
9

Ask now the beasts, and they shall teach thee. . . .

—J OB 12:7

I'll never forget the moment I first laid eyes on Millie.

Actually all I saw was her wet black nose poking out of a puppy kennel stacked on an airline luggage cart. My wife Julee and I lifted the kennel to the ground and opened the door. After some hesitation our little golden retriever emerged, looking both relieved and overwhelmed at the activity around her. *Millie,* I thought, *you have so much to learn, and I'll teach you.*

Well, wouldn't you know it, she's probably taught me as much as I've taught her. A few lessons from Millie:

- *When you're happy, let the world know.* For such a sweet, gentle dog, Millie has a monster bark. But she doesn't bark much except when she's happy. She reminds me that joy is contagious and there's no reason to keep it in.

- *Hold your tail up.* A trainer observed that Millie exhibits confidence by walking with her tail held high. "It makes other dogs feel relaxed around her." I should hold my head up when I walk down the street.
- *Play, play, play.* Learning to be a city dog is *serious* business. It takes a lot of concentration and practice. But don't forget to play like crazy whenever the opportunity presents itself.
- *Be thankful.* For every meal, every walk, every nap, every friend. With a nuzzle or a lick, Millie says "Thank you." I should remember to be grateful in all things too.
- *Stay in the now!* Millie greets each day as if it's the greatest adventure of her life. Her whole body wags at the prospect of a morning walk. For me, staying in the moment is the only way to experience God in my life. He is here now, in the moment, the greatest adventure life holds.

THANK YOU, GOD, FOR MILLIE AND ALL THE WAYS YOU USE HER TO TEACH THIS OLD DOG NEW LESSONS. —EDWARD GRINNAN

Bear ye one another's burdens, and so fulfil the law of Christ.
—GALATIANS 6:2

There was a picture of Dr. Steve and his family on a table in the exam room where I was waiting for my annual physical. When Steve arrived in his white lab coat to begin the exam, I asked him how his children were doing. I knew his four kids from church, but I didn't know them well. As Steve thought about them, his expression was softened by that special smile that all fathers recognize, the smile that says, "Thank God our children are more than what they learn and inherit from us."

Steve told me that he had come home late one evening when everyone but his youngest son Matthew was downstairs. Even with his limited awareness of his dad's work, Matthew knew his father was having a really difficult time. Matthew didn't understand what a doctor goes through when a young patient dies, but he knew that his father had been sad all week.

When Matthew came downstairs, he was proudly wearing his dad's much-too-large-for-him lab coat. "Look, Dad, I'm you!" Matthew said.

"That's real cute, Matthew," Steve said absentmindedly.

"No, Dad, you don't understand. Let me be *you* for a while. If I'm you, then you don't have to be!"

DEAR GOD, MAY I HAVE THE COMPASSION TO CARRY THE BURDENS OF THOSE I LOVE. —TIM WILLIAMS

THU 11

"The God of heaven will give us success. . . ."
—NEHEMIAH 2:20 (NIV)

It was spring, and Kiernan, our sixth child of seven, would soon be headed to college. A hot cup of tea and fresh scones in front of me, I sat with his financial aid papers in my hand. Suddenly a little voice in my heart whispered, *Patti, it's time! Why not get your bachelor's degree?*

Back in high school, when all I had wanted was to marry my sweetheart Bill, I settled on an associate's degree. *Someday,* I thought, *I will get that bachelor's degree.* Well, here I was, thirty-seven years later, with a strong faith, a loving husband, seven children and a successful small farm bed-and-breakfast. I was blessed for sure. What could this diploma give me that I didn't already have?

I prayed for the Lord to guide me. I talked to Bill, contacted an adult degree program in Brattleboro, Vermont, and sent in my application. At fifty-four I was going to get that degree, knowing it wouldn't be easy to hit the books while caring for my family and our B&B, and struggling with a chronic illness that had plagued me for years. Each step of the way, I prayed for strength and wisdom.

On graduation day I slipped into my black robe, donned my mortarboard and joyfully walked down the aisle as the oldest student in the program. I was grinning as I looked at my husband and children. I knew at that moment that the knowledge (spiritual, intellectual and emotional) I had acquired during the past two years was one of the greatest gifts God had ever given me.

LORD, I KNOW THAT IF YOU BRING ME TO IT, YOU WILL BRING ME THROUGH IT.
—PATRICIA PUSEY

*Forgive as quickly and completely
as the Master forgave you.*

—Colossians 3:13 (MSG)

Years ago my father, who had been an alcoholic, accepted Christ as his Savior and stopped drinking. It was a time of great celebration for our family. Gone was the tormented man his children had long feared. In his stead was a giving man who now loved and served God.

At a social gathering around that time, a man lashed out at me on hearing the news of Dad's conversion. "Your dad's a hopeless drunk, Roberta. Always has been, always will be." His words attracted a great deal of attention, and even his children looked on in disbelief. I was mortified.

Daily I replayed the man's words in my mind. And as I did, unforgiveness took up residence in my heart. After the man died, I continued to nurse the grudge by being cool and distant with his family.

WITH ETERNITY IN VIEW

Ask for Forgiveness

Twenty-five years passed, and still I held resentment in my heart for the man's piercing words. "I can't stop thinking about this, Lord," I prayed. "Please help me."

One morning I spotted the man's son having a cup of coffee in our hospital cafeteria. It reminded me of Dad's own early morning ritual. *Dad would want you to forgive, Roberta*, an inward voice urged.

I sat down in the booth across from him. "I need to ask your forgiveness for something," I began. He reached for my hand, guessing the words that were to follow.

Forgiveness never felt so sweet.

LIVING WITH ETERNITY IN MIND IS A GREAT PLAN, LORD. HELP ME NEVER TO FORGET THAT EARTH IS NOT MY FINAL DESTINATION.   —ROBERTA MESSNER

SAT
13

*O Lord, our Lord, how majestic is
your name in all the earth! . . .*

—Psalm 8:1 (NIV)

I've never been one to sit still for long periods of time. After a while my mind begins to weave in and out, and I shift in my chair like a restless three-year-old. During one of my choir's annual retreats in the country, I experienced one of my "Get me out of here!" moments. I was trapped in a cabin with a hint of mildew in the air, listening to yet another speaker drone on. Of course, I felt guilty. Everyone else seemed content in the chairs they'd been occupying for almost four hours. *Forgive me for wanting this to be over, but please, Lord, let it end now!*

The choir director thanked the speaker and announced we'd have to skip our free time since we were behind schedule. "Grab a bite to eat at the cafeteria," he said, "and we'll meet back here in about forty-five minutes. Sister Cheryl will discuss the meaning of worship." I wanted to cry. After the closing prayer I was the first to bolt through the doors. At the cafeteria I grabbed a plate of food and ate alone under a tree. I couldn't bear to be surrounded by walls again.

After I finished eating, I still had time to take a short walk in the woods—a city girl's treat. I climbed over rocks, skipped stones in the creek, and let the sun wash over me as I lay on a bed of grass and leaves. Time flew by and I knew I'd missed the workshop, yet I felt no guilt. Instead, I felt a sweet and peaceful understanding between God and me. He, more than anyone, knows me and molded the restless spirit that I am.

DEAR GOD, THANK YOU FOR ALLOWING ME TO HEAR YOUR VOICE THROUGH YOUR CREATION.   —KAREN VALENTIN

SUN 14

We have this hope as an anchor for the soul, firm and secure. . . .
                                        —HEBREWS 6:19 (NIV)

After Hurricane Katrina I went out to gather footage of one of our hardest-hit schools for a TV documentary. Brock Elementary, more than one hundred years old, had been a stately two-story brick structure with an oak-shaded playground. But Katrina had pushed four feet of water into it, overturning desks, file cabinets and bookshelves. Strong winds had forced doors off their hinges and blown glass out of the windows. Textbooks and schoolwork now lay in wet heaps on the floor.

After getting the footage inside, I walked down the steps into the school yard. I was devastated. I'd attended school here as a child; so had my mom. Now it looked like the school would be closed forever. *It would take a lot of hard work by a lot of people to rebuild this school,* I thought.

As I was about to step over some debris, I stopped; under it lay a flag. Strong winds had shredded and twisted it, knotting twigs and small branches into its tattered and faded red, white and blue. I reached down and picked it up. Instantly, I felt a quickening of my heart. Although it was almost completely destroyed, this flag was still a powerful symbol of the perseverance and can-do attitude of the American people.

A surge of hope rushed through me. I looked up at the school. One day children would again run up and down its steps; Boy and Girl Scouts would once again raise the flag every morning. I looked down at the torn flag in my hands. In spite of what it had been through, it had not lost its glory.

FATHER, ON THIS FLAG DAY, MAY WE HONOR OUR FLAG AS AN ENDURING SYMBOL OF STRENGTH, UNITY, LIBERTY AND HOPE. —MELODY BONNETTE

"Thou didst clothe me with skin and flesh, and knit me together with bones and sinews."

–JOB 10:11 (RSV)

Some years ago I had what the queen of England once called an *annus horribilis,* an awful year, when every bad thing that could happen happened: love died, relatives died, jobs died, cars died, things were as bleak as they could get. But oddly enough I learned a great happy lesson that year: I learned the simple joy of the body.

I remember one night in particular, when I was drowned in loss, I grabbed my basketball and dribbled down the street to the park and shot baskets all night long until the sun crawled up. I remember shooting and shooting until I thought my arm was going to fall off. This sounds like a totally ridiculous male way to deal with a crisis, but everyone has places they go when they are scared and exhausted, and that was mine then.

In the years since, through the deeper and harder losses of middle age, I have realized, year by year, almost day by day, the utter astounding gift of the sweet creaky vehicles issued to us by the Coherent Mercy. The intricacies of your fingers! The dart and dance of your tongue! The throb of your heart, the flash of your mind, the fact that your knees and elbows work! Isn't it astounding, when you think about it, that despite all the sickness and injury and wear and tear, we get these totally cool mammalian miracles to drive?

DEAR LORD, WELL, I HAVE SOME QUESTIONS ABOUT THE DESIGN OF THE SPINE, AND IS THIS REALLY THE RIGHT SIZE NOSE FOR THIS BODY? BUT OTHER THAN THAT, BOY, AM I GRATEFUL FOR THIS BODY.   —BRIAN DOYLE

TUE
16

I wait for the Lord, my soul
waits, and in his word I hope.
—PSALM 130:5 (RSV)

Last fall my wife Carol and I decided to spruce up our yard with a patio, new plantings and a small pond with a waterfall. I was especially excited about the pond, about feeding the fish, listening to the frogs, watching the sunlight glint on the water. We called up contractors and signed a contract. They did a beautiful job, and before we knew it, our yard had been transformed from a dull lot into an inviting landscape.

The only trouble was I didn't like the pond. Although only six or seven feet wide, it looked too large in our little yard, more like a misplaced ocean than the elegant feature that I had pictured. It looked dangerous, too, as if a heavy rain would cause it to overflow and engulf the yard. And the waterfall was noisy, more like Niagara Falls than a friendly neighborhood trickle. I couldn't sleep at night, wondering why we had dug such a big hole in our backyard and filled it with water.

Eventually, however, things improved. Maybe it was the squirrels scampering happily over the rocks or the dragonflies darting across the water. Maybe it was the way the fish came up to feed when my children tossed in their flakes. Maybe it was the sound of falling water soothing away my cares. Or maybe I was just learning the value of patience. For in time, I came to love the pond. Now I spend as many hours with it as I can, glad to know that gifts can take a while to mature.

LORD, TEACH ME ALWAYS TO BE PATIENT, TO LET THINGS RIPEN ACCORDING TO YOUR WILL.   —PHILIP ZALESKI

"Good morning, Lord. With what will You fill my cup today?" A friend whom I always thought must be an angel on earth once told me that she said these words on waking each morning. Beginning my day with them lets me acknowledge God's presence and not just rush hurriedly into the day's events.

—*Carlisle Parsons, Oxford, Mississippi*

Feed me with the food that is needful for me.

—Proverbs 30:8 (RSV)

I took Maggie to the dentist yesterday. At six years old, she's had more dental bills than the rest of my children combined. While three-year-old Stephen and I waited for the drilling to be done, I read him a book in which rather saccharine animals preached oral hygiene. Brush twice a day. Floss. Drink tap water. Don't eat sweets. Don't eat sticky snacks like dried fruit or granola bars.

Wait a minute—raisins are dried fruit. Can't my kids eat raisins? The thought gave me a headache. We've already done away with candy and most sweets. I take into account low fat, good vs. bad cholesterol, a balance between Omega-3 and Omega-6 oils, and limited use of processed foods. I eliminated the foods to which my children are allergic (fortunately, only nuts and shellfish). Then I have to factor in what we can afford to eat, and the likes and dislikes of seven individuals. Oh, and don't forget how much time I have available to prepare the food. That goes into the equation too. It's impossible even if raisins aren't a forbidden fruit.

But after mentally banging my head against the wall, I settled down to itemize what was left for my shopping list: a variety of meat, poultry, fresh vegetables, fruit and two eggs a day; dried beans, honey, molasses; whole-grain bread; milk, yogurt and cheese; sweets and carbs in moderation. Good stuff, food my great-grandmother ate, with ingredients whose names she'd recognize. I cook it with less fat and better equipment, but maybe feeding a family isn't any harder today than it used to be.

LORD, HELP ME TO BE THANKFUL FOR THE SIMPLE GIFTS YOU GIVE.

—JULIA ATTAWAY

He that keepeth thee will not slumber.

—PSALM 121:3

I flicked on my flashlight and looked at the clock; it was only midnight. I plumped my pillow. My mind was spinning out of control with "what ifs." Earlier that day my mare had given birth to Wind Dancer, a gangly-legged, floppy-eared red mule—my dream mule. The owners of the guest ranch where I worked had let me electric-fence a separate pasture away from their huge herd. It was the safest—and only—option available. But I knew the dangers of newborn colts and electric fences.

I rolled on my back, my eyes open wide. *What if Wind Dancer gets tangled up in the wire with the current shocking her? What if a deer runs through the fence and knocks it down and Wind Dancer escapes? Maybe I should check on them.* As I sat up in bed, my German shepherd groaned loudly, as if to say, "*Ahem*, I'm trying to sleep."

"Exactly, Tess, I'm trying to sleep too." Or was I? I had created a drama of "what ifs," and nothing had happened—everything was fine.

There was one thing I hadn't done. *Lord, I'm worried about this electric fence, but there isn't anything else I can do. Please guard and protect them.* Immediately God's peace flooded my spirit, and within minutes I fell asleep.

The next day I watched Wind Dancer zipping around the pasture. As soon as she approached the electric fence, her mom blocked her way. I pulled up my green plastic lawn chair and watched. Every time that red mule neared the fence, the mare herded her away.

I guess I'll never know if God gave the mare wisdom or if it was conditioning or instinct or His angels, but I did learn that when I gave my dramatized "what ifs" to God, I could finally sleep.

THANK YOU, LORD, FOR REMINDING ME THAT THERE'S NO SENSE IN BOTH OF US BEING AWAKE.

—REBECCA ONDOV

And, lo, I am with you always,
even unto the end of the world. . . .

—MATTHEW 28:20

I like surprises, little unexpected things that pick me up on a lonely or difficult day. When I get home, I always look in the mailbox before opening the front door. I'm eager to know if I've received a letter from a friend. I'm thrilled when my hopes are fulfilled and disappointed when only bills greet me.

When I work at my computer, I fight the urge to pause and check my e-mail. I want to find out if someone has reached across the expanse of cyberspace to contact me, to say hello, ask a question, share a thought.

This same thing is true in my spiritual life. I long to feel the presence of God. I often open my Bible seeking a "letter from God," a special word addressed to me. Early in the morning or late at night, I take long walks and talk aloud to my Creator. Many times it's a monologue, and I can only hear the sound of my own voice. But occasionally the monologue is transformed into a dialogue. I hear no heavenly voice, but I know that God is talking to me. And when that happens, it's a joyous surprise.

And so I guess I have a choice: I can sit and wait for others to communicate, or I can take the initiative and write the letter, flash the smile, give the gift or share the touch. Above all, I can faithfully talk to God, knowing that in His own good time He will speak to me.

FATHER, IN THE MIDST OF LONELINESS, MAY I REMEMBER THE WORDS OF ST. FRANCIS: "FOR IT IS IN GIVING THAT WE RECEIVE." AMEN. —SCOTT WALKER

The land produced vegetation. . . .
And God saw that it was good.

—GENESIS 1:12 (NIV)

When my husband Travis and I moved into our first home, he seeded the lawn and planted azaleas, roses and berry bushes. A little jealous of his success in the garden, I decided to raise succulents. I kept several around the house and resisted the urge to reach for the watering can, since they seemed to thrive when I neglected them. As they outgrew their tiny pots, I moved the cuttings to the yard. They flourished; it seemed the trick was to let them be.

When Travis decided to tackle the bamboo on the embankment below our house, we knew we would have to plant something in its place. Large jade plants were running riot elsewhere, so we hatched a plan to propagate about twenty small ones. I potted cuttings, set out my baby bushes among Travis' azaleas and roses, and checked them regularly.

Every morning I found my pots tipped over by the local critters and the cuttings strewn about. I replanted them, but before they could take root, rain pelted us for two weeks. My bushes were overturned, scattered and in pieces. "They're totally overwatered now," I told Travis. "They'll rot before they root!"

Travel and weather kept us out of the yard for a few weeks. Then one sunny Saturday I picked up one of the broken branches and found a whole series of fat, happy roots growing along the stem.

My tried-and-true recipe of neglect had worked again. The plants weren't growing the way I had intended, but they were growing. I straightened up the planter a bit and left the new jade bushes to manage on their own. In another couple of months, we'll move them to the hillside, where I'll try hard to continue not to pester them so that they can do their work in peace.

LORD, YOUR MAGNIFICENT DESIGN HARDLY NEEDS MY FUSSING. HELP ME RECOGNIZE WHEN TO LET THINGS BE.   —KJERSTIN WILLIAMS

SUN
21

O Lord, thou hast searched me and known me! Thou knowest when I sit down and when I rise up. . . .
—PSALM 139:1–2 (RSV)

Father's Day and not a word from Timothy—not even a quick "Happy Father's Day!" at the breakfast table. It was not like him to forget Father's Day.

It made me nostalgic for Father's Days of the past when both boys were around. I could remember magical days at the ball field, cheering them on. I could recall picnic suppers in the park and handmade cards and clay creations. But not this year: William had a summer job in California, and in the afternoon we would be taking Timothy upstate to his job as a camp counselor. The day would be spent behind the wheel of a car. After the long drive, Carol and I would come home, eat dinner, and I'd watch Tim's and my favorite TV show all by myself.

That's all right, I told myself. *The boys are busy doing other things—as it should be at their ages.*

William called on the cell phone as we were driving back from camp. I was touched. But Timothy hadn't mentioned anything, even when I hugged him good-bye. The house seemed deathly quiet. I washed dishes, brushed my teeth and went to watch TV. I was just about to plop myself down on the sofa when I noticed a bright turquoise envelope on my usual spot. "Papa," Timothy had written on the card inside, "I hope it's a good episode tonight, even without me there. Happy Father's Day!"

When someone loves you, they know you well . . . and know just where to find you.

LORD, LET ME BE DEPENDABLE—AND FULL OF SURPRISES—TO THOSE I LOVE.

—RICK HAMLIN

MON
22

It is God himself who has made us what we are and given us new lives from Christ Jesus. . . .
—EPHESIANS 2:10 (TLB)

There's a showboat in the driveway adjoining ours. An exact replica of a Mississippi sternwheeler built to scale, twenty-five feet long and fourteen feet high, it's the stage from which our neighbors Nancy and Jack present the marionette show that takes them crisscrossing the country during county fair season. When the antique whistle goes off and the smokestack belches steam, "Come on, y'all, the fun's about to begin!"

Nancy is a ventriloquist. She's part of a family of puppeteers who have brought joy, laughter and wonder to millions of people for three generations. It's my good fortune to live next door, with firsthand access to the workshop where puppet life is always in the making. Millie, the bicycle-riding monkey, is my favorite. She rides around by remote control, mingling with the crowd, wisecracking and talking to children who fall all over themselves in awe.

"As you design and create each individual character, do you ever feel a bit like God?" I ask Nancy.

"I guess," Nancy says with a smile. She winks as she holds up a red-headed girl in a frilly skirt. "This one has taken on a personality of her own. Sometimes she blurts out words that I had no intention of saying!"

Nancy puts her heart into each of her creations. A carefully placed dimple here, a crooked smile there: Sassy, sweet, fierce, comic, from fun-loving clowns to creepy-crawly caterpillars, they are her much cherished family. *Hmm,* I think, *kind of like us in the family of God!*

"Thou art the Potter, I am the clay," I pray with hymnist Adelaide Pollard (1862–1934). "Mold me and make me after Thy will . . . Christ only, always, living in me."   —Fay Angus

---

TUE
23

Jesus wept.
—John 11:35 (NIV)

It's been five years now since our son Reggie was killed in a car accident. Ever since that time, Rosie and I have become familiar with a sound like a grunt, a kind of half sob. We can hear it at night in bed or when riding in the car or coming from whatever room one of us is in. We can hear each other make this little grunt, and almost always we ask the question, "What's wrong?"

The grunts come especially around birthdays or holidays. But they can also come out of nowhere when we hear a particular word or song. There are times that a little grunt turns into weeping, and we remember John's words, "Jesus wept." We're learning that it's okay to remember, it's okay to grunt and it's okay to weep.

After five years, the grunts don't come as often, but they still come. The challenge Rosie and I have is to give each other the space to have our moments and simply say, "I understand . . . I understand." In those times, God takes over and gives us the assurance that, despite the pain, we are incredibly blessed because He loves us.

Lord, continue to give us strength to trust You through the pain and to celebrate Your goodness.   —Dolphus Weary

"I was hungry and you gave me something to eat, I was thirsty and you gave me something to drink. . . ."

—Matthew 25:35 (NIV)

Once a week a neighbor and I join about forty volunteers who call themselves the Gleaners (www.fvgleaners.org). We meet in a large warehouse, taking our places at tables stationed on either side of trolleys laden with bright yellow and red peppers, mounds of onions, carrots, cabbages and other vegetables. We cut up the vegetables, which kind farmers have donated, and then they are dried and made into nutritious soup mixes.

There's a buzz of excitement throughout the warehouse. Someone whistles a tune; people are talking and laughing. Many of us seniors have come through hard times, like the Depression and World War II, and we've learned not to waste anything. Then, too, we're reminded that the food will go to hungry children in more than thirty countries. Their smiling faces are looking down on us from bulletin boards on the walls.

When our family were refugees in Austria, it was like Christmas in our small room every time another care package arrived from America. Lost in wonder, we'd lift the cans of Spam and sardines, chocolate bars and dried fruit and other foodstuffs out of the box. What a treat to be able to augment our meals of boiled potatoes and bread!

Now it's our turn to give back. We're told that one volunteer hour generates the equivalent of more than 120 food servings. What an awesome return for our time!

Dear God, thank You for this opportunity to take seriously the words of Jesus when He said, "I was hungry and you gave me something to eat."

—Helen Grace Lescheid

A time to get, and a time to lose. . . .

—ECCLESIASTES 3:6

When my husband Robert proposed to me, he gave me a gold necklace with two beautiful pearls, each one set on a gold strand, with the two strands intertwined as a symbol of our lasting love. It became my most precious possession.

One night six years later, I fell from a porch, badly twisting my back. At the hospital the radiologist asked me to remove my necklace for X-rays. I handed it to Robert, who put it in his shirt pocket.

It wasn't until we were back from the hospital that we realized my precious necklace was gone. Robert called the hospital and looked everywhere without finding it. The loss seemed so great that I cried myself to sleep. I awoke with these words: *God has given you true love. You have the real thing! Let the symbol go!*

A TIME TO EVERY
PURPOSE

Is this letting-go what Koheleth meant when he wrote "a time to get and a time to lose"? As I wait in prayer, this answer comes:

> *In the far vaster order beyond time,*
> *nothing is ever truly lost.*
> *It's safe to let go*
> *with tranquility and trust,*
> *for your truest treasures*
> *are forever preserved for you*
> *in eternity.*

I wouldn't be honest if I said I no longer have moments of sadness about the loss of my necklace and the many other worldly things that have slipped beyond my grasp. But whenever I have a loss, I sit in prayer and say, "With God's help, I can let go." And I find that most of the time I can.

BOUNTIFUL CREATOR, HELP ME TO SEE MY LOSSES AS TEMPORAL AND MY TREAS-
URES AS ETERNAL.   —MARILYN MORGAN KING

*For no other foundation can any one lay
than that which is laid, which is Jesus Christ.*

−I Corinthians 3:11 (RSV)

Bankhead is a ghost town north of Banff, Alberta—once a thriving coal-mining town housing immigrants from all over Europe. Built by the Canadian Pacific Railway at the turn of the last century, it was Canada's first planned community, with running water and electricity, sports arenas and schools, and Holy Trinity Church. Built atop a knoll between Upper Bankhead (where the miners and their families lived) and Lower Bankhead (where the mining operations were located), the church was visible from home or work, the center of the religious and social life of this peaceful Rocky Mountain town.

Though it was Catholic, the church allowed Protestants worship time whenever they could find a minister. On Saturday nights the various nationalities took turns sponsoring ethnic dances in its basement. Funerals for the miners killed below were held here; weddings too. What's left for us is its foundation, and each time I wend my way to this place I have to search harder to find it, for the forest has slowly crept up the knoll, hiding it from view.

But here it is, its massive foundation rising out of the ground, framing the basement and topping out some ten feet high. Here the wide cement stairs climb to long-ago doors that once opened beneath a simple steeple and summoning bell. No walls now, no ceiling, no steeple or bell, just the foundation and stairs that meet the sky and heaven beyond.

Last summer I climbed the stairs, and sat, feet dangling into the basement. Slowly I began to sing a hymn: "The church's one foundation is Jesus Christ her Lord. . . ." Just me and the trees, the chipmunks, the grazing elk, the breeze, and the presence of God Who lingers here still.

Dear Lord, You are my one foundation, yesterday, today and forever.

−Brenda Wilbee

In the image of God He created him;
male and female He created them.

—GENESIS 1:27 (NKJV)

I recently returned home from New York City where I saw John, a friend of thirty years. The visit spotlighted changes that unsettled me. Known for his intellect, John is suffering memory loss. What day is it? He checks his calendar-watch. Which bus does he take? Well, he's always found his way home—so far. But he's losing ground. Will I recognize him in a year's turning?

Like me, John is invigorated by art. "Let's go to the Metropolitan," I suggested. At the museum, we lingered at a familiar Impressionist scene, painted by Claude Monet: the sun-bathed, beige-toned front of a French cathedral. But the colors weren't quite as I remembered them. "I've seen another version of this," I said.

John concurred, "Yeah, he painted it again, a lot."

Before we left, I bought commemorative note cards depicting the Rouen Cathedral "in sun."

After unpacking my bags, I pulled out my art-card storage box. As I suspected, I discovered a Monet print of the cathedral "at dawn," the caption says. The façade is blue, the shadows dark. In an art book I discovered a third rendering, luminous and golden, "at sunset." Online I viewed more: "in morning light," "in full sunlight," "in gray weather." Monet painted this cathedral entrance thirty times, I learned, each reflecting a different degree of light.

Monet once said that "everything changes, even stone." But the more I look at his Rouen painting series, the more I recognize a deeper constancy: the cathedral's crafted magnificence. It gives me assurance that I'll always recognize John for what he is at heart: a most beloved son of his Creator-Redeemer-God.

LORD, EVEN AS THE COLORS OF MY LIFE CHANGE, COMFORT ME WITH THE KNOWLEDGE THAT MY IDENTITY REMAINS CONSTANT IN YOU.   —EVELYN BENCE

*I have written unto you, young men,
because ye are strong, and the
word of God abideth in you. . . .*

–I JOHN 2:14

For years now, while sitting in church, I've imagined that my grown sons would burst through the doors, find me and sit down next to me, one on each side. At long last, they'd have returned to God, and I, along with all those who have prayed for them so steadfastly, would rejoice.

Actually, Jeremy has returned to the very church my husband Gene and I attend. Each Sunday he sits with us, and I rejoice. Still, I long and pray for his twin brother Jon to be on the other side of me. When the local newspaper published a picture of Jon at the butcher shop where he works, I studied it long and hard. My eyes lingered on his large, square-shaped hands. The freckles didn't show. He wore a shirt I'd given him beneath his apron. Jon's addictions have taken a tremendous toll, and he rarely communicates with us.

I can't seem to relinquish my prayer of Jon sitting with us. I've placed the newspaper picture of him in my Bible, right by one of his favorite Scriptures: "I am the vine, ye are the branches" (John 15:5). Jeremy continues to sit by me. And in a way Jon does, too, nestled in God's Word.

BECAUSE NOTHING IS TOO HARD FOR YOU, FATHER, I'M GOING TO CONTINUE TO SEE MY SONS SITTING ON EITHER SIDE OF ME AT CHURCH.   —MARION BOND WEST

---

*"I'm telling the solemn truth: Whenever you
did one of these things to someone overlooked
or ignored, that was me—you did it to me."*

—MATTHEW 25:40 (MSG)

After several busy years of preaching, my spirit turned gray. I felt less intimate with the Lord. One day, as I read the dramatic account of the judgment day scene in Matthew 25, I got a simple picture of how to spend more time really getting to know Jesus.

The "Son of Man" divided the crowd into two groups: the sheep on His right and the goats on His left. He told the sheep they would be with Him forever because they had cared for Him, clothed and fed Him, and visited Him. The sheep said, "What are you talking about?" The Lord replied, "Whenever you did one of these things to someone overlooked or ignored . . . you did it to me."

Keith, Jesus seemed to be saying, *I'm with you Sundays at church. But during my workweek, I live with the poor, lonely, sick and imprisoned— especially people who are at the end of their rope. If you want more intimate time with me, that's where you can find me.*

Soon after that I visited a friend in the hospital. As I listened to him share his experience of dying from cancer, I began to picture Jesus sitting inside my friend, cradling his heart. I could almost see the Lord smile and silently say, *Keith, I'm glad you came. I've been waiting for you.*

DEAR LORD, THANK YOU FOR OFFERING ME ON-THE-JOB TRAINING FOR HEAVEN WITH YOU, LEARNING YOUR QUIET WAYS OF LOVING THE LITTLE ONES YOU DIED FOR. AMEN.   —KEITH MILLER

> *How precious to me are thy thoughts,*
> *O God! How vast is the sum of them!*
> —PSALM 139:17 (RSV)

"I'm *bad*! I'm the worst person in the world!"

It's bedtime, and I've been sitting with eleven-year-old John, trying to help him deal with his latest ant attack. Whenever John is punished—or just admonished—for doing something wrong, the litany begins. In his mind every infraction is a major offense and every setback is an unredeemable disaster. His therapist calls them "ants"—*a*utomatic *n*egative *t*houghts. Julia and I are trying to help John set out ant traps to short-circuit his negative thinking. Usually that means trying to help him sort out his feelings and deal with some of the underlying fears that bring on his ants.

In working with John, I've come to recognize ants in my own thoughts too. Ironically enough for someone who works in an organization based on positive thinking, my first reaction to setbacks is often to assume the worst: If I'm having trouble with a work project, then I'm just showing that I'm untalented. If Julia is irritated by something I've done, then our marriage is in danger. Neither of these things is true, but

I have to step back and look at them rationally to know this. If I just go with the emotional flow, I'm opening the door to anger and depression.

I try telling John about my ants. After fifteen minutes of talking, both our ants have fallen into the trap and John is feeling better. "Thanks for telling me, Dad," John says. "Can we say evening prayers?"

I get my prayer book and Bible. We share some Psalms and other Scriptures and prayers. Then I put my arm around John's shoulder and walk him to bed.

LORD, YOUR WORD IS THE BEST ANT TRAP OF ALL. —ANDREW ATTAWAY

MY LIVING WORDS

1

2

3

4

5

6

7

8

9

10

11

12

13

14

15

16

17

18

19 _____

20 _____

21 _____

22 _____

23 _____

24 _____

25 _____

26 _____

27 _____

28 _____

29 _____

30 _____

JULY

*The words of the Lord are
pure words: as silver tried
in a furnace of earth,
purified seven times.*

—PSALM 12:6

A man's heart plans his way,
But the Lord directs his steps.

—Proverbs 16:9 (NKJV)

When I was graduating from college in 1965, I didn't know what I wanted to do with my life. I was qualified for several things, but when I asked God to lead me, I saw no signs of His answer.

For the time being I took a church-related job, but two years later I was just as confused and unhappy as when I had started out.

"Why doesn't God just show me what to do?" I complained to my wife Sharon.

"He will in time, I'm sure of it. Perhaps you just need more time to be prepared for what He has in mind for you."

That summer we went on vacation to the East Coast. We were almost to North Carolina when we decided to pull into a grove of beautiful pine trees and eat lunch from our cooler. I turned into the grove and shut off the motor. When I looked up, there was an old, red, one-room schoolhouse, perfectly preserved from the 1800s. Suddenly, something clicked inside me, and I blurted out, "That's what I want to be! I want to be a teacher!"

GOD SPEAKS THROUGH PROVIDENCE

A few weeks later I got a call from a former professor at my alma mater, asking me to assist him with a few classes. This time I said *yes* with no misgivings. Now, forty classroom-years later, I can see that God did indeed guide me in His own time to the place I was wondering about.

I guess sometimes we have to find out what we don't want to do, before we are ready to do what God had in mind for us all along.

LORD, MAKE ME PATIENT IN MY SEARCH FOR YOUR WILL.   —DANIEL SCHANTZ

Through him and for his name's
sake, we received grace. . . .

—Romans 1:5 (NIV)

This has been a summer of babies for our family. In July my niece and her husband arrived from Birmingham, Alabama, with their newborn Finn and his fourteen-month-old brother Aiden. While they were here, my first granddaughter was born, Isabelle Grace. Next came my niece Scarlet's baby, Lillian. They, along with my grandsons Drake and Brock, are sure to put the "din" in family dinners for years to come!

My daughter-in-law Stacy has already begun to play baby-friendly versions of hymns for her wee one. "Isabelle's favorite song is 'Amazing Grace,'" she told me recently. "She always gets quiet when it comes on."

When I hold a newborn and look into those eyes, I can't keep from believing in a divine Creator and in His grace—unmerited favor—from the minute we're born. Maybe Isabelle Grace, so fresh from those mysterious realms, knows this in a way we don't . . . or can't.

Grace. What's so amazing about it? Everything! How blessed I am that my new granddaughter will help me remember that every day.

I PRAISE YOU, FATHER, FOR THE MIRACLE OF NEW LIFE AND FOR LIFE RENEWED THROUGH YOUR TENDER AND CONSTANT CARE.   —MARY LOU CARNEY

When I am weak, then am I strong.

—II CORINTHIANS 12:10

My mother drinks from the same Alice-in-Wonderland teacup every morning. She bought it many years ago when we were on vacation in Florida. My parents had just divorced, and the trip was planned so that we could get away and begin our new lives.

Unfortunately, the entire time we were at Disney World it rained. At first we tried to do indoor things, but on the third and final day, we put on raincoats and tried to tough it out. But the wet got the better of us, and after a huge argument over what to do, we decided to leave.

On the way out, we collected gifts for everyone back home. As Mom piled T-shirts and hats onto the counter, she added a half-priced Alice-in-Wonderland teacup as an afterthought.

That evening we drove to the ocean for one last look. The rain had let up and the mosquitoes were brutal, but the water was warm and we stayed to watch the sunset.

"I'm sorry," Mom said. "I guess this vacation wasn't such a good idea."

I looked off into the distance and pretended not to hear. It seemed lately all we had was disappointment, and I needed something to be all right.

"We tried," she said. "That's the important thing."

When we got home, instead of giving away the cup as she had planned, Mom put it in our cabinet. Soon it became a special part of her morning. Since then, the gold rim around the edge has worn off and the Cheshire cat is missing teeth, yet the cup grows more precious every day.

LORD, SO OFTEN MY WEAKEST MOMENTS BECOME MY STRENGTHS. THANK YOU FOR THE LITTLE THINGS THAT HELP ME TO REMEMBER TO PUSH ON.

—SABRA CIANCANELLI

SAT
4

Behold, the Lord thy God hath set the land before thee . . . fear not, neither be discouraged.

—DEUTERONOMY 1:21

A couple years ago I was visiting two of my children in California, Jeanne and Andrew, and their families. Jeanne's Adeline was three years old and Andrew's Ethan was two and a half. We drove to a little town to watch the fireworks on the Fourth of July and ended up sitting on a brick ledge in front of a grocery store for the best view.

When the booms and flashes began, Ethan started shaking and was soon in tears. I tried to comfort him, but even Grandma's lap couldn't provide shelter from the sensory overload.

Then Jeanne put the two little ones together in the front seat of a huge grocery cart shaped like a big toy car. Adeline put her arm around Ethan, and before long they were giggling and staring at the fantastic light show with glee.

Sometimes I'm afraid of things too: noisy politicians, war, rising taxes, hurricanes, health problems. Then I remember: Today is the Fourth of July, Independence Day, the day we officially became a nation under God, indivisible, with liberty and justice for all. We're in this together and our government, our democracy, *under God*, is designed to give us a chance to tackle the problems, big and little, that concern all of us.

Just like Adeline and Ethan, I find strength in numbers and comfort in the shared goals that we Americans enjoy. God bless America!

FATHER, KEEP ME THANKFUL FOR THIS NATION THAT PROTECTS US WHILE KEEPING OUR FREEDOMS INTACT. —PATRICIA LORENZ

I will boast all the more gladly of my weaknesses, so that the power of Christ may dwell in me.
—II CORINTHIANS 12:9 (NRSV)

Our annual Fourth of July celebration is our liveliest community event; everyone comes out, rain or shine. But the fireworks display requires darkness and that has become a problem for me because my children no longer sit with me on a blanket in the grass. When we arrived for the fireworks this year, my teenage daughter found one or two of her friends within half a minute and disappeared into the chaos. "Meet me back here as soon as it's over!" I yelled, not even sure if Sarah heard me.

A couple years ago I wouldn't have allowed her to run off like that. *Why did I allow it this time?* As most parents know, I didn't *allow* it; I didn't really have a choice.

There came a time—not very long ago—when I simply had to learn to let go. I would have been happy if the children sat quietly by my side forever. "May I, Dad?" "Would you like to go for a walk, Dad?" But it doesn't quite work that way anymore.

God has shown me that not only can't I keep things that way, but I shouldn't even try to. God wants me to let go gradually. Just when I thought I was a strong father, there are small ways now that I must become weak.

Sarah was perfectly fine that evening. In fact, she met me back at the spot where she had left, within ten minutes of the end of the fireworks.

Christ walks with Sarah, and He is better for her than I will ever be.

I KNOW THAT YOU CARE FOR ME, LORD, AND THAT YOU WANT WHAT IS BEST FOR ME. SHOW ME THE WAYS TO DO THE SAME FOR THOSE I LOVE. —JON SWEENEY

MON
6

For lo, he who forms the mountains, and
creates the wind, and declares to man what
is his thought; who makes the morning
darkness, and treads on the heights of the
earth—the Lord, the God of hosts, is his name!

—Amos 4:13 (RSV)

I woke up this morning in a motel, feeling exhausted from two weeks of traveling. Now, as my husband Larry headed the car toward the Colorado border, I sat listlessly staring out the window at the Kansas landscape. I felt so drained that I'd skipped my morning prayers. *Maybe we should just give up the rest of our trip and head for home,* I thought.

Our car topped a rolling hill and I looked off across the prairie, startled by the sight of dozens of tall silvery towers with rotating windmill arms. They marched across the countryside in all directions, looking like drum majorettes twirling batons.

"Wind farm," Larry said.

I'd heard of those wind farms, and I'd read that just one of those windmills could generate enough energy to power hundreds of homes. Here were at least a hundred windmills. I sat in awe, thinking about that. Wind. A nonpolluting source of energy and power. You can't see it, but it's always there, available to everybody.

"Okay, I get the message," I whispered and settled back in the seat, focusing on my morning prayers. Soon I felt the renewed energy that comes from connecting with the Higher Power.

HEAVENLY FATHER, KEEP MY SPIRIT OPEN TODAY TO THE POWER OF YOUR GUID-
ANCE AND STRENGTH. —MADGE HARRAH

TUE
7

"There is no one besides You, Nor
is there any rock like our God."

—I Samuel 2:2 (NAS)

Fifty years of marriage!

The family insisted we mark this milestone with a special celebration. Soon the e-mails were floating back and forth as plans were made to rent two cottages at the lake and have a family reunion.

Two families planned to fly, and the third would be making a three-day drive. "The locals" (ourselves and our oldest son's family) would be figuring out what to put where and where to put whom. Finally all eighteen of us were settled in for a week's worth of visiting and eating and laughing and swimming and boating.

Our anniversary gift was unique. One son had found a big rock weighing between one hundred and two hundred pounds, and together with his brothers had heaved, hoisted, levered and wrestled it into position. At that point their wives took over, painting our names with a gold 50 on the top of the rock. A green trailing vine with each person's name written on a leaf was then painted around the edges.

The rock now sits in a prominent place in our flower garden. Every time I pass it, the rock brings back fond memories of our celebration. And it reminds me that over the course of fifty years, when the rains descended and the floods came, when the winds blew and burst against us, our marriage did not fall because it was built upon the Rock of Ages.

THANK YOU, LORD, FOR BEING THE SOLID FOUNDATION OF OUR MARRIAGE.

—ALMA BARKMAN

Editor's Note: "Since my wife Shirley and I reached retirement age," writes Fred Bauer, "we've taken our children, their mates and our grandchildren on several family reunion trips. (We tell our kids we are spending their inheritance.) Our adventures have taken us to Germany, Hawaii, England, Costa Rica, China and, most recently, Greece." Fred's Greek trip, a seven-day cruise to Turkey, several islands in the Aegean, plus three days in Athens, brought him to several important sites in Christian history, and over the next four days he'll share his discoveries there with us.

WED
8

> *For who hath stood in the counsel of the Lord,*
> *and hath perceived and heard his word?*
> *who hath marked his word, and heard it?*
>
> —JEREMIAH 23:18

As we sail into Istanbul, two of the city's landmarks—the 1,400-year-old Hagia Sophia, the Church of Holy Wisdom, with four towering minarets, and the famous Blue Mosque with six (the mosque at Mecca is the only

Islamic shrine with more minarets, seven)—punctuate the late afternoon skyline, majestic reminders that Turkey's population is ninety-nine percent Muslim with fewer than one percent Christians and Jews. But such was not always the case. The Hittites controlled the land for nearly a thousand years, followed by the Assyrians and Persians before it was incorporated into the Roman Empire at the end of AD 100. That's when Constantine, one of the most important rulers in history, came to power.

SAILING THE SEA OF FAITH

Day 1: Holy Wisdom

He founded Constantinople on the site of the former Byzantium in AD 330, and through conquest became the sole ruler of the Roman Empire. At age forty Constantine converted to Christianity and did much to promote the faith. Most significantly, he called the first Ecumenical Council of the church to meet in Nicaea, now Iznik, in AD 325. More than three hundred bishops from throughout the empire met to resolve some of the doctrinal conflicts that were fragmenting the church. Discussions about Christ's relationship to God, His humanity and divinity, resulted in the concept of the Trinity as expressed in the Nicene Creed, which many of us recited in church last Sunday. It begins, "I believe in one God, the Father Almighty, maker of heaven and earth. . . ."

REMIND US, LORD, OF OUR GREAT DEBT
TO HISTORY'S FAITHFUL, LEST WE FORGET.
—FRED BAUER

THU
9

"This fellow Paul . . . says that man-made gods are no gods at all."
—ACTS 19:26 (NIV)

The place I most anticipated visiting on our cruise was Ephesus, Turkey, about 110 miles southeast of Istanbul. In the ancient world it was renowned as the location of the Temple of Artemis, the goddess of hunting and plenty. One of the Seven Wonders of the World, it was a huge edifice that measured 425 feet in length, 220 feet in width and sixty feet in height with 120 pillars. Inside was a wooden statue of the goddess. Alas, like five of the other ancient wonders—only the Pyramids in Egypt remain—there is little left of the Greek shrine. Today a pool of stagnant water and one pillar are the only remnants of the enormous structure.

According to the book of Acts, Paul spent two years and three months teaching and preaching in Ephesus, and he might have stayed longer if not for a run-in with the silversmiths of the city, who took umbrage with him over his criticism of idol worship. When Paul tried to speak at the huge 25,000-seat stadium, which, amazingly, still stands, proclaiming that "man-made gods are no gods at all," the artisans protested long and loud. They made their living fashioning images of the goddess and were worried that Paul would hurt their livelihood. "Great is Artemis of the Ephesians!" they shouted, and soon the city was in an uproar. In the end Paul was arrested and ordered out of town.

> **SAILING THE SEA OF FAITH**
>
> *Day 2: Overturning the Idols*

In the short term Paul seemed to have lost. The Ephesians chose Artemis over the Christ, Whom Paul presented to them. But today the Temple of Artemis lies in ruins and Christ . . . you know the rest.

THANK YOU, LORD, FOR THOSE OF FAITH LIKE PAUL,
WHO GAVE THEIR SOULS, THEIR LIVES, THEIR ALL.

—FRED BAUER

FRI 10

I, John, your brother and companion in the suffering and kingdom and patient endurance that are ours in Jesus, was on the island of Patmos because of the word of God and the testimony of Jesus.

—REVELATION 1:9 (NIV)

On the third day of our cruise, we visited the tiny island of Patmos. Though the place has a beautiful harbor at Skala, its rocky and barren terrain does little to recommend it, and only about 2,500 people call it home. The main attractions of Patmos are the Monastery of St. John, which sits pristinely on the pinnacle of the island, and a little cave, the Sacred Grotto, where tradition has it that St. John the Divine wrote

Revelation after being exiled from Rome in AD 95 by the emperor Domitian.

Some scholars believe that Revelation was aimed exclusively at first-century Christians, who were anticipating Christ's imminent return.

SAILING THE SEA OF FAITH

Day 3: Island of Vision

Others see it as a book of timeless prophesy for all believers, a fore-telling of the end times. What we do know is that the book was sent to the seven churches of Asia Minor and that it is highly symbolic, with the number seven, the number of completeness, occurring again and again.

Why was John's vision included in the New Testament? My take is that Revelation serves two purposes: as a warning to Christians to be prepared, and in the last chapters as a promise of a New Jerusalem when good shall overcome evil and the Kingdom of God will prevail.

Seeing the place where John "heard . . . a great voice as of a trumpet" (Revelation 1:10), commanding him to write about his vision, certainly made Revelation come alive for me. But I left wondering what John would say today. Even though Christ's return did not come quickly as first-century Christians hoped, I think John would admonish us to heed Jesus' advice to keep watch, for "no one knows about that day or hour, not even the angels in heaven, nor the Son, but only the Father" (Matthew 24:36, NIV).

HELP US LORD, FROM YOUR WORD TO GLEAN
WISDOM AND TRUTH UPON WHICH TO LEAN.

—FRED BAUER

SAT
11

While Paul was waiting for them in Athens, he was greatly distressed to see that the city was full of idols.

—ACTS 17:16 (NIV)

The last stop of our family journey was Athens. Of course, we visited the Acropolis with its famous temple, the Parthenon, dedicated to the goddess Athena. After the Acropolis my main interest was the Agora on Mars Hill, one of three knolls at the base of the historic landmark. *Agora* in

Greek means a marketplace where people meet, and from it comes the word *agoraphobia*, which afflicts those who have a fear of such open, public spaces. The Agora was the commercial center of Athens, and it was here that merchants, legislators and philosophers met to do business and discuss the issues of the day.

It was in the Agora that Paul preached the good news of salvation to the Athenians. His message is recorded in Acts 17. "Men of Athens!" he began, "I see that in every way you are very religious. For as I walked around and looked carefully at your objects of worship, I even found an altar with this inscription: To an Unknown God" (Acts 17:22–23, NIV). Then Paul told them about a god who does not live in temples built by man, a god who "now . . . commands all people everywhere to repent" (Acts 17:30, NIV).

SAILING THE SEA OF FAITH

Day 4: The Hill of Mars

One thing is for sure: Paul did not suffer from agoraphobia. He spoke fearlessly and articulately in this vaunted intellectual capital of the world, promising eternal life to all who repented of their sins and believed. Many scoffed, but some didn't, and from such small seeds came the universal church.

GIVE US COURAGE, LORD, OUR FAITH TO SHARE,

AT TIMES WHEN WE ARE WONT TO DARE.

—FRED BAUER

SUN
12

. . . My fellow workers, whose names are in the book of life.
—PHILIPPIANS 4:3 (RSV)

Walking into the church parlor the other day, I saw that our Walter Clark plaque had disappeared. An innocent act, I'm sure. Why clutter up the wall with the names of people no one remembers? But I remember.

Almost single-handedly, Walter saved Hillsboro Presbyterian Church from extinction. When hard times came and there was talk of dissolving the congregation, he refused to give up. He gave his time, his money and his energy to make it work. His own father had been the minister here fifty years earlier, but Walter was not caught in the past. He moved forward, realizing that to survive, a church must be relevant to the times. Walter saved our church, and it would make me sad if the next generation never knew his name.

On cold nights homeless people find a warm bed at Hillsboro. Desperate mothers look to us for rent money and food. In Guatemala children go to school and drink clean water. In Zimbabwe AIDS orphans live in a safe home. An unending number of self-help groups meet at our church, disabled adults are housed here, all kinds of people are comforted, cared for and loved. No one mentions Walter's name, but our church lives because of him. His name is indelibly written on every good work.

Scripture speaks of a book where God writes the names of His workers—not just the people who make big things happen, but those who take time to be kind, who make the earth nicer, who love people— the Book of Life. I know Walter's name is there, and that's what really matters.

FATHER, FOCUS MY EYES AND MY HEART ON THE WORK YOU HAVE FOR ME SO THAT MY NAME WILL BE WORTHY OF YOUR BOOK OF LIFE.   —PAM KIDD

MON
13

For thus says the Lord God, "Behold, I Myself will search for My sheep and seek them out."
—EZEKIEL 34:11 (NAS)

The youth choir rehearsal had almost ended when the lights suddenly went out in the church. There was a lot of commotion as people left the building. At first I thought only our church had lost electrical power, until someone yelled, "The whole city is in the dark." My siblings Sandy and Orland and I quickly walked home. Everything looked different without light.

At home my mother was anxious about us. She grabbed her flashlight and rushed out of the apartment into the dark hallway and down the stairs. She walked down several steps before she slipped and tumbled. She got up and continued down the stairway and into the neighborhood searching for us. We all arrived safely home shortly after, but later that night my mother's left foot began to swell. The next morning she went to the hospital—she had broken her ankle.

When I remember the blackout of 1977 in New York City, it's not the chaos or the darkness that comes to mind, but my mother's love for us. She let nothing get in the way, risking her own safety to search for her children before anyone or anything could harm us.

DEAR GOD, EVEN IN MY DARKEST MOMENTS, WHEN ALL SEEMS DIM AND BLEAK, YOUR LOVE IS SEEKING ME OUT. —PABLO DIAZ

TUE 14

Do not withhold good from those to whom it is due, When it is in your power to do it.
—PROVERBS 3:27 (NAS)

I was out to dinner one evening when a five-year-old girl with long platinum-blonde hair stopped by my table. "One more inch and my hair will be long enough for Locks of Love," she announced.

Her mother took her hand and bent down to kiss her forehead. "That's all Alicia talks about," she confided. "She loves her hair more than anything, but she wants it to go to a child who's lost hers."

That evening all I could think about was that little girl's glistening hair. It was her finest possession and she was willing to give it away.

"Show me that kind of love, Lord," I prayed. An image formed in my mind that would not let me go: I was standing before Jesus and all I had to offer Him were the things I had given with a cautious hand.

Today I was wearing an intricately designed turquoise and rhinestone brooch when I visited a

WITH ETERNITY IN VIEW

Give from the Heart

friend. She fingered it in admiration. I noticed that it would complement the chocolate-brown suit with turquoise piping she was wearing. *Be like that little girl and give it to her*, an inner voice urged.

But a conflicting voice reminded me how I'd watched the brooch on a clearance table until it went down, down, down. *It's mine*, the voice continued.

The other voice won out: *It's in your power to give that brooch away, Roberta. Do it now.* I removed the brooch from my lapel. Joyfully, I fastened it to my friend's suit. It seemed tailor-made for her . . . the way giving from the heart now seemed tailor-made for me.

I WANT TO GIVE THE WAY YOU DO, LORD—COMPLETELY. —ROBERTA MESSNER

READER'S ROOM

Though I'm a native of northern Wisconsin, I've never been so exposed to nature as I have this season. There's been a myriad of birdlife this year: bluebirds, hummers, wild canaries, redwing blackbirds, crows, loons crying on their way to Hanson Lake. Recently a bear and three cubs fed at the forest's edge at twilight. We've got red foxes and coyotes. Each fresh, brand-new, spanking day shares new delights of God's creation.

—*Kurt Sampson, Rhinelander, Wisconsin*

WED 15

As servants of God we commend ourselves in every way: through great endurance, in afflictions, hardships, calamities. . . .
—II Corinthians 6:4 (RSV)

My sister has survived forty-two years as a quadriplegic. A Las Vegas bookie would laugh at those odds and tell you to pray for a miracle. Truth is, our time in waiting rooms has been borrowed time.

Forty-two years ago a doctor gave my dad the sad lesson: "Quads don't live long. Your daughter will make it five, maybe ten years." Instead, my sister finished high school, completed college and made a life for herself. She's battled pneumonia and insurance companies and doubt. My mother and father and aunt and brother and a cadre of nurses and neighbors have made this possible, but mostly it was my sister's simple refusal to die. And now she gives lessons to doctors, who must rethink their weighty calculus.

She gives lessons to all of us—and not in the subjunctive case, not with the conditional "If you consider that she's quadriplegic . . ." No. Forget the label. Tenacity knows no label. Tenacity is a choice, not a diagnosis. Tenacity is strength and courage and renewal and responsibility, where you wake up every morning and pack your lunch (casserole leftovers) and steer your car through whatever traffic brings, maybe finding the occasional shortcut because maybe you're wiser than you think, and maybe you realize that you don't need to know the word for everything, and maybe with some guidance and some impromptu prayer, you can make it through another day.

LORD, WHATEVER TODAY BRINGS, GIVE ME THE STRENGTH TO KEEP HOLDING ON TO YOU. —MARK COLLINS

Many, O Lord my God, are the wonders which You have done, And Your thoughts toward us. . . .

—PSALM 40:5 (NAS)

It was summer in Minnesota, and the birds were nibbling at the feeder—only not at ours. Seven-year-old Hannah, visiting Grandma and Grandpa, decided to hang an invader—a fine mesh bag filled with more seed—from the post. I had doubts about the idea, but it seemed essential to her that we try. Instead of eating from the bag, the birds were frightened by it and stayed away. Several days later, with Hannah's permission, I took it down.

Two weeks later, back home in Alaska, where I'd accompanied her, Hannah was about to don a lavender sundress on a cool rainy day. "Hey, Hannah," I suggested, "why don't you try the little purple shirt with the heart buttons under your sundress. It would look cute . . . and keep you warm."

Hannah had her own ideas—and they didn't include wearing that shirt. Then I remembered the birdseed bag we had tested at my house. I kindly reminded her that I'd tried her idea then and was asking her to try mine now.

Hannah popped on the shirt and dress, glanced in the mirror, exclaimed, "Grandma, it looks great!" and skipped off to play.

We had learned from each other. We had each tried an idea important to the other. One was successful; one was not. But we had cared for one another enough to be a team and extend the gift of giving our ideas a chance.

Isn't this what our gracious God asks, that I care for Him enough to open my life to His ideas? Ideas that *always* work!

DEAR GOD, FROM A FAR-FLUNG UNIVERSE TO A SAVIOR BORN AMONG US TO LIFE WITHOUT END, YOUR IDEAS ARE SPECTACULAR! —CAROL KNAPP

Let the people praise thee, O God. . . .
—PSALM 67:5

When I moved from Wyoming to New Hampshire, I found myself driving in a state the size of my former county with about one million more people. Not only did I see thousands more cars, I saw hundreds of vanity license plates. Maybe it was the word *vanity* or the extra cost—or the nailing July heat—but today the messages annoyed me. 4 KICKS. L8AGN. WOOF. Couldn't that thirty-five dollars be better invested?

While waiting for a perpetually red light to change on my evening commute, I pulled up behind a compact car bearing a New Hampshire license PSALM 67. *Hmm . . .* I didn't recognize that one. I repeated "PS 67" for the short ride home so I would remember to look it up.

Over an iced drink I read all of Psalm 67, which begins, "God be merciful unto us, and bless us." Imagine, a praise plate! In one year, for about ten cents a day, some faith-filled driver could advertise God's goodness while idling in traffic, even while parked.

So I'm rethinking my attitude toward vanity plates. One driver's foresight brightened my day. Perhaps I can do the same. When it's time to renew my license plate, which Scripture shall I choose?

LORD OF THE JOURNEY, THANK YOU FOR THOSE AMONG US WHO PRAISE WITHOUT CEASING. —GAIL THORELL SCHILLING

Suddenly an angel of the Lord appeared and a light shone in the cell. He struck Peter on the side and woke him up. "Quick, get up!" he said. . . .
—ACTS 12:7 (NIV)

Last weekend I walked out my front door in Durham, North Carolina, and found myself in Baton Rouge, Louisiana.

Well, it really wasn't quite that simple, but almost.

Late last year I made a list of people whom I'd like to meet, sit down with and talk to, people who have been where I hope to go in my career and could guide me. I whispered a prayer and then I set up an alert on my computer that would e-mail me each time the name of award-winning author Ernest Gaines appeared in print. I hoped I'd find out about some event where he was speaking and that I'd be able to make my way there.

Months passed and most of the e-mail alerts I received were useless. In fact, I was about to cancel the alert when I got good news: Ernest Gaines was going to be speaking in a tiny town in Louisiana about one hour outside of Baton Rouge. I called the library sponsoring the event; the librarian was tickled that I would come all the way from North Carolina and gave me all kinds of information. I got a flight and a hotel room.

There were flight delays and I was sleep-deprived, but on Saturday morning I was sitting at a table right across from the man I'd dreamed of meeting. I talked to him; I asked a question; I even got my books signed! It was worth everything it took to get there.

The experience, though, wasn't simply about an improbable meeting; it was a reminder to keep dreaming and believing and to wait for "impossible" things to happen in my life. Because sometimes the unlikeliest thing can come true in the twinkling of an eye.

GOD, YOU ARE REMARKABLE! I AM PRAYING FOR WONDERFUL, IMPOSSIBLE THINGS TO HAPPEN IN MY LIFE AND THE LIVES OF OTHERS.   —SHARON FOSTER

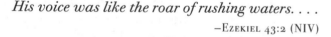

SUN 19

His voice was like the roar of rushing waters. . . .
—EZEKIEL 43:2 (NIV)

Last night five friends gathered around my table. I served up a simple meal—potato salad and saucy chicken—that prompted compliments. I asked a leading question about career paths and the conversation took off. Over dessert, my mother's special pear upside-down gingerbread, the storytelling turned to laughter and finally to someone gently acknowledging God's presence among us. Guests lingered until well past eleven. After church this morning, one of them summarized the evening's success. "If that had been my party, I'd be feeling *Yes!*"

By early afternoon, though, my spirits had dipped. My friends felt far away, my apartment quiet, my world small. Praying for a brighter perspective, I headed out. Where? I wasn't quite sure. To the buttressed cathedral? To the park? I felt drawn toward a chapel courtyard to sit beside its centerpiece fountain with twin jets shooting as high as eight feet.

At first I just watched the fountain: the fluid dance of its forceful sprays, the brief high-step jet fluctuating to more subdued splashes. In the water's rhythm I could see my hours and my days: flashes of success followed by down times. I could hear that both the high points and the letdowns were complementary, equally full of grace.

LORD, GRACE ME WITH REMINDERS OF YOUR PRESENCE.   —EVELYN BENCE

MON
20

When anxiety was great within me, your consolation brought joy to my soul.

—PSALM 94:19 (NIV)

Elizabeth is away at MathPath, a camp made in heaven for children like her. Yesterday, while I was out, she called home. Amid cheerful chitchat with her dad, she told him that today the camp would be going to a park with a pool. Elizabeth is a city kid whose water experience is with sprinklers; she doesn't know how to swim. Proud of a recent accomplishment, however, she happily said, "Don't worry, Dad. I know how to tread water, so I won't drown."

When Andrew reported this, my heart froze. I am not a worrier by nature, but the thought of a child who can't swim but is confident she won't drown terrified me. I said a prayer, tried to shake off my trepidation and went about the rest of my day. Then last night at two-thirty, three-year-old Stephen pattered into our room because of his own nightmare. He quickly went back to sleep. I did not.

I prayed, but I didn't know what to pray. My imagination enacted horrifying scenes, each made vivid by the dark room. Ever practical, I made up a mental list of the people I'd have to inform about my daughter's death. I cried. I begged God to keep Elizabeth safe. I remembered every instance in which God had said no to a prayer and pleaded with Him to take this cup from me. I didn't want to add "but Thy will be done." Finally, just before sunrise, I did. And with that, I fell into a brief but exhausted sleep. When I awoke, I e-mailed the camp to have someone keep an eye on Elizabeth at the pool.

Later that evening, the phone rang. "Hi, Mom!" Elizabeth said. "We had a great time at the pool—even though it was only three feet deep."

LORD, HELP ME REMEMBER THAT YOU HOLD ME JUST AS SECURELY WHETHER OR NOT I WORRY.   —JULIA ATTAWAY

TUE
21

. . . A time to keep, and a time to cast away.

—ECCLESIASTES 3:6

When I moved out of our family home, I had a garage sale. My friend Dorothy stopped by and saw the little pump organ I got for Christmas at age seven. She remarked, "Oh, don't sell your memories!" I looked around and saw other things I wasn't ready to part with. It was "a time to keep."

Seven years later, when I moved from Nebraska to Colorado, it was "a time to cast away." I gave the little organ to my granddaughter Saralisa and found something for each family member that I knew they'd cherish. I took several loads of things to a charity. Then I threw away broken toys, musty books, boxes, string, jars, clothes hangers and such, and I stopped saying, "I might use that someday."

A TIME TO EVERY PURPOSE

How does one decide what to keep and what to cast away? Here's the answer that helped me:

> *Ask three simple questions:*
> *"Have I worn it or used it in the last year?"*
> *"Is there someone who could or would use it?"*
> *"Could this become an heirloom?"*
> *Then make a decision and let it go,*
> *knowing some choices will be mistakes.*

Did I make mistakes? You bet I did! But never mind the things that are gone. I'm richer now that I've let them go.

> I still have the silent stars and the silver moon;
> phone calls and visits from my children
> and my children's children.

> I have music to listen to in the dark,
> golden aspens to color my autumn,
> trusted friends who truly care,
> and my husband Robert to sit with by the fire
> when winter's first snow gently flocks the pines.

I have work I love and ways to serve,
some aches and pains, losses and gains,
and a Holy One to guide me home.

CREATOR GOD, MY GRATITUDE CUP IS SO FULL IT SPILLS OVER.

—MARILYN MORGAN KING

And he that sat upon the throne said,
Behold, I make all things new. . . .

—REVELATION 21:5

How did we get from being a cozy family of five to being an unruly crew of ten on our way to a two-week vacation? The short answer is a son-in-law, a daughter-in-law and three small grandsons heading to a large house in the Loire Valley of France with multiple cribs on site.

Everyone got along just fine—except in the kitchen. He wanted to cook spaghetti; she wanted a vegetarian menu. Her two-year-old wasn't allowed any refined sugar; a three-year-old announced he would only eat peanut butter; an emergency bottle of ketchup was located in a local grocery store.

When it was all over and we grandparents were recuperating, life got even more complicated: 1,300 quite wonderful digital pictures showed up in my e-mail from four camera-happy parents. Grandma, they thought, would love to make an album.

The challenge felt daunting, but I found a program, then I clicked and dragged, deleted and pasted through 272 pictures (computers love numbers). One final click and everything flew through cyberspace and was turned into a lovely book with a green linen cover. A few days later, five copies came in what is now scornfully known as "snail mail."

I've always believed in miracles, that there were indeed enough loaves and fishes for the five thousand and that water turned into wine at the wedding in Cana. But no one expects miracles in the twenty-first century. Imagine how the printers of the Gutenberg Bible would have reacted to my sixty-two-page instant book. But as I turned the brightly colored pages, I realized that the miracle in these pictures was timeless: the love and laughter that binds a family together even when they can't agree on the menu.

LORD, MAY WE ACCEPT THE NEW AND PRESERVE THE OLD, AND USE BOTH TO STRENGTHEN OUR CARING FOR EACH OTHER. —BRIGITTE WEEKS

"But I say to you, Love your enemies and pray for those who persecute you, so that you may be children of your Father in heaven. . . ."
—MATTHEW 5:44–45 (NRSV)

When I need to remember something and don't have a notepad nearby, I take off my wedding ring and slip it in my pocket or put it on my desk where I can see it. It may sound ridiculous, but since the ring represents the second-most-important relationship in my life, I'm very aware of it. Like my marriage, the ring is a part of me, and I often touch or turn it around my finger during the day. So when it's off, I'm sure to remember why I took it off.

Recently I folded my hands in prayer and noticed that my ring *was* off. I reached into the pocket where I'd put it earlier that day and remembered why it was there. I'd been hurt by a colleague and I wanted to make sure I remembered every rotten detail so that I could tell my husband Charlie and we could discuss various ways to, well, get revenge. And all this came flooding back simply because I'd routinely folded my hands in prayer. Except that with God, nothing about prayer is routine.

I can't say that my anger and hurt evaporated right then and there, but when I finally did see Charlie later that evening, I had more than one interesting thing to remember to tell him.

FATHER, WHEN I'M DETERMINED TO GO IN A NEGATIVE DIRECTION, PLEASE TURN ME GENTLY AROUND SO THAT I CAN SEE A BETTER WAY. —MARCI ALBORGHETTI

Keep on doing the things that you have learned
and received and heard and seen in me,
and the God of peace will be with you.

—Philippians 4:9 (NRSV)

I was already sitting in my usual aisle seat. "Mister, this is gonna be fun," a towheaded boy announced to me as he pointed past me to his seat in the middle. "Are you excited, mister?"

Well, no, I wasn't excited. I was tired and cranky, stuck on a cramped airplane likely to sit on the runway for an hour before it took off. Observing the somber faces of the people around me, it was clear I wasn't the only one who felt that way.

None of that was a problem for Benji, a fussing, fidgeting cauldron of seven-year-old energy. His boarding pass was great; the safety demonstration was great; the runway delay was great (more time to watch other planes take off, he told me); even the meal—a small bag of pretzels—was great. At one point, his mom leaned over to me—I was probably looking just a bit annoyed—and said, "You'll have to excuse Benji. This is all new to him."

"I guess I've been on too many flights to think this is fun," I said.

"I guess he's not old enough to take things for granted like we do," she replied.

Have you ever met a person who never intended to change your life but changed it anyway? I did—on a hot, crowded airplane more than three hours late. There, a boy helped me to see something that I too often miss: the remarkable, exciting opportunities that God puts in front of me every day. They're there, if I'm not too busy or cranky or taking things too much for granted to see them.

Thanks, Benji.

Let today be different, God. Give me eyes to see Your wonder in a place I've been missing it lately.   —Jeff Japinga

SAT 25

"The kingdom of heaven is like a king who prepared a wedding banquet for his son."

—Matthew 22:2 (NIV)

"This is not the way I dreamed of spending my Saturday," I mumbled under my breath. My husband Jacob had to work, so here I was doing all the household chores on a beautiful summer weekend. *What I should be doing is swimming at the lake,* I said to myself, pulling off the yellow gloves I wore to do the dishes.

I was feeling pretty sorry for myself and more than a little annoyed as I picked up the bottle of spray bleach and headed into the bathroom. A small voice brought me to an abrupt halt.

"Mommy, what is heaven?"

I looked down at Trace, my four-year-old. He was staring up at me, a serious look in his big gray eyes. I swallowed and knelt down, so I could look into his face.

"Well," I said, trying to think of all the correct biblical answers but drawing a blank, "heaven is . . ." I looked down at the bleach in my hands. "Heaven is . . . a big party."

"A party?" He looked confused.

"Yes. A big party, where we get to be with God and all the people we love. Remember how much fun you had at Jeremiah's birthday party? Remember the cake and presents and games?" Trace nodded. "Heaven is like that: a big, wonderful party."

A smile spread across his face. "Awesome, Mommy," he said. Then he hugged me and ran off to play.

Lord, when I get caught up in the daily grind, help me remember the wonderful party You have planned.

—Amanda Borozinski

SUN 26

And in thee shall all families of the earth be blessed.

—Genesis 12:3

As I entered church that July morning, I glanced toward the altar and saw Wes Jr., who was preparing to serve as lay reader and Eucharistic minister. He would be reading the Scripture lessons from the lectern; then at Communion he would help the pastor by passing the chalice. His wife Linda would be serving as usher-in-charge. They had driven thirty-five miles from their summer home to attend the nine o'clock service.

Also ushering would be their daughter Nancy and her brand-new husband. This was his first time, but he was in good spirits. Nancy's children would bring the bread and wine to the altar for Communion. Here, for the first time I could remember, was an entire family serving at church. I felt blessed.

During the collection my mind raced back more than thirty years ago to another Sunday, when I was ushering. After the service a newcomer approached me and said, "I saw something beautiful this morning. A tiny tot in the choir lost her place and became quite embarrassed. Quietly, the little girl beside her smiled and helped her for the rest of the service. I don't think anyone noticed." That helper was Nancy, now a mother, a new bride, a nurse—and still serving.

HELPING FATHER, BLESS ALL WHO FOLLOW YOUR WORD AND SERVE IN QUIETNESS.

—OSCAR GREENE

But for that very reason I was shown mercy so that in me, the worst of sinners, Christ Jesus might display his unlimited patience as an example for those who would believe on him and receive eternal life.

—I TIMOTHY 1:16 (NIV)

I'm seldom idle; my schedule is packed with meetings, travel and appointments. When I do sit down, I have either a pair of knitting needles in my hands or a book. I'm not a patient person; it's simply not in my genetic makeup to gaze at a sunset for more than a few pleasurable moments. It's lovely, but there's dinner to cook and things that need to be done.

But last year I injured my rotator cuff and needed surgery. The surgeon said I'd need six to eight weeks to heal properly and several months of physical therapy. I listened and nodded at all the right times, but I figured I'd be back in the office within a week or two. I was wrong.

I tried to work, but my energy level was so low that after a short while I needed a nap. Surely the Lord knew about my deadlines; didn't He care about the commitments I'd made and the people who relied on me?

After five weeks of staying at home, attending physical therapy three days a week and napping every day, I'm here to tell you that God *does* care. The time at home rejuvenated my marriage, inspired my creativity and gave me a renewed appreciation of life.

LORD, I'M GRATEFUL THAT YOU'RE NEVER IDLE IN YOUR CARE FOR ME.

—DEBBIE MACOMBER

TUE 28

I have set before thee an open door, and no man can shut it. . . .

—REVELATION 3:8

My mother died eight years ago at the age of ninety-two. Some days I miss her more than others, but truth be told, the thing I really have a hard time with is the fact that I can't go home again. I've ridden by the old house three times; I no longer belong there. Still, some part of me can't accept that.

While shopping for a greeting card, I was drawn to the section marked *Mothers.* My heart thumped wildly, tears filled my eyes and I blinked rapidly. Unexpectedly, a smile brightened my face, for I was suddenly home again, about to run up the three steps to the open door and be welcomed by my mother, probably wearing her red apron. We'd hug at the door and she'd light up like a Christmas tree because I was home.

I picked up a card hesitantly. The bungalow house was amazingly like Mother's, but the thing that stole my heart was the open front door and the amber glow from inside the house—the unmistakable love that spilled through it and the curtained windows. The front porch beckoned me. Twilight approached; lightning bugs would be out. Pink camellias bloomed near the porch. The lawn was Easter-basket-grass green.

Carefully, I read the words on the front of the card: "For me, home will always be an open door." Almost reverently, I opened it. "And you'll be standing in it with a welcoming smile. Happy Birthday, Mom."

The card's been sitting on my desk for several years now. Whenever

I feel the need, I go home again through that open door, if only for a few precious seconds.

FATHER, BLESS YOUR HOLY NAME FOR DOORS YOU KEEP OPEN FOREVER.

—MARION BOND WEST

My flesh and my heart faileth: but God is the strength of my heart, and my portion for ever.

—PSALM 73:26

I spent a fascinating afternoon a few years ago wandering the Picasso Museum in the artist's hometown of Barcelona, Spain. The Museu Picasso is found on Carrer Montcada in Barri Gòtic, the ancient heart of Barcelona, a warren of cobbled streets and medieval structures. The museum itself occupies a row of five gothic palaces, and the architecture alone is worth the visit.

Pablo Picasso wasn't actually born in Barcelona but moved there in 1894 when his father, an art teacher, found work in the city schools. Picasso was certainly precocious—he had his first exhibition at fifteen— and didn't even bother to sign his work in the beginning. The museum is full of those early pieces, room after room of them. And there is one thing that struck me about most of it: It was really bad.

No wonder he didn't sign anything, I thought to myself. Finally, after looking at some awkward paintings of the Barcelona shoreline, I mentioned my impressions to a guard. He chuckled and said, "Well, sometimes you have to be bad before you can be good."

Picasso became more than good. He was arguably the greatest, and certainly the most influential, artist of the twentieth century, though it would be some time after his Barcelona years that he would finally sound his genius in Paris. So maybe he had to be really bad before he could be really great.

GOD, OUR PATHS ARE LITTERED WITH COURAGEOUS FAILURES. LET ME ALWAYS REMEMBER THAT OFTENTIMES I HAVE TO BE BAD BEFORE I CAN BE GOOD.

—EDWARD GRINNAN

THU
30

And this is his command: to believe in the name of his Son, Jesus Christ, and to love one another as he commanded us.

—2 JOHN 5 (NIV)

When our dog Cookie was about eleven years old, we got a puppy, another white puffball named Dolly. I was used to my comfy old dog and had forgotten how mischievous an energetic puppy is. Every day I chased after Dolly with my shoe in her mouth, or yelled at her to not pull Cookie's tail, or picked up the tissue snowstorm after Dolly had emptied and shredded an entire box.

One rainy day after Dolly had burst through the doggy-door with mud-covered feet, I yelled to our daughter Maria to catch her before she painted half the house with mud. Maria grabbed her as I reached for a towel. "What am I going to do with this dog?" I asked in frustration.

"Love her, of course," Maria answered, hugging Dolly tightly as she carried her to the kitchen sink. Her simple admonition was absolutely right. No matter how I may feel about what Dolly has done, I need to love her. Discipline and train her, yes, but at all times, love her.

Even with her adorable puppy face, that's easier said than done, because she simply isn't lovable all the time. Who is? Yet I know God loves me always, not just when I please Him. Jesus' command is to "love one another, as I have loved you" (John 15:12). I need to remember that when I get annoyed with my husband or frustrated with my children.

God's love for me never changes. How comforting to know He simply loves me, no matter what.

GRACIOUS GOD, AMID LIFE'S MESSES AND IRRITATIONS, HELP ME TO LOVE AS YOU HAVE LOVED.   —GINA BRIDGEMAN

FRI
31

Feed the flock of God which is among you, taking the oversight thereof. . . .

—I PETER 5:2

The 101-degree heat wasn't nearly as hot as the rage that boiled inside me. I reached into the stall and gently ran my fingers over the bony horse's hide. Three emaciated gray-and-brown horses crowded the stall. They could only be fed small amounts of low-energy food at a time because rich food would kill them.

Some of the herd had starved to death before the sheriff's department seized more than thirty others and brought them to the Hamilton, Montana, fairgrounds. Local veterinarians and a number of us volunteers were nursing them back to health.

As I scratched the horse's forehead, an inquisitive man wearing a tan cowboy hat peered into the stall. "What kind of person would willingly starve them?"

I nodded my head in agreement and was going to say some unkind words when my spirit arrested me and a still, small voice said, *Look at the people around you. Many of them are starving to death spiritually. Will you have compassion and feed them?*

I blinked my eyes and looked at the folks crowding the fairgrounds. I'd never thought about people being spiritually emaciated. I could apply the same guidelines to their spiritual hunger as we did to the horses: If someone was spiritually starving, I could give him or her a teaspoon of God's love.

That afternoon a business contact mentioned that his son was soon to be stationed in Iraq. Even though I wasn't familiar with his beliefs, I asked if he would like me to pray for his son. It was a morsel of God's mighty Word.

TEACH ME, LORD, HOW TO MAKE OPPORTUNITIES TO FEED YOUR SHEEP.

—REBECCA ONDOV

MY LIVING WORDS

1 _____

2 _____

3

4

5

6

7

8

9

10

11

12

13

14

15

16

17

18

19

20

21

22

23

24

25

26

27

28

29

30

31

AUGUST

*Thy words have upholden him
that was falling, and thou hast
strengthened the feeble knees.*

—JOB 4:4

> *Do not overwork to be rich. . . . For riches*
> *certainly make themselves wings. . . .*
> —Proverbs 23:4-5 (NKJV)

I know all about God's promises to take care of us, to supply all our needs. After all, I was raised in a believing home and knew those promises by heart. But one year, when the college where I teach was going through hard times, and paychecks were delayed, I fell into a panic.

My car was wearing out, our daughters needed money for college and I couldn't see how God could supply, so I took matters into my own hands. I began taking on extra work and stayed up late to meet deadlines.

GOD SPEAKS THROUGH FREE WILL

"You're making yourself sick," my wife warned, and trips to the doctor verified her judgment. I began to be short with Sharon and the girls, even with my students and colleagues. My teaching suffered from a distracted mind.

At the end of the year, Sharon figured up our taxes. "Your extra earnings put us into a higher tax bracket," she noted. "And all these medical bills, they just don't stop coming."

In the end, everything extra I earned that year was wiped out. I had put my health, my marriage and my job in jeopardy for nothing. And yet, strangely, I'm glad that God let me find that out for myself. I knew His promises by heart, but not by experience.

Like a wise Father, God sometimes allows me to touch the hot stove, to see for myself what *hot* means. I doubt that we would ever be fully happy without the freedom to find out the hard way.

You gave us a great gift, Lord, when You gave us our freedom in Christ.

—Daniel Schantz

> *I believe that I shall see the goodness*
> *of the Lord in the land of the living!*
> —Psalm 27:13 (RSV)

A lone traveler in Paris, I was living a dream, a birthday present from my mother and stepfather. For years I'd longed to test my wings and travel alone. This was it. I could walk for miles, stopping whenever I wanted to take photos. When it rained, I wrapped my camera in plastic and walked on. I lingered in ancient cemeteries searching out marble angels, and no one said, "Hurry!" There were no schedules—just me, my camera, a tiny hotel room a block from the Eiffel Tower and a city to explore.

The time had gone quickly, and this was my last day—my Mona Lisa day. "Small, dark, disappointing," I'd heard people say about the painting, but I was undaunted.

I trekked along the Seine toward the Louvre and found a crowd waiting to get in. "It's Free Day," someone explained. "Half of Paris is here."

Oops. I circled back and sat down to think. I remembered reading that the Louvre had a back entrance. *Worth a try,* I thought.

Soon I was chatting with the guard at the back door. He was young and sweet and liked my Southern accent. I was in!

I walked from exhibit to exhibit until finally I stood before her, transfixed. She was familiar, like a good friend. And why not? She'd been riding around in my head practically all my life. My eyes filled with tears. I looked at the guard standing watch. "She's beautiful," I said.

"Ah," he said, "you came believing. Yes?"

Father, wherever I go in life, believing makes all the difference. Open my eyes and let me see the best Your world offers.   —Pam Kidd

---

MON
3

Jesus said: "I'm telling you once and for all, that unless you return to square one and start over like children you're not even going to get a look at the kingdom, let alone get in."
—Matthew 18:2–5 (MSG)

I sat up in bed, unable to get back to sleep. "God," I prayed, "I love You. But to be honest, my prayer life is just not working. Please give me a hand."

I opened the Bible at Matthew 18 and tried to read, but my spirit wasn't in gear. Then I had a strong nudge: *Focus on what you're reading. It's for you!*

Jesus was saying to His disciples, "I'm telling you once and for all,

that unless you return to square one and start over like children you're not even going to get a look at the kingdom, let alone get in." *Keith*, God seemed to be saying, *you can't see reality from My perspective—or what to do—unless you become like a little child again.*
Immediately I remembered the Lord's Prayer, the only prayer that Jesus gave as a model. Although our translations begin it with "Our Father," in Aramaic, Jesus' native language, it began "*Abba*" ("Daddy"). I bowed my head. "Daddy, I'm a lost little boy trying to control everything instead of listening as Your little child." Instantly tears came, and I grasped the problem with my prayer life. When praying to "Our Father," I prayed adult to adult, as if God were a peer with expertise in an area I hadn't mastered (and Whom I could fire if I didn't like His advice). But when I prayed to "Daddy," I prayed as a listening child. Simply saying "Daddy" brought me what all my studying and meditation had not: a new set of ears.

DADDY IN HEAVEN, THANK YOU FOR TEACHING ME TO COME TO YOU CHILDLIKE, EYES WIDE OPEN AND EARS LISTENING. AMEN. —KEITH MILLER

Be openhanded toward your brothers and toward the poor and needy in your land.
—DEUTERONOMY 15:11 (NIV)

One day I accompanied Edna, a visiting nurse, on her rounds through the South African township of Khayelitsha. As we drove along, Edna was dismayed at how many children wandered the dusty streets. The social worker for the area had resigned, so in addition to her nursing work, Edna helped people get school fees waived and uniforms provided. "Education is their only hope to escape this," she said, gesturing at the poverty all around us.
In a one-room brick house with no electricity or running water, we visited a young HIV-positive mother. She looked very frail; Edna made sure she was taking her antiviral drugs. Back in the car, Edna shook her head. "I'm afraid she started the medicines too late."
In the next house we found an elderly woman all alone, shivering in bed on this hot summer day. We scoured the neighborhood, but couldn't find her caregivers. The woman gratefully sipped some water;

she didn't remember when she had last eaten. Edna promised to return that evening to check on her. Edna told me that visiting nurses often use their own funds to buy food for patients or to provide transportation to the hospital. "We can't just leave them in the state they're in. If we don't care for them, who will?"

With such overwhelming needs, I wondered how Edna did this heart-wrenching work day after day without burning out. Then, while Edna was filling the gas tank, I noticed a small shelf underneath the glove compartment. It held two books: One was the Bible; the other was a slim volume titled *The Body of Christ.*

LIKE EDNA, LORD, HELP ME TO SEE YOU IN EACH PERSON I MEET TODAY AND TO LOVINGLY GIVE OF MYSELF. —MARY BROWN

WED
5

The memory of the just is blessed. . . .

—PROVERBS 10:7

My bachelor son Phil and I were rolling down an Alaskan highway during my summer visit. "I'll have to clean this messy handprint off your side window, so I can see the scenery better," I said.

There was a pause before Phil replied. "Actually, Sarah made that a long time ago . . . and I was leaving it for a memory." Sarah, three at the time, is my granddaughter and Phil's niece.

I was speechless over his display of tenderness. Here was a guy driving a big four-wheel-drive pickup truck that he likes to keep shined, and its accessory package included five tagalong sticky fingerprints.

Months later, back home in Minnesota, my three-year-old grandson Clay, playing with my loon collection, added a stubby beak to those already broken. He mixed up the birds on the shelf to suit himself, even stacking a smaller one in the hollowed back of a larger one.

I won't rearrange the loons or repair its stunted beak. Thanks to Phil, I don't see damage or disorder; I see imagination—and a dear little face engrossed in play. I'm leaving those loons just as they are . . . for a memory.

JESUS, BY YOUR GRACE, MAY THE PRINTS I LEAVE BEHIND BE THE KEEPING KIND.

—CAROL KNAPP

THU 6

When I was a child, I used to speak like a child, think like a child, reason like a child; when I became a man, I did away with childish things.

—I Corinthians 13:11 (NAS)

When I was a little boy, I sometimes woke up in a bad mood, which made life miserable for our family. Fussing about every little thing that didn't please me, I'd shuffle to the breakfast table to darken everyone's day. Even now I can see my mother lean across the table and say, "Scott, I think you got up on the wrong side of the bed. Why don't you tuck yourself back in and get up on the other side?"

When I heard those words, I knew it was time for an attitude change. My mother's nearly inexhaustible patience had reached its limit.

Recently I fell back into that childish mood. Things weren't going my way and hadn't for several days. Furious, I sat down in my easy chair and tried to recover my equilibrium. Out of my memory came the image of the writer and missionary Elisabeth Elliot. As a young woman Elisabeth lived with her husband Jim in Ecuador and worked with an indigenous tribe, the Huaorani. In 1956 her husband was killed by Huaorani warriors, leaving Elisabeth to raise their ten-month-old daughter alone.

Returning to the United States, Elisabeth became a well-known writer and speaker. Some years ago I read one of her books and memorized this passage: "It is always possible to be thankful for what is given rather than to complain about what is not given. One or the other becomes a habit of life."

As I sat in my chair, I decided that it was time to listen to my mother one more time before a few days' funk became a lifetime habit.

FATHER, HELP ME CHOOSE TO BE POSITIVE RATHER THAN NEGATIVE, EVEN IN THE WORST OF TIMES. AMEN.   —SCOTT WALKER

FRI 7

These things that were written in the Scriptures so long ago are to teach us patience and to encourage us. . . .

—Romans 15:4 (TLB)

A couple of summers ago, a once-in-a-hundred-years storm dumped nine inches of rain over parts of central Oklahoma in just three hours. During the next weeks my sister Amanda did double duty: She worked hours each day helping her son Jeff and his family clean their flooded home, and she volunteered through the American Red Cross and her church to arrange housing and food for families left homeless.

One woman who'd lost her home was in very poor health. After helping her with the basics, Amanda asked, "Is there anything else you need?"

The woman hesitated a moment, then said, "I wish I had my Bible."

"Let's look in the church library," Amanda suggested. "We have plenty of Bibles to share."

"I need one with large letters," the woman responded wistfully. "I just can't read small print anymore."

All the Bibles stacked on the library tables were regular print. Then Amanda pulled a Bible from a library shelf. The Bible was in large print; it had belonged to a church member now in a nursing home. Stuck to the cover was a note: "Nonie Burge wants this Bible to go to a person who really needs it."

"The Lord is so good to me!" the woman said when Amanda placed the Bible in her hands. "He is just *so* good!"

THANK YOU, LORD, FOR ALL WHO GIVE AND RECEIVE YOUR PRECIOUS HOLY WORD. —PENNEY SCHWAB

SAT
8

The whole multitude of the disciples began to rejoice and praise God with a loud voice for all the mighty works that they had seen. . . . And some of the Pharisees in the multitude said to him, "Teacher, rebuke your disciples." He answered, "I tell you, if these were silent, the very stones would cry out."

—LUKE 19:37, 39–40 (RSV)

For six thousand years Canadian Natives ran buffalo herds over a cliff they called Head-Smashed-In. Once, the cliff stood twice the height it is today. The "fill" is millions of buffalo bones, layered and silted through with prairie soil. People come from all over to this World Heritage Interpretive Center to see and better understand our past.

A trail winds along the bottom of the cliff. Walking through the high grasses last August, I wondered if my own personal excavation might prove as fruitful as the ongoing digs that are part of Head-Smashed-In.

For health reasons my parents had sent me to live with friends in Arizona when I was seventeen. Mum placed me under the care of a doctor, and what happened in his office I have never been able to speak of. Bones of fear and shame litter the cliff of my soul.

I stooped to pick up a stone. To the skilled, stones speak the truth of many hidden things. Was it time to dig? To listen? To hear what they say regarding the part of me that was buried in 1969? I put down the stone. I would go back to Arizona, to seventeen. I would trust the stones to speak.

I have my ticket. I don't know what I'll find next month or how painful it may be, but I know I'll discover who I once was and still can be.

JESUS, YOU TELL US THE VERY STONES WILL CRY OUT WHEN TRUTH IS DENIED. HELP ME TO FIND THE STONES THAT BURY MY PAST, WHATEVER THEY MAY BE, AND HEAR THEM. —BRENDA WILBEE

Jesus answered, "I am the way and the truth and the life. . . ."

—JOHN 14:6 (NIV)

My grandson Drake and I were standing outside church one Sunday morning, waiting for the rest of the family to join us. I was, as is my custom, dressed up—a lacey top, a gauze broomstick skirt, and a great straw hat with a band of tulle and a cluster of silk hydrangeas. Suddenly, the sun disappeared and it started to sprinkle. "Oh no," I wailed, "my beautiful hat will get wet!"

Drake looked at me, considering this for a moment. Then, with perfect three-year-old logic, he said, "Nana, your flowers will like it. They need rain!"

I laughed, even as the drops became thicker. All Drake knew about flowers was that they needed water. And in this summer of drought, he had watched his mother and me water, water, water. He wasn't aware that silk blossoms this perpetually full could be had for $3.99 at craft stores.

Knowing what's real and what's not is pretty much a lifelong quest, whether you're seeking true love, testing the waters of a new friendship or choosing which tub of butterlike substance to buy for your morning muffin. I'd like to say that age has rendered me an expert at sniffing out the fakes in life—the friend who will desert you just after you tell her your dearest secret, the designer blouse that will fray the third time you wear it, the "special offer" that isn't quite as special as it claims—but I still make mistakes in judgment.

I have learned, though, to cling tightly to those things that have proven themselves good and true and real: my husband Gary, my family, my closest friends and, most of all, my faith. There's nothing fake or fleeting about the way God has seen me through the traumas and temptations of my life.

IN THIS WORLD OF CONFUSING DECISIONS AND CLAMORING OPTIONS, YOU, LORD, ARE THE ONE TRUE THING. —MARY LOU CARNEY

MON
10

Finally, brethren, farewell. Be perfect, be of good comfort, be of one mind, live in peace; and the God of love and peace shall be with you.
—II CORINTHIANS 13:11

Visiting family is always a blessing, but when the clock announces that it's time to go, the struggle to say good-bye almost overshadows the joy of the time spent together. On this particular visit to Long Island to celebrate our son Noah's and his daughter Avery's birthdays, we lingered over last-minute hugs when we should have been heading north to Vermont.

Finally on the road, we reflected on our visit while enjoying the warmth of a summer drive in our little convertible. Hours later, after the hot sun had set, we turned north onto the quiet country road that was just a few miles from the comforts of our farm. Bill slowed to drive over a small bridge as I gazed heavenward to look at the bright gleaming stars.

All of a sudden, out of the corner of my eye, I caught a glimpse of a moving object galloping up the hill from the stream. Within seconds a large bull moose headed for our little car and came so close I could almost feel his breath on the top of my head. We swerved and missed hitting him by mere moments.

I may never learn the art of saying timely farewells, but those long, drawn-out good-byes are precious . . . and that last one may even have saved our family from having to say a *final* good-bye to us.

LORD, THANK YOU FOR WATCHING OVER US AND KEEPING US SAFE.

—PATRICIA PUSEY

In confidence shall be your strength. . . .

—ISAIAH 30:15

There's nothing like a bathing suit to make me feel inferior—short, plump, not particularly striking—and there I was on the Colorado River with Pat, a lean, athletic blonde without an ounce of fat on her frame, and Kate, the kind of beautiful redhead that makes heads turn.

The river was one thing. But I felt entirely outclassed a few months later when Kate came to town to visit, and after calling Pat, invited my husband Keith and me to go out to dinner with them. At first I tried to find excuses not to go, but finally we agreed to meet them at a nearby restaurant and I spent a long time trying to decide what to wear so that I wouldn't just vanish.

Then we saw them in the restaurant parking lot, and my heart sank. Each of them was so lovely in her own way, and there I was, kind of nondescript. When we walked into the restaurant, I saw people stare at Kate, while Pat seemed entirely comfortable.

Keith took my arm, and suddenly I realized that of the three of us I was the one with a man. Astonished, I started to smile.

When we finally got home, Keith said, "You seemed to have a good time, even though you didn't want to go."

"I thought I'd just sort of be background to Pat and Kate," I said. "They look so wonderful."

Keith stared at me as if I'd lost my mind. "How could you think that?" he asked. "You're beautiful."

I didn't think he meant my looks, but suddenly that was okay with me.

LORD, THANK YOU FOR SHOWING ME YOUR LOVE THROUGH MY HUSBAND'S EYES.

—RHODA BLECKER

WED 12

Give me understanding, and I shall live.

—Psalm 119:144

Our daughter Elizabeth is back from a visit to her mother's cousin in Vermont, and in a few days she'll turn thirteen. It's been an exciting summer for Elizabeth; she spent July at math camp in Colorado, her longest stint on her own, and she'd barely gotten home when she was off to spend a week with Cousin Susan.

It's been a strange time for me. As our firstborn has grown, she's gone in directions where this math-challenged philosophy major has had trouble following her. But after her month in camp, I've given up entirely. Oh, I can parrot some of the formulas she's shared with me (she's taught her siblings a song with the refrain, "e to the pi i equals negative one"), but I have no real conception of what they mean. I can pick up a reference book and struggle through definitions of hyperbolic geometry and linear algebra, and I can listen attentively as she tries to explain set theory to me, but I know I'll never see them the way she does—as miracles of beauty and elegance.

For most of my life I've been a good learner, able to follow the threads of most conversations, whether in person or in books. But Elizabeth reminds me of my limitations, of just how far my abilities don't go. I need that reminder; I need to know that there's more in everything, not just math, than I can ever comprehend. When I'm reading a passage from the Scripture, I need to remember that no matter how well I know the definitions of the words on the page, I may be missing their meaning entirely. If I'm to look into the Word and come to know its Author, I can't rely on my own understanding. That's a good lesson to learn, no matter how young the teacher.

LORD, LEAD MY DAUGHTER AND ME INTO ALL TRUTH, FOR YOU ARE TRUTH ITSELF.

—ANDREW ATTAWAY

THU 13

And to stand every morning to thank and praise the Lord. . . .

—I Chronicles 23:30

Watching Lovey, my golden retriever/Labrador, grow old unnerved me. As she approached thirteen, she slowed down considerably.

When her eyes met mine, they were dim. Still, she wagged her tired old tail and came to me when I called her name. She barked at imagined trouble but had ceased chasing the practically tame squirrels and chipmunks that enjoy our backyard.

Early each morning when Lovey heard the back door open, she'd lumber out from the coolness underneath the porch, her beige coat speckled with red Georgia clay. She knew I'd visit with her for a bit before the sun came up and maybe give her a piece of watermelon, her favorite food.

One hot, muggy August morning, she didn't appear. I tried to imagine that she was merely sleeping late and continued to call, "Here, Lovey! Here, girl!"

When she didn't come, I searched all over our large, fenced-in backyard. Finally, I made myself stoop down and look underneath the porch as the sun rose. There she lay, unmoving, gone in her sleep.

As an avalanche of sorrow and grief came down on me, I begged, *Lord Jesus, help me thank You and praise You that we don't have to make the dreadful decision to put her down. Thank You for the memories. Thank You that I gave her watermelon yesterday.*

Slowly, despite the pain, gratitude rose up in my heart.

MY FATHER, HOW HARD IT IS—AND HOW POWERFUL—TO PRAISE AND THANK YOU IN ALL CIRCUMSTANCES! —MARION BOND WEST

FRI
14

. . . The birds of the air, and the fish of the sea. . . .
—PSALM 8:8 (RSV)

Almost every summer we go back to the same bay in Southern California for a week of vacation. You might think it would get boring year after year, the same family, three generations now, sitting on our beach chairs, reading our books and magazines, swimming out to the buoy, paddling a kayak across the water, jogging along the ocean, biking on the boardwalk. But every year something's a little different. The blue house down the sand might be painted yellow, or our rental will have a new rug. We'll spot birds we haven't seen before or see a sunset that paints the sky with a stunning shade of gold.

Last year, for instance, I was taking a lazy swim out to the buoy, floating on my back. All at once, my relatives on the beach stepped out from under the umbrella and waved. *How friendly*, I thought, waving back to them. They kept waving and pointing. *They seem to be making a big deal out of this swim.* Finally I heard them shout: "Behind you!"

I turned, thinking there might be a large boat entering the bay or a gondola passing. Instead, just five feet from me, was a sea lion staring at me, a small octopus in his mouth. My first instinct was to wonder, *What are* you *doing here?* Sea lions don't usually come into the bay. But then it occurred to me, it probably wondered the same about me: *What are* you *doing here?*

After a few seconds it raised its head and swallowed the octopus, then plunged into the deep. As for me, I swam a little faster back to shore.

How great is Your handiwork, God.

—Rick Hamlin

SAT
15

> *And do not neglect doing good and sharing,*
> *for with such sacrifices God is pleased.*
> —Hebrews 13:16 (NAS)

Last summer, on the hottest Saturday in August, I held a yard sale at my log cabin. I'd worked for weeks getting ready, and on the day of the sale, I got up at 5:00 AM to set up tables, display my merchandise and post signs throughout the neighborhood. By the time noon came, I was famished and I'd failed to plan anything for lunch.

About that time my friend Debbie stopped by to see how my sale was going. I'd met Debbie eight years before when she was my mother's hospice nurse. From the morning she happened by, just when I was having trouble managing Mother's pain, I noticed Debbie had a knack for knowing when her help was needed.

With Eternity in View

Look for Ways
to Help

"I came to see what you want for lunch," she said. "What about a salad or a sandwich? I'll run down and pick it up for you."

Twenty minutes later Debbie returned with a turkey-and-provolone sandwich on whole wheat and a large soda. "When I heard you were having a sale," she said, "I thought back to the day I had mine. I wanted to do something to help you, and when I asked God about it, He seemed to say, 'Nothing big, Debbie. Just take Roberta something to eat.'"

That refreshing lunch gave me a second wind for the afternoon. As I folded up tables after the sale in record speed, I knew that Debbie's kindness was something I wanted to emulate. Ever since, I've been trying to follow her example by looking for simple ways to help others. It's becoming a joy-filled way of living.

LORD, SHOW ME HOW TO COMMUNICATE CARING IN SIMPLE, LOVING WAYS.

—ROBERTA MESSNER

And at the ninth hour Jesus cried out in a loud voice, "Eloi, Eloi, lama sabachthani?"—which means, "My God, my God, why have you forsaken me?"

—MARK 15:34 (NIV)

I hate to admit this, but earlier this summer I was not on speaking terms with God.

My saga started with a trip to the emergency room and a diagnosis of intestinal blockage, a result of scar tissue from my first cancer surgery. From that moment on, everything that could go wrong seemed to go wrong. I was admitted to the hospital, but my doctor was out of town, which delayed the scheduling of my surgery.

During the endless waiting two of my children and their families canceled their summer vacations to be close by. I endured many painful medical procedures, including a tube down my throat, which meant I couldn't eat. The long dark nights seemed the worst as I felt paralyzed in that narrow bed, hooked up to monitors and IVs.

Surely I should have felt a oneness with God through all those circumstances; that would be the spiritually mature and obedient response. But I did not. I felt totally abandoned, especially when my daughter suffered her third consecutive miscarriage right before my surgery. The ceiling of that hospital room seemed an impenetrable barrier between God and me. I simply could not pray.

After fifteen long days I finally came home on a Sunday afternoon and lay on the couch, savoring simple pleasures: hearing the sounds of family in the kitchen, preparing dinner; listening to three little grand-daughters arguing over the possession of two baby dolls; licking warm buttery mashed potatoes from a spoon, the first real food I'd had in two weeks. But my favorite was crawling into my own bed that night next to my husband Lynn and pulling our lightweight down comforter up under my chin. I was finally home.

LORD, THANK YOU FOR THE REMINDER THAT YOU ARE MY COMFORTER. YOU KNOW ME. YOU KNOW ABOUT MY SOMETIMES SHALLOW FAITH AND MY DOUBTS. YET YOU STILL LOVE ME, IN SPITE OF MYSELF. —CAROL KUYKENDALL

Pure and undefiled religion before God and the Father is this: to visit orphans and widows in their troubles. . . .

—JAMES 1:27 (NKJV)

Early that August afternoon our telephone rang and Virginia's voice boomed through. "Oscar," she said, "you're still collecting, aren't you?" Yes, I was always seeking donations for our seven Trash & Treasure tables at our fall church fair.

"I've put all Don's books outside," Virginia continued. "If you're here in fifteen minutes, they're yours. Otherwise don't bother!" Don, her late husband, died five years ago at age forty-eight. Her loss was still painful.

Minutes later I pulled into Virginia's driveway. I blinked; the books were neatly piled in stacks three feet high. I had never seen so many books. This was Don's library, years in the gathering. After two hours the books were packed and nestled in the car. I tried to thank Virginia and say good-bye, but she remained in the house. It had taken courage for her to part with those books. I knew her heart was breaking.

After we sorted the books, we donated the technical ones to the local library; the rare and out-of-print books went to friends. The remainder went to the church fair, much to the delight of book lovers and dealers.

On that August afternoon Virginia taught me a lesson I will remember all my life: No matter how hard it is, there's a time to let go and trust.

HEALING SHEPHERD, PLEASE BLESS VIRGINIA. AND HELP ME TO BE ALWAYS READY TO REACH OUT AND SHARE. —OSCAR GREENE

**TUE
18**

Every way of a man is right in his own eyes. . . .

—PROVERBS 21:2

We had seven more stops to go on the subway when three-year-old Stephen decided that he wanted to put fresh blackberries into the roll he was munching. I looked at his yellow shirt and beige shorts, and suggested that berries and clothing shouldn't mix. "But I won't stain them! I *have* to put berries in my roll!" Stephen wailed. "I have to!"

We were heading for a rut that we'd already visited several times that day. I took a deep breath and squatted down in front of Stephen's seat. "Buddy," I said, "I think you've got to be a bit more flexible here."

"But I can't bend my legs that far like my stretchy rabbit can!" he protested.

Hmm . . . wrong word. Let's try again.

"Okay. I can see you have an idea about the blackberries that you like a lot. But you need a backup plan. A lot of times in life your first idea won't work. In fact, it's usually good to have a whole bunch of other ideas. That way you don't get stuck."

Stephen pondered my words. His eyes narrowed suspiciously as he weighed the sense of my words against his impulse to reiterate, "But I have to put berries in my roll!" another five hundred times. I took advantage of his indecision to point out that the lady across the aisle had purple hair. The distraction worked, at least for a moment. Then Stephen noticed his blackberry-less roll.

"Mommy," he said, "I want those berries to *smush* into my roll." I groaned inwardly, thinking of the remaining three subway stops that would be filled with wailing. I opened my mouth to speak, but Stephen continued, "Can I have the berries when we get to the playground?"

LORD, I GUESS I DON'T REALLY *HAVE* TO DO EVERYTHING MY WAY. I COULD DO IT YOUR WAY INSTEAD. —JULIA ATTAWAY

For we are strangers before thee, and sojourners, as all our fathers were. . . .

—I CHRONICLES 29:15

Last summer my family and I went on vacation to Martha's Vineyard, a lovely island off the southern coast of Massachusetts. I should say that most of my family went, because my older son John was away at college and couldn't join us. We love the Vineyard, with its long sandy beaches, its white picket fences, its old-fashioned ways. But this was the first time that we'd gone on vacation without John, and we missed him terribly.

We stayed at a nice hotel, staffed mostly by summer workers from Caribbean islands. Soon after arriving, I got to chatting with one of them, a young man from Jamaica. At first we were reserved with each other, perhaps worrying about our differing roles or ages or cultural backgrounds. Soon enough, however, Paul was telling me about his family, whom he had left behind to take this well-paying summer job. "I love it here," he said. "But I miss my children. That ache doesn't go away." Paul had two little ones, both under five years of age.

"I know what you mean," I said. "My son John is away at college now. He's a lot older than your children, but I miss him just the same."

To which Paul said, "That's what life's about. Sometimes we have to give up a good thing today to get a better thing tomorrow." He gave me a wistful smile, and in that moment something passed between us: a mutual recognition that employee or guest, young or old, black or white, none of those categories mattered much.

LORD, TEACH ME TO BE AWARE OF THE KINSHIP WE ALL SHARE THROUGH THE SORROWS AND JOYS LOVE BRINGS. —PHILIP ZALESKI

*When people are saying, "All is well,
everything is quiet and peaceful"—then,
all of a sudden, disaster will fall upon
them as suddenly as a woman's birth
pains begin when her child is born.* . . .

—I Thessalonians 5:3 (TLB)

Living in Florida is very different from living in any other part of the country because of our vulnerability to hurricanes every June through November. Once a hurricane is spotted, even if it's a thousand miles away, the weather reports dominate the news for days.

Unlike those who are suddenly shocked by an earthquake, flood, volcanic eruption or fire, we can at least see a hurricane coming and prepare. We fill containers with water and freeze them in case the power goes out. We buy nonperishable food, flashlights, lots of batteries, a weather radio, and if the hurricane is heading in our direction, we board up our homes and move to higher ground.

Although God hasn't told us when, He has given all of us advance notice that we'll have to give an account of our lives to Him. Sometimes when I do something I know I shouldn't, like getting caught up in gossip at the pool, I can see I'm on a destructive path, take cover and redirect my energies. All I have to do is change the subject or excuse myself and go swim laps.

Lord, give me strength during the bad weather times and remind me to prepare well for life here and for life in eternity.   —Patricia Lorenz

---

*"For man looks at the outward appearance,
but the Lord looks at the heart."*

—I Samuel 16:7 (NAS)

This summer I volunteered to teach a Bible study at a women's shelter. Initially it sounded like fun, but I'd begun to dread it. How would I be able to relate to the women?

I drove to the shelter in the sweltering afternoon sun. Inside, stifling heat greeted me. The air conditioner repairman hadn't come, though none of the women complained. They invited me to eat dinner with them—hot dogs and watermelon. We made polite conversation at the worn Formica table.

Then we went into the tiny den for the Bible study. At first it was too quiet, just the sounds of the oscillating fan and women clearing their throats. I sat down on the braided rug with a few of the others. I'd been a Sunday school teacher for fifteen years, so I'd carefully prepared a lesson.

As I stared at my handwriting, I knew I couldn't teach from my notes. Instead, I told them the truth. I shared the struggles in our family—drug addiction, abusive relationships, mental illness and jail time. I told them that some people in my family had come close to homelessness.

After I opened up with them, they opened up with me. Several had drug histories and most had been in abusive relationships. God's sweet spirit began to move among us.

When it was time to leave, I asked one of the women to close with a prayer. Every single word of her prayer was for me, for my family, for our needs.

Oh, Father, bless that woman for her great kindness.   —Julie Garmon

---

SAT
22

No one whose hope is in you will ever be put to shame. . . .

—Psalm 25:3 (NIV)

The heat in Alabama was oppressive. We'd gone eleven weeks without rain, and a break or a storm cloud wasn't anywhere in sight. I began to feel guilty about the gallons of water I poured on my potted tomato plants each week.

The plants were a gift from my father. His mother had grown tomatoes, then Dad and now me. The green thumb hadn't quite made it to my generation, but a love for growing things did, and I tended the plants daily. But they withered and drooped in the sun, and I knew I had to let them go and start again next season.

Days went by and it became too painful for me to go out on the back porch. The plants had been my connection back home, where my parents were tending to my grandmother, the very one born with a green thumb for tomatoes, who was in critical, failing health. During my morning walks I prayed for Grandma, who seemed to weaken by the day, and trained my eyes to avoid the view of my porch, where dry sticks stood in place of lush, leafy plants.

One day, after hearing that Grandma was back in the hospital, I felt as though my prayers were just floating away to deaf ears. Then something on the porch caught my eye—something red. *Surely not,* I thought. *It's been more than a week since I watered and the temperature has averaged 105 degrees!* But there amid brown stalks and crumpled leaves was a petite but perfectly round, red tomato.

Grandma pulled through just fine.

THANK YOU, LORD, FOR TEACHING A VERY THANKFUL GRANDDAUGHTER A VALU-
ABLE LESSON ABOUT FAITH AND HOPE. —ASHLEY JOHNSON

SUN
23

And Adam said, This is now bone of my bones,
and flesh of my flesh. . . . Therefore shall a
man leave his father and his mother, and shall
cleave unto his wife: and they shall be one flesh.
—GENESIS 2:23–24

We always make a big deal out of birthdays, anniversaries, graduations and holidays in our family. We think it's important to gather and celebrate. Last year on this date, the kids helped Shirley and me mark our fifty-fourth wedding anniversary. Oh, one other thing: We're particularly fond of homemade gifts.

I have a friend who is great with wood and makes beautiful samplers for special occasions. An artist I know expresses her wishes with little drawings. As one who has worked with words all his life, I try to write poems for my loved ones. Last year when Shirley and I celebrated our anniversary, one of my gifts was a verse I composed for my "Ever Luvin'."

> First you were lover extraordinaire
> Then you were wife beyond compare,
> Next, a mother whose children were blessed—
> Loved, nurtured, hugged and caressed.
> Now in your golden, grandmother years,

You laugh with your heirs, dry their tears,
And me, the husband, you still attend,
Sees not only lover, but closest friend.

With thanksgiving I echo that old chorus:

I REALLY THINK THAT GOD ABOVE
CREATED YOU FOR ME TO LOVE.

—FRED BAUER

As well the singers as the players on instruments
shall be there: all my springs are in thee.
—PSALM 87:7

It was a dreary Monday morning, sticky and overcast, a crummy way to start the week. Yet all of a sudden there he was, being swept up the escalator from Penn Station and virtually ejected onto the streets of Manhattan with the thousands of other morning commuters—men in sharp suits, women in no-nonsense heels, students shouldering bulging backpacks. And this guy, in a sequined jumpsuit, guitar slung over his back, mirrored sunglasses, carrying a conservative briefcase that could have been a lawyer's, was going to work like anyone else braving the daily throng, except that he looked like he just came from Graceland.

I have a friend, otherwise quite conventional, who is an Elvis freak. I never have to worry about what to get her for a present; anything Elvis will do. "Everyone loves Elvis," she says. Her mother does. So did her grandmother. Their family Christmas tree is dominated by Elvis ornaments. The children have Elvis lunch boxes. My friend even has a singing Elvis on her desk that croons and shimmies when it's turned on (I admit, a gift from me).

I wanted to run up to the commuter Elvis and ask him what it all meant, but he was soon swallowed up by the crowds on Seventh Avenue, a man with a job to do.

God gives us everything, so He must have given us Elvis and, by extension, Elvis imitators. Certainly He's given most of us a need for pop-culture heroes, people whose accomplishments we admire and celebrate, whose legends we somehow want to share in, if sometimes a bit obsessively. Through these icons people of all sorts connect; they derive a quirky exuberance from them. And that is a gift; that is grace.

PEOPLE, LORD, ARE FUNNY, BUT YOU KNOW THAT. LET ME ALWAYS FIND GRACE, QUIRKY AND OTHERWISE, IN EACH OF THEM. —EDWARD GRINNAN

"Listen and understand."
—MATTHEW 15:10 (NIV)

When the grown son of a friend of mine took his own life last year, I didn't know what I could say that would help her. I got an armload of books about grieving and chased down support groups on the Internet. Then I prayed about it and felt led to speak to Ellie, one of my coworkers who used to be a counselor.

I headed into her office and mentioned something I'd seen on her bulletin board—a Band-Aid in a beautiful oak frame, labeled "The Golden Band-Aid." "I don't want to take up your time," I said, "but I know you used to be a counselor, and . . . well, I see you have this Golden Band-Aid. Is that an award you got for knowing how to help people?"

To my astonishment, Ellie laughed. "No! It's a reminder to keep my mouth shut, even if I have to clap a Band-Aid over it! What do you think is the hardest thing a counselor has to learn?"

I shrugged.

"It's just to listen. That's our best and hardest job. And if there's some advice I feel I must give, that means I need to listen all the more!"

And so I listened to my friend. I heard about her son's first day at kindergarten and the time he stole a Mars bar and she marched him back to the store. I heard about the award he'd been given for citizenship in first grade. And much, much later, I listened in amazement as my friend told me how helpful I'd been. "You're the only one who sat with me as long as I needed it and listened. Everyone else wanted to fix me or get me through it."

I blushed, remembering how close I'd come to doing just that. And that's why I always keep a Band-Aid or two in my purse . . . to remind me just to listen.

GOD, HELP ME APPROACH PROBLEMS WITH AN OPEN MIND AND OPEN EARS, BUT NOT AN OPEN MOUTH. —LINDA NEUKRUG

Today if ye will hear his voice, Harden not your heart. . . .

—PSALM 95:7–8

I was working outside one summer day a few years ago when a ninety-foot-tall spruce tree suddenly fell to the forest floor. While pulling weeds among the tomato plants, I heard the loud, creaking, staccato sound of the sinews of a great tree rapidly separating from each other. Then, *Bang!*

The fall of that tree has puzzled me ever since. Why would it suddenly crash to the earth?

"Woodpeckers," my neighbor Bob said, when he walked by the following afternoon. "Got to be woodpeckers." But a glance at the fallen trunk, straight as a telephone pole, revealed no holes.

A month or so later I was telling another neighbor about my mysterious tree and he said simply, "Rot. Sometimes a tree rots from the inside out and you never know it until, *bam*, it falls."

Now, I don't know what makes trees rot from the inside out, but I think I have an idea of how it can happen to human beings. We can harden before falling over. Each of us requires love from others, caring for others, kind words and regular time spent quietly with our Creator in order to be whole. We need each other in more ways than we know, and my mysterious tree reminds me to attend to those needs in every way I can.

HOLY COUNSELOR, BRING PEOPLE INTO MY LIFE WHO WILL NEED ME, AND DON'T ALLOW ME TO MISS THE OPPORTUNITY OF SERVING THEM. —JON SWEENEY

They shall call on my name,
and I will hear them. . . .

—ZECHARIAH 13:9

On a warm summer night I lay in the dark in my apartment, grateful to be home after hip replacement surgery. Vaguely I heard my cat Sheila racing around the living room, and when she bounded into the bedroom, I wondered if I should turn on the light and check on what she was doing. Nope, I was too tired. But when I heard a thump and then a rustle, I reached over, clicked on the light and sat up. Sheila was on the floor at the foot of my bed, her paws holding tight to a shadowy form with velvet brown wings.

My heart skipped a beat. A bat. I like bats, they're interesting—from a distance. But up close and flapping around in my small city space when I was still fairly incapacitated? I groaned and eased myself out of bed.

The bat flapped its wings against the rug; the cat held it down with her paw, proud of bagging it. What to do? *Don't panic, take a deep breath, say a prayer: Dear God, help me get a grip.*

The gripper! At the hospital I'd been told I mustn't bend over, and I'd been given a metal tool to pick things up from the floor. It looked like a four-foot-long shoehorn with a kind of claw at the end. When you squeezed the top, metal fingers closed on the bottom.

I didn't really want to get close. *Think of Stellaluna,* a voice told me, *the gentle bat in the children's books.* I reached for the gripper on a nearby bookshelf. In one smooth stroke I pushed away the cat, gripped the stunned brown bat, limped my way to an open window and flung it out into the night, where it darted away.

A nature crisis in the big city, a fast but fervent prayer, and a sensible answer—yet again.

LORD, WHENEVER I SUDDENLY HAVE TO THINK CLEARLY, REMIND ME THAT A LITTLE PRAYER GOES A LONG WAY. —MARY ANN O'ROARK

Then he told them many things in parables,
saying: "A farmer went out to sow his seed."

—MATTHEW 13:3 (NIV)

Rosie and I both grew up in farm families, and we're accustomed to seeing things grow when planted. So late last spring we decided to create a small garden to grow a few tomatoes and collard greens.

The ground was harder than we thought, and I had to bring out a chair to rest in between intervals of digging. After we prepared the soil, we planted eight collard plants and two tomato plants. We thought that with proper fertilizing and watering, we could grow enough collards for quite a few meals.

I strategically planted the tomato plants about sixteen inches apart, but for some reason, I put a collard plant in between the tomatoes. As the tomatoes grew, they took over the entire space, and by midsummer they had choked out the collard plant. Jesus' parable of the sower came to mind: "Other seed fell among thorns, which grew up and choked the plants" (Matthew 13:7, NIV).

Sometimes good things in life can crowd out other good—or better—things. Having too many things on my to-do list or too many appointments on my schedule can keep me from enjoying the things that are really important. I have to make sure that I always have room to grow.

LORD, HELP ME TO BALANCE MY LIFE SO THAT THE GOOD ISN'T THE ENEMY OF THE BETTER.   —DOLPHUS WEARY

A time to rend, and a time to sew. . . .

—ECCLESIASTES 3:7

We just returned from my hometown in Nebraska where we attended the funeral of my brother's wife. They'd been married only eighteen months before her death from acute leukemia.

Don rarely shows his emotions, so I was surprised to see him drying his eyes on his handkerchief all through the service. Later, his eyes grew teary whenever he tried to talk about Doris.

Sometimes I think it would help, when we're hurting deeply, if we could do something explosive to get the pain out. I'm not advocating tearing one's clothes, as was the custom in Koheleth's day, but just some harmless physical action that could help relieve that bottled-up pain.

What I like about this passage in Ecclesiastes is that after the intensity of clothes-tearing, there is "a time to sew" (though I'd prefer the word *mend* because it suggests healing). Before Doris died, she said to Don, "Be happy please. Do it for me." So my prayer question today is, "How do you sew up a broken heart? How can I help my brother heal?"

A TIME TO EVERY
PURPOSE

The answer is short—HELP—but the medicine effective:

Hold *the torn cloth, the hurting one.*
Encourage *him to talk about his pain.*
Listen *with all your heart, soul and spirit.*
Pray *for his wholeness.*

LOVING FATHER, MAY I REMEMBER TO *H*OLD, *E*NCOURAGE, *L*ISTEN, *P*RAY.

—MARILYN MORGAN KING

SUN 30

> *I rejoiced with those who said to me,*
> *"Let us go to the house of the Lord."*
> —PSALM 122:1 (NIV)

Wearing matching T-shirts, we settled into our seats on the plane full of excitement. Several churches in Spain had sponsored a ten-day concert tour by our choir, and we were beyond thrilled. Yet by the time we stepped off the plane, excitement had given way to jet lag.

We arrived at the hotel, aching for a nap, but were told to get ready to sing for one of our host churches. We filed into the bus like zombies, unaware that this would be the pace for the rest of the trip.

"When are we going to sightsee?" I asked as I looked at our packed schedule. The outlook seemed bleak. Every day at the crack of dawn we would journey for hours to a small town. After sound checks and a long concert, we'd travel back to our living quarters and go to bed way after midnight. The hotel was thirty minutes from Barcelona, but it seemed as if we'd never have time to see the city.

Toward the end of the trip I reached the point of delirium. I was bored, sleep-deprived and sick of long bus rides with people as cranky as myself. All I wanted to do was bolt out of the bus and hail a cab to the nearest airport, but instead I sat there in tears of self-pity and disappointment.

Everything changed when we pulled up to one of our host churches. A little girl in a white dress jumped up and down and waved her hands wildly. "They're here!" she shouted as she celebrated our arrival. Her excitement over the gift of song we were about to bring lifted the heaviness I was feeling, and I remembered the real reason that I was in Spain: God had given us a mission to share His word through music. I was now more than happy to answer His call.

LORD, THANK YOU FOR THE REMINDER YOU GAVE ME THROUGH THE INFECTIOUS JOY OF ONE LITTLE GIRL. —KAREN VALENTIN

"Still other seed fell on good soil, where it produced a crop. . . ."
—MATTHEW 13:8 (NIV)

For the boys in our Scout troop, the thrill of being in the woods, the profusion of acorns and the abundance of interesting targets create an irresistible temptation. The first acorns fly as we hike along a ridge near our campsite. The boys suggest an all-out acorn war with their friends.

My stern words and appeals to reason bring about a ceasefire, but only until a boy with idle hands spies an acorn too plump to resist. "It doesn't matter if you *want* to be pummeled with acorns," I scold them, "it's dangerous!"

Cooking and eating dinner is an excellent distraction, but the Scouts not on dish duty secretly fill their pockets again. Plans for the reenactment of the Great Acorn War are made in whispers. When everyone is safely zipped into sleeping bags, all is quiet. Soon, though, the distinctive hiss of acorns against nylon tents and the muffled laughter of boys not quite ready for sleep jostle the adults awake.

The Scoutmaster confiscates the acorn arsenals, the boys apologize and silence settles in again. Gazing out my tent at those stars you never see in the city, I worry that our message of outdoor fun has been drowned out by the acorn controversy. Then the whispers begin again:

"Man, that hike was so cool! I could see all the way out over the valley—maybe we can explore down there tomorrow!" "Dude, did you see the size of that grasshopper on the trail? I think it was bigger than our Chihuahua! We should definitely go camping more often!"

Nature is speaking loudly, and the Scouts are listening. I smile and think that when the mighty oaks dropped those acorns, surely it was with the hope they might find their way away from the rocky ridge, whether carried by a bird or lobbed by a boy with a good pitching arm.

LORD, THOUGH ENTHUSIASM AND COMMON SENSE MAY SOMETIME SEEM AT ODDS, THANK YOU FOR THE BEAUTIFUL, COMPLEX WORLD IN WHICH THEY COEXIST.

—KJERSTIN WILLIAMS

MY LIVING WORDS

1

2

3

4

5

6

7

8

9

10

11

12

13

14

15

16

17

18

19

20

21

22

23

24

25

26

27

28

29

30

31

SEPTEMBER

*How sweet are thy words
unto my taste! yea, sweeter
than honey to my mouth!*

—PSALM 119:103

TUE
1

And the songs of the temple shall
be howlings in that day. . . .

—Amos 8:3

The worst culture shock of my lifetime has been the loss of my kind of church music. I was raised on the great hymns of faith, written by the best poets and musicians in the world. Now, happy hymns like "Love Lifted Me" and choruses like "It's Bubbling in My Soul" have given way to melancholy choruses that I find vague and hard to sing. Pianos and organs have been trumped by electric guitars and drums played so loudly that my bones buzz.

No, I don't like all the old hymns, nor do I dislike all the new music. Much of it is lovely. I'm just happy for the rich lyrics and melodies that drift through my mind from a childhood spent in church.

In the morning I find myself singing, "Some golden daybreak, Jesus will come. . . ." When the day gets hard, I'll be humming, "I need thee every hour, most gracious Lord." And when I'm too upset to sing, I'll think of the song that says, "And Jesus, listening, can hear the songs I cannot sing."

GOD SPEAKS
THROUGH MUSIC

One afternoon I was walking around town, thinking about doing something I shouldn't have (never mind what). At that very moment the neighborhood church bells began to play, "Savior, like a shepherd lead us . . . keep thy flock, from sin defend us, seek us when we go astray." With blurry eyes of repentance, I turned toward home.

Whether you prefer the old tunes or the new ones, music is a heavenly language that enables us to tune out the din around us. I recommend it for whatever ails you.

SAVIOR, LIKE A SHEPHERD LEAD ME, BECAUSE I TEND TO WANDER.

—DANIEL SCHANTZ

Trust in the Lord with all your heart,
and do not rely on your own insight.
In all your ways acknowledge him
and he will make straight your paths.

—PROVERBS 3:5–6 (NRSV)

My husband Charlie and I seldom fight, but when we do, it's usually devastating for both of us. We're just not very good at it. We usually end up drained and much more distressed about hurting each other than we were about the original problem.

A few months ago we were anxious about what appeared to be a looming crisis. My style in a situation like that is to plan obsessively for all contingencies so that we'll be ready for whatever disaster I imagine will strike. Charlie's way is to wait and see what happens, confident that he will be able to handle whatever occurs.

On this particular occasion we clashed big time. When, after an exhaustive review of the possibilities, I told him what I planned to do, he looked at me wearily and said, "You're not doing that."

Everything came to a screeching halt. The ensuing crisis had nothing to do with the one we'd been discussing. My determination to "worry about tomorrow" despite Jesus' warning (Matthew 6:34) ended up ruining an entire night, causing us both heartache and grief.

Oh, and that looming crisis? It never happened.

FATHER, FORGIVE ME FOR WORRYING. PLEASE LET THE PAINFUL LESSONS THAT YOU TEACH ME LEAD ME TO PEACE IN YOU.   —MARCI ALBORGHETTI

A friend loveth at all times, and
a brother is born for adversity.

—PROVERBS 17:17

Driving through a dense dark night by the ocean, I ask my oldest and dearest friend, "Hey, man, how're you doing?" He is quiet for a few minutes because he knows I mean the black dog, *Mr. D. Pression,* and he's an honest guy, and he wants to answer without lies. I wait, the ocean murmuring in my window as we zoom along.

"The tide isn't all the way out," he says finally. "I carry a piece of paper in my wallet with all the names of all the things I love. It's a really long list. The other day I got it laminated because it was getting messy. People must think I'm some kind of crackpot or lost and checking directions, because I pull it out all the time. But I sure need to read that map, you know?"

There's a long silence in the car after that, and then out in the ocean there's an incredible moaning bellow, really loud and long, a tanker or a barge or a ferry or something, and I say, "Man, that sounds like a whale passing a kidney stone or a lighthouse mooing." He and I start laughing, and the rest of the trip we laugh and tell stories, which is so often how we say the things we don't say.

I don't say what I want to say, which is that I love him, and I pray for joy in his heart, and I thank God for the shaggy humor and oceanic generosity and piercing intelligence of a friend I have had for more than thirty years. But the laughter and the stories are eloquent and articulate, and by the time we arrive at our destination he is laughing as I haven't heard him laugh in a year. There are so many ways to serve each other.

Dear Lord, I've never, not once, thanked You enough or properly for the astounding, amazing, incredible, invaluable gift of my friends. Without them, I would be lost and lonely and small. —Brian Doyle

---

FRI
4

The eternal God is thy refuge, and underneath are the everlasting arms. . . .
—Deuteronomy 33:27

One of the compromises the men in our family have made with their mother, my wife Kathy, has to do with our four-wheel-drive vacations. She'll bump along almost anywhere as long as there's a comfortable bed and a good dinner at the end of the day.

After eight hours of off-road driving, we were nearing Chelan, Washington. Early the next day we were going to take the ferry to Stehekin, a remote village at the far end of Lake Chelan.

"Mom, just one more loop off this trail." This was Cooper Mountain. Joel knew that because her maiden name was Cooper, his mother would probably cave in.

After consulting the trail map, we decided to take this last detour before driving the final miles to our destination.

The climb up the side of the mountain resembled a goat path. The mountain rose sharply on one side of the SUV and dropped away severely on the other, with switchbacks every few hundred feet up the barren ledge. A huge boulder blocked any hope we had of completing the loop. Only by the grace of God and answered prayer did we back down to the closest hairpin turn, where we spent the next half hour turning around, inches at a time.

I awoke early the next morning to get gas for the SUV; it was leaning seriously to one side. The front tire on the passenger side had been slashed by a sharp rock somewhere on the unmarked mountain trail. Now, whenever I hear the Scripture "underneath are the everlasting arms," I remember the day God cradled the Nace vehicle on Cooper Mountain.

THERE ARE NO WORDS TO THANK YOU SUFFICIENTLY FOR THE TIMES YOU HAVE CARRIED US, FATHER. NEVER LET ME STOP TRYING TO EXPRESS MY GRATITUDE.

—TED NACE

SAT
5

Therefore, as we have opportunity,
let us do good to all. . . .
—GALATIANS 6:10 (NKJV)

I stacked the breakfast dishes on my arm. As I turned to take them into the kitchen, I almost ran into Sarah, an adorable eight-year-old guest, who stood squeezing her cowboy hat with both hands. She looked at me with big blue eyes and timidly asked, "Can I see your baby mule?"

I winced. "We'll see. Maybe after dinner." I took her cowboy hat and settled it down on her head and said, "Now scoot."

Wind Dancer had been the hit of the guest ranch where I worked. Everyone had wanted to pet the baby—all the time—for the last couple of months. At first I loved showing off my little mule, but as the demands became overwhelming, I limited the visits to after dinner. Then a couple days ago I was in an accident and severely burned both my feet with a pan full of boiling grease. A large blister covered each foot. I wrapped and tucked them into a pair of oversized water shoes.

I balanced the dishes and slowly and painfully shuffled to the kitchen. *I'm tired of the baby thing, and I've got so much work to do. Besides, I just want to lie down and put up my feet. Why do I feel guilty?* Then I remembered horse-crazy me at Sarah's age.

Just before sunset I met Sarah and her mom at the pasture. I showed Sarah all of Wind Dancer's favorite spots to get scratched. When Wind Dancer expressed her gratitude by scrunching up her face and curling her lips, Sarah burst out laughing and I forgot about my feet. Every night for the rest of the week we met in the pasture.

When we said our good-byes, Sarah's mom said, "Your mule was the highlight of our whole vacation. Sarah will cherish these memories forever."

LORD, HELP ME TO PUT OTHERS FIRST, WHATEVER THE CIRCUMSTANCES.

—REBECCA ONDOV

SUN
6

"I will make you into a great nation and I will bless you; I will make your name great, and you will be a blessing."
—GENESIS 12:2 (NIV)

I've been a member of the Peale Center's Positive Thinkers Club for the last seventeen years. A few years back, Ruth Stafford Peale wrote about simplifying our lives. The first step in making that leap is to determine what is really important to each one of us. One way to accomplish this is to create a mission statement.

I'd been thinking about creating such a statement for a long while, but I had put it off. I'd toyed with a number of ideas, but they felt clumsy and wordy. When I'm stuck, what sometimes works best for me is to put things aside and let the Lord direct me.

It shouldn't come as any surprise, but I found the answer in my Bible. I was reading Genesis 12, where God makes His covenant with Abram. God tells Abram that He will make him into a great nation and that He will bless him. The last part of verse 2 was what caught my eye: "You will be a blessing." I read those words twice as they gripped hold of my heart. This was my mission statement, simple, profound and direct.

THANK YOU, HEAVENLY FATHER, FOR DIRECTING MY PATH AND SHOWING ME HOW YOU WANT ME TO LIVE. —DEBBIE MACOMBER

Thus says the Lord: "Keep your voice from weeping, and your eyes from tears; for your work shall be rewarded. . . ."

—JEREMIAH 31:16 (RSV)

It's difficult to find full-time work these days, particularly for someone my age. For four years, like many of my friends, I've had to cobble together multiple part-time jobs. Ironically, for all our hard work, we weren't getting our bills paid and our stress levels were high. Our discouragement was also high, for it was becoming increasingly clear that middle-aged women were being passed over for the younger generation with less skill but sharper presentation. *I need to find a job,* I told God, *where my abilities are seen instead of my age. Can You work on that?*

Last year I took a seasonal position at a company I'd worked for nearly ten years before. To my delight I discovered that Kay, my former trainer, was still there, working in a different department. I was even more pleased to find that her boss was my neighbor Lori. Even more surprising, many in the department were middle-aged.

One Saturday I was wrestling with the seeper hoses for my rose garden when Lori came along the trail that runs beside my house. "Hey, you," she called through the sweet peas. "Any chance you're looking for year-round work?" She needed someone who could write, teach and design, and Kay had talked me up.

I've been on the job a month. I love it! And though I still fret because the job offers no benefits or job security and pays only a part-time wage, I know God sees through it all and intervenes.

DEAR LORD, IN THESE TROUBLED TIMES IN A DOWNSIZING, PART-TIME WORLD, HELP US KEEP OUR FAITH IN YOU, KNOWING YOU NEVER OVERLOOK WHAT WE HAVE TO OFFER. —BRENDA WILBEE

Teach me thy way, O Lord;
I will walk in thy truth.

—PSALM 86:11

Seeing the neighborhood children walk toward the bus stop on this first day of school prompted me to pull out a notebook page on which I keep an A to Z list culled from my Bible. As a child I memorized many of the short sentences. The rest I intend to learn this fall. They're reminders of how I want to live out the Word by what I do, what I know and what I pray.

A Awake, awake; put on thy strength. . . . (Isaiah 52:1)

B Be ye kind. . . . (Ephesians 4:32)

C Create in me a clean heart, O God. . . . (Psalm 51:10)

D Do all to the glory of God. (I Corinthians 10:31)

E Every perfect gift is from above. . . . (James 1:17)

F Fear not: for I am with thee. . . . (Isaiah 43:5)

G Give us this day our daily bread. (Matthew 6:11)

H Hear my prayer, O God. . . . (Psalm 54:2)

I In the beginning God created. . . . (Genesis 1:1)

J Jesus himself drew near. . . . (Luke 24:15)

K Keep thy tongue from evil. . . . (Psalm 34:13)

L Let us love one another. . . . (I John 4:7)

M Mercy shall follow me all the days of my life. . . . (Psalm 23:6)

N Now is the day of salvation. (II Corinthians 6:2)

O O sing unto the Lord a new song. . . . (Psalm 98:1)

P Pray without ceasing. (I Thessalonians 5:17)

Q Quicken me, O Lord. . . . (Psalm 143:11)

R Rejoice in the Lord your God. . . . (Joel 2:23)

S Seek ye first the kingdom of God. . . . (Matthew 6:33)

T Trust in the Lord. . . . (Proverbs 3:5)

U Unto thee, O God, do we give thanks. . . . (Psalm 75:1)

V The very hairs of your head are all numbered. (Matthew 10:30)

W We are labourers together with God. . . . (I Corinthians 3:9)

X   Exercise thyself... unto godliness. (I Timothy 4:7)
Y   Yield yourselves unto the Lord. . . . (II Chronicles 30:8)
Z   Zion heard, and was glad. . . . (Psalm 97:8)

MASTER TEACHER, I WANT TO BE YOUR LIFELONG STUDENT.   —EVELYN BENCE

"Well done, good and faithful servant!
You have been faithful with a few things;
I will put you in charge of many things. . . ."

—MATTHEW 25:21 (NIV)

The delicate brown-haired waitress at the breakfast place seemed to blend in with the heavy white coffee mugs and plates of steaming pecan pancakes. I'd never paid much attention to her until the Saturday morning she commented on the novel I'd brought along to read.

"Wow! She followed a dream!" she said when she read the author's name.

"What's *your* dream?" I heard myself asking. The words were out of my mouth before I had a chance to ponder them.

It was as if the young waitress had been waiting to share her heart with someone for a very long time. Quickly I learned that her name was Anna, that her job waiting tables was one of three she held down in addition to attending college, and that she wanted to be a social worker and help children more than anything in the world.

WITH ETERNITY IN VIEW

Notice the People
in Your Path

I need to reach out to her, Lord,
but I don't know how. An idea began to form in my mind. *In my job at the hospital, I work with a dozen social workers. Why not arrange for Anna to meet one of them?*

When I related my proposal to Anna, she acted as if I'd just presented her with three weeks' paid vacation. "That's perfect!" she exclaimed. "I have a class where I'm supposed to interview a role model."

I thought of Jeanine, the consummate social worker, and how just last week she'd smoothed out every little detail so an elderly man could return home to die surrounded by his grandsons. Suddenly I couldn't wait to get Anna and Jeanine together. Something told me this was just the first of many steps in helping Anna reach her dream.

HELP ME, LORD, TO REACH OUT TO PEOPLE EVERYWHERE ON LIFE'S PATH.

—ROBERTA MESSNER

THU 10

. . . The simplicity that is in Christ.
—II CORINTHIANS 11:3

During my early morning walks I inevitably became bored as I huffed and puffed. A jogging friend explained that she fought the boredom by praying for her neighbors as she passed their homes.

Approaching Bobby and E.J.'s house the next morning, I asked God to do something simple for my friends of more than forty years. E.J. had been diagnosed with Alzheimer's and ALS (Lou Gehrig's disease). Bobby, his wife of almost fifty-seven years, cared for him at home with astounding love and patience. "Lord, give them laughter," I prayed. "Let E.J. remember something funny today."

Every morning as I passed their house, I prayed for Bobby and E.J. Then one day Bobby confided to me, "I just want him to go to heaven from our home, not some facility." It didn't look likely. Just to get E.J. to eat, Bobby had to feed him, one spoonful at a time. I wasn't sure how long she could handle it alone.

One day E.J. waved to me from their open front door, smiling. "Thank You, Lord," I prayed. "He's still at home. Content and kind—just much leaner." Early Easter morning, walking by their lovely brick home, I left a small basket filled with jelly beans. E.J. and I both adored them.

The sun was barely up one sultry summer morning when I passed Bobby and E.J.'s house, unable to think of what to pray for. Finally I said, "Lord, do something brand-new for E.J. today."

After I got home, I checked my phone messages. One had been left early that morning. "Marion, Bobby wanted you to know that

E.J. left this life from his beloved recliner in the bedroom around six thirty. She's okay, and she knows he is too."

FATHER, YOU STAND READY TO ANSWER EVEN THE SIMPLEST, MOST HURRIED PRAYERS IN YOUR MAGNIFICENT WAY! —MARION BOND WEST

Therefore Eli said unto Samuel, Go, lie down: and it shall be, if he call thee, that thou shalt say, Speak, Lord; for thy servant heareth. . . .
—I SAMUEL 3:9

Historians of the 9/11 tragedy will most certainly focus on the monstrous horror of that day, but there are also stories to be told that remind us that in a world of woeful words and deeds, courage, love and hope also exist; good can come out of evil; and even in the most negative circumstances, something positive can result.

Recently I heard about a Washington, DC, police officer who, with no regard for his own life, entered the Pentagon inferno and rescued a host of people. The man was Isaac Ho'opi'i, a native Hawaiian living in McLean, Virginia. According to newspaper accounts he helped eight people to safety (carrying several of the injured out of the carnage), then returned to the smoke and fire to guide others who were blinded and confused. "If you can hear me," he shouted, "head toward my voice!" Five crawled toward him and were saved.

If you can hear me, head toward my voice. Young Samuel heard God's voice and at Eli's prompting he answered. And as a result of Samuel's faithfulness, God used him in a mighty way: He helped establish the kingship of David and Saul.

I think that by learning to listen, His "still small voice" becomes clear. To act on His marching orders is the hard part. But by doing what He asks and going where He directs, we grow daily in spiritual understanding and wisdom.

WHEN A NEED REQUIRES IMMEDIATE ACTION,
GIVE US COURAGE, LORD, AND LOTS OF TRACTION.
—FRED BAUER

"Do not hinder them from coming to Me; for the kingdom of heaven belongs to such as these."

—MATTHEW 19:14 (NAS)

At the children's story time in the bookstore where I work, I'd been reading stories to pretty much the same group for some years, and now six or seven of my wee regulars would be heading off to kindergarten. Of course, they'd be having so much fun in school—and hearing so many stories—that they wouldn't be coming to hear me on weekends anymore. I'd miss them!

I was hesitant about facing a new group of cherubs. It always took a while for new children to get used to me. And how would they—and their parents—feel about story time? What if they never showed up? Even worse, what if they showed up once and then never again because they didn't like my storytelling?

Then Mai Lee came back from kindergarten to visit me. "We were passing the bookstore," her father said, "and she just had to come in to say hello."

"How's school?" I asked. She'd been very worried about starting "big school."

"I like it!"

"What's your teacher's name?"

"Mrs. Miller."

"Is she nice?"

"Yes." Then she added, "I have three friends! I play with them."

"Three friends? Already?" I said, surprised and happy for her. "What are their names?"

She looked puzzled, then shrugged. "I don't know."

Her father and I laughed, but I didn't miss the lesson. I had new friends too: the children and parents who'd be coming in to hear my stories. And even though I didn't know their names yet, I'd do just as well with them as Mai Lee was doing in kindergarten with her new friends.

GOD, TEACH ME THAT THE BUTTERFLIES IN MY STOMACH MEAN EXCITEMENT, NOT APPREHENSION, WHEN I'M STARTING SOMETHING NEW. —LINDA NEUKRUG

READER'S ROOM

God is so good, and He tells me every day how much He loves me, even when I feel unloved. The faith deep within me whispers, "I love you, My child." As I repeat this thought, my heart is overjoyed and tears come to me. Oh, how good is my God!

—Vicky Orlowski, Beaver Falls, Pennsylvania

SUN
13

For I have come to have much joy and comfort in your love. . . .

−PHILEMON 7 (NAS)

My mother tells a story about her younger brother Bob, as a child in the late 1920s, running to lock the front door when it was time for his beloved grandmother to leave. A tiny Norwegian lady who wore her white hair swept up in a bun, my great-grandmother's arrivals were highly anticipated by her grandchildren and her departures were deeply regretted.

No one has ever tried to lock me in to prevent me from leaving, but I also get chagrined end-of-visit reactions from my grandchildren. Sarah, three, disagreed when I announced I had to go. "No, Grandma, you do not have to go."

When my husband interrupted our play, three-year-old Clay, whose home is near ours, said, "No, Papa, Grandma can't go home yet. We're playing our game."

One time Caleb, five, rattled off his telephone number as I was leaving and said, "Maybe you can call my dad and he can give you a ride back here." A ride from Minnesota to Alaska is a long ride!

Hannah, seven, reminded me as I was dropped off at the airport, "When you love someone, they're in your heart forever."

Yes, they are. The love between grandparents and grandchildren is like the Old Testament story of the oil in the widowed woman's lamp: No matter how much is poured out, it stays full.

GOD OF THE GENERATIONS, WHETHER IT'S 1929 OR 2009, A GRANDPARENT'S LOVE SPREADS JOY AND COMFORT.

—CAROL KNAPP

This is the day which the Lord has made;
let us rejoice and be glad in it.

—PSALM 118:24 (RSV)

This year our golden retrievers Beau and Muffy had a litter of nine puppies. We kept two of the male pups and named them Bear and Buddy. They are now six months old and chewing up everything they can fit in their mouths.

This morning I awoke and looked out the window into our backyard. There were Bear and Buddy, side by side like bookends, gazing intently at a large oak tree. They were tracking a squirrel high in the shadowed branches. With their mouths open and their tongues hanging out, these young retrievers were beautiful and full of life. Their morning was filled with purpose and joy.

Sitting drowsily on the side of my bed, facing my own day, I heard the Psalmist whisper, "This is the day which the Lord has made; let us rejoice and be glad in it." I didn't feel as chipper and energetic as my two young pups, and I had more squirrels to chase than I could count. But I was reminded that gladness is a choice and that attitude is the key to happiness.

I looked again at those two gangly puppies and smiled. It was time for me to choose to be glad, to get up and take a shower, to walk outside and chase one squirrel at a time, to rejoice in the gift of another day of life.

FATHER, PLEASE TAKE THIS MATURE DOG AND TEACH HIM NEW TRICKS. HELP ME TO FEEL THE JOY OF MY SALVATION AND CHOOSE TO BE GLAD. AMEN.

—SCOTT WALKER

The Lord will fulfil his purpose for me. . . .

—PSALM 138:8 (RSV)

Do you ever feel that no matter how hard you pedal, you'll never catch up with life, and no matter how much you do, you'll always leave something undone?

I was feeling pretty much that way as I scurried through the house, looking for copies of *The New Yorker* to take to Claude O'Donnell. "Claude's birthday: buy socks, take magazines," my to-do list said. The drive to the extended-care facility where he was recovering would take a ridiculous chunk out of my day.

As I drove, I remembered Claude's reaction the year we gave him a cake. *What's a couple of more minutes?* I thought. I swung into the grocery parking lot and found a sugar-free apple pie. Claude was diabetic now.

Socks wrapped, pie in hand, I found Claude's room. I went in singing "Happy Birthday to You" in my off-key way. By the look on his face, I might have been Celine Dion.

Claude was in a wheelchair, but he insisted that we travel down the long corridor to the lounge area. I think he wanted people to see that someone had come for his birthday. So I played it up big, announcing his birthday and his accomplishments playing the viola with the Nashville symphony.

In my car, with no time to go back, I discovered the magazines.

For weeks the magazines rode around in my car, taunting me. One more thing undone. And then, out of the blue, came a call: Claude had suffered a massive stroke. He was gone.

Distraught, I went to the car and gathered the magazines, expecting also to find a heap of guilt. But the memory of Claude waving and smiling as he escorted me down the corridor sent a different message. *You made me the birthday king,* Claude seemed to say. *Let go of what you didn't do. Think about what you did!*

<small>FATHER, HELP ME TO ACCOMPLISH WHAT I CAN AND LET GO OF THE REST.</small>

—PAM KIDD

Except ye utter by the tongue words easy to be understood, how shall it be known what is spoken? . . .

—I CORINTHIANS 14:9

When my son Tom decided to trek Brazil for three months, my heart was in my mouth. No news was good news—or so I thought. He didn't tell me about the car wreck until he had been home for a week.

Apparently Tom, always a cautious driver, had driven his rental car into the left lane, signaling to make a left turn. The light changed and a driver whizzing past on his left broadsided him and spun the car. Tom wasn't injured, but since he had been speaking Portuguese for only three months, he couldn't make the police understand him. In fact, the other driver convinced officials that Tom had caused the accident. Though the insurance claim was still a tangle, I felt weak with relief that Tom had been spared serious harm in a foreign land.

A few months later Tom packed his aging pickup truck to move to graduate school in California. With the precision of a true scientist, he had constructed his itinerary with little wiggle room. I prayed for both his safety on the journey and his peace of mind. Tom was a stickler for schedules and chafed when they went awry.

All too soon after he had left, he phoned. Within 150 miles of home, his transmission had gasped its last breath. He had about 2,800 miles left to go, his carefully calculated schedule now useless. I felt myself bracing for a frustrated tirade. Instead, he talked casually about the tow truck driver who had brought him to a garage where the staff dropped what they were working on to help him. The crew had even directed him to a diner with home cooking.

Finally I ventured to ask Tom about his new schedule.

"Hey, Mom, not a problem. It will only be two days. Besides, these guys speak English!"

LORD OF THE JOURNEY, THANK YOU FOR THE BEAUTIFUL WAYS YOU BLESS MY CHILDREN AS THEY TRAVEL TOWARD MATURITY. —GAIL THORELL SCHILLING

THU
17

Now therefore ye are no more strangers and foreigners, but fellow-citizens with the saints, and of the household of God.
—EPHESIANS 2:19

My route to work takes me through New York City's Little Korea on West 32nd Street, roughly between Fifth and Sixth avenues. There are nail salons, super-modern teahouses, karaoke clubs, newsstands, hotels, twenty-four-hour BBQ restaurants (for Korean businesspeople traveling at all hours), and a couple of churches (South Koreans are predominantly Christian). The air is suffused with exotic aromas, and the street is crowded with groups of young, trendily dressed folks.

I have some Korean friends, and I was a little jealous when I learned that when many of them came to the United States they chose American first names to supplement their Korean ones. One woman chose Doris because she loved Doris Day movies.

On the other hand, my mother used to tell stories about how her father Jack Rossiter would go down to the docks in Philadelphia to meet the immigrant boats carrying the Irish to America. With brogues as thick as sod, some of them could barely make their names understood to the harried immigration agents who, for the sake of expediency, would sometimes rechristen whole families "Smith" or "Black." That's where Grandpop came in. He would wade through the throng and mediate. He did not like the idea of a family—especially an Irish family—losing its name.

We are having a national conversation about immigration that is sure to go on for some time, but I think we all agree that immigration, properly managed, is good for the country. After all, most of us are of immigrant stock, and our forebears came to these shores for the same reason people still come—to build better lives for themselves and their families, to participate in the great experiment of democracy, to worship God as they see fit, and even to change—or not—their names.

You bring us, Father, to this place of freedom and opportunity whose greatest gift is our freedom to worship You. —Edward Grinnan

---

FRI
18

As for God, his way is perfect. . . .
—II Samuel 22:31

Every year at the High Holidays, we're asked to reflect on our lives during the past year so that we can resolve to do better in the coming one. As I walked toward the synagogue for the first Rosh Hashanah service, it was hard not to think about all the medical and dental problems we'd had to deal with in the past twelve months. If there was anything I wanted to leave behind, it would have to be the messiness and chaos. I wanted a perfect next year.

I didn't think I was being unrealistic. Yes, I was going to services without my husband Keith, who'd had two teeth extracted that morning, but that was the last of the old year, after all, not the start of the new year. There was still a chance everything could be wonderful.

Ushers were handing out the special prayer books for the High Holiday services as we entered the sanctuary. I took a book without looking at it and found a seat with some other women. We chatted until the rabbi began speaking.

Then I looked at the prayer book I'd been handed. A large white label was pasted at the top of its cover. "The cover of this book is upside down," it read. For a moment I was just startled and then I began to laugh. The book was not put together right, but it still had all the prayers in it, and it was being useful, just like all the other books. And I accepted that the next year would be what it would be.

HELP ME TO STRIVE FOR WHAT PERFECTION I CAN, LORD, AND THEN HELP ME TO ACCEPT THAT YOU CAN TAKE CARE OF THE REST.   —RHODA BLECKER

SAT
19

"He who is faithful in a very little thing is faithful also in much. . . ."
—LUKE 16:10 (NAS)

This is the time of year when baseball gets exciting. The World Series looms and fans switch loyalties to the teams that still have a chance.

Columnist George F. Will once reported that there were 3,180 home runs hit during the 1988 professional baseball season. Seems like a lot, doesn't it? But that same year, 25,838 singles were hit. Eight times more singles than home runs. It makes sense, then, that more games are won by singles than homers.

I know one thing: When it comes to my life, I'm not a home run hitter; I'm a singles kind of gal. Sometimes I get discouraged because I don't accomplish great things. I won't be invited on *Oprah* because I haven't done anything truly spectacular. But life has taught me that if I accomplish little things here and there, those little things add up to a winning lifestyle.

I work in my home office, pay my bills, cook meals, invite friends over for dinner, clean out my desk, organize the arts-books-crafts fair for the clubhouse across the street, do a lot of swimming and biking for exercise and entertainment, redecorate a room, attend church, watch movies, go to plays, visit art shows, travel, do some volunteering, spend time with my family and friends. Little things day after day after day. Nothing spectacular, but joyful nonetheless.

Hitting singles is what I do best. And somehow, through all those single hits, my game of life is being won with great gusto and pure happiness.

HEAVENLY FATHER, ON THE DAYS WHEN I WISH MY LIFE WAS MORE EXCITING, HELP ME APPRECIATE MY SMALL DAILY ACCOMPLISHMENTS.   —PATRICIA LORENZ

"Six days you shall labor and do all your work, but the seventh day is a Sabbath to the Lord your God. . . ."

—EXODUS 20:9-10 (NIV)

After we graduated from college, four of my friends and I found jobs near Washington, DC, and rented a house together. We liked being employed—no more scraping together loose change to afford a pizza. But with the pickup soccer games of college replaced by sedentary desk jobs, several of my housemates began noticing burgeoning waistlines. I had just received my personal training certification, so I offered to design an exercise and diet plan for the house.

First, we bought used exercise equipment and converted our basement storage room into a gym. Then we replaced all the junk food in the refrigerator with fresh fruits and vegetables. We all started eating smaller, healthier meals.

After three months, we stepped back on the scales. Two roommates had lost nearly twenty pounds each, and all together we'd lost more than fifty!

What was our secret? Our diet included a "day off" when we could eat the foods we'd been craving all week—ice cream, soda, French fries. The day off made the other six days manageable because it provided a break from the discipline and stress involved in following a diet.

Thank God for the "day off" concept; He rested on the seventh day and His people have been doing the same ever since.

LORD, THANK YOU FOR THE DAY OF REST WE NEED TO OVERCOME THE CHALLENGES OF THE OTHER SIX DAYS EACH WEEK.   —JOSHUA SUNDQUIST

Behold, I will do a new thing;
now it shall spring forth. . . .

—Isaiah 43:19

Planning a college visit during our son Ross's senior year in high school, I made an interesting self-discovery. As I made flight and hotel reservations for Nashville, Tennessee, a city we'd never visited, I realized I couldn't remember the last time I'd been to a new place. Our family vacations are usually to Ohio to visit relatives or to the San Diego beach where my parents keep a condominium. My travel scenery looks very familiar.

But it's more than that: I saw other ways I'd fallen into comfortable ruts, from driving the same routes to the usual places in my daily schedule to ordering the same cheese bagel and iced tea each time I get together with friends at a neighborhood café. God has given me many gifts, but I guess a sense of adventure isn't one of them.

Still, thinking about all of the possibilities in God's creation made me determined to cultivate my sense of wonder—something as simple as asking myself, *Where does the road lead if I drive straight, leaving my neighborhood on the way to church, instead of always turning right? What will I see there?* The first time I took the new route, I discovered a small farm that I had never known about, with horses and goats and even a llama!

Opening up to the possibility of change brought a new feeling to my days. In fact, today, at age forty-six, I got my ears pierced for the first time, at my twelve-year-old daughter's urging.

See, I *can* do a new thing. Now I can't wait until tomorrow.

DEAR GOD, GIVE ME THE COURAGE TO TRY NEW THINGS AND SAMPLE MORE OF ALL YOUR INCREDIBLE CREATION HAS TO OFFER.   —GINA BRIDGEMAN

. . . A time to keep silence, and a time to speak.

—Ecclesiastes 3:7

When all of our family was at home, there were six of us plus our two dogs, and the noisy chaos often made it hard for me to pray. Then I read about Susanna Wesley, the mother of

John and Charles, who had a large family—nineteen children, ten of whom reached adulthood. When she wanted to pray, she'd pull her ample apron up over her head as a signal to her family, who would quiet down or leave the room.

So I made a little sign that read: Quiet please. Silent Prayer. I punched holes in the top corners and tied a string into them, so I could hang it over the door of the master bedroom. Then I'd go in, prop myself up in bed and drop into silence. After resting in the arms of the Holy Spirit, I'd be ready to listen to the family's problems and complaints, hear about the happy events of the day, and help harmonize any discord among them.

A Time to Every Purpose

So my question today is, "What causes that transformation to happen?"

Silence has its own magic.
When you let yourself fall into the vastness,
your soul is held and embraced by the Spirit,
and all of the day's tangles and wrinkles
are combed out and ironed to smoothness
so that your heart and soul and spirit
are tranquil and ready to speak
from that place deep
where the Wise One dwells within.

HOLY ONE, PLEASE HELP ME TO VALUE SILENT PRAYER ENOUGH TO MAKE TIME FOR IT, NO MATTER HOW CHAOTIC MY LIFE MIGHT BE. —MARILYN MORGAN KING

WED 23

Strengthen ye the weak hands,
and confirm the feeble knees.

—ISAIAH 35:3

Six years ago when I first started going to the gym, I turned to a couple of exercise magazines for guidance. They spelled out different routines for every week. *Okay, I'll give this a go,* I thought. Three sets on that machine, a few reps on this one. Crunches, push-ups, pull-ups. I went to the high bar to try the latter. "Two sets of ten," the magazine said. I grabbed the cold bar and dangled from it like a monkey. "One, two, three . . ." I grunted and groaned. After three and a half, I had to give up, dropping from the bar in defeat. "I can't do it!" I barked at the magazine with its glossy photos of incredibly sleek and impossibly toned models doing what I couldn't do.

I stayed away from pull-ups after that. But every once in a while I'd try to do just a few. And then maybe some more. On my jog through the park, I ran past a high bar in the playground. *Do a couple of pull-ups at the end of each loop*, I challenged myself. And even though I was older and not apparently in any better shape, I got in the practice of doing two sets of pull-ups every time I jogged. Somehow over the years the number of pull-ups in each set increased. Four, five, six, seven, eight. Finally it dawned on me that I could do eight pull-ups at once! Count 'em, eight of those impossible-to-do, don't-ask-me-to-try pull-ups. It makes me wonder how many other things I've told myself I simply can't do that I might be able to . . . even at *my* age.

I'll let you know when I get to ten.

LORD, GIVE ME THE PERSISTENCE AND DETERMINATION TO REACH GOALS I NEVER KNEW I COULD REACH.
—RICK HAMLIN

I lift up my eyes to the hills—where does my help come from? My help comes from the Lord, the Maker of heaven and earth.

—PSALM 121:1-2 (NIV)

Many years ago a friend shared her favorite tidbit of wisdom with my five-year-old son. "When in doubt, look up," she advised him. He immediately looked up at the sky. She smiled. "That's right, Christopher. If you're ever in doubt of what to do, just look up. The answer always comes when we remember to ask our Father in heaven."

A few weeks later I took Christopher to the county fair. We rode kiddy rides, visited the pens of farm animals and finished off the day with some cotton candy. Sunburned and exhausted, we made our way to the parking lot. I dug around in my purse for the car keys. After a few minutes of searching, I peered into the car; my keys were still in the ignition. "Oh no," I groaned, "we're locked out of the car! Now what?"

"When in doubt, look up," Christopher said.

"Not now, honey," I said. "I've got to figure out what to do."

"Mommy, when in doubt, look up," he repeated.

"Okay, honey," I sighed, "you're right. Let's pray." I took his hand in mine. "Lord, we're stranded here at the fairgrounds. Please help us find a solution to our problem. Amen."

Just then, we heard a loud roar overhead. It was a small biplane pulling a banner advertising a locksmith! I quickly wrote down the phone number. "Let's go find a pay phone!" I said.

A few hours later we were back in our car, headed home. I looked into my rearview mirror at Christopher buckled into his car seat, sound asleep. I said a prayer of thanks for this little boy, whose simple faith had led me to just the right answer.

LORD, MAY I ALWAYS REMEMBER TO LOOK UP TO YOU FOR THE ANSWERS IN MY LIFE.
—MELODY BONNETTE

FRI
25

"Is not this the kind of fasting I have chosen . . . to share your food with the hungry and to provide the poor wanderer with shelter. . . ?"
—ISAIAH 58:6–7 (NIV)

My daughter Lanea works for the city of Durham, North Carolina, as part of a two-person team on a project called the Ten-Year Plan to End Homelessness.

It's been a hot, dry summer and early fall in North Carolina. The entire state has been under a severe drought. In the midst of it, Lanea has sweated, working on a one-day event called Project Homeless Connect to cut red tape and make services available to some of our most needy citizens.

She has been planning, meeting, cajoling, coordinating and talking about the event even in her sleep. "It's so big, Mama. There's so much need," she tells me. I can see that she feels overwhelmed and responsible for everything. As the day draws closer, I can see the telltale signs of stress, but she has worked with the team to secure volunteers, social workers, doctors and services from public and private organizations. Everything that could be done has been done. What could go wrong?

The night before the event, after months of drought, it begins to rain. The next morning it's still drizzling. We pray. "Well, we have tents," she smiles, trying to sound optimistic as she heads out the front door.

When she walks back in the door in the evening, she is glowing. "We fed hundreds of people, Mama! They came in the rain. We handed out toiletries and clothes. There were showers for people and flu shots. There were lines of people to see the doctors and lawyers and to apply for housing and jobs. The barbers and the pet groomers were really big hits!"

I am so proud of my daughter.

LORD, HELP ME TO SERVE YOU IN THE WAY THAT YOU DESIRE. —SHARON FOSTER

Moses listened to his father-in-law and did everything he said.
—EXODUS 18:24 (NIV)

I awoke before dawn one morning, tired and frustrated from a persistent cold. My wife offered some loving medical advice, which I grumpily ignored. Then I stomped outside to feed the dogs and heard an elk bugle. I quickly herded the dogs back to their pen, grabbed my binoculars and my flutophone, and began hiking to a ridge north of our house.

A flutophone is a plastic imitation of a flute, barely more sophisticated than a kazoo. The bugle of a mature bull elk is magnificent, spans several octaves and can be heard for miles. I can coax two squeaky octaves from my flutophone and the resulting sound wouldn't fool any elk, not even a young one with hearing disabilities. But for one or two weeks in September, a bull elk is so full of rage and jealousy that he would probably charge a car if the driver honked the horn.

I watched the bull cross the Animas River, run toward my ridge and bugle a loud challenge when he arrived in the trees below me. The herd of cow elk that followed him sensed my presence and bolted before ever coming out from the trees. The huge bull ignored their advice and stomped into the open from behind a stand of juniper trees. Had I been a hunter, his boldness would have cost him his life.

I watched the elk awhile and then turned back to the house. It was time to do something about that cold.

DEAR GOD, PLEASE HELP ME TO ACCEPT ADVICE FROM THOSE WHO LOVE ME, ESPECIALLY WHEN I NEED IT THE MOST. —TIM WILLIAMS

Come near to God and he will come near to you. . . .
—JAMES 4:8 (NIV)

I'd been out of town for several days, so it had been a while since I'd seen my three-year-old grandson Drake. Now he and I were at my kitchen table, late in the afternoon, eating apple slices. Since I only have two chairs at my table, we were sitting across from each other.

Drake paused as he reached for an apple. "I want to sit there." He pointed across the table to the place nearest me.

"Oh no, sweetie, you're fine where you are," I said. "Besides, there's no chair there."

Without hesitation, Drake climbed down and with great care and effort moved his heavy chair to my side of the table. Now our elbows were almost touching. Drake didn't say a word. He just munched loudly on his apple slice and smiled. Being near me—really near me—was important to Drake.

I thought about that when I read my Bible that night. *I want to be nearer to God.* I closed my eyes and pictured myself climbing down out of my chair and into the arms of my heavenly Father. *Let's talk about how to make this happen more often,* He said. And I resolved to listen closely.

DRAW ME NEARER, NEARER, NEARER, PRECIOUS LORD! —MARY LOU CARNEY

They . . . went without food all day
as a sign of sorrow for their sins. . . .
—I SAMUEL 7:6 (TLB)

Today is Yom Kippur, the Day of Atonement and the culmination of the ten Days of Awe of the Jewish new year. A week ago I asked one of my Jewish friends to join me for lunch, and when she told me she wouldn't be available until after Yom Kippur, it led her to explain these holy days of her faith.

"This is the time when we search our souls and try to find ways to better obey God's commandments. We repent of our sins and ask forgiveness from those we have offended."

"Do you fast on Yom Kippur?" I asked.

"Not only from food but even from water." There was a pause at her end of the phone. "It's so we can better focus spiritually and also show ourselves that if we can discipline ourselves this way, we can control other things in our lives that may be leading us away from God."

I was impressed. It had been a long time since I'd taken a day for fasting and prayer. I decided that quietly, in my own way, I'd make Yom Kippur an opportunity to search *my* soul.

IN THOUGHT, WORD AND DEED, FOR ALL MY TRANSGRESSIONS, FORGIVE ME, LORD JESUS, MY REDEEMER. CREATE IN ME A CLEAN HEART AND STRENGTHEN MY RESOLVE TO MORE CLOSELY FOLLOW YOUR COMMANDMENTS.   —FAY ANGUS

Dear friends, I am not writing a new
commandment, for it is an old one you have
always had, right from the beginning. This
commandment—to love one another—is the same
message you heard before. Yet it is also new. . . .
—I JOHN 2:7–8 (NLT)

The other day I watched brightly dressed children exiting a yellow school bus. They reminded me of autumn leaves, blowing down the street and then swirling into clusters. I particularly noted one "leaf": a boy standing alone.

He reminded me of a classmate back during my grade-school years.

Amazingly, after all this time, his name, *Vernon*, remains tattooed on my memory. Another mental picture surfaced: playground games. The "in" kids were chosen first, but Vernon never garnered a spot on anyone's side. At least, not until he was the only one left. And when we all filed back in, following recess, the line invariably gaped where Vernon stood.

At least, I didn't avoid him, I told myself. But my conscience reminded me, *You weren't brave enough to buck the crowd either. Even at that age, you were well aware that befriending him risked your own social status!*

I shrugged off my uneasiness by reasoning, *Children can be cruel and thoughtless,* and was startled when my conscience replied, *So can adults.*

I then remembered that just the day before a stranger had hesitantly come into the church foyer alone. I didn't really avoid the woman, you understand, but did I welcome her? No, I was too busy with the brightly dressed others in the "in" group.

LORD, PUT INTO MY HEART THE RIGHT THING TO DO AND THEN GIVE ME THE STRENGTH AND THE "WANT TO" TO DO IT. —ISABEL WOLSELEY

Editor's Note: Last year, as John Sherrill's wife Elizabeth (Tib) pulled into a downward-sloping parking space at a store near their home and put her foot on the brake, the pedal shot to the floor. Her fifteen-year-old car smashed into a wall and came to a hissing stop. "No one was hurt, that's the main thing," says John. But the right front fender of her car was caved in, the headlight smashed, the bumper dented, the passenger door sprung.

Because Tib loved "Old Red," John spent days trying to determine the repairs needed to make the car safe to drive again. For the next six days in "Lessons from an Automobile," John shows us how the experience had surprising parallels in his spiritual life.

How long will it be ere they believe me, for all the signs which I have shewed among them?
—NUMBERS 14:11

Tib was on the phone, her voice shaky with shock. "I've had an accident. I'm okay, but the car hit a wall."

Half an hour later we were following a tow truck down the highway toward the dealership. The service manager quickly discovered the problem: The car had lost its brake fluid.

"Brake fluid?" asked Tib, who likes to know as little as possible about the inner workings of machinery.

Early automobiles, the manager told her, had steel cables running from the brake pedal back to pads on the rear wheels. When the cables tightened around the pads, the car slowed. "Today," he went on, "your foot pressure is sent to the wheels by a viscous fluid. That's what leaked out of your car. Chances are there was a yellow stain on the garage floor. That's your car trying to tell you there's trouble ahead."

LESSONS FROM AN AUTOMOBILE

Warning Signs

We left Old Red at the dealership while its computers examined the car for further problems. *A yellow stain*, I thought that night, *was a warning signal. Does God give us signals, too, warnings of hidden spiritual dangers?*

I get furious when someone honks at me as a traffic light changes. Am I really that incensed at somebody's bad manners or am I angry at something else, something deeper that I should pay attention to? My stomach churns as inflation eats away our retirement savings; have I stopped trusting God's provision? I feel put upon by a long wait at the dentist's; is this the sin of self-importance?

If an automobile can warn of trouble ahead, how much more must our heavenly Father try to warn us of dangers to the spirit.

MAKE ME ALERT, FATHER, TO THE DANGER SIGNALS THAT COME FROM YOU.

—JOHN SHERRILL

MY LIVING WORDS

1 _____

2 _____

3

4

5

6

7

8

9

10

11

12

13

14

15

16

17

18

19

20

21

22

23

24

25

26

27

28

29

30

OCTOBER

*I wait for the Lord,
my soul doth wait,
and in his word do I hope.*

—PSALM 130:5

THU
1

But Jesus withdrew himself. . . .
—MARK 3:7

Even before the accident, Tib occasionally had trouble starting Old Red. Now the dealership called to say the computer indicated that the starter was wearing out. The price for a new one: five hundred dollars! I was dismayed—until I remembered Alf. When I was ten, back in 1933, I looked forward to Alf's visits. This balding, stubble-faced man helped my father with the heaviest digging on the small farm Dad had bought so we could grow vegetables during the Depression.

You could hear Alf coming well before his kerosene-fired Tin Lizzie sputtered up the farm's gravel drive. When it was time to leave, Alf always had to fight to get the car started. He used a hand crank, which, if the engine misfired as it often did, could kick backward and break an arm. How often I heard Alf lament, "Oh, if only I had one of them starter things!"—usually muttered just before his car finally coughed into life and he drove away in a cloud of blue black exhaust.

There are two ways I can get myself started. One is by hand crank—my own efforts. Those are the days when I get up in the morning and begin immediately to "accomplish" things. When I do this, I've noticed, the day is often filled with pressure, tension, poor timing.

LESSONS FROM AN
AUTOMOBILE

The Starter

On the other hand, I can begin the day by finding a quiet corner—the porch in good weather, the living room when it's raw outside—and writing out a prayer, a conversation between myself and God. This dialogue time acts as a sort of internal starter, built right into the functioning of my whole system. Even with my kerosene-fired old body, it gets me going on my day with ease and joy.

FATHER, HELP ME REMEMBER THAT I GET STARTED BEST WHEN I START WITH YOU.

—JOHN SHERRILL

There is a time . . . for every work.
—ECCLESIASTES 3:17

The computer revealed another problem with my wife Tib's car. "Your timing belt is cracking," the service man told me. A timing belt, he explained when I looked blank, makes the spark plugs fire at the right moment.

Immediately I was back on the farm again, now age twelve. Dad's birthday was coming up, and I knew what I wanted to give him. Dad had bought a big, old, secondhand mower, a self-propelled monster that had lately been running rough. "Needs cleaning and oiling," he said. I'd surprise him by doing the job myself!

Alone on the farm one morning, I set about taking the mower apart. Laying out a sheet on the shed floor, I carefully put down each piece in exactly the order I'd taken it out, reversing the sequence as I put them back together, shining and sleek. Late that afternoon, imagining Dad's amazed delight, I jerked on the lanyard. The machine coughed and wheezed, but start it would not.

It was then I heard our car coming up the drive. Dad walked over to where I stood next to the silent mower.

"Looks like we'll have to call a mechanic," he said. It was one of his better fathering moments.

The mechanic was complimentary: "Pretty good job for a twelve-year-old." I'd done everything right except for one detail. He pointed to two small chisel marks, one on the flywheel and one on its casing. "Those have to be lined up exactly or your timing will be off," he said. "Timing is everything. If your timing is off, the machine just isn't going to run."

LESSONS FROM AN AUTOMOBILE

The Timing Belt

Timing is everything indeed! When I rush into a situation too fast or when I procrastinate until an opportunity has passed, it's because I've failed to listen to the still, small voice whisper, *Now!*

HELP ME LISTEN FOR YOUR PERFECT TIMING, LORD, IN ALL THAT I SAY AND DO THIS DAY.
—JOHN SHERRILL

<table>
<tr><td>

SAT

3

</td><td>

"He took our infirmities and bore our diseases."

—MATTHEW 8:17 (RSV)

At the dealership they replaced the brake fluid and put in a new starter.

</td></tr>
</table>

Before racking up further expenses, it was time to get the bad news about the cost of repairs to the body. They gave me the address of a shop they used.

I found Marcello's Auto Body Shop on a dead-end street. As I pulled into the lot, a man in his thirties came out, wiping grease from his hands and introducing himself as the owner. Marcello looked at the crumpled

LESSONS FROM AN
AUTOMOBILE

The Impact Absorber

front end, then raised Old Red's hood—metal screeching against metal. "Looks like the impact absorber's shot."

I'd heard of shock absorbers but not impact absorbers. "A shock absorber," Marcello explained, "smoothes out the little bumps of a ride. An impact absorber cushions a crash."

Tib and I have a whole repertory of little shock absorbers in our lives: a daily walk, a scheduled time to look at priorities, an end-of-the-workday backgammon game, a division of labor to ensure that each of us has time off. I like to cook; Tib makes arrangements for all the travel we must do. These habits smooth out the daily ride.

When a "crash" occurs, though—an operation, a crisis with one of our children, an accident—then the impact absorber comes into play. When the situation is too big to handle by ourselves, we turn to a circle of praying friends, counting on Jesus' promise that where two or three are gathered in His name, He Himself is among them. It's Jesus Who absorbs the impact of the crashes in every life that would otherwise overwhelm us.

MAY I LEARN TO TURN TO YOU QUICKLY, LORD JESUS, IN CRISES I NEED NEVER HANDLE ALONE. —JOHN SHERRILL

SUN 4

Thou . . . hast redeemed us . . . out of every kindred, and tongue, and people, and nation.

—REVELATION 5:9

Marcello's estimate of the cost of repairs came to more than the book value of the car. So began the always daunting task of visiting dealers' showrooms. We'd look for an American car, we decided, thinking of the layoffs in Detroit.

American? Each car had a "Country of Origin" sticker on the side window, specifying where the components had been made: United States, Canada, Japan, United Kingdom, Korea, Mexico, China, Germany. There are some 3,800 parts in a modern automobile, one salesman told us, coming today from everywhere under the sun.

Not long ago Tib and I were researching a story in the mountainous Basque country between France and Spain. Among the undecipherable Basque words on the bulletin board of the small Protestant church next to our hotel in Pamplona, one phrase was given in English too: "World Communion Sunday."

During that service Tib and I understood not a word. The singing, though, was magnificent! The man next to me was off-pitch, but never mind—his enthusiasm was contagious. I recognized the melody of the Communion hymn, "Let Us Break Bread Together," and joined in with my neighbor, each of us

LESSONS FROM AN AUTOMOBILE

The Country of Origin Sticker

singing lustily in his own language. As the tray of tiny cups was passed along our pew, he lifted one and served me.

Outwardly, everything was different from services in our Episcopal church back home. Yet, just as the Country of Origin stickers indicate that it takes the whole world to turn out a car, so the Body of Christ reveals itself, in experiences like this, as a whole made up of members from every corner of the globe.

Leaving the little church, I remembered Jesus' prayer to His Father "that they may be one, even as we are one" (John 17:22).

JESUS, HELP ME TO CELEBRATE THE GREAT DIVERSITY OF YOUR FOLLOWERS, EACH ONE OF US NECESSARY TO MAKE UP YOUR WHOLE AND UNDIVIDED BODY.

—JOHN SHERRILL

MON
5

"It is sacred, and you are to consider it sacred."

—Exodus 30:32 (NIV)

We were driving to Marcello's body shop in Tib's "new" car. The price tags on the showroom models we'd looked at were so astronomical that she'd settled on this four-year-old white one. She liked it fine, but she missed Old Red, and I knew why.

For Tib an automobile is not a thing; it's a very personal place retaining something of the people it has carried and the events it has taken her to: driving kids to ball games, going to a wedding, taking her mother to the hospital, filling the trunk with groceries for a family Thanksgiving. When we go on a trip, we use car time as a place to discuss stories, pray, play word-games.

LESSONS FROM AN
AUTOMOBILE

The "New" Car

Now we were going to Marcello's to pick up Old Red and dispose of it in some way or other. There on the lot stood her beloved car. And next to it, to our surprise, was Marcello himself, pointing out something under the raised hood to an older man.

Marcello saw us and straightened up. "This is my dad," he said. "Dad's always wanted one of these, and always a red one. I was wondering if you'd sell it to me. Let me fix it up for him?"

Half an hour later, paperwork underway, we were again in Tib's white car, leaving the lot. "I'll always be grateful," she said, "for the look on the face of Marcello's dad when we agreed. I think he's going to love Old Red as much as I did!"

And with those words I could see that already her new car was becoming for Tib one of her places; her happiness for Old Red was entering the very fabric of the new car. Then and there we started to fill Young White with praise.

GIVE ME THE GRACE, FATHER, TO SANCTIFY OUR EVERYDAY TIMES AND EVERYDAY PLACES.

—JOHN SHERRILL

TUE
6

By the sadness of the countenance
the heart is made better.

—ECCLESIASTES 7:3

In my later forties I first noticed the losses of middle age: the loss of energy and looks; the empty nest; the loss of friends and dreams; problems with my feet and knees, my eyes and teeth.

I pretended these losses just didn't matter, but they did. One day I went to the dentist about a problem tooth. He worked on it awhile, then said, "I'm sorry, but I can't save this tooth."

"That's okay," I said nonchalantly, "teeth don't last forever." He extracted it; I paid the nurse and headed out the door. It was a beautiful day, and there is no greater feeling than that of leaving the dentist's office. I was whistling as I walked briskly to the car.

Suddenly, I felt moisture on my left cheek. I looked up to see if there were rainclouds, but there weren't. Then I realized

GOD SPEAKS
THROUGH OUR LOSSES

that I was crying—crying over the loss of a tooth. It was the tipping point.

I managed to make it to the car before I broke down. I sat there in the front seat, like a little boy sitting on his father's lap, seeking comfort. Like getting the first olive out of the bottle, the loss of my tooth enabled me to extract all my other griefs and to present them to God.

When at last I regained my composure, I felt a hundred pounds lighter. That cry was probably worth a year's therapy.

Now when I experience a loss, I go to God first, instead of waiting until my load is so heavy that it interferes with my happiness.

THANK YOU FOR NOT LEAVING ME, GOD, WHEN OTHER THINGS ARE GOING AWAY.

—DANIEL SCHANTZ

WED
7

Love one another earnestly from the heart.

—I PETER 1:22 (RSV)

I'm a Southerner. I make mean cheese grits, have an iron skillet reserved exclusively for corn bread and will happily spend half a day picking blackberries for a cobbler with a life span of three minutes.

For some, the South has a bad reputation. A few years ago I was involved in a political campaign where the opposing camp, lacking anything bad to say about my candidate, attacked him for having a Southern drawl. Amazingly, that was right here in Nashville, Tennessee, and it worked!

Good thing I'm not set on running for office, since I've been accused of turning *pie* into a three-syllable word. But I don't mind my accent. For me, it's just one more thing to love about the South.

Here we still say "please" and "excuse me" and our words lack sharp corners. We talk a lot about tomato plants in the summer and find time to catch lightning bugs and take night walks. In the winter, snow is still scarce enough to close the schools and keep us home from work. We make snow cream and hot chocolate from scratch.

We still pull over to the side of the road when a funeral procession passes. We love porches and being neighborly. We teach our children to call their elders Miss Linda and Mr. Bob. We take chicken soup to sick friends.

Every section of our country and every nook and cranny of our world has its own defining characteristics. God made us different, not to divide us, but to delight us. Kindness isn't regional; it doesn't matter whether we say "y'all" or "youse guys" or *"tus individuos."* He's made our hearts multilingual, and that's one more thing to love about being alive!

Father, help us to delight in our differences and love one another as You have asked. —Pam Kidd

---

THU
8

But there is a spirit in man, And the breath of the Almighty gives him understanding.
—Job 32:8 (NKJV)

I pulled my red and gray pickup off I-90 onto the Reserve Street exit. I hadn't been to Missoula, Montana, in a year, but today I had to come. There was an urgency inside me: I planned on buying some doorknobs for my kitchen cupboards, which had been knobless for more than six years.

I pulled into a gas station, jumped out and pulled a copy of the local classified paper out of the rack. I was on a tight schedule and planned only to buy knobs and immediately drive home. Instead, I bought a diet cola, sat in a booth and paged through the ads in the paper. Tucked away in the horse-and-tack section was an ad for a Tennessee Walker mare. My heart skipped a beat. I'd been looking for another horse for two years. *Lord, is this the one?*

Within a half hour I was riding a majestic black horse whose tail was so long it swept the ground. I knew she was mine, so I signed the papers and a check.

I didn't have time to shop for doorknobs. But I knew now that the urgency I'd felt wasn't about them. It was God's Spirit getting me where I needed to be, and He used the knobs to do it.

Lord, thank You for leading me where I need to go.   —Rebecca Ondov

---

FRI
9

He provides food for those who fear him;
he remembers his covenant forever.

—Psalm 111:5 (NIV)

As a gymnastics coach I'm constantly lifting mats, moving equipment and helping children as they swing, climb and somersault through the air. When my husband and I found out I was pregnant, I asked the doctor about the potential dangers at work. "You don't have to worry right now," she'd said, "but the bigger you get, the more risk you'll have for back problems."

I thought about leaving my job after my fifth month of pregnancy, but I was worried about our financial stability. "We'll be fine," my husband assured me, but I still had my doubts.

During a weekly Bible study, I explained my situation as we went around the room, sharing prayer requests. "I've never had to depend on someone else to take care of me," I admitted. "What if it's not enough?"

Aliza, an older woman in the group, smiled at me and shook her head. "God is your provider. He always has been." She wrapped my hands in her own. "You can't depend on yourself or your husband. God will take care of your family, and it will always be enough."

After her encouraging words I made a decision to leave after the fall semester. I didn't know how everything would work out, but I knew I could trust in the One Who had always taken care of me.

Then, just weeks after I gave my notice, I received an e-mail: A company was interested in some work I'd done years before. They wanted to give me a contract at three times the usual rate!

When I calculated the income and the amount of time I'd be out of work, it was more than enough. I thanked the Lord, not just for the financial blessing and peace of mind, but for confirming Aliza's words so quickly.

LORD, YOU ARE MY PROVIDER. YOU HAVE ALWAYS TAKEN CARE OF ME, AND IT WILL ALWAYS BE ENOUGH.   —KAREN VALENTIN

May the Lord cause you to increase and abound in love for one another. . . .
—I THESSALONIANS 3:12 (NAS)

I'd been feeling left out of my own family. Our daughters, in their twenties, were out on their own, and Thomas, our sixteen-year-old son, preferred his father's company to mine. If Thomas and his dad weren't playing basketball or baseball or fishing, they were talking about sports.

Thomas and I had been close when he was little; he loved to go to the library with me. But books weren't important to him anymore.

One Saturday night I peeked through the den window and saw them at it again—playing basketball. Thomas had grown a tad taller and a bit quicker than his dad. I decided to go outside and watch. Opening a lawn chair, I sat down under the lights.

"Want to play, Mom?" Thomas asked. He made a difficult-looking shot.

"You *really* want me to?"

"Yeah, let's see what you've got."

The coolness of the evening and the feel of the basketball in my hands took me back to when I was a teenager. After supper, my dad and I would shoot baskets in the driveway. I never played organized sports, but for those few minutes we were a team—Daddy and me. He's in heaven now, but under the stars with my husband and son, I remembered our sweet time together.

My long-lost dribbling rhythm returned that night, and I even made a few baskets. The guys *ooh*ed and *aah*ed, but something bigger happened: I rediscovered the common ground I had shared with my father and now shared with my almost grown-up son.

FATHER, CONTINUE TO SHOW ME HOW TO CONNECT WITH THOSE I LOVE.

—JULIE GARMON

Jesus said to him, "If you want to be perfect, go, sell what you have and give to the poor, and you will have treasure in heaven; and come, follow Me." But when the young man heard that saying, he went away sorrowful, for he had great possessions.

—MATTHEW 19:21–22 (NKJV)

Jim came to me feeling anxious. He was raised in a wonderful home and had offered his life to Christ. Yet he felt God wouldn't listen to him. He was baffled.

I remembered feeling as Jim did. Then someone had pointed me to the story of Jesus and the rich young man. "The story tells us that Jesus wasn't primarily interested in what we do to 'be good,' but whether we put God first. Anything other than God that we put first, when we make our decisions, that is our real god."

Jesus asked the rich man first to give everything to the poor. The young man could not do that and left sorrowfully. He already had a god: his wealth.

I told Jim about the rich young man and how I realized Jesus was saying to me, *Keith, you can't follow me as a disciple, because you already have a god that you obey when the chips are down. To follow me in the way I taught, I must be the one that you obey.*

I wrestled quite a while before I could finally say, "Okay, God, I surrender my whole life to you, including the secret gods I've been hiding. I love You more than these."

LORD, THANK YOU FOR SHOWING ME THAT EVEN THE GOOD THINGS IN LIFE WILL BE RUINED IF I PUT THEM BEFORE YOU AND MAKE THEM RESPONSIBLE FOR MY HAPPINESS. AMEN. —KEITH MILLER

. . . Beyond measure astonished. . . .

—MARK 7:37

My husband Gene adores the ducks that come and go on the lake a couple of doors down from our house. For seventeen years he's left cracked corn for them, talking to them as if they understand him. "Hi, guys. Here's breakfast!" he says, and many of them come to meet him, squawking gratefully.

A few years ago we fell in love with an odd couple at the lake. The female duck had a twisted bill from which a bit of her tongue protruded. The male seemed quite protective of her. Then we noticed that the female had a wounded leg. One of the large turtles in the lake had bitten her. We'd seen this happen to other ducks; the wound becomes infected, and as the infection spreads, the desperate mate stays close until the end.

We could see enough to determine that the female's leg was indeed infected. When she stopped eating, her mate did too. Our hearts broke for the doomed pair. The day the female disappeared, her mate swam alone on the quiet lake. Finally, he, too, disappeared.

On a summer day when we were walking past the lake, I confessed, "I prayed so hard, Gene. I asked God to heal the infection."

"Me too," he said softly.

One Monday morning in October, Gene came rushing into the house shouting, "They're back! Come and see!"

Not believing him, I hurried to the lake. Sure enough, there they were—the female with her twisted mouth and protruding tongue and her devoted mate. They waited at the old feeding spot. Gene appeared, running down the hill with a large sack of cracked corn, calling out ecstatically, "Here, guys! Here's breakfast! Here I come!"

HELP ME, HOLY SPIRIT, TO BELIEVE, ESPECIALLY WHEN THERE'S NO REASON TO.

—MARION BOND WEST

READER'S ROOM

I have a twelve-year-old daughter, an only child. When I read the piece by Julia Attaway about writing down encouraging notes in a book for each of her daughters, I decided to give this a try. My daughter and I are both into arts and crafts, so the book became more like a scrapbook, with pictures, stickers and notes. My daughter just loves flipping through the book. I feel like I'm giving her a little piece of me to carry with her always. It helps me see the positives as she moves into her teenage years, and it also reminds her how much she is loved. And even more, it has brought us closer to God. —*Diane Francis, Keizer, Oregon*

| TUE |
| 13 |

Wisdom and knowledge shall be the stability of thy times, and strength of salvation. . . .
—ISAIAH 33:6

It's six weeks into school, and friends and neighbors are asking, "How are the kids adapting?" No matter how many times I'm asked the question, I pause. It's hard to articulate how different life is after eight years of homeschooling.

"I think they're all doing well," I begin slowly.

Academically, this is true. It's also true that the teachers are full of compliments about how well the children fit in. Yet something feels vaguely amiss, and I've been struggling to put my finger on it. Partly it's our new schedule. In the mad morning rush to get lunches packed and hair brushed, and to find the shoe or homework that's not where it's supposed to be, there isn't time to savor one another. There's a whole lot of Martha and too little Mary in our lives right now. I haven't quite figured out how to get our day focused before we're all out the door.

There's also a sense of dislocation now that everyone is centered in a different place. At 6:45 AM, Elizabeth heads off to high school. John's bus arrives at 7:30 AM to take him to the Bronx, and then the no-longer-little girls, Mary and Maggie, begin their trek up to the church school with Stephen and me. It feels as if we're scattered about on different paths, when we used to be companions throughout the day. The children miss being with one another. They miss spending time with me. I miss them.

I know by faith that God is with us in our new schedule as much as He was in the old. But we Attaways are used to recognizing His presence in familiar routines that no longer fit on the daily agenda. Part of what's new this year is finding other ways to spend time with the Lord. We're learning to seek Him where we are, even if we're not in the usual places.

LORD, HELP ME DISTINGUISH BETWEEN WHAT'S UNCOMFORTABLE BECAUSE IT'S DIFFERENT AND WHAT'S UNCOMFORTABLE BECAUSE IT'S NOT YOUR WILL.

—JULIA ATTAWAY

Command them to do good, to be rich in good deeds, and to be generous and willing to share.
—I TIMOTHY 6:18 (NIV)

I love tomatoes. So when my wife Carol decided to plant cherry tomatoes along the sunny side of our garage last spring, I was all for it. She purchased three little plants and some wire cages to protect their growth and set to work.

Then one day a couple of weeks later, she came in from her garden, exclaiming, "You won't believe this, but we have tomato plants coming up all over the place!" Sure enough, the plot alongside the garage had sprouted nearly a dozen "volunteers," plants that had sprung from the seeds of last year's crop. We hadn't known about them because we had only moved into the house in January.

By midsummer the plants were spilling out over the walkway. Tomatoes, all of them of the cherry variety, began dragging down the plants and even tipping the wire cages. Soon we were eating tomatoes in salads, with sandwiches or just as snacks almost every day.

"We can't eat all these!" Carol said one day, setting another batch on the kitchen counter, and as much as I love tomatoes, I had to agree. "Let's give some to the neighbors," she said.

In the following weeks we gave bags full of cherry tomatoes to neighbors on both sides of us and to those across and down the street. Everyone welcomed us and happily accepted them. Smiles and thanks were just as profuse as the tomatoes. "I love taking them to work to have for lunch," said our next-door neighbor. "They're delicious!"

Right now we're still eating cherry tomatoes, even though the first frost has already killed the plants. A batch of green tomatoes continues to ripen on the kitchen counter. What a harvest we've enjoyed—and I don't mean only tomatoes!

FATHER, THANK YOU FOR THE ABUNDANCE YOU'VE ALLOWED US TO SHARE.

—HAROLD HOSTETLER

Love is patient, love is kind. . . .
—I CORINTHIANS 13:4 (NAS)

I can set my watch by their calls. No sooner have I snuggled under my warm quilt with a book than the phone begins its relentless ring: dinnertime telemarketers hawking subscriptions to magazines I've never heard of, property in Florida, a new Internet service.

"I'm not interested," I hear myself snarl into the telephone. I don't know this person who is suddenly impatient and inconsiderate.

But then a friend took a job as a telemarketer. His job was to query homeowners about remodeling projects they'd undertaken in the past year. For this father of

WITH ETERNITY IN VIEW

Be Patient

three small children, telemarketing was a way to put food on the family table. He took his job seriously, exceeding his quotas with pride.

Suddenly, telemarketing wore a face—Aaron's face, a face with a smile and a big dimple. "So many people cut you off on the phone," he told me. "It's like you're not a real person with a real job because you're a telemarketer."

Listening to Aaron, I could sense God speaking to my heart. *The next time the phone rings at five thirty in the evening, put a face with the words, Roberta: the face of a single mother trying to scrape together a little extra money for Christmas, a college student struggling to pay for tuition.*

When a telemarketer with a chipper voice called this week to try to interest me in insurance, I declined, explaining that I already had all the policies I can use. But as I complimented her boundless enthusiasm, I could hear the appreciation in her voice. "Thanks for being so nice," she said. "It's been a long evening already."

I'M SO, SO GLAD, LORD, THAT ON CALVARY YOU LOOKED AHEAD IN TIME AND SAW MY FACE.   —ROBERTA MESSNER

That their hearts might be comforted, being knit together in love. . . .
—COLOSSIANS 2:2

My mother knew how to do Aran knitting, the unbelievably complicated combination of stitches that creates diamonds, knots and twists of yarn. Imagine twenty-four rows, each with different instructions and no margin of error—even one wrong stitch destroys the whole sequence. I've been knitting sweaters for Guideposts Knit for Kids for more than twelve years, but I've never even attempted the advanced Aran pattern. My good friend Ellen wrote this wonderful set of instructions, but I knew they were much too hard for me.

But somehow there was a connection in my heart between this craft and my mother, apparently effortlessly creating sweater after spectacular Aran sweater for every member of the family. How did she learn it? Why did she knit so faithfully for us all? There were no soft words of love from this difficult lady, but did we realize we were all wearing outward and visible signs of her inward and spiritual affection?

Every time I saw a fisherman's sweater in a catalog, I felt the tug of those memories. So one peaceful day last year I found myself on a porch, looking out toward the Blue Ridge Mountains of Virginia, with a sheet of instructions on my lap. I'd decided to attempt an Aran sweater for a child, unknown and faraway. Four times I started, and four times I looked at the lopsided lines of stitches full of strange holes, unraveled the whole thing and started over.

It took me almost a week, but on the fifth attempt I managed a respectable little dark green sweater complete with diamonds and cables.

As I held it in my hands, I felt I had finally, after many false starts, knitted a bond with my mother that I never achieved in her lifetime. Did she see my struggles and feel my woolen outreach? I think so.

LORD, WITH THE WORK OF MY FINGERS MAY I WEAVE TOGETHER MEMORIES OF THE PAST AND HOPE FOR THE FUTURE. —BRIGITTE WEEKS

The ways of man are before the eyes of the Lord. . . .
—PROVERBS 5:21

I was at Michigan Stadium, cheering for my beloved Wolverines. My sister and I were on our annual pilgrimage to Ann Arbor for a football game. This year it was against highly ranked Notre Dame, extra incentive to cheer my team on.

The first half was tight, and as halftime arrived my voice was getting hoarse. I decided to brave the hordes and get a soda. I inched my way down the long, narrow bench with painted-on numbers that passes as a row of seats in the "Big House" and was about to squeeze into the aisle when a hand shot out and tugged at the elbow of my maize and blue sweatshirt.

"You're Edward from *Guideposts*," said a woman.

"We recognized you from your picture in the magazine," chimed in a man I presumed to be her husband.

How incredible that in a crowd of 111,000 screaming fans, this couple had picked me out. A little startling too. I normally try to be on my best behavior, but I have to admit that sometimes things slip out of my mouth at a Michigan game that ordinarily wouldn't and shouldn't.

The couple was from Ohio. They happened to be driving across the country and a pair of tickets to the game fell into their hands. "We decided it would be an exciting way to start the journey, and here we are meeting the editor of our favorite magazine," the woman explained.

We chatted for a while, and I returned to my seat where I turned to my sister and asked, "I didn't say anything I shouldn't have during the first half, did I?"

Mary Lou laughed. "No, you were fine."

Enthusiasm is a good thing, and I have it when it comes to Michigan football. But I've also got to remember to behave myself. You never know who might be watching.

GOD, WE'RE ALWAYS VISIBLE TO YOU. LET THE LOVE OF CHRIST SHOW FORTH IN ALL MY WORDS AND DEEDS, EVEN IN THE HEAT OF WOLVERINE FOOTBALL AT THE BIG HOUSE. —EDWARD GRINNAN

If . . . you seek the Lord your God, you will find him if you look for him. . . .
—DEUTERONOMY 4:29 (NIV)

My four-year-old son is busy. He climbs on furniture, has trouble sitting still for more than five seconds and runs everywhere.

Most of the time I don't mind Trace's activity, but when he wiggles and giggles and squirms during church, I lose my patience. Not only does he talk nonstop to anyone who dares to sit next to us, but he also dances during hymns and stands on the pew and says, "Amen!" as loudly as he can. I worry constantly that he is distracting the other worshippers. "Church is a time for quiet reflection," I whisper.

One Sunday our pastor asked Trace if he'd be willing to light the candles during the opening prayer. I was about to decline (picturing candle wax dripping down the aisle) when Trace said, "Please, Mommy, I know I can do it." He looked so excited that I didn't have the heart to say no.

The candles got lit. But it took two trips because Trace walked so fast the first time that the flame on the candlelighter went out. And he managed to get everyone laughing when he skipped back to his seat. *That's the last time I let him do that,* I thought.

Three days later I was getting the mail when I noticed a card addressed to Trace from Nancy, a member of our church. "Dear Trace," it said, "Thank you for the wonderful job you did helping your church family last Sunday. We all love the joy and enthusiasm you bring. You are a blessing."

DEAR LORD, HELP ME TO REMEMBER THERE IS A PLACE FOR ALL OF US IN YOUR FAMILY. —AMANDA BOROZINSKI

MON 19

If we love one another, God dwelleth in us, and his love is perfected in us.

—I JOHN 4:12

One of the gifts that I've received this year is to learn about the life of St. Thérèse of Lisieux (1873–1897). Thérèse was a young French Carmelite nun. Suffering from tuberculosis, she never left her convent after the age of sixteen and died at twenty-four. Despite the brevity of her life, she is considered by many to be, with St. Francis of Assisi, the most beloved of saints.

As a sickly young woman Thérèse's world was limited and confined. Yet in the midst of her limitations, she developed a rule for living called "the little way." Simply put, you cannot always choose your circumstances or the company that surrounds you. But you can choose to love each person with whom you come into contact each day. As Michael Novak explains, Thérèse of Lisieux believed that "no matter what spiritual darkness you find yourself in, choose as your North Star a tender love for the persons that life's contingencies have put next to you."

For the last few months I've tried to make Thérèse's "little way" my guiding star. Whenever I feel frustrated, limited or overwhelmed, I simply try to love the person closest to me. I'm amazed at the huge difference this "little way" has made in my life.

LORD, HELP ME ALWAYS TO LOVE THE PERSON YOU'VE PUT NEXT TO ME. AMEN.

—SCOTT WALKER

TUE 20

I will tell of all your wonders.

—PSALM 9:1 (NIV)

My daughter Kendall recently took up painting and immediately became smitten with her new hobby. She watched classes on TV and covered canvas after canvas with mountains and rivers and trees and cloudy blue skies. When she came to visit, she sometimes brought her paints.

"You've got to try it, Mom!" she urged enthusiastically.

"I can't!" I told her just as emphatically.

"Why not?"

"Because . . . ," I sputtered, searching for the right reason, "because a blank canvas scares me."

A few days later I watched my five-year-old granddaughter sitting at our kitchen counter, a crayon in her hand, gleefully filling blank white pages with stick figures, houses, flowers and pointy-edged suns. Obviously, blank pages didn't scare her; they represented endless possibilities.

When in the process of growing up did I lose that ability to create without fear of the results? When did self-confidence get replaced by self-consciousness?

Those are questions I can't answer, but this I know: I don't want to grow so far "up" that I get fearful of trying something new, regardless of the results. So the next time Kendall brought over her box of paints and her easel and several blank canvases, I didn't say, "I can't." Instead, I picked up a brush and began dabbing some color onto a blank canvas.

The result? Well, let's just say Grandma Moses would have nothing to worry about from me. But I'm ready to try another painting, and that feels pretty good.

LORD, HELP ME TO SEE THE POSSIBILITIES IN ALL THE BLANK CANVASES IN MY LIFE.

—CAROL KUYKENDALL

Many waters cannot quench love, neither can the floods drown it. . . .

—SONG OF SOLOMON 8:7

For six months this past year, our twenty-year-old son William was far away. I mean really far away. He did a semester of college in Melbourne, Australia. That's twenty-some hours of flying and fourteen time zones away! If he called us during the evening, it was late morning the next day for him! Yet he did call and e-mail us, the messages arriving instantly. I thought back to my college travel days when the only way to call home was to go to the post office of a foreign city, pay a hefty sum and have an operator put you through. You had to holler to be heard—"My flight has been changed to Tuesday!"—across the Atlantic with waves of static rolling through the wires. But with William, we signed up for a service that wasn't expensive at all, and it was as if he was in the next room.

"What's that?" I would say, hearing a birdcall. *Some exotic Australian budgie?*

"I'm outside, Dad," he would say. "It's a beautiful day." Outside on a day that hadn't even gotten to us, talking on his cell phone.

But the best part was to hear the excitement in his voice about the koala bears in the eucalyptus trees, the kangaroo that kicked him, the nighttime sky in the outback, the game of footie (a sort of Australian football) he played with his classmates on a day that was spring for him, autumn for us. He wanted us to know that he was doing okay—better than okay—and I felt reassured that thousands of miles couldn't separate me from a love that's always there.

"Love you," I said, signing off.

"Love you too," he said.

Some amazing things aren't so newfangled after all.

THANK YOU, LORD, FOR THE LOVE—AND TECHNOLOGY—THAT KEEPS MY LOVED ONES CLOSE.   —RICK HAMLIN

Kind words are like honey— enjoyable and healthful.

—PROVERBS 16:24 (TLB)

Several years ago I was car-shopping via the newspaper classifieds when a black-bordered display ad caught my attention.

> TOMORROW IS MY 60TH BIRTHDAY.
> I LIVE ALONE AND WOULD
> LOVE TO CELEBRATE WITH
> CALLS FROM PEOPLE OF ALL AGES.

I cut out the notice. I prayed that the woman would have a happy birthday and receive lots of nice calls. I picked up the telephone three times. But I didn't dial the number to say, "Happy Birthday!"

I had occasion to remember that ad on my birthday last year. Why? Because only my daughter Rebecca wished me a happy day. My husband

Don's midmorning e-mail to my office didn't count. "Sorry I forgot your birthday," it read, "but I got you a card." Translated (as only someone married forty-plus years can do), that meant he'd made a quick trip to the dollar store.

At sixty-plus I'm old enough to understand that forgetting my birthday is trivial compared to the love and kindness with which my family and friends typically surround me. I hope I'm also old enough to understand that every opportunity to brighten another person's day is a gift from God.

LORD, NEXT TIME—EVERY TIME—GIVE ME THE COURAGE AND COURTESY TO SPEAK WORDS OF LOVE AND CHEER TO ONE OF YOUR LONELY CHILDREN.

—PENNEY SCHWAB

FRI 23

He found him in a desert land, and in the waste howling wilderness; he led him about, he instructed him, he kept him as the apple of his eye.
—DEUTERONOMY 32:10

At some point—let's say 4:37 AM—the phone will ring; it won't be a wrong number. Or maybe it'll be a knock on the door or a telegram. The receptionist will say, "The doctor will see you now." A baby will arrive, wet and crying. Or your daughter will wed and you'll be crying. It'll happen. And for the millionth time you'll muster your resources—and for the millionth time they'll assemble: family, friends, people . . . until one day when they won't.

For some sudden reason you're alone. Who knows why? Bad timing, bad luck—but the folks you counted on aren't there. No malice aforethought; they just couldn't make it.

You're alone, utterly. But you're not utterly alone. Every prophet, every pauper has taken this journey—forty days in the desert or forty years.

But that's not the end of it. All of these lonely, painful journeys share something else: shedding your old self. Not only shedding the usual suspects (possessions, prepossessions, presumptions), but shedding your old way of thinking. Maybe your friends didn't abandon you; maybe they're on their own journey and you were too tired to lift your head to notice.

Maybe you think you cannot—*can not*—soldier on. Yet here you are, reading this, soldiering on against all odds.

And maybe that's where you find God—in the desert, in this new life that has emerged unasked, against all odds. And maybe that's grace, showing up unsolicited at 4:53 AM, carrying solace and holiness and redemption like a small precious child.

LORD, I SEE YOU NOW, IN THE REARVIEW MIRROR, TRACING MY WAYWARD TRACKS THROUGH THE DESERT. AND NOW THAT THE DUST HAS SETTLED IN FRONT OF ME, I HAVE SOME IDEA OF WHERE I'M GOING. AGAINST ALL ODDS. AMEN.

—MARK COLLINS

Editor's Note: Monday, November 23, one month from today, is Guideposts' fifteenth annual Thanksgiving Day of Prayer. Please plan to join all the members of our Guideposts family in prayer on this very special day. Send your prayer requests (and a picture, if you can) to Guideposts Prayer Fellowship, PO Box 8001, Pawling, NY 12564.

After this I looked, and there was a great multitude that no one could count, from every nation, from all tribes and peoples and languages, standing before the throne and before the Lamb. . . .

—REVELATION 7:9 (NRSV)

I work for and belong to the denomination that used to be known as the Dutch Reformed Church. Our first church in this country was started in 1628 in a little settlement known as New Amsterdam, at the mouth of a river named after Dutch explorer Henry Hudson. That church? Marble Collegiate in New York City, the one Dr. Norman Vincent Peale served for half a century.

The *Dutch* came out of the name Dutch Reformed Church two centuries ago. So imagine my surprise when a colleague said, "Yep, went to a Sunday worship service in Dutch yesterday."

"Where?" I asked, imagining a small, rural church, an oasis of tradition far from our rapidly changing society.

He smiled. "Brooklyn," he said. "New York City."

I've since visited that congregation, and they look nothing like any Dutch-speaking congregation I've ever known. That's because it's an immigrant church from a Caribbean island where Dutch is still spoken— descendants of African slaves speaking the original language of that first New Amsterdam church and of my own forebears.

Maybe it's fitting that both the original Dutch church and this new one are only miles from New York City's United Nations building. Because on this day designated as United Nations Day, I find myself thinking about all those immigrants who have made not just New York City but so many of our communities seem like a little United Nations, and what I can do in the places where I live and work to promote the United Nation's stated purpose: "To live together in peace with one another as good neighbors."

Maybe that even means learning Dutch!

IN WHATEVER LANGUAGE, GOD, MAY OUR LOVE FOR YOU GROW AS QUICKLY AS YOUR CHURCH DOES THROUGHOUT THE WORLD. —JEFF JAPINGA

And God said, Behold, I have given you every herb bearing seed, which is upon the face of all the earth, and every tree, in which is the fruit of the tree yielding seed. . . .

—GENESIS 1:29

I've taught a children's Sunday school class for several years now. Because our congregation is small, all the children, ranging in ages from four to twelve, come to my class. Lately I've been wondering if I should turn the class over to someone younger than I am. Maybe someone else could do a better job.

Recently I took a brown paper bag to Sunday school and held it up for the children to see.

"I've got one of God's great miracles inside this bag," I said.

When I pulled out a big red apple and placed it on the table, one child asked skeptically, "That's a miracle?"

"Yes," I said. "Just watch."

I carefully cut the core out of the apple and extracted eight black seeds. Spreading the seeds out before them, I said, "Each of these seeds contains an apple tree."

"No way," another child said.

"Yes, way," I said. "God has created His own special computer program inside each seed that tells it how to become a tree. Eight seeds, eight trees inside this one apple. And each of those eight trees has the ability to grow thousands of apples during its lifetime. All of that inside this apple."

"Wow!" exclaimed a third child. "That *is* a miracle!"

When the children left the class that day, one of them said, "You're a good teacher."

Maybe I'll hang in there a little longer.

DEAR LORD, I WANT TO SERVE YOU IN THE BEST WAY I CAN. PLEASE MAKE ME AWARE TODAY OF YOUR WILL FOR MY LIFE, AND GIVE ME THE WISDOM AND COURAGE TO FOLLOW THROUGH.   —MADGE HARRAH

MON 26

> *Have salt in yourselves, and have peace one with another.*
> —MARK 9:50

Tony works behind the counter in one of our neighborhood luncheonettes. I usually say hello to him when I order my morning coffee, but he never does anything but grunt. So after a while I gave up and ignored him, placing my order with one of the other employees.

But I felt bad about giving Tony the cold shoulder. It seemed clear to me that God wants us to be neighborly toward everyone we meet, whether we like them or not. So one day I gathered up my courage, went over to Tony and said, "Good morning."

No response.

"How's it going?"

Grunt.

"You know, Tony, you make great coffee."

Grunt.

So I decided to go for broke.

"In fact, you make the best coffee in town. If it weren't for you, I'd switch to tea."

That did the trick. Tony turned to me, laughing, and said thanks. It didn't cost me anything, and I earned not only that smile but a friendly nod every time I go into the café. Don't get me wrong. Tony is still grumpy and we still don't talk much. I don't like him any more now than I did before. But something's opened between us—a chink for God's light to shine through.

FATHER, TEACH ME TO TREAT ALL THE PEOPLE I MEET AS MEMBERS OF ONE FAMILY THROUGH YOUR LOVE. —PHILIP ZALESKI

"Be strong, and let us be courageous for the sake of our people, and for the cities of our God; and may the Lord do what seems good to him."

—II SAMUEL 10:12 (NRSV)

Twelve turkeys walked into my yard one late October afternoon and began nibbling on something in the abandoned garden. If you've never seen a wild turkey, imagine something much taller and skinnier than a Butterball. I've never picked one up, but they must weigh five or six times as much as my house cat.

My cat happened to be outside when the turkeys emerged from the woods. I watched her stealthily approach the birds and then burst in among them. I think she was expecting scared flight, but instead, four of them quickly turned and pecked at the top of kitty's head. Bushy-tailed and still looking tough, she turned her back only slightly, one eye fixed steadily in the birds' direction, took three slow steps and then quickly ran under the porch.

I know how she feels. I'm tall and fairly big (bigger than I should be!), and my voice tends toward the deep end. But when I'm faced with having to be courageous, I've often fallen short. Kitty and I, we're not very different.

In traffic the other day, I accidentally cut off a young man who was speeding up to get in front of another car. He was clearly upset with me, making his feelings known in a variety of ways familiar to the frequent commuter. There are times when I might have shrunk away from the situation entirely. But this time I looked at the man, put my palms together in a gesture of blessing I'd seen from Archbishop Desmond Tutu and mouthed the words, "I'm sorry." He paused and gave me a thumbs-up sign.

Maybe that's what courage really looks like.

HEAVENLY FATHER, ALL GOOD THINGS COME FROM YOU. PLEASE GIVE ME THE GIFT OF COURAGE TODAY.   —JON SWEENEY

WED 28

. . . A time of war, and a time of peace.
—ECCLESIASTES 3:8

I've always believed that God's will is for peace on earth.

Yet as I write this, there are wars going on in many places around the world. Sons and daughters, brothers and sisters, fathers and mothers are being killed every day, and when I watch the news, my heart aches for them and for their families.

I recently heard a speaker say, "Only about ten percent of the soldiers in World War II actually aimed their shots at people. Most of them just shot in the enemy's direction. So the army started using dummies as targets on the rifle range to get soldiers used to shooting at other human beings."

A TIME TO EVERY PURPOSE

So I ask the stinging question that's in my heart: "Why? Why must we keep fighting wars when we have an inborn sense that it's wrong?" Yet no clear answer comes. Instead, out of the sacred silence I hear:

Some hard questions are shrouded in mystery
too deep for human minds to understand;
the hidden answers aren't meant to be unlocked
until the soul is ready to see life whole.
Every good thing has its shadow
and every dark night is the back side
of a new day waiting to dawn.

FATHER OF ALL GREAT MYSTERIES, I'LL TRUST YOUR BALANCING GRACE AND CONTINUE, STILL, TO PRAY FOR PEACE. AMEN.   —MARILYN MORGAN KING

> *And now, brethren, I commend you*
> *to God, and to the word of his grace,*
> *which is able to build you up. . . .*
> —ACTS 20:32

It had been a trying week, and things were not going well. Both Maggie and Stephen had had bad dreams the night before, and not even a few cups of strong coffee had been able to wash the cobwebs from my eyes. We'd been going through many changes at work; increased rounds of meetings had disturbed my usual routine and it wasn't easy to get back into it. And I'd just passed one of those birthdays with a nine in it, and I was feeling every bit my age.

Given the circumstances, it's no wonder that I started revving up the self-pity. By the time I'd finished answering the morning's e-mail, I was feeling thoroughly sorry for myself. Then I took some papers into my colleague Stephanie's office.

Stephanie sat at her desk, surrounded by open Bibles, pencil in hand, checking the Scripture verses on a batch of devotionals. She looked up at me, smiled and said, "What a blessing to be able to spend time working with Scripture!"

I smiled back at her, left the folder in her in-box and went back to my office. I looked around. On the right side of my desk was a row of Bibles—KJV, NIV, NAS, NKJV, ESV, RSV. In the bookcase to my left were concordances, Bible dictionaries and a dozen other reference books. Not a day goes by at my job when I don't open a Bible to look up a reference or find an appropriate verse for a devotional or a book project. Not a day goes by without a reader or writer sending an inspiring story or sharing a prayer. It doesn't matter how many meetings I have to go to or how many forms I have to fill out; I'm blessed—more blessed than I can ever deserve.

Thank you, Stephanie, for the reminder!

LORD, THANK YOU FOR BLESSINGS—FAMILY, WORK, GOOD FRIENDS AND THE BEAUTY OF YOUR WORD.   —ANDREW ATTAWAY

FRI

30

*"I will give you the treasures of darkness
And hidden wealth of secret places. . . ."*

—Isaiah 45:3 (NAS)

The people of Plum Coulee, Manitoba, dream big—so big they could foresee a future for the tall grain elevator that towered over their little village. For decades the elevator had been a central collection point for local farmers, who each autumn hauled their truckloads of grain into its holding bins, awaiting shipment by rail to distant points. But now, like many "prairie sentinels" of its kind, the elevator was facing demolition.

The local heritage committee wanted to turn the elevator into a tourist attraction. There was just one problem: money.

The company that owned the elevator was cooperative, agreeing to sell the building for the token sum of one dollar. When the massive job of cleaning began, however, community volunteers discovered that the company had inadvertently missed two large bins of grain stored away in the dark recesses of the elevator. Notified of the oversight, the company laid no claim to the grain since the building had been sold "as is." What was a minimal loss to a large elevator company thus became a much-needed gain for the heritage project.

I sometimes think God delights in letting us discover "the hidden wealth of secret places." Yesterday it was a pair of sandals I found in a sale bin, the only pair my size, reduced to one-quarter the original price. A few months ago it was a stash of quilt patches unearthed in a recycling store in just the colors I needed. Several years ago it was discovering the joy of lilies, "treasures of darkness" bursting forth from bulbs buried in the rich black earth. And years before that, it was discovering "the secret wealth" (and health) of baking our own bread, the yeast hidden in the warm, fragrant dough.

Lord, thank You for granting me life "as is," and the unexpected treasures You allow me to discover and enjoy. —Alma Barkman

SAT
31

A word fitly spoken is like apples of gold in pictures of silver.

—Proverbs 25:11

For years, when daylight saving time ended in the autumn, my heart sank. As every day got darker earlier, so did my spirits. "It's depressing. I hate the dark in the winter," I told my sister last year. "Oh," Jeannie said, "I think it's cozy."

Cozy. I'd never thought about it like that. Suddenly I saw my winter blues in a whole new light. Now when it got dark at four thirty in the afternoon, instead of feeling sad, I clicked on lamps with a warm glow and pulled a nubby blanket over me while reading or watching TV. It *was* cozy.

The power of words never fails to amaze me. A few months ago when I was bemoaning a difficult work project, an acquaintance surprised me by saying, "That sounds like fun!" Once during a European trip, the airline I was traveling on went on strike and I was about to panic, until my traveling companion announced, "Guess we'll be having an adventure." *Hmm*, a different way of looking at things.

Best of all was several years ago, when I was making changes in my life from a nine-to-five office job to freelancer. I e-mailed a good friend and told her several times how scared I was. When I later reread the e-mail, I was shocked to see a recurring typo: Instead of typing *scared* I'd typed *sacred*. Once again my perspective took a turnaround: from being scared to opening my horizons to a whole new sacred dimension in my future.

In fact, that's why I sometimes write words to myself on index cards and tape them around my apartment. This morning I woke and through my bleary eyes saw the word *Rejoice* taped to my bedroom wall—another sacred fun adventure of a cozy winter day coming up!

Holy Spirit, keep me aware and renewed by the words that influence and nourish my life.

—Mary Ann O'Roark

MY LIVING WORDS

1

2

3

4

5

6

7

8

9

10

11

12

13

14

15

16

17

18

19

20

21

22

23

24

25

26

27

28

29

30

31

November

Thy word is a lamp unto my feet,
and a light unto my path.

—Psalm 119:105

A gracious woman retaineth honour. . . .

—Proverbs 11:16

I suspect that everyone knows someone in the category of a saint, someone whose example of suffering and service is an icon for the rest of us.

"She was a saint" could be said about my Grandma Schantz, who lived in a little brown house in Springfield, Ohio, where I was born. She had deep-set French eyes filled with kindness, a mischievous smile and a laugh that filled the house with music. Because of Grandpa's disabilities, Grandma worked in an electric motor factory till the day she died. She had everything but money, yet her hallmark was generosity.

When we went to see her, she fixed all our favorite foods. She knew them by heart. Always she had something for us boys. "Here is some copper wire I salvaged from work. You boys can use it for your amateur radios." She saved old postage stamps and cigar boxes for us to keep them in.

> God Speaks
> through Examples

Sunday night was the highlight of our week, when my dad would take all of us for a drive around town. Sooner or later we would end up at the A&W Root Beer stand, where teenage girls would bring trays of frosty mugs to our windows. The sassafras fragrance of the liquid would attract bees and butterflies.

"How about some popcorn for these boys?" Grandma would say. "I'll pay for it." She knew my parents would never buy such a luxury. To this day the smell of popcorn or the taste of root beer floods my brain with memories of Grandma.

She is just one of millions who quietly go about making the world a sweeter place for all of us. They are the kind of people who, without a word, make me want to be a better person.

Lord, You gave me my grandma's eyes. Now may I see as well as she did.

—Daniel Schantz

MON
2

"I will not leave you as orphans;
I will come to you. "

—John 14:18 (NIV)

I've often wished for the special ability to comfort people as Jesus did. As a nurse in an acute care hospital, it was my job to give support to dying patients and their families and I often felt inadequate to the task.

On this particular morning, my patient Paul, a tall man suffering from leukemia, had worsened during the night. A death-pallor lay on his handsome face, and he had drifted into unconsciousness. His wife Susan was bending over him, trying to coax him to open his mouth for a drink. "Paul!" she called to him. "Honey, can you hear me?" She put down her glass and cradled his head in her hands.

As I watched Susan, I prayed, *Lord Jesus, please comfort her and show me how I can help.*

Suddenly, I remembered the hymnbook I had tucked into my large black purse. The previous day, Susan had told me about her husband's love for music; how, when he was well, he would sit for hours at the piano or organ playing hymns. So I had brought along a hymnbook, just in case.

I reached for my purse and pulled out the book. Handing it to her, I said, "Susan, do you think we could sing one of Paul's favorite hymns?"

"Here's 'Amazing Grace,'" she said, "Paul's favorite." Then, turning to his unresponsive face, she said, "Honey, the nurse and I are going to sing for you."

"Amazing grace . . . ," she began. Her voice quavered and broke in giant sobs. Then she took a deep breath and bravely continued, "how sweet the sound." But tears overwhelmed her again. She looked at Paul's face and managed to get through the song. Then she chose another hymn. This time there were fewer sobs. During a third hymn, I noticed that her voice was becoming stronger.

For the next two hours we sang hymn after hymn. Staff nurses tip-toed in to check the machines, or to give medication. We scarcely noticed.

What I did notice was a Presence in the room. Susan's anguished face had become relaxed and radiant. Then, with a voice full of confidence, she said, "Paul, this is not defeat. This is victory."

HELP ME TODAY, JESUS, TO BE SO IN TUNE WITH YOU THAT I SHALL BE ABLE TO BRING OTHERS THE COMFORT OF YOUR PRESENCE. —HELEN GRACE LESCHEID

Work hard and cheerfully at all you do, just as though you were working for the Lord....
—COLOSSIANS 3:23 (TLB)

Although I didn't always agree with his political opinions, the late Senator Hubert Humphrey was a man I admired enormously. In good times and in bad, he was a chronic enthusiast. Not only did he win enthusiastically, he lost enthusiastically. After conceding an election, Humphrey said, "I have done my best. I have lost.... The democratic process has worked its will, so now let's get on with the urgent task of uniting our country."

It's hard to be enthusiastic about losing. After five years of working on a community project, I, together with many others, was on the losing side of the city council's decision. I took a tip from Humphrey. "We did our best and we lost. At least we can go on record as having tried."

Humphrey believed that life is to be enjoyed, not merely endured. His attitude has helped me to focus on enjoying the process of living, even in the most mundane tasks, such as dumping the trash or cleaning out a mucked-up oven.

The word *enthusiasm* comes from the Greek root *en theos*, meaning "in God." It is in Him that we find our enthusiastic joy.

ANOINT ME WITH A ZEST FOR LIVING, BLESSED LORD. I CONSECRATE MY DAILY TASKS TO SERVING YOU WITH JOY AND GLADNESS. —FAY ANGUS

Like as a father pitieth his children, so the Lord pitieth them that fear him. For he knoweth our frame; he remembereth that we are dust.

—PSALM 103:13–14

Wednesday night: basketball tryouts, seventh grade. I am pinning the number ninety-two on my son's shirt. You have to pin a number on because there are a hundred kids here and only twenty make it. My son's back is tense, and there's a dagger of sweat down the middle of his shirt. I try to cut the tension by saying, "Man, ninety-two. What are you, a defensive tackle?" But he's not exactly in the mood, which I can tell just from the tone of his silence.

I get three pins in quick and clean, but fiddle around for a while with the last one, because I'm totally overwhelmed with nerves and love and joy and trepidation. I love this boy more than I can ever tell you or explain even to myself, and I want him to do well and make the team.

But he might not, and then I'd have to give him the Speech about how to mill pain into joy, how to turn it on the lathe of your will, etc. You know the Speech—you got it from your dad, I got it from mine. Every dad has to give that speech eventually, because every child sooner or later feels the hot lick of disappointment and pain: The girl says *no*, your name's not on the roster, you punt the test, you miss the shot.

I click the last pin into place and cup his face in my hand and say, "Dude, I love you," and we touch fists like cool guys, and he runs off with the other players. I stand there shaking, and out I go into the wild wet air whispering, "Thank You, thank You, thank You. Take care of my boy. Thank You, thank You."

DEAR LORD, I CANNOT IN A THOUSAND YEARS THANK YOU ENOUGH FOR THE SWEET CHAOS OF MY CHILDREN. BUT I WILL REALLY, REALLY TRY.

—BRIAN DOYLE

THU 5

A woman . . . touched the hem of His garment. For she said to herself, "If only I may touch His garment, I shall be made well."

—MATTHEW 9:20–21 (NKJV)

After my friend Patricia received a distressing diagnosis of metastasized cancer, I cooked, cleaned and chauffeured for her. I also prayed, for her as well as for myself, but in a vague way that didn't feel meaningful—until I stopped and took a nap.

After lunch one day, I ran out of steam. Anticipating the rejuvenating power of a catnap, I pushed away from my computer and kicked off my shoes. As I stretched out on my bed, some garbled revision of the Matthew 9 "if only" passage came to mind: "If only I could touch the edge of . . . sleep."

I quickly nodded off. I awoke fifteen minutes later, refreshed physically, if not spiritually. But even before I opened my eyes, I felt the warmth of my tabby Kitty, herself napping on the quilt. She'd rested her cheek on the back of my hand and extended her front paw across my shirt-cuffed wrist. Before I disturbed her pose or resumed my routine, I lingered a moment. Her quiet touch settled my spirit and coaxed the biblical "if only" from my memory: "If only I may touch Jesus' garment." It's a woman's faith-full prayer for health.

My prayers for Patricia—and myself—are more focused now.

DEAR JESUS, BE AT OUR SIDE TO HEAL AND GUIDE.   —EVELYN BENCE

FRI 6

Our mouths were filled with laughter, our tongues with songs of joy. . . .

—PSALM 126:2 (NIV)

My high school had a tradition: The day before the homecoming football game was Crazy Hair Day. So my senior year I wrapped my hair in curlers and applied the chemicals from a "seven-day perm" kit. After an hour, I removed the curlers and—voila!—my hair was curly. It was so curly that it stood out in every direction like a giant ball of cotton.

Needless to say, it was a big hit at school on Friday. But when I woke up Saturday morning, it was still just as curly; Sunday morning, the same thing. After seven days had passed and the curls remained, a friend dared me not to get a haircut until it straightened out. I took the dare. I finally cut it all off when I couldn't stand it anymore—nine months later!

My next goal? Getting my car to run on whatever was in that seven-day perm.

LORD, THANK YOU FOR THE FUN TIMES THAT YOU PUT IN OUR LIVES. MAY I ALWAYS APPROACH LIFE LIGHTLY, BUT WITH FEWER CURLS! —JOSHUA SUNDQUIST

I am Alpha and Omega, the beginning and the ending. . . .
—REVELATION 1:8

I forgot to check the calendar when the forms for parent-teacher conferences came home. *Oops.* With one conference scheduled for 4:45 PM and another at 5:00 PM on Monday, I have to figure out how to get Maggie to play rehearsal (uptown) at 5:00 PM and Mary to Nutcracker rehearsal (downtown) at the same time. Plus I just received an e-mail reminding me of a five o'clock fund-raising committee meeting at the school around the corner that I *have* to attend. My husband Andrew can't help; he'll be at work. I need him to pick up Elizabeth when *she's* done with choir anyway.

After the initial shock of discovering my scheduling megadisaster, I forced myself to take a deep breath. There's only one thing that helps me when I'm faced with mind-boggling conundrums like this and that's to remember that logistical problems aren't actually problems, they're puzzles. They belong in the crossword-solving part of my brain, not the worry center. No one is going to die or be scarred for life or even require a trip to the doctor if I don't figure this out. The only true danger is that I'll stress out and start being unpleasant to my family. So I tossed the problem onto the back burner, where so many insoluble difficulties simmer into solutions.

Last night, around midnight, I think I figured out a way to handle Monday. The logistics require higher math to follow and a cast of thousands to execute, but the plan will probably work. And if it doesn't, then it doesn't. It's neither the beginning nor the end of the world.

LORD, HELP ME TO REMEMBER THAT THE WORLD WON'T FALL APART IF I'M NOT ABLE TO MAKE THINGS RUN PERFECTLY SMOOTHLY. —JULIA ATTAWAY

SUN
8

"You shall know the truth, and the truth shall make you free."
—JOHN 8:32 (NKJV)

Large numbers have always shielded me from the enormity of human pain and suffering. Once the word *million* is applied to a statistic, my mind freezes up and I can't get my cognitive and emotional arms around the size of the problem.

Recently I read that 850 million people struggle with chronic hunger each day. My mind shut down; the number was beyond my capacity to understand. As I continued to read, I learned that eighteen thousand children die each day around our world from hunger or diseases caused by malnutrition.

Our church sanctuary can seat a thousand people, I thought. *If we placed the bodies of all the children who die of hunger inside our sanctuary, we would have to fill and empty it eighteen times every day!* For the first time the horror of world hunger gripped me, and for a brief moment I perceived the truth.

It has been said that a modern man or woman is a person who does not lack information but cannot comprehend the meaning. Perhaps the future of our world depends on our willingness to get beyond statistics and to make real to ourselves the fact that children are dying from hunger, which could be avoided; that the polar caps are melting from climate changes that can be prevented; and that diseases are rampant that sufficient effort could cure.

FATHER, HELP ME TO NOT BE A PERSON WHO IS WELL-INFORMED ONLY, BUT A PERSON WHO CAN COMPREHEND THE TRUTH. AMEN. —SCOTT WALKER

MON
9

*Don't let anyone look down on you because you
are young, but set an example for the believers in
speech, in life, in love, in faith and in purity.*

—I TIMOTHY 4:12 (NIV)

Kristina, the youth director at our church, asked me if I could teach her high school Bible study. I agreed, but I wanted to meet her students and observe her class first.

She introduced me to the three students who were attending that week's study. Kristina asked about their week, prayed and then jumped onto a chair. "I want two of you to grab my hands and see if you can pull me off this chair." All three of the students were boys, two of them large enough to lift Kristina and the chair easily if they chose. Only one shyly stood up to take Kristina's right hand, so I volunteered to take her left hand. With very little effort, we pulled her forward and she had to jump from her chair to keep from falling.

Kristina climbed back onto the chair and said, "Now I'm going to lift Tim up to my level." She couldn't, of course. "It's a lot easier to pull someone down to your level than it is to lift someone up," she added.

Kristina had four students that evening. I know the spirit of her oldest student was lifted high.

DEAR GOD, THANK YOU FOR THE GIFT OF FAITH THAT IS MEASURED BY DEPTH, NOT BY YEARS.

—TIM WILLIAMS

TUE
10

Rejoice always, pray without ceasing.

—I THESSALONIANS 5:16-17 (NRSV)

Do you ever have trouble figuring out what the Bible means for your everyday life? When the participants in a Bible study I was leading pressed me one day on the above passage, I had to swallow hard and say, "Pray without ceasing? I really don't know how to do that."

How do you pray all the time? Not just when someone is sick or you have something to say to God, but all the time? I knew my prayer life wasn't like that. I felt that I had failed as their teacher. Worse, I wondered if I was also failing as a man of faith.

That night while watching the news, I was mesmerized by the story of a photographer from the *Los Angeles Times* who took stunning pictures of some firefighters deploying their silver emergency shelters when a devastating Southern California wildfire overran their position. When asked what was going through her mind when she was taking the photographs, she said simply, "I would stop shooting and start praying."

Pray all the time? Figuring out what the Bible means sometimes is as simple as doing what the Bible says, as best you can, as often as you can, in as many places as you can.

TEACH ME SOMETHING NEW ABOUT YOUR WORD TODAY, GOD, SO THAT I MAY LIVE IT OUT TOMORROW IN PRAISE OF YOU.　　　　　　　　　　—JEFF JAPINGA

WED 11

Now may the Lord of peace himself give you peace at all times and in every way. . . .
—II THESSALONIANS 3:16-17 (NIV)

When my mom and dad were newly married, my mom was startled awake one night and saw my dad crouched at the foot of the bed, stealthily crawling around the edge.

"Karl, what's going on?" she asked. No response. Finally, Dad reached the pillow and lay back down, still sound asleep. The next morning Mom asked him, "What were you dreaming about?"

At first he didn't remember, but as Mom described his slow crawl around the bed, he shuddered. He explained that he had been dreaming about being stalked by the enemy in the Philippine jungles during World War II. He shuddered again, remembering the jungle snakes, and said his terror of them was almost as great as his fear of being discovered by the enemy.

I had forgotten about Dad's nightmares of war until my friend Noni mentioned that her husband Rich, a Vietnam veteran, had painful memories of his tour of duty. Unlike Dad's generation of vets, Rich did not receive a hero's welcome when he came home. He struggled to fit back into society and was sometimes criticized by those opposed to the war.

When my mom was a girl in the 1920s, every city and town had a grand parade on Armistice Day, as it was called then. Nowadays, Veterans Day passes quietly in many places. But let's make a gift of appreciation for all veterans by taking a few moments to offer a special prayer. May our Lord see a "parade of prayers" today—for healing for those who experienced firsthand the horrors of war, and for peace in the world.

O LORD, GRANT PEACE TO YOUR WORLD AND TO ALL YOUR PEOPLE. HELP EACH OF US MAKE PEACE WITH THE PAST AND WITH ONE ANOTHER.   —MARY BROWN

I press on toward the goal to win the prize for which God has called me. . . .
—PHILIPPIANS 3:14 (NIV)

For years I was in awe of the "hard" Bible study at my church. They met for an hour longer than my class next door, and when I'd peek in as I walked by, they'd be poring over the Bible with highlighters and marking pens. I'd heard they even had hours of homework each week! They seemed to know so much about the Bible. *I could never be like that*, I thought. *Where would I start?*

Then our son Ross, learning about the world's religions in a history class, came home with some questions I couldn't answer: Were the Gospels close to eyewitness accounts or written many years later? Did Jesus ever really say He was God? I knew I had to dig deeper into God's Word and find the answers to help Ross strengthen his faith. So I signed up for the hard Bible study, promising myself that I'd attend the first day and see if I could handle it.

That was four years ago. Since then I've come to know God much better. But I've also learned a simple plan for facing intimidating situations, one that's worked for me whether it's taking a hard class, sticking to an exercise regimen or giving up a bad habit:

Go. Make an effort to get started, even if it's only a baby step.

Stay. Don't quit that first day; stick with it, even if you can't keep up.

Return. Keep going back and making one more try. Soon all those "just one more day" attempts pile up, and you've made a lot of progress.

STAY CLOSE BY ME, LORD, SO THAT WHEN I FEEL WEAK OR MY WILL BEGINS TO FAIL, YOUR GENTLE NUDGING HELPS ME PRESS ON. —GINA BRIDGEMAN

FRI
13

And we know that all things work together for good to them that love God, to them who are the called according to his purpose.
—ROMANS 8:28

Our daughter Christine was in great spirits when she got home from work. Earlier in the day she had had her performance review. Elba and I were wondering how she had done, but we didn't want to bring up the subject. Christine chatted cheerfully with us for a while but gave us no news. The wait was killing me.

Before she got her job as a product coordinator in a textile business, things had been different. Several months out of college without work, she decided to try the catering industry. She took a position at a small firm, starting at the bottom with the hope of moving up. The pay was low, the hours were long and the work was grueling.

"Mom, I am never going to get a decent job," she'd complained. "I have no life."

"It will come together. Trust God," Elba responded. Christine seemed puzzled when her mother said, "Trust God." That was a tall order for our twentysomething daughter. In her world it was now or never.

I finally got tired of waiting for Christine's news. "How did your review go?" I asked.

"I got a wonderful evaluation and a larger raise than I expected. And they have plans for me to grow in my position."

Whenever one of us is facing an unexpected situation or things are not going our way, Elba never fails to encourage us: "It will come together. Trust God." And it does, often in more ways than we can expect or imagine.

LORD, WHEN THINGS DON'T SEEM TO BE WORKING OUT, HELP ME TO REMEMBER THAT IN YOUR GOOD TIME, IT WILL COME TOGETHER. —PABLO DIAZ

Thankful praise to You, God, because You've given me Your Word to guide me, Your grace and love that saved me, Your forgiveness when I confess my sins, Your light in a dark world, Your perfect plan for me in each situation, Your peace in chaos, Your comfort in sorrow, Your faithfulness in all things through Jesus my Shepherd-Savior and the leading of Your Holy Spirit.

—*Carolyn Malion, Fairmont, North Carolina*

Of making many books there is no end. . . .

—ECCLESIASTES 12:12

"Books furnish a room," my wife is fond of saying. A good thing, too, because our house threatens to be buried in books. We've got them furnishing every room: the hard covers in the dining room, the paperbacks in the TV room, the books that we intend to read on the floor by our beds, the books that we've read and intend to lend to friends on the cabinet. Every time we get a new shelf, it seems to fill up. First the books fill out rows, then get stacked in double rows and then we start laying books horizontally on top. The only hope for us is our neighborhood's annual book fair. With pleasure, I deliver bags full of used books, all for a worthy cause.

For a couple of days our shelves look neater, our floors have more space on them, the house seems to have a little more air. Then comes the actual day of the book fair. Carol stops by, "just to see what's there." I drop in, "just to check on prices and maybe run into an old friend." Almost by accident I start looking down the row of books and spot many old friends . . . and new friends. *We don't have a copy of that,* I think. *Isn't that a nice edition? Haven't I always wanted to read that?* Surreptitiously, quietly, Carol and I gather books—bargains, I tell you, fabulous finds—and we bring them home, sheepishly, apologetically. They start the journey from bedside table to shelf . . . and eventually to a bag for next year's book fair.

OPEN MY EYES TO THE WISDOM, LORD, IN ALL I READ.   —RICK HAMLIN

"For John baptized with water, but . . . you will be baptized with the Holy Spirit."

—ACTS 1:5 (NIV)

Something strange has been happening to me in the last few years: I cry in church. For no reason that I can understand or explain, right in the middle of worship my eyes will cloud with tears. I blink furiously and take deep, even breaths to keep them at bay, but it rarely helps. My husband Wayne has gotten into the habit of carrying a handkerchief with him on Sunday morning. Apparently, he recognizes the signs now, because halfway through the service he tucks the hankie into my hand and gives my fingers a gentle squeeze.

If those tears in church weren't embarrassing enough, the same thing started happening during my morning prayer time. I'm most comfortable communicating with God in writing, but these days many of my prayers are smudged with tears. I was convinced that this was a side effect of menopause, but that didn't seem to affect anything other than my worship and prayer time.

My friend Wendy came to visit recently. I casually mentioned how easily the tears flowed when I communicated with God. She smiled knowingly. "That happens to me too."

"It does?"

She nodded. "Those tears are an indication that the Holy Spirit has touched me in some way."

I pondered her words for a long time and recognized the truth in them. My tears in church don't embarrass me any longer; they're my emotional response to the overwhelming love of God as He touches my heart with His Spirit.

HOLY SPIRIT, SWEEP DOWN OVER YOUR PEOPLE AND TOUCH OUR HEARTS THAT WE MIGHT SERVE GOD. AMEN.   —DEBBIE MACOMBER

MON
16

It is good to give thanks to the Lord. . . .

—Psalm 92:1 (NAS)

The Veterans Administration medical center where I work as a nurse has a beautiful chapel with colorful stained-glass windows featuring intricate geometric designs. At the beginning of each workday, I slide into the second pew from the back and commit the day ahead to God.

There's something I encounter there that never fails to nudge my thoughts heavenward. At the chapel's entrance a small book lies open on a table for patients, families and staff to record their prayer requests. And daily one of our faithful volunteers enters the same message: "Frank Dorsey: Thankful."

With Eternity in View

Always Give Thanks

Yesterday, when everything conspired to create confusion, I found Mr. Dorsey, a World War II veteran, kneeling at the chapel's altar, his baseball cap removed in reverence. When he stood to leave, I asked him about his curious habit. "It's a high privilege to serve other veterans here," he told me. "And I've found the best way to do that is to start my day by saying thanks. Thanks for God, this great country of ours and this medical center."

Mr. Dorsey is a senior citizen of small stature who can often be seen in the hospital corridor, transporting specimens to the laboratory. For him, it's a way to thank God. And with his grateful servant's heart and quiet strength, he instructs everyone around him. Most of all, he teaches me. As I entered the chapel today with an endless to-do list, I found myself writing underneath Mr. Dorsey's neat script: "Roberta Messner: Thankful."

Dear God, I will thank You throughout eternity for Your gifts great and small.

—Roberta Messner

TUE 17

Then they brought little children to Him. . . .
—MARK 10:13 (NKJV)

My new Tennessee Walker mare rested her head on my shoulder as I brushed her. "What am I going to name you?" I asked. She batted her long eyelashes and nuzzled me. It'd been weeks since I bought her, but I still hadn't a clue about her name. I'd owned nearly a hundred horses over the years and never had a problem naming a single one until now. "You don't look like an Intrigue. Besides, that sounds too stuffy and flat."

I'd researched baby names and checked books out of the library, but nothing fit. Her personality was robust. She was curious, yet extremely feminine. I loved watching her prance, her deep black coat shimmering blue in the sunlight and her long tail sweeping the ground. And she *loved* baths, especially when I brushed the shampoo until it foamed.

That evening I was at a friend's home, and her eight-year-old daughter led me into her room. We plopped down on the floor, and she introduced me to her plastic horses. The white one was Star, the red one Ruby, and on she chattered through the pile. Then I glimpsed a black horse that looked just like mine. I picked it up and asked, "What's this one's name?"

"That's easy. She's Dazzle."

Dazzle? That's it!

WHEN I MAKE THINGS HARD, LORD, REMIND ME TO SPEND TIME WITH CHILDREN TO SEE THE WORLD THROUGH THEIR EYES.　　　　—REBECCA ONDOV

WED 18

Delight yourself in the Lord and he will give you the desires of your heart.
—PSALM 37:4 (NIV)

When I was a little girl, I was a *Romper Room* fan. *Romper Room* was a live TV show hosted in St. Louis by Miss Joan, who was a perky cross between a mother and a teacher. I ate my snack when the children on the show ate their snacks; I exercised with them; I sang with them. At one point in the show, Miss Joan would look in a mirror and say, "Magic Mirror, tell me today, have all my friends had fun at play?" Then she'd call out the names of children watching at home: "I see Bobby. I see Becky. I see Mary." But she never called my name.

One day I found out that a cousin of mine was going to be on *Romper Room* and that I could go with him to the studio. Everyone was excited; my cousin was going to be the first African American child on the show. But I was excited for another reason: Maybe I'd be able to meet Miss Joan! Maybe I could ask her if the Magic Mirror would remind her to say my name!

I sat in the green room and watched on a monitor while my cousin cavorted with the other children in front of the cameras. When the show was over, he came back to the green room and behind him walked Miss Joan. She looked down at me, smiled and said, "Would you like to be on *Romper Room?*"

I spent two weeks on the show. My mother bought me ten dresses so that I'd have a new one each day. I sang; I danced; I ate the snacks; I got to hold the Magic Mirror in my own two hands! At the end of my two weeks, I received a diploma, a *Romper Room* Do-Bee ring and a giant container stuffed with candy. And, yes, Miss Joan finally said my name.

THANK YOU, LORD, FOR BLESSING ME IN WAYS I DON'T EVEN HAVE THE COURAGE TO PRAY FOR. —SHARON FOSTER

You can trust God to keep the temptation from becoming so strong that you can't stand up against it, for he has promised this and will do what he says. . . .
—I CORINTHIANS 10:13 (TLB)

I love sweets. From my first Twinkie as a toddler to today's chocolate candy, I'm hooked.

Americans eat five hundred million Twinkies a year. Each little four-inch-long yellow sponge cake filled with creamy stuff contains twenty-eight ingredients, including cholesterol, salt, carbs and 150 empty calories. Why do we eat them? Come on, who doesn't like Twinkies? I eat one every couple of years just to remind me of my childhood.

But I also try to eat good, healthy, natural foods. Now that the produce departments are making it easy by prewashing fresh vegetables and even cutting them up in easy-to-eat, easy-to-cook pieces, I have no excuse. But still, chocolate calls my name. Brownies; hot fudge sundaes; rich, creamy dark and milk chocolate candy—I want it all, just as I wanted Twinkies when I was a child.

It's tough, trying to stay healthy. Every day I tell myself, *Eat less, eat better and exercise more.* Sometimes I have to say it over and over. In fact, sometimes I have to talk to myself out loud and quite sternly: "Put down that bag of malted milk balls and ask the Lord to give you the strength to walk to the gym. Now! Step away from the candy!"

HEAVENLY FATHER, THANK YOU FOR THIS MARVELOUS MACHINE YOU CREATED FOR ME. HELP ME TO RESPECT IT BY EATING RIGHT AND EXERCISING MORE.

—PATRICIA LORENZ

FRI
20

For as the heavens are higher than the earth, so are my ways higher than your ways, and my thoughts than your thoughts.

—ISAIAH 55:9

Solomon, my five-year-old, gets upset by things that don't follow the rules of cause-and-effect. Whenever he comes across something that doesn't seem quite right, he furrows his brow and demands an answer. So when Faith, a classmate of his, was diagnosed with leukemia, Solomon tried to make sense of it all. "Why did this happen?" "Why is Faith too tired to play?" "Why did she lose her curls?" "Will she die?" "Will I die?" "Will you die?" "When will we die?" "Does dying hurt?"

At that moment I longed for the innocent "What's that?" of Solomon's toddler years. How could I explain that I had no idea why Faith was sick, that sometimes bad things happen for reasons we can't explain? Instead, I found myself hugging Solomon tightly and being thankful that he was in my arms and healthy.

"Why are you crying, Mommy?" Solomon asked.

"I don't know," I said. "I don't know why Faith got leukemia. I don't think anyone knows."

Solomon's face perked up. "Mommy, I know who knows."

"Who?" I asked.

"God. God knows everything. He's got a plan."

"You're right," I said.

"But, Mommy, how can we figure it out? How can we know the plan?"

"I don't think we can. But we can pray for Faith and her family."

"Oh, okay," he said. "I have another question."

"Okay."

"How come the teacher never picks me to be line leader?"

I'm happy to say that Faith is doing well. Her leukemia is in remission. Her curls have grown back, her energy and smiles have returned. Aptly named, Faith has filled us all with hope and gratitude.

DEAR LORD, WHEN THERE ARE NO ANSWERS, LET ME ALWAYS TRUST YOUR PLAN.

—SABRA CIANCANELLI

SAT 21

"Why do you see the speck in your neighbor's eye, but do not notice the log in your own eye?"

—LUKE 6:41 (NRSV)

While putting out snacks for the residents of a homeless shelter where my husband Charlie and I occasionally volunteer, I noticed a newcomer. Most of us dress casually for our shifts, but he wore dress slacks, a crisp shirt and sober tie. It was the end of the day, and his hair was perfectly combed and he was clean-shaven. I listened to him complain to another volunteer about the plunging housing market and high property taxes and rolled my eyes, wondering where he thought he was. After greeting him briefly, we began distributing food and greeting the residents.

A young woman tentatively approached us. I knew her; she spent her time at the shelter alone, talking to herself. I was about to hand her whatever food was closest when the new guy said, "Hello, Delilah. How are you this evening?"

What? He knew her by name? I'd never even gotten her to meet my gaze.

Delilah glanced quickly at him and smiled; I almost dropped my fruit cup. Then he said, "I know you like baloney sandwiches, so I put one aside for you. Do you want mustard or mayonnaise?" She pointed decisively at the mayonnaise, and after asking if she'd like him to fix it for her and receiving a nod, he spread on the mayo and handed her the sandwich.

After smiling at him yet again, she walked away, clutching her special sandwich, her head held higher than ever before. Mine, on the other hand, hung low.

Lord, thank You for reminding me that when I smugly judge others, the joke's on me.   —Marci Alborghetti

The preacher sought to find out acceptable words: and that which was written was upright, even words of truth.
—Ecclesiastes 12:10

I was seated in church with my grandson Caleb, age five. He reached for the small pencil and envelope used for recording attendance and giving, and said, "This is so you can write, 'I love You, God.'"

God wrote an entire book saying "I love you" to the human race. But not once did I ever think of scribbling those words on a pew envelope to be offered at the altar in blessing to Him.

My granddaughter Hannah, age seven, once sang me a song she had learned in summer Bible school about following Jesus. She paused mid-sentence to say, "I know how you turn back on the path to God."

"How?" I asked.

"When you read the Bible and pray and obey the commandments . . . and then you stop."

Her explanation was so stark and pure I felt myself squirm. I had been experiencing a season of struggle regarding those very issues. I needed a jolt.

I found myself backing away from that abrupt edge, the "stop." I wanted once again to open my Bible and pray and have a heart to obey— to move forward on the holy path. I missed saying, "I love You, God."

Jesus, in the pages of my Bible, I find Your reassuring promises telling me that I can start following Your path anytime.   —Carol Knapp

MON
23

Where can I go from Your Spirit?. . .

—PSALM 139:7 (NAS)

My husband Gene and I were flying to a meeting in Indiana. I'd been ambivalent about going. At the last minute, problems in our family made me wonder, *Should I really be leaving now?* I felt as though I'd left my faith somewhere and couldn't find it. Gene tried to encourage me. "Look at the clouds," he said up at thirty thousand feet. "Don't you feel close to God?"

I didn't.

Gene pulled his tiny, worn New Testament from his jacket pocket and read me Scriptures. I remained keenly aware of my lack of faith in God's ability to care for the people I'd left back home.

As we rolled our luggage over the tile floor of the airport in South Bend, Indiana, the clickety-clacks of the wheels turned into a haunting question: *Where's your God? Where's your God? Where's your God?*

Suddenly, Gene stopped and grabbed my hand and together we entered a small room squeezed in between a restaurant and a souvenir shop. A sign said, Prayer Chapel. We'd nearly rushed right past it.

The instant we stepped inside, sweet comfort closed in around me. Hurriedly scrawled prayer requests were pinned to a bulletin board. There were praises, too, and favorite Scriptures. A small wooden cross stood on a simple table. Tracts were scattered around the cross. Suddenly I felt surrounded by others who'd stopped in this tiny place of prayer—believers who also had needed to reaffirm their faith. And I sensed an unforgettable welcome by the Holy Spirit, Who waited patiently in that little room for weary, worried travelers.

OH, FATHER, HELP ME REMEMBER THAT I CAN'T GO ANYWHERE WITHOUT YOU.

—MARION BOND WEST

Editor's Note: Join us today for our annual Thanksgiving Day of Prayer. On every working day, Guideposts Prayer Ministry prays for your prayer requests by name and need. Visit us online at www.OurPrayer.org, where you can request prayer, volunteer to pray for others or help support our prayer ministry.

"When the people willingly offer themselves—praise the Lord!"

—JUDGES 5:2 (NIV)

One of my morning rituals at work is a quick hello to the head custodian in my building. I always look forward to my conversations with Mr. Al, and today was no exception. "Good morning, Mr. Al," I called out when he passed by my office door.

"How are you on this great fall day?" he asked.

"Okay, I guess," I sighed. "I just opened an e-mail from a coworker asking me to fill in for her at a presentation this morning." I paused. "Of course, I'll do it, but I don't feel very prepared to talk about the points she needs me to cover."

"Oh, you'll do fine," he said. "Remember, it's really God doing the asking, and He wouldn't ask you if He didn't think you could do it."

Mr. Al took off his cap and wiped his brow. "A while back I was visiting a church down the way. They needed someone to read the Scripture to the congregation during the service. The minister walked over and asked me to help out. I did it, even though I was nervous. I figured I wouldn't have been asked if God didn't think I was up to it."

Later that day, our staff met for our annual Thanksgiving meal. Mr. Al was asked to say a blessing. Not expecting the request, he hesitated for a moment. Then he bowed his head to lead us in prayer. "Oh, precious Lord, thank You for the food before us and for all the opportunities You give us to serve You. Amen." When he was done, he looked up at me with a smile. "You see, Miss Melody? We just have to keep saying *yes* whenever God calls."

FATHER, GIVE ME A HEART WILLING TO BE USED BY YOU. AMEN.

—MELODY BONNETTE

Let us come before his presence with thanksgiving. . . .

—PSALM 95:2

It was the day before Thanksgiving, and my wife Sandee and I were arguing about . . . something. I was at work—which may have contributed to my black mood—and the shuttle to the parking garage was running late. Both the turkey back home and I were stewing in our own juices.

Then a young man and his parents walked by. The young man jumped on the shuttle, gleeful for the free ride. His parents called for him to get off the bus but to no avail. Finally the mother looked at the driver, tapped the side of her head and said, "He's not right."

They weren't walking to the garage; they were walking to Western Psychiatric Clinic. This young man was checking in. Imagine the festive holiday dinner at *their* house.

I wasn't just humbled; I felt something beyond shame. I'd been blind to the sweet routine of my wonderful life. Did I really need to see another family's suffering to recognize what I'd been given? Had I been with the disciples on the road to Emmaus, even the One beside me would have escaped my notice.

I could tell you that I went home and kissed my children and my ever-patient wife—which I did—but it's hardly a fitting end to the story. I must live with my lapses, my blindness, my . . . well, ingratitude. Thanksgiving is still my favorite holiday, and now I have another reason: I'm grateful for a second (third, fourth, millionth) chance at grace, however undeserved it might be.

THANK YOU, LORD. AND PLEASE BE WITH THAT YOUNG MAN'S FAMILY, WHO MIGHT HAVE SOME TROUBLE GIVING THANKS.

—MARK COLLINS

In every thing give thanks: for this is the will of God in Christ Jesus concerning you.
—I THESSALONIANS 5:18

It's Thanksgiving morning. The kitchen table is piled with unpeeled potatoes, and I am missing my mother.

How many potatoes did Mother peel in her lifetime? I breathe in the earthy smell of the unwashed skins and hear Mother say, "Mary Lou, run down to the basement and get us some potatoes for supper."

Mother loved feeding people—and not just family and friends. I remember many Thanksgiving meals when, as we cleared the table, Mother would say, "Let's make up plates for the Georges." The Georges were the poor family at the end of the road. Some years it wasn't the

Georges, but it was always some hard-luck case that had come to my mother's attention.

I pick up the knife and begin peeling the potatoes. It's Thanksgiving and time I started giving thanks.

My daughter and son-in-law will be arriving later with my two grandsons. They live only a mile away. *Thank You.*

My son and his wife will come with little Isabelle Grace—it's her first Thanksgiving. *Thank You.*

My mother-in-law, widowed several years ago, will contribute deviled eggs and cranberry salad to our feast. At eighty, she's still able to drive herself and help babysit her great-grandkids. *Thank You.*

I'll give my sister a call to wish her a happy day. She's the only one who shares my childhood memories, and I cherish our relationship. *Thank You.*

My husband will say a simple grace. We've been married for thirty-eight years. *Thank You.*

I'll place a mountain of steaming mashed potatoes in the middle of the table and hear Mother say, "Good girl. You used real butter and lots of it." And I'll know that Mother will be a part of this holiday and all the ones to come. *Thank You.*

Sweet Jesus, thank You for the godly ones who have come before us and for the reunion You have planned for us in heaven! —Mary Lou Carney

---

FRI
27

> *He hath made every thing*
> *beautiful in his time. . . .*
> —Ecclesiastes 3:11

So here we are again with one of those hard-to-understand lines. Koheleth, author of Ecclesiastes, has just written of fourteen pairs of opposites. In each pair, there is a positive and a negative.

A Time to Every Purpose

The negatives include such words as *die, kill, weep, mourn, rend, hate* and *war.* Yet he follows those contradictory pairs with the statement that "He hath made every thing beautiful."

But the sentence ends with "in his time." So we're back to where we started—with time, *His* time. *What,* I wonder, *is His time?* What could it be other than all time? And what could all time be but eternity, a vast and ever-expanding now? Somewhere in God's eternity are the answers to all of my questions. Today I ask the silence, "How does God transform hate, killing and weeping into beauty?"

Think about your father who treated wounded soldiers
on a Navy troopship in World War II.
Consider how gentle and caring he was when he came home.
Could it be that war had mellowed him?

Sometimes hatred is deeply buried childhood pain
masquerading as bravado, misdirected and acted out.
Asking and receiving forgiveness is the cure.
It has the power to transform hatred into love.

And tears. Is there anyone who has never wept?
Tears are the great releaser, the cleanser of pain,
healer of overburdened lives.
This is the beauty of weeping.

HOLY FATHER, I CONFESS I DON'T REALLY KNOW HOW YOU TRANSFORM THE HARMFUL INTO THE BEAUTIFUL. I ONLY KNOW THAT YOU DO IT IN YOUR OWN TIME.

—MARILYN MORGAN KING

SAT
28

I have learned to be content
whatever the circumstances.
—PHILIPPIANS 4:11 (NIV)

When my husband Travis and I purchased our first home, it was easy to tell the bathrooms apart: One was the Ugly One. Its dated, clashing hardware and strange-patterned tiles made it an eyesore.

Piece by piece, we tried to spruce up the Ugly One—a new faucet, a new light fixture, a fresh coat of paint. We couldn't afford to retile and remodel, so at first I tried to embrace the tile's strident green color and unusual pattern. *After all,* I thought, *someone must have liked it well enough to have it installed.* But wanting to like it wasn't enough.

When Travis' aunt suggested painting over the tile, we started poring over paint chips, finally choosing a serene slate blue. Over the next week we spent every moment we could spare sanding, priming, painting and finally sealing the tile. We counted the hours until we could remove the masking tape and see the effect of the face-lift.

Our moment of triumph was short-lived. The blue that seemed so restful on the paint chip was much brighter than we expected and high-lighted the fact that the tiles were not quite level. The pattern showed through in places, giving the tile a peculiar, patchy, geometric texture.

We added a coat of antiquing varnish to deepen the color and dis-guise the texture. But that just made the uneven, garish blue tiles look grimy. And when we removed the masking tape, it lifted large patches of paint with it, exposing the bright green surface underneath and leaving a jagged edge on the wall. "Did we make the Ugly One even worse?" I sputtered.

"Nope," Travis said, patting my shoulder, "we made it ours. Come on, I'll touch up the walls while you tackle the tile." He smiled and handed me a brush. "Now we can call it the Blue One."

I must admit, the Blue One is growing on me.

LORD, THANK YOU FOR THE LOVE THAT MAKES A HOUSE INTO A HOME, HOWEVER HUMBLE THE BATHROOM TILE MAY BE. —KJERSTIN WILLIAMS

Editor's Note: For all of us, there are special things—memories, deco-rations, family traditions—that make the message of Christmas especially precious. This year we invite you to take an Advent journey with Brock Kidd, as he shares the ways in which he and his family celebrate the birth of Jesus.

FIRST SUNDAY IN ADVENT	MAKING CHRISTMAS

SUN
29

A man's life consisteth not in the abundance of the things which he possesseth.
—LUKE 12:15

Ashes. I couldn't believe my eyes, even as I breathed in the stench of my parents' smoke-choked living room and touched the sooty residue scattered across the floor.

Just a few hours before, the ashes had been a finely carved wooden carousel that my grandfather had brought from Germany soon after my birth. It had several tiers—the wise men, then the shepherds, then the angels—all traveling up to the top, where Joseph and Mary knelt over the Baby Jesus.

Every year my mom would get the carousel out of the attic, gently place the wooden fan blades around the top and light the candles at the bottom. It always seemed like magic to me when the heat of the candles turned the blades and the rows of figures seemed to move slowly on their own.

Mom always joked, "When I go to heaven, Brock, your sister will get the diamonds, but you get the carousel."

But now it was gone forever. Mom had gone out to dinner and left the candles burning. The resulting fire had consumed the carousel, the table and the rug, and burned a hole in the floor. Then, somehow, it put itself out.

I felt my eyes beginning to fill with tears. Mom was even more upset. "I can't believe it's gone. Oh, Brock, I'm so sorry!"

As usual, Dad came to the rescue. "Hey, at least the house is still here. And think about it. Nothing can take all those carousel Christmases away. They're a permanent part of who we are."

I wrapped my arms around my mother. "Dad's right, Mom. Close your eyes. It's still here, even if we can't touch it or see it. We'll always have it in our hearts."

FATHER, OUT OF THE ASHES YOU'VE SHOWN ME SOMETHING TOO BIG FOR ANY-ONE TO OWN AND TOTALLY FREE TO ANYONE WHO CLAIMS IT: THE SPIRIT OF CHRISTMAS.   —BROCK KIDD

I have shown you kindness, that ye
will also show kindness. . . .

—JOSHUA 2:12

I'd always thought of Walnut Creek, California, as a safe haven, compared to New York City, where I'm from. So I was shocked last month when my groceries were stolen. I'd left the shopping cart, over-flowing with the three paper bags full of produce, bread and canned goods, outside the store while I popped back in, past people shaking their collection tins for some charity or other, to grab a forgotten quart of milk. When I came out, my groceries were gone.

I went into the store. "Did anyone turn in a basket of groceries?" I asked, to blank looks all around. I left fuming.

I was still fuming when I got to work an hour later. Everyone heard my story. "They even got the birthday cake!" I told them. I'd been appointed to pick up the cake for our monthly break-room celebration.

On my break I hurried back to the store. When the manager heard my story, he yelled, "Tim, that lady is here!"

A green-aproned boy appeared; the manager glared at him and the boy stammered, "I was supposed to give the donations to the food bank. Your cart was near the piles of cans, and I . . . I . . . loaded them into the van."

"You donated my groceries to the food bank?" I said weakly.

"I thought it was really nice that you donated that big chocolate cake. Most everything else was canned spinach and stuff . . ."

The manager looked at me. "He's only been with us a week. But don't worry, we'll give him a good talking-to. And I suppose we can give you a refund."

"No need," I said, as I started chuckling. "Tim, go back to work. Let's look at it this way: Together we made a nice donation to someone who really needs it."

DEAR GOD, HELP ME NOT TO BE SO QUICK TO ASSUME THE WORST.

—LINDA NEUKRUG

MY LIVING WORDS

1

2

3

4

5

6

7

8

9

10

11

12

13

14

15

16

17

18

19

20

21

22

23

24

25

26

27

28

29

30

DECEMBER

And the Word was made flesh,
and dwelt among us. . . .

—JOHN 1:14

*Obey your leaders and submit to them,
for they keep watch over your souls as
those who will give an account....*

—HEBREWS 13:17 (NAS)

Authority figures tend to intimidate me. With a single memo or change in procedure, my boss can make my life miserable. Fortunately, God has given me a great boss, a former student of mine.

David is a brilliant man, gifted in administration, speaking, technology and music. Such giftedness would tempt some folks to pride, but David has a servant's heart.

He's no marshmallow. He has high standards for the faculty, but he comes alongside to help us meet those goals. For example, before he makes out the semester schedule, he asks us, "What hours do you prefer to teach?" If a student comes to him with a criticism about me, he comes straight to me and asks, "What's the rest of the story on this, Dan?" When I was feeling overwhelmed by my workload, David worked out a contract that would ease my load and enable me to continue teaching.

GOD SPEAKS
THROUGH LEADERS

The best kind of communication is not that which comes from a manual, a Web site or a book. When I'm having trouble with my computer, I don't want to read a manual, I want David to come and help me—someone patient, who can answer my questions and give me encouragement.

No wonder that when God wanted to talk to us, He sent His own Son down in person to live with us and talk to us personally.

LORD, OUR LEADERS CARRY HEAVY BURDENS. HELP ME NOT TO ADD TO THEM.

—DANIEL SCHANTZ

"Your strength will equal your days."

—DEUTERONOMY 33:25 (NIV)

"I'm not handling this challenge so well," a friend told me as we sat together at my kitchen counter, drinking tea and talking about our shared experience of living with cancer. "I feel so afraid."

She had called me the day before, asking if we could get together because she needed help. "How do you do it?" she asked.

I wasn't sure I had any answers, but here we were, and so I told her something I learned almost twenty years ago from my friend Lois.

"When Lois was diagnosed with lung cancer, she shared her fears about the challenges that might lie ahead. 'What will happen when I lose my hair?' she asked me on one of our many long walks. And when she did, she enjoyed the sassy looks she could create with outrageous wigs.

"'What will happen when I'm on oxygen and can't go on our walks?' she asked. But when that happened, she willingly sat in a wheelchair with her portable oxygen tank and laughed when I did wheelies while pushing her around the neighborhood.

"'What will happen when I'm so weak I have to stay in bed all day?' she asked, and yet when that time came, she seemed peaceful and content.

"Looking into the future, Lois had fears, but when she got right up to the edge of each one, it disappeared. God gave her the strength she needed when she needed it.

"All I know is that I trust God to do the same for me," I told my friend that day. "If I face the things I fear the most, I trust that He will give me exactly what I need in that moment."

Before she left, I prayed for both of us:

LORD, HELP US TO BELIEVE YOUR PROMISE THAT YOU WILL GIVE US THE STRENGTH TO COPE WITH OUR CIRCUMSTANCES. AND HELP US BELIEVE YOU.

—CAROL KUYKENDALL

THU
3

Those who wait for the Lord will gain new strength; they will mount up with wings like eagles, they will run and not get tired, they will walk and not become weary.
—ISAIAH 40:31 (NAS)

Our golden retriever puppies are eight months old. Brothers from the same litter, Bear and Buddy have never been separated from each other. Since birth they have had free reign to romp in our large fenced backyard.

But, until today, they had never been taken to the country to run unrestrained by leash or fence.

Unloading the pups from the back of my SUV, I led them through a pasture gate and over the rise of a hill. There before us stretched rolling Texas prairie, expanding to an endless horizon. I knelt down by the pups, quietly unsnapped their leashes and stepped back. For a moment, both dogs hesitated and then realized they were free. They exploded in a burst of energy and sprinted away. After several hundred yards, they slowed, caught the scent of quail and instinctively cut wide figure eights, searching for the covey. I grinned from ear to ear, caught up in the magic of their exhilaration. For over an hour Bear, Buddy and I ambled across rich farmland together, and I felt the weight of my world lift.

Then, as the sun dropped into pink and amber, both man and beast were ready to load up and go home. We were tired, hungry and chilled. The thought of hearth and food and soft blankets beckoned. But freedom had restored our souls.

GOD, IN THE MIDST OF MY RESPONSIBILITIES, LET ME NEVER FORGET THE TASTE OF FREEDOM AND THE TOUCH OF YOUR GOOD EARTH. AMEN.   —SCOTT WALKER

Today, if you hear his voice,
do not harden your hearts. . . .

—PSALM 95:7–8 (NIV)

Frustrated with always finding my CD cases empty or with the wrong CDs tucked inside, I decided to organize my music collection. I was sitting in the middle of a couple of unsteady mini-towers when I came across a CD I hadn't listened to in years. It was my very own.

Years before I had recorded a handful of songs I'd written, completing my first and only demo. Nothing ever came of it, and I never pushed to make my music known beyond family and friends.

I popped the CD into the player. As I listened, my mind went back to the days when I'd sit at the piano, thinking, playing, scribbling, crossing out and humming until a new song was born. There was so much I'd wanted to say, always new ideas and melodies dancing around in my mind. And with each song there was a feeling of satisfaction, accomplishment and pride.

It had been a long time since I'd been inspired to do much of anything. I was in a rut, creatively, spiritually and every other way. Yet as I listened to my music, I felt God ministering to my heart. Each word gave the encouragement and counsel I needed to hear, each melody touched the emotions I'd been dealing with.

Eventually, I couldn't even hear myself in the music; my voice faded as God's grew stronger. I understood more than ever that I wasn't the one who had created these songs. God had molded the music in my heart and crafted the words that He knew would minister to my spirit so many years later.

LORD, ALL I HAVE TO DO TO GET MYSELF OUT OF A RUT IS ALLOW YOU THE FREEDOM TO CREATE THROUGH MY OBEDIENT AND WILLING HEART. —KAREN VALENTIN

SAT 5

"Do not be afraid. I am the First and the Last."
—REVELATION 1:17 (NIV)

In the South, the leaves turn color and fall from the trees a little later than they do up North. They may not be as colorful as they are in the Northeast, but they are beautiful and plentiful.

One day as I was raking some leaves, our grandson "Little Reggie" came running outside and asked, "Pops, can I play?" My instant answer was, "Boy, I'm working, and I don't have time to play." He sat down on a pile of leaves, and I piled up more leaves all around him. Each time I raked a pile, he would plop down on them and say, "Pops, can I play?" and I'd surround him with more leaves. Then he started to run and jump on the piles.

As I watched Little Reggie playing in the leaves, I began to feel fearful because there were small sticks in the leaves and I didn't want him to get hurt. My fears were starting to snowball out of the here-and-now into the uncertain future when I remembered "Do not be afraid" from Revelation 1:17. God is "the first and the last." Past, present and future are all known to Him, and I can trust that from whatever may happen, today or tomorrow, He will bring us good.

LORD, FOR LITTLE REGGIE, ROSIE, RYAN AND DANITA, HELP ME TO KEEP ON TRUSTING YOU AND YOUR WORD DAILY.
—DOLPHUS WEARY

He that hath mercy on the poor, happy is he.

—PROVERBS 14:21

"Oh boy," I mumbled under my breath as my son Harrison and I walked into the mall. Maybe I was in over my head this time. In an effort to teach Harrison about the importance of giving, we had adopted a needy family for Christmas. The father was in prison and the mother was working three jobs, trying to make ends meet. Her son was Harrison's age and her daughter was a few years younger. The mother's earnings were meager, and there was little money for presents.

On the ride over, I had done the best I could to explain things to Harrison. But walking into the store was like stepping into an instant replay of the commercials we had seen while watching Saturday morning cartoons. The shelves were groaning with things that seemed designed to fill the purest heart with greed. In an atmosphere like that, how could a seven-year-old grasp the concept of giving?

"Hey, Daddy," Harrison said gleefully, "that boy would love this game. It will make him so happy! And isn't the little sister Abby's age? [Abby was his cousin.] She'll love this doll and those books over there!"

I could feel my heart warming.

"What about the mom? I think she'd like some new clothes and maybe a purse." Before we knew it, our shopping cart was full.

But my best present ever was waiting in the checkout lane. Harrison insisted on unloading the cart himself. With a faraway look in his eyes, he picked up each item and placed it carefully on the counter. He lingered for a moment over the last item and then he turned to me and looked straight into my eyes. "Jesus is right, Daddy," he said, "It *is* better to give than to get."

FATHER, THANKS FOR LETTING ME GLIMPSE YOUR SON'S WISDOM WITH MY SON'S EYES.

—BROCK KIDD

Be ye kind one to another, tenderhearted,
forgiving one another, even as God
for Christ's sake hath forgiven you.

—EPHESIANS 4:32

"I don't think I'm very good at forgiving," I told my friend Jim as we were having lunch at our favorite pizzeria. Not that I had anything specific in mind; just a vague feeling that I held on to grudges and kept track too closely of wrongs done to me.

"I can think of one place where you're good at forgiving."

"Where?"

"In your marriage."

"There's nothing much to forgive."

"There you have it." He took a large bite out of his slice of pizza and I chased an olive around my plate, finally stabbing it with my fork.

"Okay," I said. "I can remember a couple weeks ago being really irritated at Carol for not taking out the trash, but then as I was bagging it up, I remembered that she had been annoyed with me for not telling her that I was going to be late one night because of a meeting."

"Did she get angry at you?"

"Not for long."

"Did you get angry at her?"

"Not really. . . . It all sort of evens out."

"That's because you forgive her."

I considered this insight for a moment and cut another slice of pizza. When I got home I'd have to inform Carol of this good news.

GIVE ME A FORGIVING HEART, LORD, AS YOU HAVE FORGIVEN ME. —RICK HAMLIN

For he shall give his angels charge over
thee, to keep thee in all thy ways.

—PSALM 91:11

It's always hard to say good-bye to an old friend, especially one as bright and gifted and full of merriment as Van Varner, who was my boss at *Guideposts* magazine for many years. I entered his corner office for a job interview more than twenty-five years ago, and within five minutes knew I *had* to work for him. My memories of him as a colleague and a friend are tender, compelling, laugh-out-loud ones: when he telephoned me at home when my cat died; when he called me "Cupcake" with the same respect he'd give a CEO; the way he edited articles so vigorously—and to such a high standard—in pencil that the pages ripped and crumpled.

Van and I lived several blocks away from each other on Manhattan's Upper West Side. Even after we'd both left our nine-to-five jobs at Guideposts, we'd still see each other in Central Park, where Van walked his lively and much-loved dogs. I passed his apartment building often, a large and impressive edifice facing the park and the Museum of Natural History. Van's home was on the second floor and I'd always look up at his windows—shutters slightly askew, a fern hanging in a pot—and imagine him there, enjoying the city he loved so much.

I still pass his building, heading crosstown on foot or on the bus, and I always look up at one window in particular. Van wrote about it in *Angels on Earth* magazine—his surprise and glee when he realized that directly above his apartment window, carved in stone on the building's facade, was the face of an angel, its wings spread behind it. A photo accompanied that piece, Van leaning out his window smiling his unforgettable smile, under the watchful gaze of an angel.

I still see you, Van, you and that angel, and sense its enveloping presence over us all.

DEAR LORD, ENDLESS THANKS FOR THE RICHNESS OF THE PEOPLE YOU BRING INTO OUR LIVES. AND FOR THE ANGELS THAT HOVER OVER ALL OF US.

—MARY ANN O'ROARK

The hills are clothed with gladness.

—PSALM 65:12 (NIV)

At approximately 7:35 every weekday morning, Maggie, Mary, Stephen and I begin to descend the 129 steps of 187th Street that bring us down to Broadway. Then we begin the trek up to the girls' school at the top of the opposite hill.

At the bottom of the first hill, we meet crowds of Orthodox Jewish children on their way to yeshiva. Then we puff our way up the second hill into a swirl of Hispanic parents and kids, some heading in our direction, others bound for the public school on the corner. Snatches of conversation come our way as Maggie runs to catch up with a friend: a child argues that he doesn't need a scarf, another is in tears over forgotten homework, a worried grandmother gives a last-minute lecture.

At the school door Stephen and I say good-bye to the girls, and then it's down the hill and up the hill to go home. Six and a half hours later, we set out again, this time to pick up our pupils. School has been good for my leg muscles. Stephen's too.

At the end of the day, Maggie tells me what she couldn't eat from her lunch box, whether or not she got a sticker, and who in her first-grade class is behaving better. Mary reports on what happened at recess, how annoying her classmate Anthony was and which test she has the next day. There seem to be an awful lot of tests in fourth grade.

Stephen races ahead, slaying the dragon that lives on the school hill. We cross Broadway and decide whether to climb the steps, walk up the hill, or detour a few blocks south and take the subway elevator to the top.

At home the girls change out of their uniforms and sit down to do their homework. The hills wait patiently for another day.

LORD, LET ME WALK EVERY HILL—WHETHER TO SCHOOL OR TO CALVARY—WITH MY EYES OPEN TO SEE THE WORLD AS YOU DO.   —JULIA ATTAWAY

But lay up for yourselves treasures in heaven, where neither moth nor rust doth corrupt, and where thieves do not break through nor steal.
—MATTHEW 6:20

One of my first assignments as a journalist was writing obituaries. At the time I wasn't overjoyed with the task, but later I came to appreciate "obits," because if they're well written, they offer a good synopsis of a person's life. *The New York Times*, for one, is famous for its interesting obituaries.

Larger papers such as the *Times* keep files in what is known as their "morgue." Whenever something happens to someone of note, a clipping of the story is placed in their file. Sometimes the biographical part of the obituary is prepared in advance.

One day a newspaperman gave Alfred Nobel, the Swedish inventor of dynamite, a midlife look at his obituary. Dynamite and its destructive power seemed to be the focus of the article. It gave Nobel pause; he didn't like to think that his invention summed up his life. So he decided to spend some of his time and wealth on humanitarian projects, and as a result we have the Nobel prizes given each year to outstanding people in the fields of literature, physics, medicine, chemistry and for the promotion of peace.

How would you sum up your life? By your occupation? By your family relationships? By your hobbies or avocations? By the material things you have accumulated? After all is said and done, our contribution to Christ's kingdom will be the most important thing. Though we are saved by grace, "faith without works is dead" (James 2:20).

TEACH US, GOD, THAT WHAT YOU TREASURE
MAY HAVE LITTLE VALUE BY EARTHLY MEASURE.

—FRED BAUER

Know ye not that your body is the temple of the Holy Ghost which is in you. . .?

—I CORINTHIANS 6:19

Perhaps because I recently had a physical, I'm thinking about my body today. I've been using it now for more than fifty years and abusing it at times too. There have been fractures and contusions, the usual assortment of minor illnesses plus the occasional aches and pains, a minor surgery and a couple of invasive medical procedures, a number of repaired teeth, and eyes that can no longer see things at a distance unaided.

Over the years I've subjected this body of mine to both exercise and sloth (though mostly exercise these days), a few bad habits that I pray are thankfully behind me, questionable food choices and diets, too little sleep and sometimes too much caffeine, many different time zones (jet lag shortens your life, but only by a few hours, it turns out), and stress I should have known how to avoid. Yet despite all this, I'm still breathing, walking, talking, thinking.

Maybe this is the key: God has taken better care of my body than I have. He installed me in it, after all; it makes sense that He'd keep an eye on it. And the longer I use it, the more gratitude and appreciation I have for the many incredible ways it has served me. In fact, I wouldn't mind if it lasted another fifty years or so.

FATHER, YOU CREATED ADAM FROM DUST AND GAVE HIM HUMAN FORM. I THANK YOU FOR THE GIFT OF MY PHYSICAL BEING. I PROMISE IN THE YEARS AHEAD I'LL TAKE BETTER CARE OF IT. —EDWARD GRINNAN

The Word became flesh and made his dwelling among us. We have seen his glory, the glory of the One and Only. . . .
—JOHN 1:14 (NIV)

When it comes to Christmas cards, I have three strategies from which I choose every year: proactive, reactive, inactive.

Proactive means I take the initiative. I make a list, check it twice and then get cards into the mail. *Reactive* means I tear off the return address of the card that comes to our house and, usually just before Christmas, shoot off a card to the person who's sent it to me. *Inactive* means I open the card and think fondly of the sender, but the only greeting she or he gets is the telepathic kind.

This year I find myself thinking about the whole concept of proactive, reactive and inactive. I'd like to make new friends at the church I've begun attending. Which strategy will I use? And what about everyday acts of kindness? Are they only reciprocal? How will I handle our community's new emphasis on recycling and "living green"?

God, of course, has only one strategy. You might say that He's the most proactive of all. In fact, that's what Christmas is all about: The Word became flesh and dwelt among us, and nothing would ever be the same again.

Kind of makes you want to share the good news. I think I'll send a few Christmas cards.

HOW THANKFUL I AM, LORD, THAT YOU REACHED DOWN TO US BY SENDING YOUR SON. HELP ME TO BE PROACTIVE IN TELLING OTHERS, AT CHRISTMAS AND ALL YEAR LONG. —MARY LOU CARNEY

Some years ago a young friend of mine became ill with Lou Gehrig's disease. My husband and I and another couple flew to Los Angeles to comfort her. I offered her my *Daily Guideposts*, thinking that I'd purchase another one once I got home. Tina, who'd made the trip with us, asked for a devotional as well. Tina and I formed a powerful friendship. For a few years, we exchanged *Daily Guideposts* as Christmas gifts and had the blessing of sharing our spiritual experiences. We began to personalize the books as part of the gift, adding our own handwritten personal touches to the stories. This ministry has grown, and last year I personalized twenty-one copies of *Daily Guideposts* for friends.

—*Suzanne DeBoer, Speedway, Indiana*

THIRD SUNDAY IN ADVENT	MAKING CHRISTMAS

A new spirit will I put within you. . . .
—EZEKIEL 36:26

Christmas was creeping up on me and I was so busy basking in the year's successes that I hadn't given the holiday much thought. I tallied up my clients' gains and muttered "Well done" under my breath as I shut down my computer.

That night I had dinner with some associates. "This is what it's all about," I said as I made a toast to the group. Everyone nodded in agreement.

The next day was Christmas Eve, and being the quintessential last-minute shopper, I headed to the mall. Carols were blaring through the speakers as people bustled about, but I felt empty.

The next morning I pulled up behind the line of cars parked on my parents' street. Every year my family hosts a Christmas brunch, mostly for people who have no family or no place to go. *Why can't we just have our own Christmas?* I thought as I walked through the front door. I breathed in the smell of country ham and baking biscuits. Kate, who had never missed one of these gatherings, was leaning on her walker near the fireplace, watching my niece Abby playing with her new doll. In the kitchen my mother was laughing as she dished out the cheese grits.

I recognized it first on the faces of the people gathered around her. It spread through the house and finally it filled up my heart—the spirit of Christmas, the biggest dividend of all. And in that moment I understood that investing *in* people is a lot more important than investing *for* them.

FATHER, YOU INVESTED EVERYTHING IN US WHEN YOU SENT US YOUR SON. FILL ME WITH YOUR SPIRIT AS I INVEST MYSELF IN YOUR PEOPLE.   —BROCK KIDD

By their fruits ye shall know them.
—MATTHEW 7:20

Aha! I open my front door to pick up the morning paper and see that my Snow Angel has been here again. The depressing headlines won't bother me this morning.

I had moved into this apartment about two hundred steep feet from the driveway only to learn that the landlord didn't do snow removal. He's well within his legal rights, of course, but somehow I had expected more. I was disappointed—stung, really. When my daughter Trina slipped on the ice and fell on her face, I became angry.

Enter Rudy, Trina's linebacker friend who's studying to be a nurse. Within hours of Trina's fall, he arrived in his truck with snowplow, shovel, and twenty-five pounds of sand and salt to clear our treacherous route to the door. Would he accept pay for his work? Absolutely not!

After the next snowfall I woke to find a neat trail cleared from the front door to the parked cars—and the cars brushed off too. Rudy? He wouldn't say, but when a blizzard dropped a foot of snow and sleet, I found yet another trail—and brushed cars.

I settle down, smiling with my coffee and newspaper. My Snow

Angel will probably never make the news, but he restores my faith in humanity. What a great way to start a snowy day!

LORD, THANK YOU FOR ALL THE INVISIBLE HELPERS WHO FILL YOUR WORLD WITH KINDNESS. —GAIL THORELL SCHILLING

"Be still, and know that I am God. . . ."

—PSALM 46:10 (RSV)

Years ago I wanted to be a part of everything people were doing that appeared to be God's will. But before long I had made more commitments than my calendar could possibly hold. I cut down on sleep, exercise and playtime with my family. Things got more and more chaotic, until one night I woke up in a panic.

I could see myself failing and being shamed by having to admit I couldn't do it all. Thoroughly revved up, I jumped up to another frantic day of jockeying appointments, meeting deadlines and shortchanging my family, promising that I was almost caught up. Something told me my frantic life was far from Jesus' "peace that passes understanding," but I felt guilty giving up projects that seemed to serve God.

As I tossed up a "please help me" prayer and sat on the floor to do a few sit-ups, I recalled an old newspaper story. Before dawn on a cold December morning, three duck hunters in waist-high rubber waders were thrown into the icy black water of an unfamiliar lake when their small, flat-bottomed boat capsized. All three drowned trying to swim to shore. The accident was particularly tragic since the water was less than five feet deep. Had the men not panicked but simply put their feet down, they could have waded out.

I shook my head, smiling at my own blindness. I'd been struggling so frantically to take over Jesus' job and save the world that I'd almost gone under. All I had to do was stop, be still and let my full weight down on God.

LORD, THANK YOU THAT YOU'RE ALWAYS CLOSE ENOUGH TO SAVE ME FROM MY MESSES. —KEITH MILLER

WED 16

*Friends, this world is not your home,
so don't make yourselves cozy in it. . . .*
—I PETER 2:11 (MSG)

A sign outside a church on my way to work proclaims a haunting message, Eternity: It's Forever.

Since my teen years, when I was diagnosed with the multisystem disorder neurofibromatosis, I've undergone countless medical treatments and more than twenty major surgeries. The night before each operation, I strived to settle things with God in the event that this time I would meet Him in the hereafter. I thought I had faced my own mortality.

But it's only been during this year of intense soul-searching that I've finally done so. And I haven't always liked what I've seen. I've discovered traces of pride in my heart, unforgiveness, ingratitude, impatience and a host of other characteristics that are displeasing to God. And I've learned a thing or two about

WITH ETERNITY IN VIEW

Love Living Each Day

what brings our Father pleasure: empathy, celebrating our creativity, letting go of grudges, being grateful for every precious gift.

What I've discovered is that each day is a lifetime in miniature. Living with eternity in view all boils down to how I live my life every single day, 365 days a year. Each day is all there is.

This year I've grown to love life here on earth more than ever before. But I also long to be in heaven with Jesus. One heavenly delight will be at long last meeting each of you, dear *Daily Guideposts* readers, and knowing on that blessed day that our lives have mattered.

DEAR GOD, WHAT THINGS OF ETERNAL SIGNIFICANCE DO YOU HAVE FOR ME TO DO TODAY?
—ROBERTA MESSNER

THU 17

Thy brother's anger turn away from thee. . . .
—GENESIS 27:45

The guests at the monastery we visit are like a family, sharing living space and meals in the guesthouse. Over the period of a stay—whether for days or weeks—we get to know one another pretty well. Sometimes that can be a strain.

Before Christmas some years ago, my husband Keith and I uncomfortably shared the house with another couple and their ten-year-old daughter. The girl was a sweetheart, but her father criticized her all the time, sometimes even yelling at her.

When the Christmas tree was brought in, a priest supplied boxes of ornaments, and he, the daughter and I began to decorate the tree. Her parents sat on the couch, watching us. The girl was relaxed, laughing, really enjoying herself. And then one of the glass ornaments slipped out of her hand and shattered on the floor. She froze, looking immediately at her father.

Before anyone else could say anything, I laughed and said, "Well, that's one! Last year, we broke three!"

The tension seemed to drain away. "I'll get the dustpan," the priest said. "Or do you think I should wait until we've broken more ornaments?"

THANK YOU, LORD, FOR GIVING ME THE RIGHT WORDS WHEN IT REALLY MATTERS.

—RHODA BLECKER

FRI 18

Again, the kingdom of heaven is like unto a merchant man, seeking goodly pearls.
—MATTHEW 13:45

My grandson Daniel is two, with round cheeks and a smile that nearly runs out of room and a welcoming heart. When I come to visit, he is waiting at the door with shining eyes and that amazing smile. When he wakes in the morning, he comes looking for me with that same irrepressible delight. Wherever Daniel appears, he makes me feel as if I'm the sunrise on his horizon.

David, Daniel's younger brother, just turned one. Although we don't really know him yet, he has my grandmother's dimple in his chin. She and I giggled a lot. I have high hopes for David.

Another grandson, Joshua, almost four, I call "moonchild." He and I both like the moon. One wintry evening when I was visiting him in Alaska, I carried him outdoors in bare feet and pajamas to admire its brightness. Later that night the moon glow through his bedroom window cast its luminous purity across his sleeping face.

These encounters with my grandchildren have become perfect pearls, strung together in love. For me, they're the "pearly gates" swinging wide on heavenly joys right here, right now!

JESUS, JEWEL OF GOD, LEAD ME TO MY TRUE PEARLS.   —CAROL KNAPP

Pray about everything. . . . you will experience God's peace, which is far more wonderful than the human mind can understand. . . .
—PHILIPPIANS 4:6–7 (TLB)

Oh, how I love Christmas mail! Familiar names, often with updated photos of so many dear familiar faces; intriguing stamps from faraway places; return addresses that stir the imagination: Jamboree Road, Mole Hall, Greensands, Hi Winds. I want to visit them all!

Each year I choose a favorite card, which I place on the mantle next to a figure of the Madonna and Child. Its sentiment becomes my spiritual focus through the holy season and beyond. This year I put up a greeting with a Celtic prayer:

> Deep peace of the running waves to you,
> of the flowing air, the smiling stars.
> Deep peace of the quiet earth to you,
> of the watching shepherds.
> Deep peace of the Son of Peace to you.

At harried times when I get caught up in a whirlwind of worry and stress, I pause to inhale those words. They are oxygen to my breathless soul. As I shut my eyes, I can see the foam of running waves and feel flowing air around my face. I listen to the quiet earth. Then I find myself entering into the peace that comes from the Son of Peace.

AS WE CELEBRATE YOUR COMING, LORD JESUS, THANK YOU FOR LOVING WORDS THAT GLADDEN OUR HEARTS AND BRIDGE THE MILES TO DRAW US CLOSE TOGETHER. BLESS US, EVERY ONE, AND GIVE US THE GIFT OF YOUR PEACE.   —FAY ANGUS

| FOURTH SUNDAY IN ADVENT | MAKING CHRISTMAS |

Have they not heard? Yes verily, their sound went into all the earth, and their words unto the ends of the world.

—ROMANS 10:18

By hovering near the Christmas tree for hours, I had become a master at recognizing those pesky presents by the time I was seven or eight.

As soon as I picked one up and gave it a little shake, I knew exactly what it was: an ornament. Back then I saw those neatly wrapped, light-weight boxes as necessary evils that I had to tear through and politely thank my grandmother Bebee for before I could get to the good stuff. Every year she gave ornaments to each of us grandkids. They came from her travels with my grandfather, and over time we'd received tree-hangers from all over the world. There was a wooden Great Wall from China, a tin Big Ben from London, and crudely carved mangers and stars from places I'd never heard of. On the back of each was the year and the place it came from, neatly written with a black marker.

All these years later those same ornaments have taken on a unique importance as my son Harrison and I decorate our tree. They remind me, of course, that I was always in my grandmother's heart as she traveled far and wide. But somehow they've also become symbols of the greatness of God, as they bear witness to the impact that Christ's birth has had on our world.

"Where is this one from, Daddy?" Harrison asks for the umpteenth time.

"That's a Taj Mahal from India," I reply, imagining the little shop in Agra that Bebee must have visited to find such a treasure.

"India?" Harrison replies with amazement. "I didn't know people that far away knew who Jesus is."

Isn't it wonderful to know they do?

FATHER, YOUR SPIRIT FILLS HEAVEN AND EARTH, AND YOUR WORD TRULY REACHES THE ENDS OF THE WORLD. —BROCK KIDD

MON
21

*Two are better than one, because they have
a good return for their work: If one falls down,
his friend can help him up. But pity the man
who falls and has no one to help him up!*

—Ecclesiastes 4:9–10 (NIV)

For a country girl, being in a large city away from home at Christmastime was unnerving. For days I fought the traffic in department stores, trying to find a suitable present for my mother, but I could find nothing in my price range.

"Why don't you hold a promotional party?" a woman at work suggested. "If you get enough sales, you can earn a lace tablecloth." *A perfect present for my mother!* I thought.

But who would come to the party? Being new in the city, I didn't know many people. Still, I had to try. I wrote out a guest list and made arrangements with the company.

On the appointed day a saleswoman entered my scrubbed studio, decorated with cedar boughs and red candles and smelling of chocolate brownies and coffee. She spread her wares across my bed and then we waited for the guests to arrive. None came.

Promptly at 7:30 PM, Lily, my landlady, arrived. "Where is everybody?" she asked and then hurried out of the room.

"I suppose we should call it off," the saleswoman said as she began to pack her wares.

Suddenly there was a noise at the door, and two women entered. "Hi. We live down the street. Lily tells us there's a party here," they said. Bewildered, I asked them to sit down. This scenario repeated itself until the room filled with people I'd never met before. Then Lily herself entered, gave me a wink and sat down.

Yes, I did receive the coveted tablecloth—and so much more.

Father, help me to spread goodwill to all who are lonely.

—Helen Grace Lescheid

If thou draw out thy soul to the hungry,
and satisfy the afflicted soul; then
shall . . . thy darkness be as the noonday.

—ISAIAH 58:10

It was midnight. My husband David, our daughter Keri, her husband Ben and I stood on a sidewalk on the outskirts of the city of Harare, Zimbabwe. We had come to expand our church's ministry to the street children and orphans of this ravaged southern African country where AIDS had already claimed twenty-eight percent of the population.

For several hours, we had delivered blankets and bread to children sleeping in back alleys and storm drains. All night, Keri's eyes searched for a family of three she had met one morning as we helped serve tea and bread to the street people. Keri had purchased some clothes and blankets for the couple's baby.

"One more place to look," our driver said. We got back into the car and wound through the streets. Finally, we caught sight of a mound near an alleyway. On cardboard spread with a few rags, two adults huddled together.

"It's them!" Keri exclaimed.

Our driver parked the car so that the headlights fell on the couple cradling their baby. Keri rushed from the car, but I stood back, feeling empty and blank, looking at nothing. Minutes passed. Then I felt David's hand on my shoulder turning me toward where the light shone.

"Look, Pam," he said, "it's as if we were standing at the Nativity."

My eyes followed the path of light from the car to the spot where my daughter knelt swaddling a baby in a soft warm blanket. The baby's mother and father knelt, too, as if in prayer.

Suddenly my heart was spinning back to the beginning, to the place where all our journeys begin and finally end, that place of star shine and angel's song and God's clear call: "Come, lay your gifts before My child."

We offered what we had: clothes, blankets and a few loaves of bread.

OUT OF OUR DARKNESS, FATHER, YOU COME AS NOONDAY TO SHOW US YOUR WAY. THANK YOU.

—PAM KIDD

"Learn to do good. . . ."
—Isaiah 1:17 (NKJV)

It was December, and Ruby and I were concerned. We were hoping our grandson Jeremy would join the family in New Hampshire for Christmas. He would be coming from Asheville, North Carolina, and he rarely made airplane reservations ahead of time. Then, too, we were concerned about the New England snowstorms that often blanket the area and shut down the airports.

But the weather remained calm, and two days before Christmas our telephone rang. It was Jeremy. "I'm home," he said. "It was a rough trip with the holiday crowds, delays and flight changes. But I'm home." We were relieved and delighted.

At that moment our doorbell rang. I raced down the stairs, opened the door and there stood Jeremy, grinning, cell phone in hand. His surprise capped our holiday like a gentle Christmas Eve snowfall.

Surprises can bring joy. There is no warmer way of expressing love than to surprise someone with a card, a phone call or, best of all, a visit.

Gracious Lord, let me be Your vehicle in bringing joy, not only at holiday time, but all year long.   —Oscar Greene

---

Christmas Eve   Making Christmas

I am the bread of life: he that cometh to me shall never hunger. . . .
—John 6:35

In our family, as in so many across the world, Christmas Eve is a time filled with laughter and the joy of giving. There will be homemade goodies—Tennessee cheese and my grandmother's "nuts and bolts" party mix—laid out in my parents' kitchen and piles of presents waiting under the tree.

But all this comes later. We start this night at the six o'clock Communion service at Hillsboro Presbyterian, where my father has been minister all my life. The church is candlelit, and my father waits at the altar as small groups of people come forward.

I close my eyes and see myself as a little boy standing beside his grandfather. With his huge hand laid gently on my shoulder, we wait in a holy silence as my dad passes out the sacrament.

Every Christmas Eve of my life has been the same. And even as the years have flown by, even with my hand laid on my son Harrison's shoulder, I become a child again. Somehow, in the candle glow, I can sense all those I've loved—grandparents, aunts, uncles, dear friends—gathered near, and as my father looks into my eyes and says, "This is the body of Christ, Brock, broken for you," my heart is filled with enough hope to sustain me through the year.

And so on this Christmas Eve, I will come again to the candlelit church. On this night of miracles, I'll join the great crowd of people all around the world—whoever is coming now, whoever has come in the past and whoever will come in the future—all His children, all His church.

"This is the body of Christ broken for you."

FATHER, ON THIS HOLY NIGHT, I WAIT AS A CHILD IN FAITH AND HOPE.

—BROCK KIDD

CHRISTMAS	MAKING CHRISTMAS

Prepare your hearts. . . .
—I SAMUEL 7:3

Finally our Christmas breakfast has ended and the last guest has gone. The chaos of scattered wrapping paper, breakfast dishes and extra folding chairs has been cleared away. In my parents' home this has always been the quiet time. No more company— well, maybe a friend or two will drop by—for the rest of the day.

Bebee, my grandmother, finds a comfortable spot and starts reading her new book. Herb, my grandfather, joins my dad, my brother-in-law Ben and me in the den. We trade stories, examine our gifts and chuckle over Christmases past. My niece Abby's and my son Harrison's excitement have waned as they play with their new toys. My sister Keri is in the kitchen helping Mom. The house still smells of wassail and banana bread. Most everyone will find a spot for an afternoon nap.

Later we gather for dinner. The room is candlelit, and we pop open the favors that Bebee always brings and wear the paper crowns we find inside. I look around the table and wish I could make time stop. My mother laughs and says she can't believe we held it all together and "made Christmas" once again.

In a way we do "make Christmas." We make it by attending the services at church and remembering the Christ Child and how He came. We make it by reaching out to the poor as that Child taught us to do. We make it by sharing our good times with others and by establishing family traditions and carrying them out from year to year. Finally, we make it by coming together as family and loving each other as we are.

I look around the dinner table at my family, wearing their silly paper crowns. I hold the moment close and tuck it into my heart, where I know it will live forever.

FATHER, YOU MADE THAT FIRST CHRISTMAS BY GIVING US YOUR SON. USE THE CHRISTMASES WE MAKE TO BRING US CLOSER TO HIM.   —BROCK KIDD

SAT 26

For all who are led by the Spirit of God are children of God.
—ROMANS 8:14 (NLT)

Alex, my two-year-old nephew, came running back into the church. It was time for the lighting of the candles during the Christmas Eve service and he didn't want to miss it. I scooped him up in my arms and held him on one hip while my brother lit the candle in my hand.

Wide-eyed, Alex stared at the flickering flame. He caught my eye and began to sing, "Happy birthday to you . . ."

I started to shake with suppressed laughter. Hands full, I had no hope of muffling Alex's song. He continued, singing louder, "Happy birthday to you . . ."

The people in the pews around us turned and smiled as Alex finished his song with a loud, "Happy birthday to Mommy, happy birthday to you." Holly, Alex's mom, gazed down the row at us, smiling at the little boy who had so perfectly repeated the performance he'd so carefully prepared for her recent birthday.

As we stood in the now-silent darkness, it seemed to me that Alex had been singing along with something he alone could hear: a Father, in heaven, singing "Happy Birthday" to his newly born Son.

HAPPY BIRTHDAY TO YOU, JESUS. —ASHLEY JOHNSON

Let us not be weary in well doing: for in due season we shall reap, if we faint not.
—GALATIANS 6:9

My wife Julia and I were sitting on the sofa next to the Christmas tree when the demonstration began. Six-year-old Maggie and nine-year-old Mary marched out of their bedroom, chanting and carrying signs that read, School is boring! No more school!

"I'm going to perform a musical," Maggie announced. She sat at the little table we'd used for the Christmas dinner overflow, arranged pencils and papers in front of her, and began to sing, "School is so boring, I'm so very bored. School is so easy, what can I do?" The tune wasn't recognizable, but the sentiments were. The transition from the fun and flexibility of homeschool kindergarten to the routine of a first-grade class of thirty-plus hasn't been easy for Maggie.

Maggie is bright, kindhearted and well behaved at school. She loves her teacher, and her teacher loves her. But her effervescent blend of energy, curiosity and a quirky sense of humor doesn't always fit well into a classroom. And to tell the truth, school sometimes *is* boring.

Julia is working with Maggie's teacher to make sure she's challenged and engaged at school. But one of the lessons Maggie has got to learn is that every day isn't going to be filled with excitement, no matter where she happens to be. It's a lesson I'm constantly relearning myself, when I've got to tackle some necessary but uninspiring tasks at work, when I have to put aside my book to clean up the kitchen, or when I'm tired or anxious and struggling to pray.

He or she may not have heard the angels or even noticed the star, but how rich was the gift of whoever it was who mucked out that Bethlehem stable and freshened the straw our Savior slept in. Sometimes the best I can give is the small but necessary task, no matter how boring.

Lord, help Maggie and me to face all the tasks You give us with a cheerful heart. —Andrew Attaway

---

MON
28

And you will always give thanks for everything. . . .
—Ephesians 5:20 (NLT)

That's what my mother used to say: "You *will* write thank-you letters for your Christmas gifts." Doing so almost canceled out the excitement of whatever had been in the wrapped boxes mere days before. I still recall the agony of gripping a stubby pencil in sweaty hands, chewing its eraser end and asking, "What shall I say?"

Probably since the beginning of time, mothers have required the same etiquette of their offspring. My own sons didn't escape either.

So I've come up with a solution for my grandchildren and for you. Make as many copies of this form as there are gifts, cut on the dotted lines, check the appropriate boxes, fill in the blanks, mail. Done! It may not be ideal, but it's better than nothing.

- -

Dear ☐ Mom ☐ Dad ☐ Grandma ☐ Grandpa ☐ Aunt ☐ Uncle
☐ Cousin ☐ Friend ☐ Sweetheart ☐ (Other) _____,

Thank you for the _____. It is ☐ beautiful ☐ handy ☐ just what I need ☐ my size ☐ not my size ☐ the right color ☐ not the right color ☐ something I can't wait to use ☐ a gift that will be good for me ☐ something I really like ☐ (other) _____.

Our Christmas was ☐ fun ☐ happy ☐ blessed ☐ busy ☐ disastrous ☐ (other) _____.

We had ☐ ham ☐ turkey ☐ meatloaf ☐ pizza ☐ vegetarian ☐ (other) _____.

☐ Love, ☐ Blessings, ☐ Cordially, ☐ Warmly,
☐ Sincerely, ☐ Yours, ☐ Best, ☐ (Other) _____
(Signature) _____

- -

And now, here's an already prepared thank-you prayer, but it must be said wholeheartedly and with sincere gratitude:

THANK YOU, GOD, FOR SENDING YOUR SON, JESUS—OUR SAVIOR, REDEEMER, BLESSED HOPE—CHRIST, THE CENTER OF *CHRIST*MAS! ONLY YOU COULD GIVE YOUR CHILDREN THIS PERFECT GIFT! —ISABEL WOLSELEY

When you lie down, your sleep will be sweet.

—PROVERBS 3:24 (NAS)

"Why don't you take a little nap while I ice this cake?" I asked my husband Leo. He wandered off into the bedroom.

I stood at the stove, holding my electric mixer as it fluffed up the seven-minute frosting in the top of the double boiler. Stopping the beaters to see if the mixture would hold a peak, I heard the noise of paper shuffling in the bedroom. "Are you lying down yet?" I asked Leo.

"No, the sound of your mixer is too loud."

"I'll be done soon," I told him.

When the frosting stood in stiff white peaks, I began spreading it on the cake. There was another noise in the bedroom. "Aren't you napping yet?"

"I'm waiting to lick the bowl," Leo replied. I should have known.

When the cake was iced, I took him his treat. A few minutes later he called out, "I'm finished!"

"Now you better have a nap before you get cranky," I teased.

When I went into the bedroom, he lifted his face for a kiss, an extra sweet one. There was icing around his lips.

I gave him a peck on the cheek and patted his bald head. Though we've been married for more than fifty years, in some ways Leo hasn't aged a bit.

THANK YOU, LORD, THAT EVEN THOUGH "OUR OUTER NATURE IS WASTING AWAY, OUR INNER NATURE IS BEING RENEWED EVERY DAY" (II CORINTHIANS 4:16, RSV).

—ALMA BARKMAN

He told them still another parable: "The kingdom of heaven is like yeast that a woman took and mixed into a large amount of flour until it worked all through the dough."

—Matthew 13:33 (NIV)

My neighbors Ruth and Fran were coming over for pizza. I was to make the crust and they were bringing the toppings. I could make the dough with my eyes closed; we had a bakery, the Bread of Life, in the mid-1970s, and I used to make up to one hundred loaves a day to sell to local stores. I decided to double the recipe and make some loaves of bread in addition to the pizza crust.

During the first rising I walked past the bowl. It looked a little funny, but I was multitasking, so I didn't give it a second thought. When it was time to roll out the dough for the pizza and it still had not risen, I figured it would be fine when I put it in the oven. As Ruth and Fran put on the cheese and toppings, I formed five loaves of bread and put them in their pans. Time passed, but those loaves never rose.

The Julia Child committee met in my head: *Do you remember putting in the yeast? Oh no!* Actually, I was sure I hadn't added it. How could I have left out the most important ingredient?

I took the five loaves of bread, put them back in the mixer, and then dissolved some yeast with warm water, sugar and flour. I added it to the flat bread, mixed it up and baked some of the nicest loaves ever to come out of my oven.

Lord, You are truly the yeast in my life. With You, I can rise to new heights and gain eternal life.

—Patricia Pusey

He has put eternity in their hearts. . . .

—Ecclesiastes 3:11 (NKJV)

As I come to the end of 2009 and of my questions about the pairs of opposites that exist in time, I'm met with this most exciting statement about eternity: "He has put eternity in their hearts." It seems to me that, in this one assertion, all the statements about

A TIME TO EVERY PURPOSE

time in Ecclesiastes 3 are gathered up into breathtaking timelessness. Everything I've been reading about and questioning is brought together in the sure knowledge, placed in our hearts by God, that we are already inhabitants of eternity. So I ask one more question: "How can I come to know the eternity in my heart during the coming year?"

There is a silent sanctuary
hidden from the rush of daily planting and plucking up,
beyond the push-pull of keeping and casting away,
of weeping and laughing,
mourning and dancing.
It's a holy place where war is absorbed into peace
and rending is not separate from mending;
a place where vision expands beyond the temporal,
and we escape our incessant race with time;
a place where we are lifted up to a vision of the eternal
and we know with an unhurried wisdom
that this is our truest home.

CREATOR GOD, I CAN'T KNOW YOUR PLACE OF TIMELESSNESS, BUT NOW AND THEN I GET A GLIMPSE OF ITS LIGHT BEYOND THE HILLS OF TIME . . . AND IN A BURST OF RECOGNITION MY HEART CRIES, "FATHER!"   —MARILYN MORGAN KING

MY LIVING WORDS

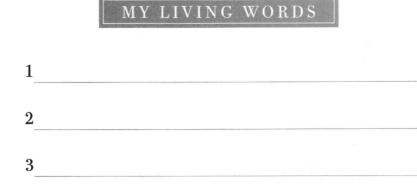

1 _____

2 _____

3 _____

4

5

6

7

8

9

10

11

12

13

14

15

16

17

18

19

20

21

22

23

24

25

26

27

28

29

30

31

If you've been wondering what our fifty-eight writers have been up to since last year, you've come to the right place: Fellowship Corner. And this year, you can learn more about them online at OurPrayer.org/DGP2009Authors. They'll share their thoughts, favorite Bible verses, the music that they love, photos and a whole lot more!

MARCI ALBORGHETTI and her husband Charlie of New London, Connecticut, try to follow Jesus' directive to help the poor wherever they are, whether it involves volunteering for a food pantry in northern California, supporting a homeless shelter in town, or trying to raise money for friends in Sierra Leone and southern India. Yet the more Marci does, the more she realizes that living the Word demands a lot. "What little we do really is never enough," she says. "For us to truly live the Gospels, we must remember how Jesus warned us that from those who have been given much, much will be required. How often does He say, 'Sell your possessions and give to the poor'? Yet how many of us manage this? It's a challenge to live the Word while living in the world. It's also the most exciting journey we can take!"

"This has been a topsy-turvy year," writes FAY ANGUS of Sierra Madre, California, "when prayerfully laid plans seem to have gone wrong and our family has had to literally live the word *trust*. After much prayer, my son made a major job change that involved relocating to Denver. Caught in the housing crunch, his home has not sold. It's been agonizing months of Dad in Denver with Mom and the four children still here in California and all-too-few weekends snatched here or there. 'We all love Denver and we're excited about the move. I don't understand. God's leading was so clear,' my son groans. We cling to Proverbs 3:5–6: 'Trust in the Lord with all thine heart; and lean not unto thine own understanding . . . and he shall direct thy paths.' We wait and trust. How long, dear Lord, how long?"

"It's been a hectic year at our house, with four of the five children in school and everybody adjusting to getting up earlier and squeezing homework into the evening schedule," says *Daily Guideposts* editor ANDREW ATTAWAY of New York City. "I'm hardly dressed before Elizabeth is heading out the door, John is sleepily eating his cereal, Mary is brushing her hair, Maggie is devising new strategies to avoid putting on her school clothes and Stephen is happily telling me about last night's dream. And it's been an eventful year at Guideposts, too, as we explore new ways to communicate our message more widely and more effectively, whether on the Internet, in bookstores or via the mail. Both at home and at work, change is a constant and sometimes a challenge. But through it all, the Word remains, guiding, restoring and strengthening all of us day after day."

"This year has seen big changes for us, with the children in school," JULIA ATTAWAY of New York City writes. "The biggest adjustment has been adapting to having less time together. Elizabeth's off at high school, the city math team and her youth choir; John and Maggie sing in a neighborhood jazz choir; Maggie's had roles in two children's theater productions; Mary dances (and dances and dances); and Stephen fills the day with his impishness and laughter, keeping me busy while I try to do freelance marketing work. With all the busyness in our lives, it's a great joy to hear Mary say at bedtime, 'But, Mom, I want to wait up so I can talk to Elizabeth!' Keeping our priorities straight—putting God and people first—is the only way to stay balanced."

"Probably without anyone realizing it," writes ALMA BARKMAN of Winnipeg, Manitoba, Canada, "our family was living the Word at a family reunion this summer when in the manner of the Old Testament, they unveiled a special stone to mark Leo's and my fiftieth wedding anniversary. The stone is decorated with all our names, and like Samuel of old, we should name it Ebenezer, which means 'thus far the Lord has helped us.' When I told a friend we were looking forward to seeing our four children, their spouses and our nine grandchildren arrive for our celebration, she teasingly replied, 'Now look what you two have done!' We say, 'Look what God has done,' for we never imagined the blessings of health, happiness and family that He would give us during five decades of marriage."

"In our Sunday school class this quarter we've been talking about what it means to be a Christian—every day, in every way," writes FRED BAUER of State College, Pennsylvania, and Englewood Beach, Florida. "One member volunteered that the world would be a lot different if Christ's followers all lived up to His high calling. Another added that Christianity hasn't failed; it just hasn't been tried. The discussion reminded me of this year's theme, 'Living the Word.' How do we do that? The Bible says we all have different gifts and callings, but love must be the centerpiece of our faith walk, and service must follow closely on its heels. To love God with all our heart, soul and mind, and our neighbors as ourselves, requires action. We need to be His hands and feet."

Highlights of EVELYN BENCE's year? "A January evening at home in Arlington, Virginia, hosting a Bleak Midwinter party. An April morning on a North Carolina beach, watching the sun rise over the Atlantic Ocean. A June afternoon, sitting behind home plate at a Washington Nationals baseball game. A July weekend in western New York, gathering with brothers and sisters around a campfire, roasting hot dogs and popcorn. Two Sunday afternoons, strolling through art museums, springtime in New York, autumn in Washington. Frequent after-church conversations, summarizing God's recent blessings. All these memories—and more—tie me to the people who inspire me, stretch me, draw out the best in me as I live out my faith, whether I'm traveling or close to home." Evelyn continues her work as a book editor and recently became a writing tutor for graduate students at a nearby seminary.

"I had to seek the right words before I could try to live them," says RHODA BLECKER of Bellingham, Washington. "This was a rough year because of my husband Keith's cancer surgery and my biopsy. So I looked for God's words where Jews have always looked for them—in the Torah (the Five Books of Moses). Torah study has kept me grounded, and struggling for the meaning of the words in Torah—using the original Hebrew, six different translations and the rabbinic interpretations in the Talmud—occupied my mind, emotions and spirit when I might otherwise have let doubt creep in. It's never easy to trust during tough times that God's plan and my own hopes will coincide. The Torah's strength became my foundation, and I lived its words by joining the 2,500 years of study that support and define my faith. Keith and I now live in the joy of the words and each other."

It's been an exciting year for MELODY BONNETTE of Mandeville, Louisiana: a new marriage, a new grandchild (beautiful blue-eyed Mia) and a new appreciation of the power of God's Word. "Johnny Swang and I married on July 1, with all of our children, their spouses and our grandchildren sharing in the ceremony—twenty-five in all! It was a day of joy, of hope and of wonderment for us to see God's Word fulfilled so perfectly. 'For I know the plans I have for you,' declares the Lord, 'plans to prosper you and not to harm you, plans to give you hope and a future' (Jeremiah 29:11, NIV)."

"This year I have really struggled with doubt," writes AMANDA BOROZINSKI of Rindge, New Hampshire. "Should I be spending more time with my family? Am I supposed to be a writer? Should I be doing more at church? In the fall my mother called to tell me my grandmother was very sick. I didn't feel we could afford the cross-country flight, and I began to worry. When my husband Jacob asked what was wrong, I broke down and told him. 'Go. We'll find the money,' he said. In the spring, I found out that I'd been accepted into the MacDowell Colony, the oldest artists' retreat in the country. For three weeks I would live in a cabin in the woods and pursue my passion of writing. 'I guess you don't have to worry,' Jacob said. 'God must think you're a pretty good writer.' Despite the ups and downs in my life this year, I see one overarching theme: God will always be there."

GINA BRIDGEMAN of Scottsdale, Arizona, went back to work part-time at her daughter's school. "I really enjoy being out in the world again after so many years as a stay-at-home, working mom," she says. Gina also returned to church choir, making worship particularly meaningful for her. "Singing hymns based on

Scripture or the Psalms set to music brings God's Word right into my heart." So does Gina's regular Thursday-morning Bible study. "Learning the history and studying the subtle meanings of the words makes God's Word as real and urgent for me as a cell phone text message." The rest of the family is doing well: husband Paul is working as technical director for Arizona Broadway Theatre; Ross, a sophomore commercial music major at Nashville, Tennessee's Belmont University, had the privilege of performing in a Christmas concert televised on PBS; and Maria, an eighth grader whose life is filled with all kinds of dance, is excitedly looking ahead to high school.

After six months overseas on sabbatical with her professor-husband Alex, MARY BROWN returned home to East Lansing, Michigan, to take an intensive workshop training her to tutor dyslexics. "I am amazed at this late stage in my life that I'm embarking on a new career, but it is profoundly rewarding. I love helping students break through barriers to decode the English language." Mary hopes to finish her degree at the same time her daughter Elizabeth graduates from Michigan State University in chemical engineering. "While overseas, battling depression and loneliness, I experienced the power of 'a word fitly spoken' (Proverbs 25:11). God comforted and strengthened me not only through His written Word, but also through the cheerful encouragement of my elderly neighbor Pat. Her kind conversation also lifted the spirits of my teenage son Mark, until he finally found friends his age."

It's been an eventful year for MARY LOU CARNEY and her family in Chesterton, Indiana. Son Brett and his wife Stacy bought a new (old!) home at the edge of the sand dunes bordering Lake Michigan. "It's a fairy-tale house," says Mary Lou, "with a rounded wooden door and vines climbing around the windows." And the family has the perfect little princess to bring there: 10-month-old Isabelle Grace. Grandsons Drake, 4, and Brock, 2, will be getting a little brother later this year when Amy Jo gives birth. "I tell Isabelle she'll have to learn how to tame her rowdy boy cousins!" Gary continues to run his excavating company but finds plenty of time to play Pa-Pa. This year Mary Lou went to part-time employment, which gives her more time for fun projects, like her new children's book that will be published this fall.

"This year my oldest son Solomon started kindergarten," says SABRA CIANCANELLI of Tivoli, New York. "Weekday afternoons my youngest Henry and I wait for the school bus. We sit on rockers on the front porch and I answer Henry's constant question, 'Wass-at?' as he points to everything in sight. Finally, the roar of the bus engine echoes down our road and all of Henry's focus shifts. His head turns and a wide smile curves on his chubby cheeks. Leaping from his chair, he jumps up and down and shouts, 'Sol-Sol! Sol-Sol!' as if they've been apart a decade. Solomon gets off the bus, his backpack strewn over one arm, collapses onto the couch, and shares the joys and woes of his day. It's a time I hold close to my heart, a blessing to watch my boys find their independence as their friendship and admiration for each other grows."

"The older I get, the more nostalgic I become," says a wistful MARK COLLINS of Pittsburgh, Pennsylvania. "But I've learned not to be critical of everything modern. I used to be suspicious of cell phones, e-mail, text messages . . . then I got a message from one of my kids that simply said, 'i was thinking of U and wanted 2 say hi.' It's amazing how a few simple words can change a day, can change a life." Mark's modern miracles include his wife Sandee and three high-tech wizards Faith, 17, Hope, 16, and Grace, 12. "The oldest will be starting college," Mark says, shaking his head. "Well, maybe I'll get a chance to return the favor. Maybe I'll send a message that says, 'i was thinking of U and wanted 2 say hi' just when she needs to hear it. Maybe that's what families do."

"This year has been about letting go and living the Word," says PABLO DIAZ of Carmel, New York. "Our family bid farewell to our sixteen-year-old schnoodle Bandit. Saying good-bye was not easy for any of us, especially for my wife. Bandit kept Elba company on many occasions while I was on the road. Elba and I are also learning more than ever to trust God that the seed of faith we sowed in the hearts of Christine and Paul when they were children will be a guiding light as they establish their careers and develop significant relationships. They're on their own faith journeys, different from each other and from us. When they were young, I heard a Christian psychologist say: 'We raise our children in love and send them into the world by faith.' Today we live by these words." Pablo is Guideposts' vice president of ministries and invites you to join the whole *Daily Guideposts* family in prayer at www.OurPrayer.org.

BRIAN DOYLE is the editor of *Portland Magazine* at the University of Portland in Oregon. He is the author of nine books of essays and poems, most recently *Thirsty for the Joy: Australian & American Voices*. He carries various tattered pieces of paper in his wallet by which he tries haltingly to live the Word. On these flitters of paper are the faces of his children, his wife's high-beam eyes, lines from St. Paul about how Christ is in us all, each and every one, a heartfelt letter of condolence after the murders of September 11 from a Muslim woman in Australia, and a shard of prayer flag on which is written E. M. Forster's great law: *Only connect.*

"My life hardly looks like the life I planned for myself," says SHARON FOSTER of Durham, North Carolina. "My family, my work and where I work are different than I dreamed. I thought I'd be married with nine children, a career executive living in New York City. I spent lots of years tired and unhappy, trying to force my life to conform to my strategic plan. Then God got involved, or maybe I finally heard the song He'd been trying to sing to me. 'For I know the plans I have for you,' declares the Lord, 'plans to prosper you and not to harm you, plans to give you hope and a future' (Jeremiah 29:11, NIV). One of the hardest things for me to do was to surrender and to believe that God loves me enough that He set in order the perfect plan for me. I adore my two children, Lanea and Chase, and I love my life—the life God planned all along."

"This summer, a friend told me to read Psalm 139 out loud every day for two weeks," writes JULIE GARMON of Monroe, Georgia. "She said not to hurry through it and to write down my thoughts. The next day I got started. 'O Lord, thou hast searched me, and known me.' I stopped at that first sentence and read it over and over. I let it soak through me. Some days, *I* don't even know me, but what a relief to know God does. No matter what, I can't fool Him and He can handle me. He never panics over my circumstances. In December I was diagnosed with celiac disease, meaning no more bread, cakes, cookies, bagels, pies, anything with wheat or gluten. So I'm relearning how to eat. Psalm 139:14 wells up daily inside me: 'I will praise thee; for I am fearfully and wonderfully made.'"

 "Our community is changing rapidly," writes OSCAR GREENE of West Medford, Massachusetts. "Longtime neighbors have relocated to the Southern states—'Less expensive and no snow,' they say. And our beloved pastor accepted a new charge in Pennsylvania." All in all, life is busier even as Oscar and Ruby become less active. "The slowing down has increased our joy. The grandchildren have visited, and we've enjoyed delicious meals and sparkling conversation. *Daily Guideposts* readers have called and we've exchanged letters. Our empty spaces have allowed God to step in with activities that we can handle and enjoy. The word we're living is *change*, and we're accepting and adjusting."

 EDWARD GRINNAN of New York City and his wife Julee Cruise have spent the last year raising a new pup, Millie, a white golden retriever. "I forgot what a handful a puppy can be, even a good one like Millie," Edward reports. There was an unexpected upside to Millie's arrival though. "I was asked to blog and vlog (video blog) on our new guideposts.com site. Millie proved a natural on camera, and her vlogs are among the most popular." Millie has also helped ease the grief of losing Van Varner, Edward's friend and mentor. "Van loved dogs almost as much as he loved people. He would have adored Millie. I sometimes find myself telling her about him. Silly maybe, I know, but it helps to talk, even to a dog. I think Van would have approved."

 "Empty nest syndrome," writes RICK HAMLIN. "Carol and I have finally hit that happy, albeit surprising stage of life. ('Are we really old enough to have all of our children out of the house?' we ask ourselves.) William is a senior in college this year, and Timothy is a freshman—both of them in California. 'Isn't it time

that you move out there too?' people ask Carol and me. Not yet. We have too much fun living in New York City. Our favorite thing to do on a Friday night is to go to the Metropolitan Museum, have dinner in the cafeteria, and then view a couple of centuries' worth of art without worrying about a babysitter or wondering where the kids are. It's the perfect date night for a couple with empty nest syndrome."

MADGE HARRAH says, "Things are going well. I'm still writing books and my husband Larry does occasional consulting work for a local materials development laboratory. During the summer we spend as much time as possible at our cabin in Colorado since the dirt road that leads into those snowbound mountains is closed during the winter. Here in Albuquerque, New Mexico, we enjoy our family and our church. We start each Sunday school session with Christ's great commandment: 'You shall love the Lord your God with all your heart, and with all your soul, and with all your strength, and with all your mind; and your neighbor as yourself' (Luke 10:27, RSV; also Deuteronomy 6:5; Leviticus 19:18). That's always been my favorite verse in the Bible, the one I've chosen to live by. I feel that Christ's entire message is summed up in that one sentence. And along with that one sentence comes an entire Bible filled with other life-changing messages. What a gift!"

"More than a year after moving back East," writes HAROLD HOSTETLER of Poughkeepsie, New York, "Carol and I are still being asked why we left Southern California. It's as if weather is the main reason for living anywhere. Of course, people understand when we say we wanted to be near the rest of our family. This past year we were present for all of our grandchildren's birthday parties and Thanksgiving and Christmas celebrations. I was also able to attend the fifty-fifth reunion of my high school graduating class in western Pennsylvania. But there's a deeper reason we believe God has led us to the Mid-Hudson Valley: a growing undercurrent of prayer here transcending churches and denominations, gatherings of people who are praying for spiritual revival. That's something a lot of us are convinced our country needs right now, and we'd like to be part of it, especially if it's going to begin right here."

If colleges can have school songs, can individual people have them too? If so, the song you'll hear JEFF JAPINGA of Holland, Michigan, singing begins like this: "'Let all things now living a song of thanksgiving to God the Creator triumphantly raise.' It's a song about a son whose impending birth was foretold in the pages of Daily Guideposts many years ago," says Jeff, "and who will graduate from Grinnell College this year. About a daughter whose game-winning hit on the volleyball floor and profession of her faith before our church were fitting bookends to her first year in high school. About a spouse whose remarkable ministry of teaching was enhanced by a nearly yearlong role as interim minister in our congregation. And, most unexpectedly, about my new calling and work as associate professor and dean for the doctor of ministry program at McCormick Theological Seminary in Chicago."

Moving from freelance and temporary employment to a full-time staff position for a magazine Web site has created a happy state of chaos in ASHLEY JOHNSON's life. "I never know what tomorrow will bring," she notes. "But that's good, because I'm a planner, and sometimes I just need to let go and trust that God has a great and wonderful plan for me." Ashley spends her free time celebrating friends' weddings, welcoming more nieces and nephews into the family (currently five under the age of four), and expanding her culinary skills in her Birmingham, Alabama, kitchen. When she has a minute to spare, she enjoys reading classic Victorian "chick-lit" novels and journaling the old-fashioned way—fancy pens in leather-bound books.

"Life is great," writes BROCK KIDD of Nashville, Tennessee. "My son Harrison is thriving and is rapidly approaching the third grade." Early last year, Brock was listed in *Bank Investment Consultant* magazine as the 13th-best producer in the country. That honor was quickly put into perspective, however, when he traveled with his family to visit the work they've been doing to change lives in Zimbabwe. "One of my best memories from the trip was meeting an entrepreneurial young man who was HIV positive. We decided to partner with him so that he could achieve his dream of having a roadside roasted-corn business. I can count that as one of the best investments I'll ever have the opportunity to make."

PAM KIDD of Nashville, Tennessee, writes, "This year my fondest wish came true when our son Brock, our daughter Keri, her husband Ben, and our granddaughter Abby all traveled to Zimbabwe with David and me. Only Brock's son Harrison, my mother and my stepfather were unable to go. But there's always next year! It took Abby, 5, less than a millisecond to bond with her African brothers and sisters, and when I looked across the lawn at an AIDS clinic and saw her playing ring-around-the-rosy with the children being treated there, I knew this was the way our world is supposed to be. Keri and I have managed to fund a number of projects in Zimbabwe with our real estate proceeds. This year we began sponsoring a feeding program at a rural school. As we served lunch to some mighty hungry children, I understood why Jesus urges us to serve others—it just makes you plain happy!"

For MARILYN MORGAN KING and her husband Robert of Green Mountain Falls, Colorado, this has been a year of reconnecting with the past and welcoming the new. "Several family members and friends visited us, staying next door in our cabin. In June we attended Robert's fiftieth Harvard reunion as well as a poetry-writing workshop in Boulder, where I reconnected with a dear friend whom I hadn't seen since junior high. July brought a family reunion, which made us deeply aware of the absence now of our parents' generation, but we were grateful for the next two generations who have come to take their places in our growing family." Marilyn was especially thankful to be able to attend her youngest grandson's birthday party in Centreville, Virginia—via Webcam! "As we walked through the year, we tried to notice and mark in our hearts the little and big moments of wonder, knowing they may not come again. They are treasures of grace, through which we felt the Holy Presence walking with us."

CAROL KNAPP of Lakeville, Minnesota, writes, "God's Word contains both lament and joy. I am learning how the two can harmonize, leading me deeper into the heart of Jesus. My mother celebrated her 85th birthday, and we were able to get historic 'Four Generations of Girls' photos, with my three daughters and their girls in Minnesota and Alaska. My son Phil surprised us on our visit by pulling into the drive of his beautiful, new, first-ever home! My husband survived a trip down several steps to a concrete floor; I survived a semitrailer scraping my car at a stoplight. Other excitements: winning big over my chief Scrabble competitor; hosting our first arrive-on-a-plane grandchildren visit; getting my picture taken under a Speed Limit 55 sign on my 55th birthday; inventing 'pancake prayers' (I'll write about them next year!); discovering *Silver Pennies*, a wonderful 1920s children's poetry book; a bald eagle skimming above me on my country walk; and finding a heated hotel pool where I can swim on cold winter mornings."

"My husband Lynn and I just marked the two-year anniversary of our duo-diagnoses of cancer and celebrated the good results of our most recent tests," writes CAROL KUYKENDALL of Boulder, Colorado. "One of the blessings of outliving our life expectancy (I was given two years) is the motivation to create a 'bucket list' of things we've always wanted to do. Last year we cruised the Inland Passage of Alaska and visited New York City at Christmastime. This year I want to walk a half-marathon and train Kemo, our still pesky eighteen-month-old golden retriever, so we can visit cancer patients in hospitals. We're also celebrating many family blessings. Our daughter, her husband and their two children recently moved into a house next door to us. We enlarged our family with the birth of one new grandchild and are looking forward to another. Lynn is still practicing law, and I still do some writing and speaking for MOPS (Mothers of Preschoolers) International. Our greatest blessing is trusting God's promise that no matter where we are in life's circumstances, the best is yet to come."

"For the past several weeks I've been meditating on Isaiah 40," writes HELEN GRACE LESCHEID of Abbotsford, British Columbia, Canada. "It's awesome to think that God, the sovereign Lord, Who sits on the circle of the earth, Who scoops up the oceans in His hands and Who brings the rulers of the world to nothing, is mindful of us. When I truly grasp these truths, I can face the day with much more confidence. Knowing God's divine diligence comforts me also when I think of my five children and five grandchildren who live in faraway places: Australia, Africa and eastern Canada. Last January we had a wonderful family reunion in Toronto. My heart burst with gratitude as I saw the fun and friendship the siblings enjoy with one another. My book *Treasures of Darkness* was expanded and reprinted. You can learn more about it by going to www.helenlescheid.com."

PATRICIA LORENZ is celebrating five years of life in Largo, Florida, where the wildlife, warm Gulf of Mexico waters, sensational sunsets and fabulous bike trails keep her enchanted with her adopted state. "When it comes to my writing and speaking career, I'm still winging it, totally trusting in the Lord to bring me opportunities. A couple of years ago I coauthored three books for the Chicken Soup for the Soul series and last year I finished my eleventh book, *The Five Things We Need to Be Happy*. I've learned that living the Word means that if I simply trust God, the work appears and life is joyous. My friend Jack is still just fifty-seven steps away, but to visit my children and their families requires air travel: Jeanne and Andrew are in northern California, Julia in Wisconsin, and Michael in Ohio."

After undergoing shoulder surgery and learning to deal with a painful back, DEBBIE MACOMBER of Port Orchard, Washington, has found herself living daily in God's Word, seeking encouragement and guidance. Looking for the silver lining to this forced time of recuperation, Debbie says, "I've got books plotted all the way to 2012." While it would take years to knit up her accumulated stash of yarn, she was able to make a major dent in it while healing at home with her husband Wayne on call as a loving and capable nurse. Debbie continues to serve on the national board for Warm Up America! and actively supports Guideposts Knit for Kids, and she and Wayne serve on the Guideposts National Advisory Cabinet. Her books continue to claim high positions on the best-seller lists, and she's convinced she has the most incredible grandchildren in the universe.

Words that ROBERTA MESSNER of Huntington, West Virginia, encountered on the Internet this past year—prompted, she is sure, by God Himself—set her on a new course of thinking. "I read that the average life expectancy for a person with neurofibromatosis is fifty-four years, and I was turning fifty-four in September," says Roberta. "It made me think of eternity in a whole new way and provided the focus for my series in this year's *Daily Guideposts*."

For the past two years KEITH MILLER and his wife Andrea of Austin, Texas, have been mentoring people who want to awaken and accomplish the dreams God has put in their lives. Keith's new book *Outpost: Jesus' Safehouses for Transforming the World* is planned for release late this year. "This is the most exciting book I've written since my first, *The Taste of New Wine*, in 1965," Keith says. His youngest daughter Mary-Keith Dickinson wrote her first book last year, *A Divine Scavenger Hunt*. Andrea and Keith are moving into a new chapter of their lives and ministry. To see what they're up to, check out www.keithmiller.com.

"Once a friend commented during a stressful time that hearing our son Ryan's uplifting sermons must surely help us when facing difficult days," says TED NACE of Poughquag, New York. "Truly, listening to the Word of God is easier than living the Word. But there is nothing like having the prayerful support of family and friends as well as a foundation of faith when navigating life's rocky roads." After a full year of exercise, dieting and heart-healthy living following quadruple bypass surgery, Ted is counting his blessings during his new lease on life. In April he and Kathy became grandparents once more, welcoming the first Nace baby girl in seventy-five years. And in July Ted had the joy of officiating at the wedding of youngest son Kyle to his beloved Alicia.

LINDA NEUKRUG lives in Walnut Creek, California, and spends her work-life surrounded by words in a large bookstore. "A friend told me that ninety-five percent of all conversation is misunderstood," Linda says. "This gave me food for thought about hurt feelings and anger—so much may be due to misunderstandings." A wrestler who came to the bookstore to promote his book was asked by a small boy, "Can you hurt someone more with your arms or your legs?" The huge man replied, "No matter how large you are, one part of the body can hurt someone else the most: your mouth—by meanness, gossip, complaining and sarcasm." The boy looked confused, but Linda got the message. So Linda says, "This year, I will try to refrain from gossip. I give you my word."

Three years ago REBECCA ONDOV of Hamilton, Montana, turned the crisis of her divorce, which was bound by her fears of facing the world as a middle-aged woman with no professional skills, into an opportunity to start over. "My journey began with a shattered life and a decision to get a Word from God about what He wanted for me—then live that Word," Rebecca says. "My biggest struggle has been to change the perception of my future and myself from one of defeat into one of total victory. It required moving to a new town, taking a job in which I had no experience and creating a whole new me. But by focusing on God's Word, my life is growing into a dream come true." By day Rebecca brokers lumber. Evenings and weekends she pursues her lifelong dream of studying and riding in an intensive horse training certification program.

This year MARY ANN O'ROARK of New York City enjoyed spending time with nephews, nieces and cousins all over the country. "That includes second and third generations too, but it's too hard to sort out, so whatever the age we just call each other 'cousin'!" A special family addition was the arrival of grandniece Paisley in Columbus, Ohio. "I'd always thought I'd name my own daughter Paisley," Mary Ann says. "It's a family name on my grandmother's side. It turned out I never did have children, but my cousin named his daughter Paisley and now my nephew's new baby is Paisley too." And then there's Tucker and Sam and Katie and Emily and Maggie and Grace and Cole and Madeline and Evan—merrily it rolls along. In the meantime, Mary Ann is working on a book about what it's like not having children of your own. "No matter what, we're all mothers in some way."

"I read, absorb and then live God's Word with every hat I wear in life," writes PATRICIA PUSEY of Halifax, Vermont. "I find a reason to utilize my faith in God to recognize the blessings as well as to grow from the hard times that come my way. As a nana, I have a new grandchild, Chloe; she joins eight other glorious grandkids. As a wife, I enjoy each day with Bill as we run the bed-and-breakfast and our small farm, raising Hereford cows and making maple syrup. As a mother, I continue to develop new parenting skills as I learn how to be there for our children. As an innkeeper, I have greater awareness of the changing economy. And as a believer, I am able to maintain a sense of peace and joy as I rely on the Lord to guide me in every area of my busy life."

DANIEL SCHANTZ's family is a writing family, and some of his devotionals come from his personal letters to God. "I like to write my thoughts to God," he says, "and then read the Word, looking for answers." His wife Sharon keeps in touch with friends by paper mail; she writes with a fountain pen on beautiful stationery. This year she started writing down memories from her childhood, to leave to her children. Dan and Sharon, who live in Moberly, Missouri, treasure the handwritten notes they get from their grandchildren, such as, "Grandma, thanks for coming to my baptism. Love, Rossetti." Daughters Natalie and Teresa are stay-at-home mothers and homeschoolers. Both graduates of the University of Missouri School of Journalism, Natalie edits for her former professors, and Teresa is a frequent contributor to the *Kansas City Star*. When Dan writes, he likes to munch on Cheez-Its and listen to the music of Frank Sinatra, whom he believes is alive and living in New Jersey.

During summer weekends, GAIL THORELL SCHILLING of Concord, New Hampshire, works as a docent at the Canterbury Shaker Village, where for two hundred years deeply spiritual believers created "heaven on earth" with their prayerful approach to simple tasks. "The Shaker lifestyle reminds me that living the Word means aligning my actions with God's desires," she says, "a real challenge in our fast-paced world. Both my children and I draw spiritual refreshment from this remarkably God-centered community. And where else does on-the-job training mean learning to use a spinning wheel?" After touring South America, Tom has begun graduate school at Berkeley; Greg builds cabinets in Los Angeles; Trina works toward her speech therapy degree; Tess and granddaughter Hannah stay busy in Brownie Scouts; and Gail's mom looks forward to her ninety birthday candles.

"For years my main arena for living the Word was through work with United Methodist Mexican-American Ministries, a medical and social service organization," writes PENNEY SCHWAB of Copeland, Kansas. "In retirement, I have remained involved via contract work, but my husband Don and I also have more time for family, church and community. Our grandchildren— and their parents—are a blessing! Ryan is in the premed program at Texas Tech, and David is a high school junior. Mark and Caleb took the big step from grade school to junior high. Olivia is a fifth grader, and Caden loves kindergarten. My prayer for myself and for all of us is Psalm 119:133: 'Order my steps in thy word.'"

Last spring ELIZABETH (Tib) SHERRILL of Chappaqua, New York, conducted writing workshops in New Zealand, Thailand and Singapore. "My theory was," she says, "that if you had your eightieth birthday on the other side of the international date line, it wouldn't count." The theme for this year's *Daily Guideposts*, "Living the Word," gave Elizabeth a new way to talk about Christian writing. "Writers deal in words—in these workshops, words about God, faith, miracles. Abstract words won't have much impact on nonbelievers. It's the writer's effort to *live* the Word of God's love, as revealed in Jesus, that give him or her the real-life stories that will touch the reader."

"I went to the Far East last spring and came home with a new perspective," says JOHN SHERRILL of Chappaqua, New York. John was traveling with his wife, who was holding writers' workshops. While Tib taught, John had time on his hands, which turned out to be a problem. John is a writer and businessman, used to dealing with deadlines, crises, planning for tomorrow . . . a lifestyle that has never left him with much unscheduled time. On this trip, however, with few external demands, he slowed down, walked for hours through unfamiliar cities and talked to anyone who could speak English. "The result was that I savored the journey as never before. And that's a lesson I hope to carry into my life journey too."

JOSHUA SUNDQUIST writes, "I (finally) finished school, graduating with a master's degree in communications management from the University of Southern California. It's wonderful to be done! I've moved back home to McLean, Virginia, and I'm living with some of my friends from college. I spend most of my time traveling the country as an inspirational speaker. It seems there are *Daily Guideposts* readers in almost every audience, and it's always a pleasure to connect with them. During my nine months in Los Angeles, I had the opportunity to visit a number of churches and hear several different ministers. I enjoyed seeing and hearing the diversity in communication and in application—in what it actually means to live the Word."

JON SWEENEY of White River Junction, Vermont, writes, "I'm the busy and often exhausted father of two teenagers. Sarah-Maria is 15 and Joseph, 13. I often feel that I am still trying to figure out who I am—but all of a sudden, it seems, I have teenagers! I work hard at my job (editing books and writing my own), and I worry a lot about my kids—where they are and what they may be doing or not doing. As a result, spiritual lessons often seem to be forced upon me; they break through my best defenses. What I have learned comes from daily experiences, failures, disappointments and the continual surprise of people who show me the Word of God. I'm learning to let go and let God be in control."

"Finding out I'm going to be a mother has been the most amazing and terrifying experience of my life," says KAREN VALENTIN of New York City. "I've always fantasized about having a family. My arms have often ached to hold my own children. But now that it's becoming a reality I'm awed by the enormous responsibility God has given me." Karen and her husband Gary await the arrival of their son in the spring. "Many wonderful and unexpected blessings have come into my life, and I'm grateful for the new seasons that are about to begin." Karen's children's book series will be released in 2009, and she is currently working on several other projects.

"Our son Luke graduated this year from Samford University," writes SCOTT WALKER of Waco, Texas. "Two days after graduation he flew to Bangkok, Thailand, to teach English for a year. Our daughter Jodi has completed her sophomore year at Furman University and is studying this summer at Oxford. Her oldest brother Drew is entering his third year of law school at the University of South Carolina. Beth continues her work with international students at Baylor University, and we're now hosting three students from China, Singapore and the Philippines. And in my spare time, I'm finishing a book, *The Edge of Terror*, which relates the dramatic experiences of American missionaries in the Philippines during the traumatic years of World War II."

DOLPHUS WEARY of Richland, Mississippi, writes, "Being grandparents and keeping 'Lil Reggie' every weekend is very challenging, but it is a great part of our healing process. Lil Reggie is now 4 and beginning to develop his own unique personality. We get the privilege of helping him understand how much Jesus loves him." Ryan is now a senior at Belhaven College, majoring in business with a minor in music; Danita is still excited about her medical practice in Natchez. Rosie continues to serve as leader of R.E.A.L. Christian Foundation. Dolphus serves as president of Mission Mississippi and has the privilege of speaking in churches throughout the state. Dolphus and Rosie have been able to travel together to various board meetings and speaking engagements, including the World Vision triennial conference in Singapore, where people from ninety-seven nations gathered.

"This has been a year of adventure in many ways," writes BRIGITTE WEEKS of New York City. "My liking for praying with my hands as well as my heart has helped to build part of a house in New Orleans and has created my first Aran sweater, completed—after many false starts and dropped stitches—for my oldest grandson Benjamin. And speaking of grandchildren, now I have four—all boys with blue eyes and blond hair—who all look just like my husband, their grandfather. Benjamin has been joined by Andrew and their cousin Hugo has been joined by Otto. It will be a whole new adventure when these little guys, ages 1 month to 4 years, get together. I'll need a crash course in grandparenting. There's been sadness as well as joy this year with the death of Van Varner, a colleague, friend and gentleman, one of the kindest souls I have ever known."

"This year, I begged God to get my twin sons Jon and Jeremy to places of safety," writes MARION BOND WEST of Watkinsville, Georgia, "where they could pursue lives of integrity—drug free. In May, Jeremy's counselor of almost seven years requested that Gene and I take him into our home for thirty days. We agreed. His humility, cooperation and gratitude resulted in his remaining much longer. Unemployed and needing a hip replacement from an old injury, Jeremy limped enthusiastically to Sunday school and church with us and plugged into a class entitled "Healed from Shame." He joined recovery groups and never missed a meeting. A local orthopedist gave him the most amazing Christmas gift—a brand-new hip! Jeremy and his beloved cat Houdini moved into an apartment near us, and an exciting job popped up. Jon, sadly, is not doing as well and has elected not to be in touch with us. I've made a resolute decision: Both my sons are in God's powerful hands."

BRENDA WILBEE lives by the sea in Birch Bay, Washington, where she writes and for the past year has worked as a graphic designer. For fun, she plays in a handbell choir at an antique Lutheran church way out in the county. "I am," she says, "F, F-sharp and G." This year Brenda is most grateful for the reconnection to old friends. Going back to Arizona to face the molestation she endured at the hands of her doctor four decades ago, she discovered God's goodness in these timely friends—both then and now. Further information is posted on her blog, BrendaWilbee.blogspot.com, and her Web site BrendaWilbee.com. As always, she welcomes correspondence.

It has been a year of changes for KJERSTIN WILLIAMS and her husband Travis. They bought their first home and moved to Los Angeles where they began new jobs: Kjerstin as a robotics engineer and Travis as a chemistry professor. They are volunteers with the Boy Scouts and often find themselves having more adventures than they might have otherwise undertaken, from rock climbing to kayaking to whitewater rafting. In between such stunts Kjerstin sings whenever she can. In addition to singing jazz, she has been living the Word with sacred music, both in concert and in worship. "Many of my most impassioned conversations with God are in song—and often in public!"

"Living the Word means praising God for every passage of life, even when we aren't ready for that passage," writes TIM WILLIAMS of Durango, Colorado. "Last year I retired from the fire department because I'm old enough to be a grandfather, even though we don't have any grandchildren. This year my wife is retiring from teaching and she'll finally have time to work in her beloved garden. She's not too old to teach, but God has blessed us with the ability to thrive on our small pensions. I hope we live in God's Word during times of drought and plenty. I hope we praise God for our health. And most of all, I hope it falls within the boundaries of living the Word when we visit our sons and daughters-in-law and plead for grandchildren!"

"Visiting the Holy Land is truly living the Word," says ISABEL WOLSELEY of Syracuse, New York, following her trip to Israel, Egypt, Turkey and Patmos. "Of course things have changed from the way they were two millennia ago, yet the terrain, the Sea of Galilee, the rocky hills are the same. Actually viewing such spots makes it more vivid and easier to understand why—whether one is north, south, east or west of this ancient city—one goes *up* to Jerusalem. It's the highest spot in the land!" Because Isabel's two sons, five grandchildren, their spouses and other relatives are widely scattered in New York, Texas, Nebraska, Idaho and Oregon, a family reunion is planned in her home state, Kansas. "In late May, Lord willing, we'll head for a bed-and-breakfast spot where we'll visit, play games and enjoy one another."

"It's been a year of challenges and changes in our family," says PHILIP ZALESKI of Northampton, Massachusetts. "My mother moved from New York City, where she has spent nearly all her life, into a nursing home near us. We're so grateful to have her close, as she lightens our lives with her irrepressible kindness and love. Our son Andy, now in middle school, is filling our home with the sound of Latin declensions, and John, in his junior year at college, is reading Homer in the original Greek. Carol and I, happily sticking to English, are making progress on our history of the Inklings (C. S. Lewis, J. R. R. Tolkien and their friends). All this bustle requires energy and hope, and for this we turn in prayer and thanksgiving to God, asking for the grace to carry out all our activities according to the Word."

Daily Guideposts is created each year by the Books and Inspirational Media Division of Guideposts, the world's leading inspirational publisher. Founded in 1945 by Dr. Norman Vincent Peale and Ruth Stafford Peale, Guideposts helps people from all walks of life achieve their maximum personal and spiritual potential. Guideposts is committed to communicating positive, faith-filled principles for people everywhere to use in successful daily living.

And now you can learn more about our *Daily Guideposts* authors online: Read their blogs and their favorite quotations and Bible passages; find out what music moves them; view their photos. Visit OurPrayer .org/DGP2009Authors. OurPrayer.org is a community of faith brimming with inspiring devotionals, firsthand accounts of the power of prayer, uplifting articles and much more!

Guideposts' publications include award-winning magazines such as *Guideposts* and *Angels on Earth*, best-selling books, and outreach services that demonstrate what can happen when faith and positive thinking are applied in day-to-day life.

For more information, visit us at www.guideposts.com, call (800) 431-2344 or write Guideposts, PO Box 5815, Harlan, Iowa 51593.